Daytrips
NEW ENGLAND

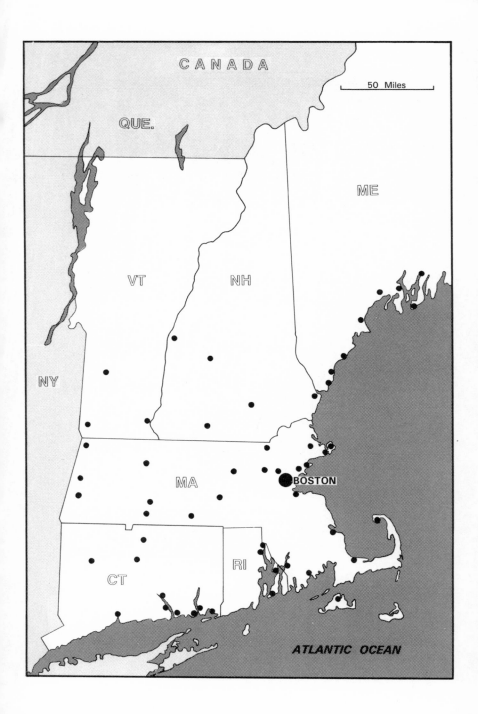

Daytrips
NEW ENGLAND

50 *one day adventures in Massachusetts, Rhode Island, Connecticut, Vermont, New Hampshire, and Maine*

EARL STEINBICKER

HASTINGS HOUSE
Book Publishers
Mamaroneck, New York

All opinions expressed in this book are strictly those of the author, who travels as an ordinary tourist paying his own way. No complimentary lodging, meals, transportation, admissions, or similar considerations were accepted.

While every effort has been made to insure accuracy, neither the author nor the publisher assume legal responsibility for any consequences arising from the use of this book or the information it contains.

We are always grateful for comments from readers, which are extremely useful in preparing future editions. Please write directly to the author, Earl Steinbicker, c/o Hastings House, 141 Halstead Avenue, Mamaroneck, NY 10543; or FAX (914) 835-1037. Thank you.

All photos and maps are by the author.

Distributed to the trade by Publishers Group West, Emeryville, CA.

ISBN: 0-8038-9379-5

Library of Congress Catalog Card Number 96-077681

Printed in the United States of America
10 9 8 7 6 5 4 3 2 1

Contents

6   CONTENTS

Introduction

So compact is New England that most of its attractions lie within easy daytrip range of its unofficial capital, Boston—or nearly anywhere else in Massachusetts, Rhode Island, most of Connecticut, or the southern parts of Vermont, New Hampshire, and Maine. A drive of just 50 miles takes you to some of America's most intriguing destinations, while extending that to 100 miles encompasses much of what the region is famous for. Although it stretches the daytrip concept just a tad, a few places are so compelling that they've also been included even though they're located as far as 140 miles from Boston's harbor.

For both area residents and visitors alike, daytrips are the ideal way to probe this treasure-filled corner of the nation. And, if you have a weekend or more at your disposal, why not combine several daytrips into a mini vacation?

Boston is, of course, a fabulous destination in itself. To help you enjoy its wonders, this book opens with four one-day walking tours that explore the most interesting corners of town, ranging from the history-strewn Freedom Trail and the thriving Waterfront to Beacon Hill and Back Bay. The bordering town of Cambridge, a very special place, is explored as well. You won't need a car for these short excursions, as all of them can easily be reached by subway, bus, cab, or even on foot.

The rest of Massachusetts is next, with 22 daytrip destinations ranging from nearby Saugus, Salem, and Lexington to as far away as the scenic Berkshires. Fully half of these are within 50 miles of Boston, and most can even be reached by public transportation.

Tiny Rhode Island follows, with a walking tour of surprisingly attractive Providence, visits to the little-known Blackstone River Valley, Bristol and Portsmouth, and two in-depth explorations of Newport.

Connecticut, perhaps the most typical of the New England states, offers a marvelously restored old seaport at Mystic, more contemporary maritime attractions at Groton and New London, and a sophisticated level of urbanity at Hartford and New Haven. Those preferring the bucolic charms of the countryside can venture up the Connecticut River Valley, explore the Tobacco Valley, and meander through the delightful Litchfield Hills.

The southern reaches of Vermont, New Hampshire, and Maine are all within daytrip range of Boston and central New England. Each has a distinct personality, with sights as varied as mountain peaks, college towns, restored historic sites, and a craggy shoreline dotted with fishing villages.

Whenever practical, the daytrips have been arranged as walking tours following a carefully-tested route on the accompanying map. This works well in larger towns and cities, and sometimes even in historic villages. In other cases, however, the attractions are just too far apart to see on foot, so their descriptions are arranged in a driving sequence from which you can pick and choose, matching site numbers with those on the trip's road map. A few of the daytrips, such as that to the Litchfield Hills in Connecticut, are designed for the sheer pleasure of driving, with just a few attractions that you might want to see along the way.

Dining well is a vital element in any travel experience. For this reason, a selection of particularly enjoyable restaurants has been included for each of the daytrips. These are price-keyed, with an emphasis on the medium-to-low range, regional cooking, and local atmosphere. Their concise location descriptions make them easy to find.

Time and weather considerations are important, and they've been included under the "Practicalities" section of each trip. These let you know, among other things, on which days the sights are closed, when some special events occur, and which places to avoid in bad weather. The location and telephone number, FAX and TDD numbers, and Web Site (if applicable) of the local tourist information office is also given in case you have questions.

Please remember that places have a way of changing without warning, and that errors do creep into print. If your heart is absolutely set on a particular sight, you should check first to make sure that it's open, and that the times are still valid. Phone numbers for this purpose are given for each of the attractions, or you could contact the local tourist office.

One last thought: It isn't really necessary to see everything at any given destination. Be selective. Your one-day adventures in New England should be fun, not an endurance test. If they start becoming that, just find your way to the nearest antique shop, gallery, or historic inn and enjoy yourself while soaking up local atmosphere. There will always be another day.

Happy Daytripping!

Section I

Scenes like this at Mystic Seaport lie within easy daytrip range

DAYTRIP STRATEGIES

The word "Daytrip" may not have made it into dictionaries yet, but for experienced independent travelers it represents the easiest, most natural, and often the least expensive approach to exploring many of the world's most interesting areas. This strategy, in which you base yourself in a central city (or its suburbs) and probe the surrounding region on a series of one-day excursions, is especially effective in the case of a region as compact as New England.

ADVANTAGES:

While not the answer to every travel situation, daytrips have significant advantages over point-to-point touring following a set itinerary. Here are ten good reasons for considering the daytrip approach:

1. Freedom from the constraints of a fixed itinerary. You can go wherever you feel like going whenever the mood strikes you.
2. Freedom from the burden of luggage. You bags remain in your hotel while you run around with only a guidebook and camera.
3. Freedom from the anxiety of reservation foul-ups. You don't have to worry each day about whether that night's lodging will actually materialize.
4. The flexibility of making last-minute changes to allow for unexpected weather, serendipitous discoveries, changing interests, new-found passions, and so on.
5. The flexibility to take breaks from sightseeing whenever you feel tired or bored, without upsetting a planned itinerary. Why not sleep late in your base city for a change?
6. The opportunity to sample different travel experiences without committing more than a day to them.
7. The opportunity to become a "temporary resident" of your base city. By staying there for a while you can get to know it in depth, becoming familiar with the local restaurants, shops, theaters, night life, and other attractions—enjoying them as a native would.
8. The convenience of not having to pack and unpack your bags each day. Your clothes can hang in a closet where they belong, or even be sent out for cleaning.
9. The convenience (and security!) of having a fixed address in your base city, where friends, relatives, and business associates can reach you in an emergency.
10. The economy of staying at one hotel on a discounted longer-term basis, especially in conjunction with package plans. You can make advance reservations for your base city without sacrificing any flexibility at all.

And, of course, for those who actually live in New England, daytrips are the key to discovering one of America's most fascinating regions—one day at a time.

CHOOSING A BASE CITY

BOSTON:

It may not be in the center, but it's certainly the hub of New England; the place from which highways, rail lines, and other transportation routes radiate out across the entire region. Most—not quite all, but most—of the area's attractions lie within comfortable daytrip range of Boston, making this the ideal base for all but the most remote of destinations. On top of that, Boston is one of the most attractive and fascinating cities on Earth, right up there in the same class with New York, Washington, San Francisco, Paris, Rome, and London! Its accommodations vary from ultra-luxurious downtown hotels to neighborhood B&Bs to inexpensive motels in the suburbs, so you're sure to find something that's both convenient and within your budget.

GETTING TO BOSTON:

By Air: Many of the world's major airlines, along with numerous small carriers, fly in and out of Boston's **Logan International Airport** (BOS). Located just across the harbor from downtown, it couldn't be easier to reach—whether by car, bus, van, subway, or ferry boat. ☎ *(800) 235-6426 for information.*

By Rail: Amtrak (☎1-800-USA-RAIL) provides fast, frequent service along the Northeast Corridor from points as far south as Virginia to Boston's Back Bay and South stations, with connections at New York, Philadelphia, and Washington for other services. They also offer somewhat more leisurely rides to Chicago and points west.

By Bus: Practically all intercity buses serving Boston wind up at or near the convenient downtown South Station. **Greyhound** serves Worcester, Springfield, Providence, Hartford, New York, Philadelphia, Washington, and many other cities, ☎ (800) 231-2222. **Bonanza** goes to Cape Cod, Fall River, Newport, Providence, Hartford, New York, and other points, ☎ (800) 556-3815. **Peter Pan** offers service to Western Massachusetts, Hartford, New York, Philadelphia, Washington, and elsewhere, ☎ (800) 237-8747. **Concord Trailways** heads north to New Hampshire and Maine, ☎ (800) 639-3317. **American Eagle** links Boston with New Bedford, ☎ (800) 453-5040. **Vermont Transit** of course goes to Vermont, ☎ (802) 862-9671. **Plymouth & Brockton** serves Plymouth and Cape Cod, ☎ (508) 746-0378.

By Car: Boston is encircled by the infamous Route **I-95** to the west, and the even worse Route **I-93** going through downtown. Venturing inside that ring during rush hours exposes you to monster traffic jams, quirky traffic patterns, and aggressive drivers. Try to avoid driving inbound on weekdays from 6:30–9 a.m. and outbound from 4–6:30 p.m. Downtown parking lots are very expensive, and free spaces virtually non-existent. You'll certainly need a car for most of the out-of-town daytrips, but in the city you're better off sticking to public transportation.

ACCOMMODATIONS IN AND NEAR BOSTON:

Unless you live in or around Boston, you'll need a place to stay. Although the city has many fine hotels, they're often heavily booked, making advance **reservations** advisable. Discount **package deals** that combine transportation with hotel rooms are offered by several airlines as well as by Amtrak. Many hotels offer deeply discounted **weekend packages**; check your travel agent about this. Visitors can save a considerable amount of money and avoid traffic by staying at an inn or motel in the **outskirts**, such as along Route I-95. Many of these are close to commuter train stations, which makes getting downtown easy.

For adventurous travelers, **Bed & Breakfast** stays are becoming an increasingly popular way of cutting costs while enjoying a much more personalized service. Ask the tourist office for a current list of booking agencies. Short of sleeping in a park, hostels are probably the least expensive of all accommodations. A favorite is the **Hostelling International-Boston** at 12 Hemenway Street in Back Bay, ☎ (617) 536-9455.

OTHER BASES:

By consulting a map and making a few modifications, all—or nearly all—of the daytrips can be made from just about anywhere in central New England.

CHOOSING DESTINATIONS

With fifty trips to choose from, and several attractions for each trip, deciding which are the most enjoyable for you and yours might be problematic. You could, of course, read through the whole book and mark the most appealing spots, but there's an easier way to at least start. Just turn to the index and scan it, looking out for the special-interest categories set in **BOLD FACE** type. These will immediately lead you to choices under such headings as Art Museums, Restored Historic Villages, Revolutionary War Sites, Boat Trips, Children's Activities, Railfan Excursions, and many others.

The elements of one trip can often be combined with another to create a custom itinerary, using the book maps as a rough guide and a good road map for the final routing.

Some of the trips, listed in the index as **SCENIC DRIVES**, are just that— they are primarily designed for the pure pleasure of driving, with just enough attractions along the way to keep things lively. These are especially enjoyable if you are blessed with a car that's fun to drive.

GETTING AROUND

The driving directions for each trip assume that you're leaving from Boston. Chances are, however, that you live (or are staying) elsewhere in central New England, so you'll need to modify the routes a bit.

The route **maps** scattered throughout the book show you approximately where the sites are, and which main roads lead to them. In many cases, however, you'll still need a good, up-to-date road map. An excellent choice for a single-sheet map that covers all of the destinations is the *New England Regional Map* published by Rand McNally. AAA members can get free single-sheet road maps for *Boston*; for *Connecticut, Massachusetts, and Rhode Island*; and for *Maine, New Hampshire, and Vermont*. The free maps distributed by state tourist offices vary greatly in quality, so if the one they give you isn't clear enough, head for your bookstore and look over their selection.

The majority of daytrips in this book are designed to be made by **car**, and do not really lend themselves to public transportation. If you've arrived without wheels, you'll have to rent, borrow, buy, or steal a vehicle; or else limit yourself to those 20 trips that *can* be done *easily* by **subway, train,** or **bus**. Besides the four trips within Boston itself, these are: Cambridge, Salem, Cape Ann, Plymouth, Martha's Vineyard, New Bedford, Fall River, Worcester, Springfield, Providence, Newport (2 trips), Mystic, Groton & New London, New Haven, and Hartford. Of course, a true public transit fanatic will find ways of getting *anywhere* by train or bus, but unless you're willing to spend over two hours each way just arriving at a destination, and then walking long distances, it isn't recommended.

Specific information about transportation within Boston and Cambridge will be found in Section II. In addition, each daytrip has a "Getting There" section outlining the most practical routes and, when applicable, public transportation services.

FOOD AND DRINK

Several choice restaurants that make sense for daytrippers are listed for each destination in this book. Most of these are long-time favorites of experienced travelers, are open for lunch, are on or near the suggested tour route, and provide some atmosphere. Many feature regional specialties not generally found elsewhere. Their approximate price range is shown as:

$ —Inexpensive.
$$ —Reasonable.
$$$—Luxurious and expensive.
X: —Days closed.

If you're really serious about dining you should consult an up-to-date restaurant and hotel guide such as the annual *Mobil Travel Guide—Northeast* or the appropriate AAA TourBooks, issued free to members.

Fast-food outlets are, of course, nearly everywhere, and have the advantage of not taking up much of your sightseeing time. In warm weather, why not consider a **picnic**? Many of the attractions have picnic facilities that you can use; these are indicated in the practical information for those sites.

PRACTICALITIES

WEATHER:

New England is famous for its long, cold winters, when walking from one heated interior to another is just about all some people can endure. Others thrive on the marvelous opportunities for skiing and other winter sports, for the special Christmas programs at historic sites, for the great cultural events, and for the chance to experience life here without the tourist throngs.

Late spring, summer, and early fall are the best seasons for the entire region, and therefore the most crowded. This is a good time to explore the less-famous attractions in the outlying countryside.

OPENING TIMES, FEES, AND FACILITIES:

When planning a daytrip, be sure to note carefully the **opening times** of the various sites—these can sometimes be rather quirky. Anything unusual that you should know before starting, such as "don't make this trip on a Monday," is summarized in the "Practicalities" section of each trip.

Entrance fees listed in the text are, naturally, subject to change—and they rarely go down. For the most part, admissions are quite reasonable considering the cost of maintaining the sites. Places with free entry, especially those not operated by governments, are usually staffed with unpaid volunteers and have a donation box to help keep the wolves from the door. Please put something in it.

Any special **facilities** that a site may offer are listed in the *italicized* information for that site, along with the address and phone number. These often include restaurants or cafeterias ✗, cafés ☕, information counters ❶, gift shops, tours, shows, picnic facilities, and so on. **Telephone numbers** are indicated with a ☎; relevant **area codes** are given in the "Practicalities" section of each trip.

HANDICAPPED TRAVELERS:

Access varies with each individual's needs and abilities, so no firm statement can be made about any site. Those that are generally accessible without much difficulty are indicated with the symbol &, but when in doubt it is always best to phone ahead.

GROUP TRAVEL:

If you're planning a group outing, *always* call ahead. Most sites require advance reservations and offer special discounts for groups, often at a substantial saving over the regular admission fee. Some sites will open specially or remain open beyond their scheduled hours to accommodate groups; some have tours, demonstrations, lectures, and so on available only to groups; and some have facilities for rental to groups.

SUGGESTED TOURS

Two different methods of organizing daytrips are used in this book, depending on local circumstances. Some are based on **structured itineraries** such as walking tours and scenic drives that follow a suggested route, while others just describe the **local attractions** that you can choose from. In either case, a town or area **map** always shows where things are, so you're not likely to get lost. Numbers (in parentheses) in the text refer to the circled numbers on the appropriate map.

Major attractions are described in one or more paragraphs each, beginning with practical information for a visit. **Additional sites** are worked into the text, along with some practical information in italics. All are arranged in a logical geographic sequence, although you may want to make changes to suit your preferences.

Walking tours, where used, follow routes shown by heavy broken lines on the accompanying map. You can estimate the amount of time that any segment of a walking tour will take by looking at the scaled map and figuring that the average person covers about 100 yards a minute.

Trying to see everything at any given destination could easily lead to an exhausting marathon. You will certainly enjoy yourself more by being selective and passing up anything that doesn't catch your fancy, and perhaps planning a repeat visit at some other time.

Practical information, such as opening times and admission fees, is as accurate as was possible at the time of writing, but will certainly change. You should always check with the sites themselves if seeing a particular one is crucially important to you.

*OUTSTANDING ATTRACTIONS:

An * asterisk before any attraction, be it an entire daytrip or just one exhibit in a museum, denotes a special treat that in the author's opinion should not be missed.

TOURIST INFORMATION

The addresses and phone numbers of local and regional tourist offices as well as major sights are given in the text whenever appropriate. These are usually your best source for specific information and current brochures. On a wider scale, state tourist offices offer free "vacation planning kits," maps, and brochures that are often useful. You can contact them at:

Massachusetts Office of Travel & Tourism
100 Cambridge St., Boston, MA 02202
☎ (800) 447-7277 or (617) 727-3201, FAX (617) 727-6525
Web Site: www.magnet.state.ma.us/travel/travel.html

Rhode Island Tourism Division
7 Jackson Walkway, Providence, RI 02903
☎ (800) 556-2484 or (401) 277-2601

Connecticut Division of Tourism
865 Brook St., Rocky Hill, CT 06067
☎ (800) 282-6863 or (860) 258-4355

Vermont Travel Division
134 State St., Montpelier, VT 05602
☎ (800) 837-6668 or (802) 828-3236
Web Site: www.genghis.com/vermont/discover.htm

New Hampshire Office of Travel & Tourism
Box 856, Concord, NH 03302
☎ (800) 386-4664 or (603) 271-2343
Web Site: www.visitnh.gov

Maine Publicity Bureau
325-B Water St., Box 2300, Hallowell, ME 04347
☎ (800) 533-9595 or (207) 623-0363

Section II

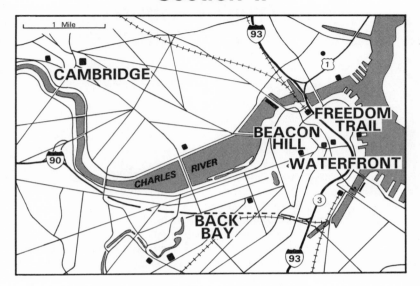

DAYTRIPS WITHIN
BOSTON and
CAMBRIDGE

Before heading off on daytrips to the rest of New England, you'll probably want to explore some of Boston and its neighbor, Cambridge. The five walking tours described in this section can guide you to both the most famous sites and also to some rather obscure attractions—always by way of enjoyable routes. The walks average less than three miles in length and each should take roughly four hours or so to complete, assuming that you visit some of the museums and other attractions along the way.

Proper Bostonians may think of their city as the "Hub of the Universe;" to others it's the "Athens of America." "Beantown" is another name that comes to mind. Whatever your take, you'll surely have to admit that this is one of the most enjoyable cities on Earth, and just about the most walkable. Its attractions range from the Colonial to the most sophisticated of Post-Modern offerings, and are enlivened with fun-filled activities such as harbor cruises, hands-on science museums, and special treats for sports fans as well as for culture mavens.

GETTING AROUND
BOSTON AND CAMBRIDGE

Although all of the tours are designed for walking, you'll still need to use some form of transportation to get to their starting points, and then back home. Here are the options:

SUBWAY:

Known simply as the "**T**" and operated by the **MBTA**, America's oldest subway system is usually the fastest and easiest way to get around Boston, Cambridge, and outlying areas. There are four color-coded lines, some using conventional subway trains and others trolley cars. All come together downtown, where passengers can change from one line to another on the same fare. The system operates from around 5 a.m. until about 12:30 a.m. "Inbound" trains are headed for the center; "outbound" away from it. Fares are currently quite low, but expected to increase in the near future: Adults 85¢, seniors (65+) 20¢, children (5–11) 40¢. Trips into the far suburban reaches cost more. **Visitor Passports**, valid for unlimited local travel on subways and buses, currently cost $5 for 1 day, $9 for 3 days, or $18 for 7 days. *For further information* ☎ *(617) 722-3200, TDD (617) 722-5146.*

BUSES:

The "**T**" is extended by a complex bus system, with maps available at major subway stations and some bus stops. Fares are 60¢ (exact change) for local service, with no free transfer to/from subways. Express suburban buses cost more.

COMMUTER RAIL:

Visitors staying in the suburbs, and those headed for some of the daytrip destinations in eastern Massachusetts and to Providence, RI, can make good use of the MBTA's excellent commuter train service. Lines to the north leave from Boston's North Station, connected to the Green and Orange subway lines; those to the south and west from Boston's South Station, connected to the Red subway line. Tickets may be purchased at major stations, or on the train without penalty if no ticket sales are offered at the boarding station. Service is frequent on weekdays, infrequent on weekends and holidays. ☎ *(617) 722-3200, TDD (617) 722-5146 for further information.*

BY CAR:

In a word, **don't**. Wise people avoid driving in downtown Boston at all cost. The streets are a confused mess, parking is practically impossible, and the local drivers (and pedestrians!) are the nation's worst. Park your car and take public transport, or walk. Those staying in the suburbs can ride the train in and skip the whole nightmare.

TOURIST TROLLEYS:

Actually tour buses in disguise, these quaint vehicles offer fully-narrated, hop-on, hop-off services along popular tourist routes, with unlimited boarding and reboarding for a fixed daily fare. Check out their offerings at one of the many sales booths (you can't miss them!); they might turn your walking tour into a riding tour. Some of the operators are: **Beantown**, ☎ (617) 986-6100; **Boston Trolley**, ☎ (617) 876-5539; and **Old Town Trolley**, ☎ (617) 269-7010.

ORIENTATION:

Downtown Boston's streets supposedly follow the meanderings of Colonial cows, possibly very drunken Colonial cows. You'll need a map to navigate this maze. The area is bisected by the hideous, elevated **Central Artery** otherwise known as the John F. Fitzgerald Expressway, or routes I-93, US-1, and MA-3. Construction is now underway to bury this leftover from the 1950s into a deep tunnel; until completed you can expect some inconvenience, noise, and confusion.

Each of the five walking tours covers a specific area, with hardly any overlap. The map on page 17 gives a general idea of where these are, while the individual walking-tour maps for each trip show all of the sites and major streets in the relevant neighborhoods.

SHOPPING

Three of the walking tours take you past areas that are especially rich in unusual shopping opportunities. The **Freedom Trail** route touches on the **Downtown Crossing** district along Washington Street, home of the original Filene's Basement, Jordan Marsh, and many other popular stores. Beyond that, it passes through the historic **Faneuil Hall Marketplace**, famous for its unusual shops and wonderful food experiences, a great place for lunch. More elegant, and much more self-indulgent, are the boutiques, galleries, and shops of the **Back Bay**, especially those along Newbury Street, around Copley Square, and in the Prudential Center. **Cambridge** boasts a multitude of trendy, youthful shops around Harvard Square.

TOURIST INFORMATION

For further information about Boston, contact the **Greater Boston Convention & Visitors Bureau**, Prudential Tower, Suite 400, Box 490, Boston, MA 02199, ☎ (800) 888-5515 or (617) 536-4100, FAX (617) 424-7664. Web Site: www.dvm.com/users/dvm/boston

Trip 1
Boston

*The Freedom Trail

Just about everyone who comes to Boston walks the Freedom Trail. Since its inception several decades ago, this well-trodden urban route has led count-less travelers along a two-and-a-half-mile exploration of Boston's—and America's—history. This is where the colony's first yearnings for freedom were expressed, and where the Revolutionary War with England began.

Along the way you'll visit the graves of famous patriots, New England's first Anglican church, the meeting house where protest rallies began, and the old British headquarters building. Historic Faneuil Hall is now the heart of a restored market area, brimming with exciting eateries and shops. Meander-ing through the colorful North End, you can traipse through the oldest house in Boston, where Paul Revere lived for 30 years, and the Old North Church, from whose steeple the famous lanterns shone. Crossing the river, you can board a ship that fought the Barbary pirates, and climb the Bunker Hill Monument for a grand panoramic view of it all.

Those making in-depth visits to many of the sites along the way may prefer to do the walk in two segments, on two separate days. The most logical spot for a break is at Copp's Hill Burying Ground, sparing you the walk to Charlestown—which can be reached by bus from the Haymarket subway station when you resume the trek.

The official route is well marked with a painted red line, or red (some-times gray) bricks set in the sidewalk. The route described in this book makes a few minor variations, especially at the beginning, and other small detours may be necessary as construction work on Boston's Central Artery project continues.

GETTING THERE:
By subway, take the Red or Green "T" line to **Park Street**, where the walk begins.

Returning from Charlestown, board an MBTA Route 92 or 93 **bus** at City Square in front of the John Harvard Mall. This will take you to Haymarket Station on the Green or Orange "T" subway lines. Alternatively, you can board a **ferry boat** at Pier 4 of the Charlestown Navy Yard for a ride to Long

Wharf, near the Aquarium stop on the Blue "T" subway line. *Boston Harbor Cruises,* ☎ *(617) 227-4321.*

By car, if you must, park as close to the Common as possible, ideally using the underground facility whose entrance is on Charles Street.

PRACTICALITIES:

Nearly all of the sites along the way are open daily, except that the Paul Revere House is closed on Mondays from January through March.

Paul Revere's famous ride is reenacted every year on **Patriots' Day**, the third Monday of April, starting at the Paul Revere Mall. For your convenience, the Midnight Ride happens at 10 a.m., and is followed by both the world-famous Boston Marathon and the opening of the Swan Boat season in the Public Garden.

Wear comfortable walking shoes. While not excessively long, the Freedom Trail is rather hilly in spots.

For further information, contact the **Boston Common Visitor Center**, 147 Tremont St., ☎ (800) 888-5515 or (617) 536-4100. You could also check the **Boston National Historical Park Visitor Center**, 15 State St., opposite the Old State House, ☎ (617) 242-5642.

FOOD AND DRINK:

There seems to be no end to the number of eateries along this popular route. More than a few are tourist traps, to be sure, but several do offer good food and atmosphere:

> **Mamma Maria** (3 North Sq., near the Paul Revere House) Northern Italian cuisine graciously served in a romantic town house. Reservations suggested. ☎ (617) 523-0077. X: Sun. lunch, Mon. lunch. $$ and $$$

> **Union Oyster House** (41 Union St., on the Freedom Trail a block north of Faneuil Hall) Calling itself America's oldest restaurant, this seafood mecca has been family-owned and little changed since 1826. For landlubbers, there are a few meat dishes. ☎ (617) 227-2750. $$

> **Durgin-Park** (North Market Bldg., Faneuil Hall Marketplace) Real New England cuisine, and lots of it—served family-style since long before the tourists arrived (1827 to be exact). ☎ (617) 227-2038. $ and $$

> **La Famiglia** (112 Salem St., near the Old North Church) Join the line waiting for huge servings of tasty Italian dishes at modest prices. ☎ (617) 367-6711. $ and $$

> **Quincy Market Food Court** (Faneuil Hall Marketplace) A large variety of self-service food counters offering all sorts of dishes, ethnic and otherwise. The tables upstairs in this historic building are less crowded and more pleasant. Hugely popular with visitors and locals alike. ☎ (617) 338-2323. $

SUGGESTED TOUR:

Numbers in parentheses correspond to numbers on the map.

Begin your walk at the **Boston Common Visitors Center** (1), where you can get free information, brochures, and maps; or purchase more detailed guides. The 48-acre **Boston Common** has been public land since 1634, and is in fact America's oldest public park. Down through the centuries it has seen use as grazing land, a training ground for the militia, a prime location for the pillory and gallows, and a venue for other public entertainments. A stroll through it is described in the Back Bay daytrip, beginning on page 40.

The **Freedom Trail** has its official beginning here, heading north through the park to the State House. Since the latter is thoroughly covered as part of the Beacon Hill daytrip (page 35), you'll find it more convenient to head up Tremont Street to the **Park Street Church** (2). Built in 1809 in the manner of Sir Christopher Wren's London churches, it is noted for its graceful spire. Gunpowder was stored in the crypt during the War of 1812, perhaps enhancing the church's reputation for hellfire-and-brimstone sermons. William Lloyd Garrison, the great abolitionist, gave a particularly fiery speech from the pulpit in 1829, for which he was nearly lynched. Three years later to the day, July 4, the patriotic song "America," a.k.a. "My Country, 'Tis of Thee," was first sung here. ☎ *(617) 523-3383. Open July–Aug., Tues.–Sat. 9–3:30. Free.*

Adjacent to the church is the **Old Granary Burying Ground**, a particularly atmospheric graveyard established in 1660. Among its permanent residents are three signers of the Declaration of Independence—John Hancock, Samuel Adams, and Robert Treat Paine—along with the parents of Benjamin Franklin (Ben himself is interred in Philadelphia), eight governors, five victims of the Boston Massacre, and Paul Revere. A curious old tombstone proclaims "Here lyes ye Body of Mary Goose, Wife to Issac Goose, Aged 42 Years, Deceased 19 Oct. 1690." According to dubious tradition, this is the grave of Mother Goose, who told tales to her many, many children. *Open daily, 8–5. Free.*

Continue up Tremont Street to the **King's Chapel** (3), the first Anglican church in New England. The earliest chapel on this site was built in 1688 over the objections of Puritans by a despotic Royal Governor, who then fled back to England. King William III and his Queen Mary II presented it with gifts that still remain in use. The present structure was completed in 1754, but never received its intended steeple, lending it a very strange appearance. In the aftermath of the Revolution, the congregation severed its ties with England and King's Chapel became the new nation's first Unitarian church, albeit retaining the Anglican *Book of Common Prayer* to this day. Step inside to admire the magnificent ***Georgian interior**, possibly the finest in America. ☎ *(617) 523-1749. Open June–Oct., Mon.–Sat. 9–4 and Sun. noon–4; Nov.–May, Tues.–Wed. 11–1 and Sat. 10–4. Donation.*

Next to the church is the **King's Chapel Burying Ground**, Boston's oldest

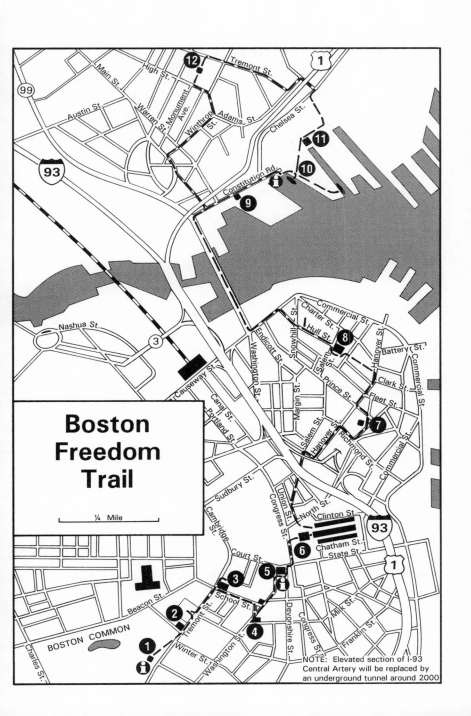

Boston
Freedom
Trail

¼ Mile

BOSTON COMMON

NOTE: Elevated section of I-93
Central Artery will be replaced by
an underground tunnel around 2000

cemetery. This quiet, almost romantic spot has been in use since 1630 and is the final resting place of virtually all of the early Puritan settlers, a passenger on the *Mayflower*, the first governor of Massachusetts, and William Dawes, who accompanied Paul Revere on that Midnight Ride.

Turn down School Street, passing the **Old City Hall**, an ornate 1865 structure that now serves as a fancy French restaurant. In its forecourt is a statue of Benjamin Franklin, who was born nearby. This was also the original site of the Boston Latin School, America's first public school, which opened in 1635.

At the intersection of Washington Street stands the **Old Corner Bookstore**, first built in 1712 as a residence and apothecary shop. In 1828 it was bought by a firm of booksellers and soon became the center of literary life in Boston, attracting the likes of Oliver Wendell Holmes, Ralph Waldo Emerson, Nathaniel Hawthorne, John Greenleaf Whittier, Henry Wadsworth Longfellow, and Henry David Thoreau. Put to other uses after the turn of the century, the shop was thoroughly restored in the 1960s and is once again a bookshop.

Head diagonally across the street to the:

*OLD SOUTH MEETING HOUSE (4), 310 Washington St., Boston. MA 02108, ☎ (617) 482-6439. *Open April–Oct., daily 9:30–5; remainder of year, Mon.–Fri. 10–4 and weekends 10–5. Adults $2.50, seniors $2, children (6–18) $1. Closed for renovations until mid-1997.* ♿.

The first meeting house on this site was a puritanical affair, as the original congregation equated religious decoration with the despised Church of England or, even worse, with the Pope. Times changed, and in 1729 the 1669 structure was replaced with a rather fancy one. Its fame, however, centers on political rather than ecclesiastical events. It was here that the Boston Tea Party got off to a spirited start in 1773, and in the years leading up to the Revolution it was the scene of many an impassioned rally. When war began the British took their revenge, turning it into an officers' club, riding academy, and pig sty. Now fully restored, it serves as a museum of those troubled times. Don't miss the ***model of Boston in 1775**.

Head north on Washington Street to the:

*OLD STATE HOUSE (5), 206 Washington St., Boston, MA 02109, ☎ (617) 720-3290. *Open daily 9:30–5. Closed Thanksgiving, Christmas, New Year's, and Easter. Adults $3, seniors & students $2, children (6–18) $1.50.*

Boston's oldest surviving public building was erected in 1713 as the seat of the British Colonial government, its façade adorned with symbols of the Crown. It was, however, always a rebellious place, the scene of several major events leading to the Revolution—including the reading of the Declaration of Independence. After the war it became the capitol of Massachusetts, where in 1780 John Hancock was sworn in as the state's first governor. In 1798 a new State House was opened on Beacon Hill, with the older structure being put to commercial use, and later serving for a decade as Boston's City Hall. Almost demolished in the 1880s, it was instead restored and saved for posterity as an interesting *museum of local history. Bostonians were reminded of the building's British origins in 1976, when Queen Elizabeth II spoke from its balcony, perhaps unaware of the decidedly unroyal goings-on that occurred here two centuries earlier.

The site of the 1770 **Boston Massacre** is marked with a ring of cobblestones set in a traffic island just east of the Old State House. Opposite the south side of the building is the **National Historical Park Visitor Center**, where you can get information, take a tour, rest your weary feet, and use the facilities. ☎ *(617) 242-5642. Open daily 9–5. Free.* ♿.

Follow the map to historic *Faneuil Hall (6)(pronounced FAN-yul), a lively and almost miraculously beautiful spot just opposite the brutally ugly City Hall of 1968. Originally built in 1742 by a wealthy merchant named Peter Faneuil as a central market for the growing city, it burned down in 1761 and was quickly rebuilt, apparently to the same design. Its upstairs meeting hall was known as America's "Cradle of Liberty" for the fiery anti-British speeches given there by Samuel Adams and others. Enlarged in 1806 by the noted architect Charles Bulfinch (of U.S. Capitol fame), it has continued its dual role as a marketplace of both food and ideas right down to the present.

Enter the ground floor, filled with eateries, shops, and a post office. At the east end (actually the front of the building), under the original grasshopper weathervane of 1742, visitors can go up to the restored *Meeting Hall of 1806 for a look around. On the wall behind the stage is a huge painting of Daniel Webster addressing Congress, with all the great Americans of the day in the audience. Oddly, the canvas was commissioned by King Louis-Philippe of France, who lost his throne before it was completed, so it remained in Boston. ☎ *(617) 242-5642. Open daily 9–5. Free.* ♿. Climbing higher, you can also visit the third-floor museum and armory of the **Ancient and Honorable Artillery Company of Massachusetts**, America's oldest military organization, founded in 1638 and resident here since 1746. Four of its members have gone on to become President of the U.S.: James Monroe, Chester Arthur, Calvin Coolidge, and John F. Kennedy. ☎ *(617) 227-1638. Open Mon.–Fri. 9–5.*

Three long buildings of the **Quincy Market** stand behind the hall, and together with it comprise the vibrant *Faneuil Hall Marketplace. Since the 1970s, this area has witnessed one of the earliest and most successful transformations of a blighted urban scene into a thriving attraction for locals and tourists alike. The central Quincy Market building dates from 1826 and looks like a very long Greek temple; one filled with a vast assortment of eateries centering on a two-storied food court under a great rotunda. More restaurants, bars, cafés, and all sorts of shops fill the equally old north and south buildings, spilling outdoors with pushcarts and sidewalk entertainers. A visit here is a highly enjoyable experience that should not be missed. ☎ *(617) 338-2323. Shops open Mon.–Sat. 10–9, Sun. noon–6. Restaurants and pubs open late every evening.*

Head up Union Street, passing the venerable Union Oyster House of 1826, which bills itself as America's oldest restaurant. Actually, the brick building is much older than that. Dating from around 1714, it was at one time home to the future King Louis-Philippe of France, who supported himself in exile by giving French lessons here.

Follow the map (or the red line) through a colorful old part of town, passing under the hideous elevated Central Artery highway. This will soon be decently buried in an underground tunnel now under construction. The route leads through the predominantly Italian **North End**, a neighborhood famous for its restaurants, to the:

*PAUL REVERE HOUSE (7), 19 North Sq., Boston, MA 02113, ☎ (617) 523-2338. *Open mid-Apr. through Oct., daily 9:30–5:15; Nov. to mid-Apr., daily 9:30–4:15. Closed Mondays in Jan., Feb., & Mar.; Thanksgiving, Christmas, & New Year's. Adults $2.50, seniors 62+ and students $2, children (5–17) $1. Partially ♿, call ahead.*

When Paul Revere (1735–1818), at the time a "middling" artisan, bought this home in 1770 it was already some 90 years old and completely out of style. He and his growing family (he had 16 children!) lived here until the early 1790s, after which he rented it out. Later used as a tenement, a cigar factory, and a grocery store, the structure became increasingly dilapidated until 1907, when his great-grandson led a movement to restore and protect this rare example of early Colonial urban architecture. This is, in fact, the oldest surviving dwelling in Boston.

It was from here that the great patriot left on that moonlit night of April 18, 1775, to be rowed across the river to Charlestown, where he received the "two if by sea" signal and set off for the Midnight Ride on a borrowed horse. The whole story is told, if somewhat inaccurately, in Henry Wadsworth Longfellow's lengthy poem of 1863, which you may have been subjected to in school.

Restored to its original appearance of 1680, the house is filled with period furnishings, a few of which belonged to the Revere family. Visitors can walk through on a self-guided tour and have their questions answered by attendants. On the same property is the **Pierce-Hichborn House** of 1711, the oldest surviving *brick* residence in Boston. It is shown on guided tours on certain days only; inquire in advance if interested.

The route now leads to **St. Stephen's Church** at Hanover and Clark streets. The only surviving church in Boston to have been designed by Charles Bulfinch, it was erected in 1804 as a Congregational meeting house,

The Paul Revere Mall

and became Unitarian in 1816. As the population of the North End changed, the church was sold to the Roman Catholic diocese and, in 1965, restored to its original appearance.

Turn left into the **Paul Revere Mall**, a pleasant bit of greenery leading up to the Old North Church. Plaques embedded in the side walls tell the stories of North End residents who played a role in Boston's history. The famous equestrian ***statue** of Paul Revere is here as well, and makes a fine photo subject with the church in the background. At the end stands the:

*OLD NORTH CHURCH (8), 193 Salem St., Boston, MA 02113, ☎ (617) 523-6676. *Open daily 9–5; Sunday services at 9, 11, and 4. Free, donations welcome.* ⅃.

Also known as Christ Church, Boston's oldest surviving house of worship was built in 1723 in the style of Sir Christopher Wren's London churches. It played a pivotal role in American history, for it was from the steeple here that two "lanthorns" signaled the news of the Redcoats coming by sea on the night of April 18, 1775—the spark that ignited the Revolutionary War. Ironically, the church remained loyal to the Crown and was supposedly used by the British commander, General Thomas Gage, as a vantage point to observe the disastrous Battle of Bunker Hill on June 17, 1775. The American Bicentennial celebration began here on April 18, 1975, with a visit by President Ford, followed by another by Queen Elizabeth II. Despite being in a decidedly non-Protestant neighborhood, the church remains Episcopalian to this day.

Continue up Hull Street to the **Copp's Hill Burying Ground**, overlooking Charlestown across the river. Begun in 1659, the cemetery is home to many famous Bostonians including the Mather family: Increase, a president of Harvard; Cotton, infamous as a puritanical witch-hunter; and Samuel, a minister of the church. Several hundred blacks, both slave and free, are also buried here. Copp's Hill was used by the British in 1775 as an artillery platform from which to bombard Charlestown.

If you're tired, this is a good place to stop before completing the walk on another day. Otherwise, bounding with energy, you can carry on by following the map across the Charlestown Bridge.

The second half of this walk begins along Charlestown's waterfront, where you'll pass the **Bunker Hill Pavilion** (9). This modern multimedia presentation uses the latest technology to re-create the Battle of Bunker Hill, fought nearby in 1775. ☎ *(617) 241-7575. Open daily 9:30–4, remaining open until 5 from June–Aug. Closed Thanksgiving and Dec 1 to Apr. 1. Adults $3, seniors $2, children $1.50.* ♿.

Continue into the decommissioned **Charleston Navy Yard**, now operated by the National Park Service as an historic site. From the early 19th century until 1974 this was an active shipyard, building and repairing warships for the U.S. Navy. It was especially active during World War II, employing some 50,000 workers to produce about 150 ships. Stop by the Visitor Center and then head directly to the prime attraction, the:

*USS *CONSTITUTION* (10), Pier 1, Charlestown, MA 02129, ☎ (617) 242-5670. *Tours daily, 9:30–3:50; self-guided visits 3:50–dusk. Free. Partially* ♿.

The world's oldest commissioned warship to remain afloat, the USS *Constitution* was launched in 1797 in Boston. She is popularly known as "Old Ironsides" because cannon balls just bounced off her 20-inch-thick oak sides. In all her years of active service she never lost a battle, even after fighting in some 40 of them. A participant in the so-called Pseudo-War with France, *Constitution* saw its first real combat against the Barbary pirates of North Africa in 1803. The War of 1812 proved to be her greatest moment, capturing or sinking many a British warship from Nova Scotia to Brazil. By 1830, however, her hull needed more repairs than the Navy was willing to pay for, so the proud ship was nearly scrapped. A poem by the young Oliver Wendell Holmes entitled "Old Ironsides" aroused public indignation to the point that the vessel was saved, making voyages until 1931. The USS *Constitution* has been restored so many times that today only about 10% of the original timbers exist, but she looks exactly as she did in 1797. On the Fourth of July of every year the proud warship slips out into the harbor on its annual turnaround cruise, firing a salute to the nation's birthday. She is still manned by U.S. Navy personnel wearing replica uniforms from the War of 1812, who take visitors on guided tours.

Close to the *Constitution* is another warship that you can board, the World War II Destroyer USS *Cassin Young*. Although built in California, she was modernized for the Korean Conflict here in Charlestown, where 14 other identical destroyers were produced during the 1940s. Near the Visitor Center is the:

USS *CONSTITUTION* MUSEUM (11), Box 1812, Charlestown, MA 02129, ☎ (617) 426-1812. *Open June–Labor Day, daily 9–6; March–May and Labor Day–Nov., daily 10–5; and Dec.–Feb., daily 10–4. Closed Thanksgiving, Christmas, and New Year's. Adults $4, seniors $3, children (6–16) $2. Gift shop.* &.
The history of the USS *Constitution* is brought to life in this large, modern museum of artifacts, hands-on displays, interactive exhibits, videos, and other experiences.

If you're really, totally pooped out by now, you can enjoy a leisurely ferry boat ride back to Long Wharf in Boston, near the Aquarium and Faneuil Hall. It leaves from Pier 4. Otherwise, follow the map uphill for one last sight.
The Battle of Bunker Hill ought to be called the Battle of Breed's Hill, because that's where it was fought, and that's where the **Bunker Hill Monument** (12) stands to commemorate the first major engagement of the Revolutionary War. It seems that the commander of some 1,200 American militiamen, given orders to defend Bunker Hill against the newly-arrived British forces, decided that nearby Breed's Hill was more defensible. He was obviously right, for the battle fought on June 17, 1775, was a terrible blow to British prestige, even though they technically won it.
At the top of the hill is a small lodge with dioramas and exhibits, and next to it the distressingly high obelisk marking the site of the battle. Climb it if you can—there are 294 steps and no elevator—for a spectacular *view and to give your legs a really good workout. Park rangers are on hand to tell you about the battle and how the monument came to be built. ☎ *(617) 242-5641. Open daily 9–4:30, lodge until 5. Closed Thanksgiving, Christmas, and New Year's. Free. Lodge is* &.
From here it's all downhill. You can get a bus to the Haymarket/Faneuil Hall area at City Square, opposite the John Harvard Mall; or an Orange Line subway at Community College, Austin Street near I-93.

Trip 2
Boston

The Waterfront

It would be a shame to visit Boston and not stroll its intriguing waterfront. Parts of this are still imbued with an old-time ambiance, while other sections radiate prosperity with their elegant, postmodern structures. Nearly all of it is easily accessible on foot. This amble takes you from the edge of workaday South Boston, through the booming Aquarium neighborhood, and well into the colorful North End, finishing there or at nearby Faneuil Hall in plenty of time for dinner.

Along the way you can relive the Boston Tea Party, treat your kids to their very own museum, walk through a giant computer, eat a fish, take a cruise, or explore the ocean depths without getting wet.

GETTING THERE:

By subway, take the Red "T" Line to **South Station**, where the walk begins. **Returning**, the nearest subway stations are at Aquarium (Blue Line), State (Blue and Orange lines), and Haymarket (Orange and Green lines).

By rail, take an MBTA commuter train or Amtrak to South Station.

PRACTICALITIES:

Good weather will greatly enhance your enjoyment of this trip. It may be taken on any day, but note that the Tea Party Ship is closed from December through February, and that both the Children's and Computer museums are closed on Mondays from Labor Day through June. Most attractions are closed on Thanksgiving, Christmas, and New Year's.

For further information, contact the **Boston Common Visitor Center**, 147 Tremont St., ☎ (800) 888-5515 or (617) 536-4100.

FOOD AND DRINK:

The prosperous waterfront area has only a few reasonably-priced lunch spots; fortunately you're within easy walking distance of Faneuil Hall and the North End, described on the Freedom Trail walk. For a light meal, you can always stop at the "milk bottle" concession outside the Children's Museum, or the snack bars in the Aquarium. Some good restaurants along the route are:

Rowe's Wharf Restaurant (70 Rowe's Wharf, in the Boston Harbor Hotel) Regional American cuisine with a creative touch, elegantly served overlooking the harbor. Dress well and reserve. ☎ (617) 439-3995. $$$

Cornucopia on the Wharf (100 Atlantic Ave., at Commercial Wharf) Creative American cuisine with a view. ☎ (617) 367-0300. $$ and $$$

Jimmy's Harborside (242 Northern Ave., a few blocks east of the Computer Museum) This long-established favorite offers all kinds of seafood along with a few meat dishes. Every table has a view of the harbor. ☎ (617) 423-1000. $$

Eastern Pier Seafood Restaurant (237 Northern Ave., a few blocks east of the Computer Museum) Chinese cuisine in a cozy maritime setting. ☎ (617) 423-7756. $$

No Name (15½ Fish Pier, a half-mile east of the Computer Museum, along Northern Ave.) Excellent seafood (and meat) at rock-bottom prices; plenty of atmosphere, hurried service. ☎ (617) 338-7539. $

SUGGESTED TOUR:

Numbers in parentheses correspond to numbers on the map. **South Station** (1), Boston's major transportation center, is easily reached by subway (Red Line), local bus, taxi, commuter train, Amtrak, or intercity bus. Recently renovated, it makes a handy starting point for this walk. Follow the map to the Congress Street Bridge. Halfway across this is the:

BOSTON TEA PARTY SHIP & MUSEUM (2), Congress St. Bridge, Boston, MA 02210, ☎ (617) 338-1773. *Open March through Nov., daily 9–5, closing at 6 in summer. Closed Thanksgiving and all winter. Adults $6.50, seniors (62+) and students $5.20, children (6–12) $3.25.*

Climb aboard the brig *Beaver II*, a faithful replica of one of the three British ships from which the tea was dumped on that fateful night of December 16, 1773. Americans, then as now, hated to pay taxes; especially to the British, and especially without representation in Parliament. An economic boycott ensued, with colonists refusing to purchase taxed merchandise. Eventually, most of these taxes were rescinded, but a small token one remained on tea. When three ships loaded with 340 chests of British tea docked in Boston, a group of rebels dressed themselves up as Mohawk Indians and went on the warpath. With much whooping and hollering they climbed aboard the vessels and threw the hated cargo overboard. Then they went home. No one was hurt, but the message sent to the other colonies— and to London—was loud and clear.

You, too, can throw a bale of tea into the harbor, and explore all over the two-master that actually sailed here from England (with a load of tea!) in 1973. The **museum** has relevant artifacts, including a tea chest believed to be one of those chucked overboard. There is also a model of 18th-century Boston, an audiovisual presentation, and more.

Continue across the bridge and turn left onto Museum Wharf, passing an amazing snack bar in the shape of an old milk bottle, a relic of the 1930s. Next to this is the:

CHILDREN'S MUSEUM (3), 300 Congress St., Boston, MA 02210, ☎ (617) 426-8855. *Open July through Labor Day, daily 10–5, Fri. until 9; rest of year Tues.–Sun. 10–5, Fri. until 9. Closed Thanksgiving, Christmas, New Year's. Adults $7, seniors and children (2–15) $6, age 1 $2, under 1 free; all ages $1 on Fri. 5–9.* &.

Don't fail to stop here if you happen to have a kid in tow. They'll love it, and so will the child inside you. Worldwide cultures are explored in lively, hands-on exhibits, where visitors can try out different roles and experience other lifestyles. They can dress up in fantasy costumes, put on shows, experiment with science projects, and engage in a zillion other activities that encourage imagination, curiosity, questioning, and just plain old fun.

Right next door is the:

COMPUTER MUSEUM (4), 300 Congress St., Boston, MA 02210, ☎ (617) 423-6758 or 426-2800. *Open mid-June through Labor Day, daily 10–6; rest of year Tues.–Sun. 10–5. Adults $7, seniors (65+) and children (5–18) $5, 4 and under free.* &.

Even technophobes who can't set their own VCRs can learn a lot about the information revolution in this unique museum. Begin by walking through a gigantic computer so you can see how the beast works, then take a stroll in cyberspace, playing with the internet or wandering off into virtual reality at sites along the way. Kids love this place, and adults get to learn something.

Continue north along the waterfront, then turn left across the Fort Point Channel on Northern Avenue. The route leads along the water's edge to **Rowe's Wharf** (5), until fairly recently a seedy area of dilapidated buildings cut off from the rest of Boston by the ugly Central Artery highway. What a difference prosperity makes! The elevated eyesore is on its way to being buried underground, thus connecting the waterfront to the revitalized Faneuil Hall area. Where rotting warehouses once stood, the elegant Rowe's Wharf complex of 1987 offers luxurious living and a delightful waterside promenade for all to enjoy. Note the attractive little ferry terminal with its domed roof, from which the airport water shuttle departs next to several fancy cruise boats.

Follow along the water's edge past the twin Harbor Towers and India Wharf to the waterfront's prime attraction, the:

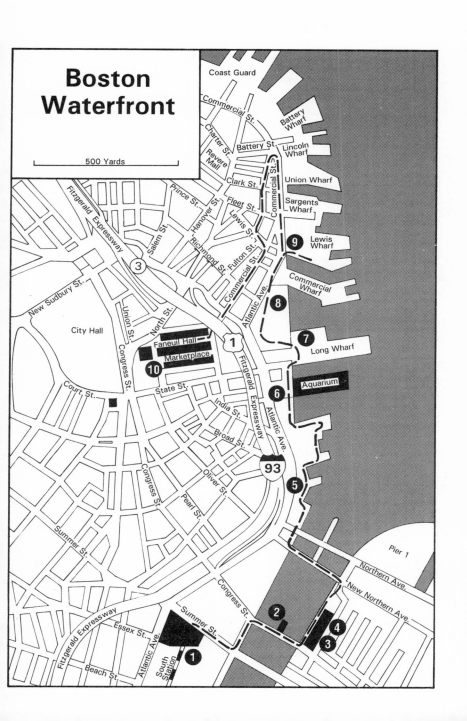

Boston
Waterfront

500 Yards

Coast Guard

Commercial St.

Battery Wharf

Charter St.

Battery St.

Lincoln Wharf

Revere Mall

Commercial St.

Union Wharf

Clark St.

Prince St.

Fleet St.

Sargents Wharf

Salem St.

Hanover St.

Lewis St.

Richmond St.

Fulton St.

9 Lewis Wharf

Fitzgerald Expressway

3

Commercial St.

Commercial Wharf

New Sudbury St.

Atlantic Ave.

8

Union St.

City Hall

North St.

7 Long Wharf

Faneuil Hall
Marketplace

1

Congress St.

10

Fitzgerald Expressway

Aquarium

Court St.

State St.

6

India St.

Atlantic Ave.

Broad St.

Congress St.

Oliver St.

93

Pearl St.

5

Summer St.

Pier 1

Northern Ave.

Congress St.

New Northern Ave.

Fitzgerald Expressway

Summer St.

2

Essex St.

4

Atlantic Ave.

3

Beach St.

South Station

1

*NEW ENGLAND AQUARIUM (6), Central Wharf, Boston, MA 02110, ☎ (617) 973-5200. *Open July through Labor Day, Mon.–Fri. 9–6, remaining open until 8 on Wed. & Thurs., weekends and holidays 9–7; rest of year Mon.–Fri. 9–5, remaining open until 8 on Thurs., weekends and holidays 9– 6. Closed Thanksgiving and Christmas. Adults $8.75, seniors $7.75, juniors (3–11) $4.75, under 3 free. Gift shops.* ♨ ♿.

Visitors here can plunge to the ocean depths without even getting wet by simply walking down the spiral ramp that surrounds the magnificent glass-sided, four-story-high, 187,000-gallon ***Giant Ocean Tank**. Exotic tropical fish, huge sea turtles, moray eels, and scary sharks glide right past your eyes, only inches away, in this re-creation of a Caribbean coral reef. Other living exhibits explore the world's waters, from Boston Harbor to the Amazon River. Special shows and events are announced frequently throughout the day, and there's a wonderful ***Sea Lion Show** aboard the floating pavilion *Discovery*.

From April to October, the Aquarium also offers **Whale-watching cruises** for an extra fee. ☎ *(617) 973-5277 for schedules and reservations.*

Outside the Aquarium, an outfit called **Boston Duck Tours** offers rides on an amazing amphibious military vehicle that waddles around town and then plunges into the Charles River for a short cruise. ☎ *(800) 226-7442 or (617) 723-3825. Operates mid-Apr. to Nov.* More cruises are offered from the nearby **Long Wharf** (7). A particularly enjoyable short one is to **Georges Island**, site of the well-preserved Fort Warren of Civil War fame. *Bay State Cruises, red ticket office, 67 Long Wharf,* ☎ *(617) 723-7800. Operates Memorial Day to Labor Day or later.* Another outfit, Boston Harbor Cruises, has inner harbor and sightseeing rides. ☎ *(617) 227-4321.*

You could finish your walk right here since you're close to the Aquarium subway stop and Faneuil Hall, but if you'd like to continue into the colorful North End just follow the map to **Christopher Columbus Park** (8). Serving as a link between the revitalized Faneuil Hall area and the renovated dockside, this lovely promenade area offers sweeping ***views** across the harbor, as well as a place to rest. A bit farther north, **Lewis Wharf** (9) provides a more intimate, and even prettier, view. First built in the mid-17th century and once owned by John Hancock, it was rebuilt in 1836 with the handsome granite buildings that grace it today. In the mid-19th century this was a center of the clipper ship trade.

Continue north along Atlantic Avenue and Commercial Street, passing Sargents, Union, and Lincoln wharfs. A hard left turn onto North Street takes you through a very old part of town. Follow it south a few blocks, then turn left on Lewis Street and right on Commercial Street. This will return you to the **Faneuil Hall Marketplace** (10) described on the previous Freedom Trail walk, a great place to end your daytrip.

Beacon Hill

Way back in 1634, the early Pilgrims erected a beacon atop one of Boston's three adjacent hills to warn of possible attack. Two of the hills have long since become landfill, but the one that remains—though truncated by some 60 feet—has changed little since the 19th century. Its quaint lanes and half-hidden cul-de-sacs, lined with brick dwellings, are still lit with gaslamps and sometimes cobblestoned. This remains the preserve of proper Boston Brahmins (who can sometimes be observed in their native habitat), although more than a few upwardly-mobile young professionals have taken up residence in recent years.

While the affluent settled on the sunny south slope of Beacon Hill, in the 19th century the colder north slope became home to Boston's growing black community. Virtually all of the historic sites connected with this settlement are covered on the walk, although not in the same sequence as the city's official Black Heritage Trail.

GETTING THERE:

By subway, take the Red or Green "T" line to **Park Street** and walk north through the Common.

By car, park as close to the Common as possible, preferably using the underground parking facility whose entrance is on Charles Street.

PRACTICALITIES:

This walk can be made at any time in nice weather, although if you wish to tour the Massachusetts State House you'll have to do so on a weekday that's not a major holiday. Those planning to visit the few houses that are open should check their schedules first.

For further information, contact the **Boston Common Visitor Center**, 147 Tremont St., ☎ (800) 888-5515 or (617) 536-4100.

FOOD AND DRINK:

Quiet, residential Beacon Hill offers little in the way of lunch restaurants; however, you're not very far from some choices on the Freedom Trail walk. Along this particular route you'll pass:

Another Season (97 Mount Vernon St.) Exceptionally fine Continental cuisine, served elegantly. Reservations advised, ☎ (617) 367-0880. $$$

Cheers (84 Beacon St.) Join the mobs of tourists waiting to get into the Bull & Finch Pub, the original inspiration for the "Cheers" TV show. Burgers, sandwiches, pub fare—even a gift shop. ☎ (617) 227-9600. $$

Rebecca's (21 Charles St.) Creative American cuisine. ☎ (617) 742-9747. $$

Ristorante Toscano (47 Charles St.) Northern Italian cuisine. ☎ (617) 723-4090. $$

SUGGESTED TOUR:

Numbers in parentheses correspond to numbers on the map. Begin at the:

*STATE HOUSE (1), Beacon St., Boston, MA 02115, ☎ (617) 727-3676. *Open Mon.–Fri. 9–5, guided tours 10–4. Closed major holidays. Free.* ♿, *use Bowdoin St. entrance.*

Charles Bulfinch (of U.S. Capitol fame) completed this state capitol building in 1798, and its front façade remains pretty much the same to this day. Its golden dome, visible for miles around, still dominates Beacon Hill. The main doors are opened only for visiting presidents and departing governors, but you can get in through an adjacent portal. Inside, there are the usual statues, cannon, flags, and paintings depicting historical events, and there is also the ***Sacred Cod**, a gilded wooden fish suspended in the House of Representatives since 1798.

Continue down Beacon Street, passing the site of John Hancock's mansion on what is now the west lawn of the State House. It was torn down in 1863. A number of handsome old buildings line the street here, overlooking Boston Common. Be on the lookout for occasional panes of purple window glass dating from the early 19th century, when some of the glass imported from Europe contained an unusually large amount of manganese dioxide. Some examples of this rarity are at numbers 39–40 and 63–64 Beacon Street. Beyond Charles Street the hill levels out as this is all landfill created when the other two hills were decapitated. Near the corner of Brimmer Street stands the Bull & Finch Pub, famous as the inspiration for the TV series "Cheers."

Follow the map around to ***Acorn Street** (2), surely the most picturesque little lane in all of Boston—and also the most photographed. At the top of the rise turn right, then left onto Chestnut Street. Charles Bulfinch designed the house at number 29A in 1800; its elegant bow front was added around 1817 and boasts the distinctive purple panes of glass. Edwin Booth, the actor and brother of Lincoln's assassin, lived here in the late 19th century. The row of houses at numbers 17, 15, and 13 were also designed by Bulfinch.

Turn left on Walnut Street. At the top, slightly to the right on Mount

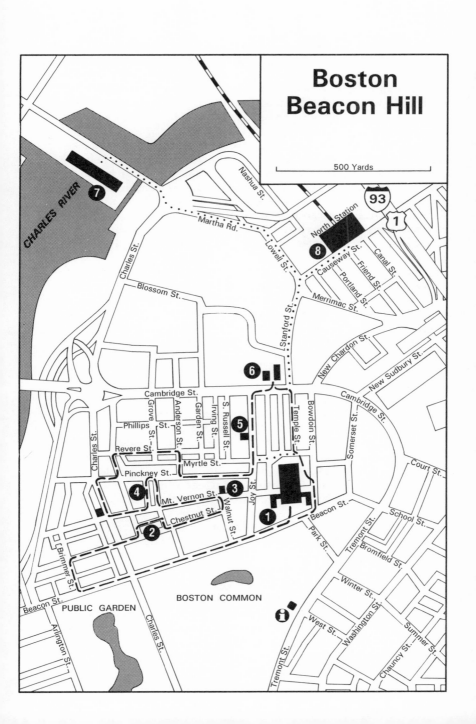

Boston
Beacon Hill

500 Yards

CHARLES RIVER

7

Nashua St.

North Station

93

1

8

Martha Rd.

Lowell St.

Causeway St.

Canal St.

Friend St.

Portland St.

Merrimac St.

Blossom St.

Charles St.

Stanford St.

New Chardon St.

New Sudbury St.

Cambridge St.

6

Cambridge St.

Grove St.

Phillips St.

Anderson St.

Garden St.

Irving St.

S. Russell St.

5

Temple St.

Bowdoin St.

Somerset St.

Court St.

Revere St.

Myrtle St.

Pinckney St.

4

Mt. Vernon St.

3

Joy St.

School St.

Charles St.

Chestnut St.

Walnut St.

1

Beacon St.

Tremont St.

Bromfield St.

2

Park St.

Brimmer St.

Beacon St.

BOSTON COMMON

Winter St.

PUBLIC GARDEN

Charles St.

Washington St.

Summer St.

Arlington St.

Tremont St.

West St.

Chauncy St.

Vernon Street, stands the **Nichols House Museum** (3). Again built by Bulfinch, this was the residence of a remarkable lady named Rose Standish Nichols from 1885 until 1960. Visitors can gain an insight into Beacon Hill social life by taking the guided tour. ☎ *(617) 227-6993. Open May–Oct., Tues.–Sat. noon–5; rest of year Mon., Wed., and Sat. noon–4. Closed Jan. and major holidays. Admission $4.*

Stroll down Mount Vernon Street, passing Beacon Hill's grandest mansion at number 85. Yes, once again, this was a creation of Charles Bulfinch, America's first professional architect. Built in 1802, it is set back from the street line. Continue past two more Bulfinch houses at numbers 87 and 89, and turn right into lovely ***Louisburg Square** (4). A private park has graced the square, virtually unchanged, since 1847. The bowfronted Greek Revival row houses are unusually elegant, and several have historical associations. Louisa May Alcott, the author of *Little Women,* lived at number 10 until her death in 1888.

Mount Vernon Street leads down to Charles Street, the main north-south artery of Beacon Hill and a thriving commercial thoroughfare rich in restaurants, cafés, art galleries, and antique shops. Across the intersection is the **Charles Street Meeting House**, built around 1807 for a dissident Baptist congregation. At that time this was next to the Charles River, in whose waters baptisms were performed. Prior to the Civil War this was a forum for such abolitionists as William Lloyd Garrison, Frederick Douglass, and Sojourner Truth. In 1876 it was purchased by an African Methodist congregation and later became an Albanian Orthodox church. It is now an office building.

Follow the map to Revere Street. Several picturesque alleyways—cobblestoned, gas-lit, and lined with old houses—lead off to the north. Find your way around to Pinckney Street, the dividing line between the affluent south slope and the more plebeian north. The small clapboard house at number 5, built around 1790 for two free black men, is regarded as the oldest surviving dwelling on the hill. A left turn on Joy Street takes you downhill to **Smith Court** (5), a short cul-de-sac that was the center of Boston's early black community. The **African Meeting House** at number 8, built in 1806, is the oldest black church building still standing in the United States. Today it houses exhibits of the Museum of Afro-American History as well as the meetinghouse proper. ☎ *(617) 742-1854. Open daily 10–4, closed holidays. Donation.* Adjacent to this is the **Abiel Smith School** of 1834, one of the first black schools in the nation.

At this point you could return to the State House (1) to finish your tour, or continue downhill to the **Harrison Gray Otis House** (6) of 1796 on Cambridge Street. This was the first of three mansions built by Charles Bulfinch for Otis, a wealthy businessman and politician. Now fully restored and a fine place to see how the really rich lived in the early days of the Republic, it also serves as headquarters for the Society for the Preservation of New England Antiquities. ☎ *(617) 227-3956. Open Tues.–Fri. noon–5, and Sat. 10–5.*

Guided tours on the hour, last one at 4. Closed holidays. Adults $4, seniors (65+) $3.50, children (6–12) $2. Next to the Otis House stands the **Old West Church**, erected in 1806 on the site of an earlier Congregational church that was badly damaged by British troops.

If the day is still young and you have energy left, you might want to make a side trip to the north of Beacon Hill before returning to the State House. Here are two interesting destinations:

*MUSEUM OF SCIENCE (7), Science Park, Boston, MA 02114, ☎ (617) 723-2500, TTY 589-0417. *Open daily 9–5, Fri. until 9; hours extended July 5 to Labor Day. Closed Thanksgiving and Christmas. Adults $8, seniors (65+) and children (3–14) $6. Omni Theater, Planetarium, and Laser Shows extra, discounted combination tickets available. Gift shop.* ✗. ♿.

One of the world's great science museums offers all manner of technological and natural wonders, presenting them in a way that even adults can understand. It's all hands-on with over 450 interactive exhibits that you can play with. Lightning strikes again and again at the monstrous Van de Graaff generator, and there are dinosaurs as well as living creatures, large and small. The Omni Theater presents one of those wraparound massive-screen shows, while the Planetarium takes visitors on a journey through the Cosmos. Allow lots of time.

FLEET CENTER TOURS (8), Causeway St., Boston, MA 02114, ☎ (617) 624-1518. *Open daily except during events, 10–4:30. Adults $6, seniors & students $4.50, children under 12 $5.*

Home to both the Boston Bruins and the Boston Celtics, the new Fleet-Center sits atop a renovated North Station. These guided tours take you through it, even visiting a locker room.

Trip 4
Boston

*Back Bay

By contrast with the earlier walking tours, this amble through Back Bay focuses on the Boston of today instead of the distant past. It could hardly be otherwise. Until the late 19th century most of the land was under water, or at least a swampy tidal flat. Serious landfill operations got underway around 1857 and continued into the 1890s. At the same time, new ideas of city planning and fresh trends in architecture were evolving, expressing themselves in some of the most beautiful streets this side of Paris. Today, Back Bay pulsates with contemporary life; smart, sophisticated, youthful, and definitely upbeat.

The walk begins with a leisurely stroll through Boston Common and the Public Garden, where you can enjoy a short cruise on one of Boston's signature swan boats. Nearby, you might take a look at the Charles River Esplanade, or visit a preserved Victorian mansion. Crossing magnificent Commonwealth Avenue, visitors are struck by the contrast between the fabulously ornate Trinity Church and its neighbor, the sleek, shiny, 60-story John Hancock Tower, perhaps ascending it for a view. Copley Square has got to be one of the most delightful public places anywhere. The route leads through decidedly upscale shopping areas to the Christian Science Center, an intensely interesting complex that serves as the world headquarters for the religion. Farther down the road, still within walking distance, are two major world-class art museums where you can finish your day amid great beauty.

GETTING THERE:

By subway, take the Red or Green "T" line to **Park Street** and stroll into Boston Common. **Returning** from the art museums or Prudential Center, board the Green "T" line (actually a sometimes-underground trolley car) that runs along Huntington Avenue.

By car, park as close to the Common as possible, preferably using the underground parking facility whose entrance is on Charles Street.

PRACTICALITIES:

This is a fairly long, though level, walk, so be sure to wear comfortable shoes. Several of the most important attractions are closed on Mondays, Thanksgiving, Christmas, and New Year's; otherwise the trip can be taken on any day in fine weather.

For further information, visit or contact the **Boston Common Visitor Center**, 147 Tremont St., ☎ (800) 888-5515 or (617) 536-4100.

Copley Square

FOOD AND DRINK:

Boston's Back Bay abounds in superb eateries. Those in a hurry might consider the Terrace Food Court in the Prudential Center.

Mirabelle (85 Newbury St., 2 blocks west of the Public Gardens) A softly elegant, cozy, contemporary restaurant featuring regional cuisine. Reservations advised, ☎ (617) 859-4848. $$$

Café Budapest (Copley Square Hotel, 90 Exeter St., just southwest of Copley Sq.) Hungarian and Continental cuisine in an Old World setting. Reservations suggested. ☎ (617) 266-1979. $$$

Top of the Hub (800 Boylston St., 52nd floor of Prudential Tower) Enjoy a spectacular panoramic view along with creative American cuisine. Reservations suggested. ☎ (617) 536-1775. $$$

Small Planet (565 Boylston St. at Copley Sq.) All manner of creative ethnic dishes; truly a Global Village of tastes and eccentricities. ☎ (617) 536-4477. X: Mon. & Tues. lunch. $$

Fine Arts Restaurant (in the Museum of Fine Arts) An unusually good museum eatery, with a menu that varies with the exhibitions. For lighter fare, there is also a café and cafeteria. ☎ (617) 266-3663. X: Mon. $ and $$

Gardner Café (in the Isabella Stewart Gardner Museum) Light lunches in a pleasantly artistic setting, with outdoor tables in summer. ☎ (617) 566-1088. X: Mon. $

SUGGESTED TOUR:

Numbers in parentheses correspond to numbers on the map.

Boston Common (1) was, of course, here when Back Bay itself was still a swamp. This 50-acre tract has been public land since 1634, and is regarded as the nation's oldest public park. At first it was used as a common pasturage, but over the years it became the site of such public functions as the hanging of Quakers and witches, and the training of militia. Mostly, however, the Common was a place where the public gathered to enjoy themselves, as they still do.

Enter from Tremont Avenue, close to both the Park Street subway stop and the **Visitor Center**, where you can get all sorts of information about Boston. Stroll through the park and exit at Charles Street, once the dividing line between water and land. The **Public Garden** (2), on the west side of the street, was laid out on the new landfill in 1859 and essentially completed by 1900. In its center is a large pond spanned by a picturesque suspension bridge, to the left of which is the dock from which you can board one of Boston's famous ***Swan Boats** for a short cruise. This irresistible treat has been operated by the same family since 1877. ☎ *(617) 522-1966. Rides April to mid-Sept., daily, weather permitting. Adults $1.50, under 13 95¢.* Continue past the splendid equestrian statue of George Washington and exit the garden.

Turn north on Arlington Street to Beacon Street. From the far corner there you can cross the Fiedler Footbridge for a look at the **Charles River Esplanade** (3), a lovely park along the river's edge. To the north is the Hatch Memorial Shell, where the beloved Boston Pops Orchestra gives outdoor concerts in July. Back on Beacon Street stands the **Gibson House** (4), one of the many Victorian town houses that grace this grand old thoroughfare. Built as early as 1859 as one of the first structures on the newly-reclaimed land, it remained in the same family, virtually unchanged, until becoming a house museum in the 1950s. Visitors today are taken on a guided tour that reveals much about the lifestyles of the rich elite who moved into Back Bay. *137 Beacon St.,* ☎ *(617) 267-6338. Open May–Oct., Wed.–Sun., tours at 1, 2, & 3; rest of year, weekends only, tours at 1, 2, & 3. Admission $4.*

Head south on Berkeley Street to the **First and Second Church** (5), a strikingly modern concrete structure that incorporates segments of the original 1868 church, which was destroyed by fire in 1968. Turn right onto Marlborough Street, then left on Clarendon Street, heading south past the **First Baptist Church** (6). This 1872 building is most noted for the frieze above the arches of its tower, sculpted in Paris by Frédéric-Auguste Bartholdi, who also created the Statue of Liberty in New York Harbor.

Next to the church runs ***Commonwealth Avenue**, a magnificent, wide, tree-lined thoroughfare clearly modeled after the grand boulevards of Paris, and every bit as elegant. In another block you'll cross **Newbury Street**, Boston's most exclusive shopping venue. Continue south on Clarendon to a

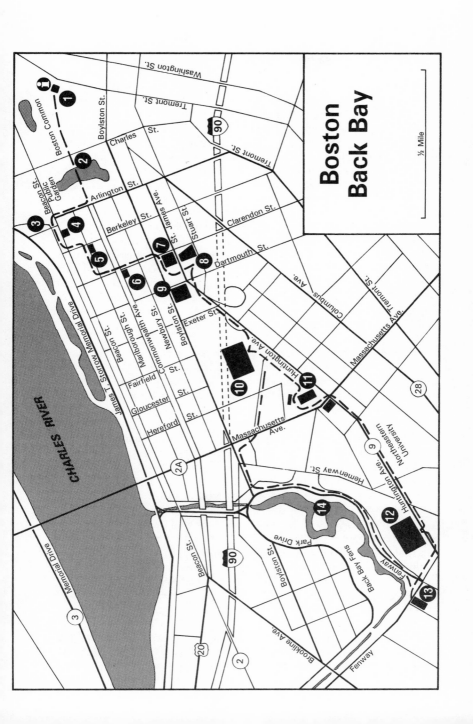

Boston
Back Bay

½ Mile

stunning sight. ***Trinity Church** (7) was the crowning achievement of Henry Hobson Richardson (1838–86), the architect who created much of Back Bay's visual splendor. Consecrated in 1877, it is a masterpiece of the Romanesque Revival style then so popular in America. Its massive ***tower** was adapted from that of the Old Cathedral in Salamanca, Spain, while the ***west porch**—richly carved with Biblical figures—owes its design to the 11th-century Church of St. Trophime in Arles, France. Step inside to view the marvelous **frescos** and stained-glass **windows**, as well as the finely-carved white-marble **pulpit**. ☎ *(617) 536-0944. Open daily 8–6.* ♿.

Trinity's medieval beauty is reflected in the sleek glass walls of its neighbor, the ***John Hancock Tower** (8), whose irregular rhomboid shape alters its appearance according to the point of view. New England's tallest building was completed in 1976, and immediately encountered a slight problem—the windows kept falling out. That embarrassment was eventually corrected, and today the tower is most noted for the fabulous ***panoramic vista** from its 60th-floor observatory. Besides the view, visitors are treated to a sound-and-light show of Colonial Boston, an audiovisual history of the city, and other exhibits. ☎ *(617) 572-6429. Open Mon.–Sat. 9 a.m. to 11 p.m., Sun. 10 a.m. (noon in winter) to 11 p.m. Closed Thanksgiving and Christmas. Adults $3.75, seniors and children (5–17) $2.75.* ♿.

Facing both buildings is ***Copley Square** (9), an unusually handsome public space that serves as Back Bay's civic center. Not only is the square attractive in itself; it is surrounded by some of the best architecture in Boston. Besides Trinity Church and the Hancock Tower, there is (to the south) the sedate Copley Plaza Hotel of 1912, and to the west the remarkable ***Boston Public Library**. Completed in 1895 by the New York architectural firm of McKim, Mead and White, it is a masterpiece of the elegant Renaissance Revival style. The rich decorations of its façade are continued inside, opening into a marvelous **courtyard** that is among the loveliest spots in town. ☎ *(617) 536-5400. Open Mon.–Thurs. 9–9, Fri.–Sat. 9–5. Free.* Finally, in the northwest corner of Copley Square, stands the New Old South Church of 1875, a somewhat exotic rendering of the North Italian Gothic style.

Head down Huntington Avenue, crossing the submerged Massachusetts Turnpike (I-90). To the right, the enormous **Prudential Center** (10) contains a convention center, department stores, apartments, a hotel, and an office tower; all tied together by a meandering, upscale shopping mall. A recent facelift has improved the dull 1960s architecture, finally bringing vitality to this early example of urban renewal. There's a fine ***360° view** from the 50th-floor **Skywalk Observatory**. ☎ *(617) 236-3318. Open Mon.–Sat. 10 a.m.– 10 p.m., Sun. noon–10 p.m. Adults $2.75, seniors, students, and children $1.75.* ♿.

Just a block or so to the southwest is another vast building complex; this one quite interesting. The ***Christian Science Center** (11) is the world headquarters of that religion, founded in 1866 by Mary Baker Eddy. Its striking buildings, dating from 1894 to 1973, are beautifully arranged around an enormous reflecting pool. The original **Mother Church** of 1894 is neatly attached to its 1904 **Extension**. Together they are made up of both Roman-esque and Renaissance elements, with a touch of the Byzantine thrown in. ☎ *(617) 450-3790. Tours Tues.–Fri. 10–4, Sat. noon–4, Sun. 11:15–2. Closed holidays. Free.* Another part of the complex houses offices of *The Christian Science Monitor,* a highly-respected international daily news-paper, and the unusual **Mapparium**, which you can visit. The latter is actually a stained-glass globe some 30 feet in diameter, through which a glass bridge enables visitors to see the world from the inside out. The world as it was in 1935, that is. ☎ *(617) 450-3790. Open Tues.–Fri. 9:30–4, Sat. noon–4. Closed holidays. Free.*

From here it's a 10-minute walk down Huntington Avenue, passing Symphony Hall and Northeastern University along the way, to the:

*MUSEUM OF FINE ARTS (12), 465 Huntington Ave., Boston, MA 02115, ☎ (617) 267-9300, TTY/TDD (617) 267-9703. *Open Tues.–Sat. 10–4:45, Sun. 10–5:45, remaining open on Wed. until 9:45. West Wing is also open on Thurs. and Fri. from 5–9:45 p.m. Closed Mon., Thanksgiving, Dec. 24 & 25. Adults $8, seniors (60+) and college students $6, youths (6–17) $3.50. Reduced prices during West-Wing-only hours. Special exhibitions may be extra. No charge to use restaurants, shop, and some other facilities. Museum shop.* ✗, ☕. ♿.

Boston is blessed with one of the world's major art museums. You could probably spend an entire day here, but even a short visit of an hour or two will prove rewarding. Whether your interests lie in Asian, Middle Eastern, Classical, European, or American art, or even in current trends, you'll surely find much to discover in these vast collections. The museum is especially noted for its fabulous ***Chinese and Japanese holdings**, ranging from Neo-lithic ceramics to the marvelous outdoor Tenshin-En ***Japanese Garden** through which you can stroll. Its ***Ancient Egyptian and Near Eastern collec-tions** are rivalled only by those of the Cairo Museum. **European art** ranges from the 12th century to the present, with an emphasis on the Romantics, the Barbizon School, the Impressionists, and the Post-Impressionists. **American paintings and decorative arts** reach back as far as the 17th century, covering a continuous stream of creativity right up to the present moment.

Just two blocks to the west is the:

*ISABELLA STEWART GARDNER MUSEUM (13), 280 The Fenway, Boston, MA 02115, ☎ (617) 566-1401. *Open Tues.–Sun. 11–5. Closed most Mon. plus Thanksgiving, Christmas, and New Year's. Adults $7, seniors and col-lege students $5, youths (12–17) $3, under 12 free. Concerts. Museum shop.* ☕. ♿.

Boston's other great—and rather quirky—art museum is perhaps just as

In the courtyard of the Isabella Stewart Gardner Museum

famous for its ambiance as for the masterpieces it contains. Nothing much has changed here since Isabella Stewart Gardner (1840–1924), a Boston socialite and art collector, opened her museum to the public in 1903. She designed the building itself, known as Fenway Court, in the style of a 15th-century Venetian palace opening inward to a flower-filled ***courtyard**. Not surprisingly, the collection is particularly rich in ***Italian Renaissance paintings**, especially those by Botticelli, Raphael, and Titian. French, German, Spanish, Dutch, and Flemish masters such as Rembrandt and Rubens are also well represented. Paintings by John Singer Sargent and James McNeill Whistler, both friends of Isabella Stewart Gardner, highlight the "modern" collection, along with works by Degas, Manet, and Matisse. A visit to this museum is a delightful experience; one you won't soon forget.

Time and energy permitting, you might want to head back by ambling through the **Back Bay Fens** (14), a string of parks following the course of the Muddy River. Turn right at Boylston Street, where you can board a Green Line subway at the corner of Massachusetts Avenue, or continue on foot back to the Copley Square area.

Cambridge

Located just across the Charles River from Boston, and sharing the same transit system, Cambridge is really a world onto itself. Although its history goes back just as far as its larger neighbor, the home of Harvard University, Radcliffe College, and the Massachusetts Institute of Technology is a more youthful, livelier town. And definitely trendier, whether in fashion or politics.

Like Boston, Cambridge was first settled in 1630, only then it was called Newtowne. Not much later, in 1636, America's first college was established there to provide for the education of clergy. In 1638 a Charlestown pastor named John Harvard died, leaving half of his estate and all of his considerable library to the new school, which was then named Harvard in his honor. Around the same time the town's name was changed to Cambridge, after the English alma mater of many of the Puritan leaders. The first printing press in the British colonies began operation there that very same year, heightening the town's status as an intellectual center.

While this walking tour focuses on Harvard, and especially on its fine museums, it also covers the historic core of Old Cambridge as well as contemporary life there. You might continue on, if you please, to the museums at MIT, and to the nearby Sports Museum of New England.

GETTING THERE:

By subway, take the Red "T" line to the Harvard stop.

By bus, if you're in the Back Bay area you can take the number 1 bus, which goes past MIT to Harvard Square. Otherwise take the subway.

By car, your major problem will be finding a place to park. Do this as close to Harvard Square as you can, even if you have to resort to a pay lot.

PRACTICALITIES:

For further information, visit or contact the **Cambridge Discovery Booth** on Harvard Square, ☎ (617) 497-1630. Information specific to Harvard University can be had from the **Harvard University Information Center** in Holyoke Center, 1350 Massachusetts Avenue at Harvard Square, ☎ (617) 495-1573.

FOOD AND DRINK:

You'll encounter an overwhelming choice of restaurants and cafés—every cuisine, every price range—around Harvard Square. Here are a few good ones:

Harvest (44 Brattle St., a block northwest of Brattle Sq.) Hidden away in a courtyard, Harvest offers fabulous, creative American cuisine. The restaurant section is fancier and takes reservations, the café section does not but is less expensive. ☎ (617) 492-1115. $$ and $$$

Grendel's Den (89 Winthrop St., a block south of Brattle Sq.) A great salad bar, veggies, and an eclectic menu from all over the world have made this a favorite. ☎ (617) 491-1160. $$

Border Café (32 Church St., a block west of Harvard Square) Tex-Mex and Cajun cooking—lots of fun at bargain prices. ☎ (617) 864-6100. $ and $$

Charlie's Kitchen (10 Eliot St., 2 blocks south of Brattle Sq.) Charlie's specializes in double cheeseburgers, and has a sports bar with 12 TVs. ☎ (617) 492-9646. $

Café Pamplona (12 Bow St., 4 blocks southeast of Harvard Sq.) The most intellectual of intellectual coffeehouses offers light lunches along with conversations in the most obscure languages. No phone. $

SUGGESTED TOUR:

Numbers in parentheses correspond to numbers on the map. Begin at **Harvard Square** (1), where you'll find a tourist information booth near the subway exit. Information about Harvard University, including free tours, campus maps, and the like can be had a block to the east on the ground floor of the Holyoke Center shopping complex on Massachusetts Avenue.

Cross the avenue and enter **Harvard Yard** (2), the oldest part of the university. **Wadsworth House**, a yellow clapboard building to the right, was erected in 1727 as a residence for the president of Harvard. George Washington used it briefly as his headquarters in July, 1775, when he came to Cambridge to assume command of the Continental Army. Today it houses university offices. Continue straight ahead into a grassy area known as Old Harvard Yard, dating back to the earliest days. The oldest building still standing at Harvard, **Massachusetts Hall** (3), was completed in 1720 and once housed Continental Army soldiers. The President and other university officials have their offices there now, and freshmen live on the upper floors. It's to your left on the path leading to the upper part of Harvard Square.

Directly across the yard stands the **University Hall** (4) of 1816, designed by Charles Bulfinch, the famous architect who also built the Massachusetts State House (see the Beacon Hill trip) and finished the U.S. Capitol in Washington. In front of this is a much-photographed bronze ***statue of John Harvard**, cast in 1884 by Daniel Chester French, creator of the statue of Lincoln at the Lincoln Memorial in Washington. Unfortunately, no one knows what the real John Harvard looked like, and the inscription contains major errors of fact.

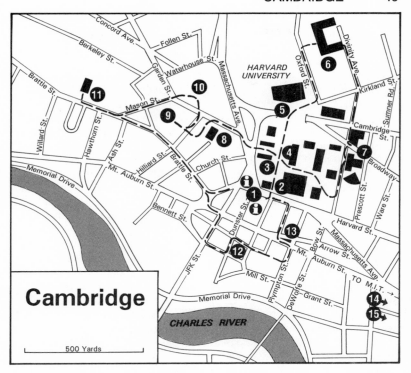

Cambridge

500 Yards

CHARLES RIVER

Continue north and exit the Old Yard. Right ahead of you is the enormous **Science Center** (5) of 1972, looking for all the world like a modern factory. The Tanner Fountain, outside, runs on timed cycles and emits steam in winter. Bear right to **Memorial Hall**, a large, looming brick building of 1878 that strongly resembles a Gothic cathedral. Commemorating the Harvard men who fought for the Union in the Civil War, it also serves as a banquet hall, theater, meeting place, and exam site. From here you might want to stroll north to the:

HARVARD UNIVERSITY MUSEUMS OF NATURAL HISTORY (6), 24 Oxford St., Cambridge, MA 02138, ☎ (617) 495-1910. *Open Mon.–Sat. 9–4:30, Sun. 1–4:30. Closed New Year's, July 4, Thanksgiving, and Christmas. Adults $4, seniors and students $3, children (3–13) $1. Museum shops.* ♿.
   Four separate museums of natural history, each covering a different aspect of the subject, are gathered together here in one building for one admission price. The old-fashioned displays in some of the halls have a charm that is largely missing from larger institutions, like stepping back into

the 19th century. Begin with the **Botanical Museum**, famous for its collection of ***Glass Flowers**. Created by two German glass blowers between 1877 and 1936, these incredibly accurate oversize reproductions of hundreds and hundreds of species of flowering plants are the museum's major draw. The adjoining **Museum of Comparative Zoology** is not as dull as its name suggests; in fact it overflows with stuffed animals from around the globe, along with an impressive collection of dinosaur bones. Visitors are especially taken with the skeletal **Kronosaurus**, a giant sea serpent from 120 million years ago. Pass through the **Mineralogical and Geological Museum**, a vast collection of over 6,000 specimens plus exhibits on meteorites, cave formations, and volcanoes. The stars here are the giant gypsum crystals from Mexico. Anthropology is the subject of the ***Peabody Museum of Archaeology and Ethnology**, where the cultures of Oceania, North America, and Central America are explored in depth. There are also collections of artifacts from other parts of the world, and a superb museum shop by the first-floor Divinity Avenue exit. Leave from here and follow the map south to the:

*HARVARD UNIVERSITY ART MUSEUMS (7), 485 Broadway and 32 Quincy St., Boston, MA 02138, ☎ (617) 495-9400. *Open Mon.–Sat. 10–5, Sun. 1–5. Admission to all: Adult $5, seniors $4, students $3, under 18 free. Museum shop. ♿, use Prescott St. entrance.*

Harvard has three separate art museums at two different addresses. The **Arthur M. Sackler Museum**, at the corner of Quincy Street and Broadway, houses a magnificent collection of ancient Asian, Islamic, Egyptian, Greek, and Roman treasures in a striking Post-Modern building. A block to the south, on Quincy Street, stands the ***Fogg Art Museum**, whose collections pretty much span the history of Western art from medieval times to the present. It is especially strong in works of the Italian Renaissance, and possesses the largest collection of paintings by Ingres outside of France. A corridor on its second floor leads into the **Busch-Reisinger Museum**, specializing in Germanic art of the 20th century, including Expressionism and the Blaue Reiter, Die Brücke, and Bauhaus schools.

Continue south on Quincy Street. The next structure on the left is the **Carpenter Center for the Visual Arts**. Built in 1963, it is the only building in North America to have been designed by the controversial Swiss architect Le Corbusier. Turn right about a block beyond this and enter New Harvard Yard, leading back into Old Harvard Yard (2).

Stroll past Massachusetts Hall (3) and exit the campus, crossing Massachusetts Avenue to **Christ Church** (8). Cambridge's oldest existing church was built in 1761. Its Tory congregation was forced to flee as early as 1774, after which the church was used as a barracks by Connecticut troops and the organ pipes melted down for bullets. George and Martha Washington worshipped here on New Year's Eve, 1775. Just beyond the church is the campus

Old Harvard Yard

of **Radcliffe College** (9), a women's school associated with Harvard since 1894. Radcliffe students are considered Harvard students, and receive Harvard degrees. **Cambridge Common** (10), across the street, has been the center of local life since the earliest times. Militia members trained here in the opening days of the Revolution, and according to tradition, George Washington first took command of the Continental Army under an ancient elm tree here on July 3, 1775. That tree was sacrificed to road construction in 1923, but its offspring carry on.

Follow the map past the Episcopal Divinity School to the **Longfellow National Historic Site** (11) on Brattle Street. George Washington slept here throughout the siege of Boston, and later on so did the poet Henry Wadsworth Longfellow (1807-1882), who was given the house as a wedding gift from his father-in-law in 1843. Longfellow actually lived here, first as a boarder, from 1837 until his death, after which it was occupied by his descendants until 1974. His furnishings and belongings are still there, and can be seen on guided tours. ☎ *(617) 876-4491. Open late May to mid-Oct., Wed.–Sat. 10:45–4. Adults $2, under 17 free.* ♿.

Brattle Street was once nicknamed "Tory Row" after the wealthy loyalists to the British Crown who lived along it prior to the Revolution. These aloof Anglicans were not exactly popular with their neighbors, mostly descendants of Puritans (and Congregationalists all), and were forced to flee back to the Mother Country in 1776. Cross over to Longfellow Park and return along Brattle Street, passing a few other Tory mansions.

The route leads through busy Brattle Square and John F. Kennedy Street. Turn left into South Street and left again on Dunster Street. A right on Winthrop takes you past **Lowell House** (12), one of several rather elegant undergraduate houses maintained by Harvard. Follow the path down steps and turn left onto Plympton Street. Across Mount Auburn Street, to the left, is a strange triangular structure of 1909 that vaguely resembles a Flemish castle. This is the **Lampoon Building** (13), home of the *Harvard Lampoon*, that infamous undergraduate humor magazine. Heading north on Linden Street returns you to Harvard Square (1).

Game for more? Two other attractions in Cambridge, both a long walk or a bus or subway ride away, might appeal to you. The **Massachusetts Institute of Technology** (14), arguably the world's greatest science and engineering school, has an intriguing 135-acre campus featuring some extraordinary structures. To get there, walk about a mile and a half down Massachusetts Avenue (or take a bus, or the Red Line subway to Central and continue on foot). A short distance beyond Main Street (before reaching the campus itself), is the **MIT Museum** with its exhibitions on scientific subjects. *265 Massachusetts Ave.,* ☎ *(617) 253-4444. Open Tues.–Fri. 9–5, Sat.–Sun. noon–5. Admission $3, seniors $1.* The **MIT Information Center**, a few blocks farther on in the Rogers Building on campus, offers free maps and guided tours. *77 Massachusetts Ave.,* ☎ *(617) 253-4795.* Several galleries of the MIT Museum, above, are located in this complex as well. A bit to the east, still on campus, is the **List Visual Arts Center**, where works by contemporary artists are displayed. *20 Ames St.,* ☎ *(617) 253-4680. Open Sept.–June, Tues.–Fri. noon–6 and weekends 1–5. Free.*

The truly energetic can follow the Charles River east along Memorial Drive and Edwin H. Land Boulevard to the CambridgeSide Galleria, a fancy shopping mall. Here, on Level 1, you'll find the new **Sports Museum of New England** (15). Interactive exhibits allow visitors to try their hands at all manner of sporting activities, and have fun doing it. There's also a vast collection of memorabilia, artwork, and videos to watch. ☎ *(617) 577-7678. Open Mon.–Sat. 10–9:30, Sun. 11–7. Adults $6, seniors and children (4–11) $4.50. Museum store.* ♿.

Section III

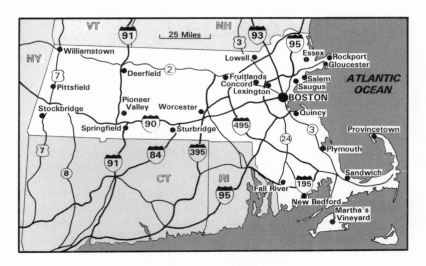

DAYTRIPS IN
MASSACHUSETTS

Just outside of Boston, and extending over a hundred miles to the west, is one of the greatest concentrations of varied sights in the nation. From the windswept dunes of Cape Cod to the bucolic joys of the Berkshire Hills, and from the earliest industry at Saugus to the peaceful quiet of Walden Pond, the rest of Massachusetts offers a host of destinations for one-day excursions. Whether your interests lie in history, art, nature, sports, dining, shopping, or simply relaxing on the beach, you'll have no trouble finding just the right daytrip to match your desires with your resources. And, if you have more than a day at your disposal, why not combine several of these trips into a mini-vacation?

Trip 6

Saugus, Lynn, and Marblehead

Looking for a short, low-key excursion without the tourist mobs? Where you won't have to stand in line for the sights, and where both early history and lovely seascapes are yours for the asking? This easy, inexpensive daytrip takes you only a few miles from Boston, but offers a wealth of enjoyment for next to nothing.

Among the places you can visit is America's first successful ironworks, begun in 1646 and now reconstructed to its 17th-century condition, an industrial town that's even older than Boston, two 19th-century homes of the religious leader Mary Baker Eddy, historic mansions, yacht basins, beaches, and spectacular maritime scenery.

For the lucky ones who can stay overnight, this outing combines well with the following trips to Salem and Cape Ann, or with the one to Essex, Ipswich, and Newburyport.

GETTING THERE:

By car, Saugus is about 10 miles north of Boston. Take **US-1** to Main St. and head east on it to the Saugus Iron Works.

Go south on Central St., then turn left on Winter St., becoming Ballard St. Make a left on Western Ave., **MA-107**, into Lynn. Turn south on Washington St., then east on Broad St., **MA-1A**, to the sites.

From Lynn head south on Nahant Road to Nahant Harbor. Return to Lynn Shore Drive, **MA-129**, following it northeast through Swampscott and into Marblehead.

Return to Boston via MA-129 and MA-1A.

All told, if you visit everything, the total round-trip distance from central Boston is about 35 miles.

PRACTICALITIES:

This trip can be made on any fine day, preferably in the warm season. Some of the minor attractions have limited times of opening; check the individual listings if you're interested. For further information contact the **North of Boston Convention & Visitors Bureau**, 48 Cabot St., Box 642, Beverly, MA 01915, ☎ (508) 921-4990 or (800) 742-5306, FAX (508) 921-4956.

FOOD AND DRINK:

The Landing (Clark's Landing, off Front St. in downtown Marblehead) Superb seafood, plus a few meat dishes, overlooking the harbor. Outdoor dining in good weather, and a pub section with lighter fare. Reservations suggested, ☎ (617) 631-1878. $$ and $$$

Hilltop Steak House (855 Broadway, on US-1 south of the Main St. intersection at Saugus) Good values in steak and seafood. ☎ (617) 233-7700. $$

East Side Mario's (1143 Broadway, on US-1 about a mile south of the Main St. intersection at Saugus) Home-style Italian cuisine. ☎ (617) 941-9090. $$

Spuds Restaurant & Pub (22 Lincoln Ave., about 2 miles south of the Saugus Iron Works) A casual place for family dining. ☎ (617) 233-2757. $

Driftwood (63 Front St., on the waterfront in downtown Marblehead) An unpretentious place for real home cooking, diner style. ☎ (617) 631-1145. $

LOCAL ATTRACTIONS:
Numbers in parentheses correspond to numbers on the map.

*SAUGUS IRON WORKS NATIONAL HISTORIC SITE (1), 244 Central St., Saugus, MA 01906, ☎ (617) 233-0050. *Open daily 9–4. Closed Thanksgiving, Christmas, New Year's. Free. Guided tours Apr.–Oct.* ♿.

American ironmaking, and by extension industry in general, had its beginnings right here in 1646, not all that long after the Pilgrims first set foot in the New World. At that time, iron was smelted by using charcoal as a fuel—and England was rapidly running out of trees to make charcoal. With its abundance of forests, ore, and water power, New England could produce plenty of iron, enough to meet local demand and perhaps even export to the Mother Country.

Alas, this initial venture at Saugus was doomed to failure. Mismanagement, high production costs, and a fixed price structure made it unprofitable, and it ceased operations within 30 years. The workers trained here, and the lessons learned, nevertheless spurred the development of other ironworks throughout the colonies, laying the foundations for the industrial growth of the United States.

What you see today is mostly a reconstruction created in the 1950s by the American Iron and Steel Institute, and turned over to the National Park Service in 1969. One building, the **Iron Works House** of 1646, is the original social and business center of the ironmaking community. Artifacts dug up on the site are displayed in a **museum**, and demonstrations are given at the **Blacksmith Shop**. Other points of interest include the **furnace**, the **forge**, and the **rolling and slitting mill**, all rebuilt on original foundations.

Drive about five miles southeast to the old industrial town of Lynn, founded in 1629 and once the shoemaking capital of the nation. Its gritty history is traced at the **Lynn Historical Society Museum** (2), located in a restored period house of 1836. One unusual display here is the medallion made of 234 different shoe soles, one for each manufacturer in Lynn, that was created for the Chicago Exposition of 1893. *125 Green St.,* ☎ *(617) 592-2465. Open Mon.–Sat. 1–4. Adults $3, children (6–16) $1.* ♿.

The nearby **Lynn Heritage State Park Visitors Center** (3), at the corner of Washington and Union streets, also tells the long story of Lynn and its people. There's a re-created shoe shop of 1830, an audiovisual presentation, and exhibits depicting local industry from early shoemaking to today's specialty of jet engines. Another part of the State Park, only a few blocks away, features a waterfront boardwalk, marina, restaurants, picnic facilities, and an unusual mural celebrating the town's story. *590 Washington St.,* ☎ *(617) 598-1974. Open Wed.–Sun., 9:30–4:30. Free.* ♿.

While in Lynn, you might want to visit the **Mary Baker Eddy House** (4), where the founder of the Christian Science faith completed her book *Science and Health* in 1875. It was here that she was ordained a minister, and later married. A few of the furnishings belonged to her; others are of similar age and type. *12 Broad St.,* ☎ *(617) 450-3790. Usually open June–Oct., Wed.–Thurs., 10–4, or by appointment. Free.*

From Lynn you might take a scenic drive to **Nahant Beach** (5) and beyond, following south on a narrow peninsula for some gorgeous views. You'll also have a chance to take a dip in the ocean.

Back in Lynn, take Lynn Shore Drive (MA-129) northeast into **Swampscott** (6), a small resort town with a beautiful coastline. As in Lynn, there is a **Mary Baker Eddy House** here. This is where Mrs. Eddy, then at death's door, experienced a miraculous healing in 1866 that led to a nine-year search culminating in the founding of the Christian Science faith. *23 Paradise Rd. (MA-1A),* ☎ *(617) 599-1853. Open May–Oct., Mon.–Sat. 10–5 and Sun. 2–5; March–Apr. and Nov.–Jan., Tues.–Sun. 1–4. Closed holidays. Adults $1.50, children 75¢.*

Continue on to **Marblehead** (7). Once a fishing port and now a great yachting center, the town was first settled by Cornwall fishermen in 1629. Its quaint ***Old Town** section abounds in historic sights, shops, and restaurants. The **Jeremiah Lee Mansion** of 1768, home of the Marblehead Historical Society, was built by a wealthy ship owner in the Georgian style. Visitors can examine decorative arts from the 18th and 19th centuries, original 18th-century wallpaper from England, rococo detailing, nautical memorabilia, toys, and much more. Such prominent personalities as Washington, Lafayette, Monroe, and Jackson were received in the Great Room. *161 Washington St.,* ☎ *(617) 631-1069. Open for guided tours from mid-May to Columbus Day, Mon.–Fri. 10–4, Sat.–Sun. 1–4. Adults $4, seniors and students $3.50.*

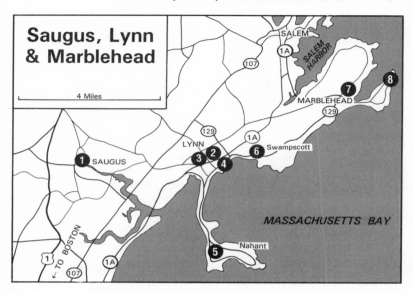

Another nearby house that you can visit is the **King Hooper Mansion**, begun around 1728. Now home to the Marblehead Arts Association and serving as their gallery, it contains a ballroom, wine cellar, and other attributes of the good life. *8 Hooper St.,* ☎ *(617) 631-2608. Open Mon.–Sat. 10–4, Sun. 1–5. Free.*

While in town, stop by **Abbot Hall**, Marblehead's Victorian town hall, for a look at the famous painting *The Spirit of '76* in the Selectmen's Meeting Room. While hardly a great piece of art, this 1876 creation of A.M. Willard is one of the most familiar patriotic icons that the country has ever known. *Washington Sq.,* ☎ *(617) 631-0000. Open June–Oct., Mon.–Fri. 8–5, Sat. 1–6, Sun. and holidays 11–6; rest of year Mon.–Fri. 8–5. Donation.*

End your day with a drive out on ***Marblehead Neck** (8), where you'll pass Devereaux Beach, fabulous mansions, and a wildlife sanctuary that may be visited. Castle Rock, reached by a pathway from Ocean Avenue, offers magnificent ocean vistas. At the tip, stop at **Chandler-Hovey Park** for the best view of the harbor, and walk along the rocks to Marblehead Light for another wonderful scene.

Trip 7

*Salem

Salem is, of course, most famous for its witches, but there's a whole lot more to this venerable town than a brief episode of mass hysteria over three centuries ago. Founded as early as 1626, it took its name from the Hebrew *Shalom*, meaning peace. Once the capital of the Massachusetts Bay Colony, Salem prospered as a shipping center, trading with exotic ports around the world. Great fortunes were generated here, as is evident from the historic homes and their magnificent furnishings. Much of this prosperous past survives to delight today's discriminating visitors, especially in the renowned Peabody Essex Museum and its associated houses. Sections of the waterfront have been preserved as the Salem Maritime National Historic Site, and the famous House of the Seven Gables offers literary memories of Nathaniel Hawthorne. Those wishing to experience the earliest days can visit the Pioneer Village, a re-creation of Salem as it was in 1630, where costumed interpreters reenact 17th-century domestic life. There's good living here, too, with many unusual shops and excellent restaurants.

Still, what brings in the tourists are those witches—the 19 who were hanged on Gallows Hill, the one who was pressed to death under stones, and the others who died in jail. You can, if you wish, relive some of that unspeakable episode—and the town will be only too happy to accommodate you. They've got witch figures everywhere, pointing the way with their broomsticks. Actually, however, the infamous trials of 1692 seemed to be more about power and politics than about any satanic goings-on; more about unscrupulous leaders and a gullible public. They have a lot to teach us today.

By staying overnight, you could combine this trip with the ones to Saugus, Lynn, and Marblehead; Cape Ann; or Essex, Ipswich, and Newburyport.

GETTING THERE:

By car, Salem is about 20 miles northeast of downtown Boston. The fastest, but hardly shortest, route is via **I-93** and **I-95** to Exit 45, then **MA-128** north to Exit 26. Follow Lowell St. and turn left onto Bridge St. (MA-127), leading into Salem.

Taking US-1 north to Peabody, then I-95 as above, is considerably shorter but not faster. The shortest route is via **MA-1A** through Lynn; scenic but slow.

There are municipal parking lots near the Peabody Essex Museum.

By train, take the MBTA Rockport/Ipswich commuter line out of Boston's North Station. The ride to Salem takes about 30 minutes, and service is fairly frequent. ☎ (617) 722-3200 or (800) 392-6100 for details.

PRACTICALITIES:

Most of the attractions are open daily throughout the year, except on Thanksgiving, Christmas, and New Year's. Note, however, that the Peabody Essex Museum is closed on Mondays from November until Memorial Day, and that the Pioneer Village closes completely from November through May.

Salem observes its **Heritage Days** in mid-August with parades, fireworks, and the like. **Halloween** is celebrated with a vengeance, with Haunted Happenings filling the last two weeks of October.

For further information, contact the **Salem Chamber of Commerce**, 32 Derby Sq., Old Town Hall, Salem, MA 01970, ☎ (508) 744-0004, OR the **Salem Office of Tourism**, 93 Washington St., Salem, MA 01970, ☎ (800) 777-6848, FAX (508) 741-7539.

FOOD AND DRINK:

Out of a vast selection, a few choice restaurants are:

Nathaniel's (18 Washington Sq., in the Hawthorne Hotel, on the south side of Salem Common) Superb dining in a casually elegant setting. Reservations suggested, ☎ (508) 745-7727. $$$

Lyceum Bar & Grill (43 Church St., 2 blocks northwest of the Peabody Essex Museum) Seafood, grilled meats, and other offerings in historic surroundings. Very popular. ☎ (508) 745-7665. $$

Victoria Station (Pickering Wharf) Prime rib and seafood, served indoors or out, overlooking the harbor. ☎ (508) 745-3400. $$

Chase House (Pickering Wharf) Seafood and steak on the harbor, outdoor dining in summer. ☎ (508) 744-0000. $$

In a Pig's Eye (148 Derby St., near the House of Seven Gables) A local favorite for casual lunches. ☎ (508) 741-4436. $

Red's Sandwich Shop (15 Central St., by the Burying Point) Locals and tourists have been getting their burgers and sandwiches at Red's for decades. Outdoor tables in summer. ☎ (508) 745-3527. $

SUGGESTED TOUR:

Numbers in parentheses correspond to numbers on the map. Begin at the:

SALEM MARITIME NATIONAL HISTORIC SITE (1), 174 Derby St., Salem, MA 01970, ☎ (508) 745-1470. *Open July–Aug. daily 9–6; Apr.–June and Sept.–Oct. daily 9–5; rest of year daily 10–5. Closed Thanksgiving, Christmas, and New Year's. Free.* ♿.

Salem's glory lies in its maritime past, and the wealth this generated. Ships like the 300-ton *Grand Turk* entered the China trade as early as 1785, making stops along the way and turning over their cargoes many times, with profits soaring. A bit of this era has been preserved in the nine-acre historic site. Stop by the **Orientation Center** to watch an introductory video and pick up a free brochure about the site, then set out to explore. Free guided tours are also offered.

Derby Wharf, begun around 1764, was by 1806 extended to a remarkable length of over 2,000 feet to accommodate all the business. It's still there today. The Federal-style ***Custom House** of 1819, a dignified structure with classical pillars, granite steps, and a cupola topped off with a golden eagle, was used to regulate shipping and collect tariffs. Author Nathaniel Hawthorne, a local lad, worked here from 1846 to 1849 as surveyor of customs. Behind it stands the **Bonded Warehouse**, filled with examples of the cargoes that were once stored here. **Derby House** was built in 1762 for Elias Hasket Derby, America's first millionaire, whose ships opened trade routes throughout the world. Its rich interior is shown on guided tours only; inquire at the Orientation Center. Several other historic buildings are also shown, one of which dates back to around 1670. The **West India Goods Store** opened in the early 19th century to sell imported merchandise, which it still does.

Head east on Derby street and turn right on Turner Street to the:

*HOUSE OF THE SEVEN GABLES (2), 54 Turner St., Salem, MA 01970, ☎ (508) 744-0991. *Open July–Oct., daily 9–6; Apr.–June and Nov.–Dec., daily 10–4:30; rest of year, Mon.–Sat. 10–4:30 and Sun. noon–4:30. Closed Thanksgiving, Christmas, New Year's. Adults $7, youths (13–17) $4, children (6–12) $3. Guided tours. Museum shop.* ♨.

Nathaniel Hawthorne (1804–64) made this strange house with its dramatically pitched roofs famous in his great novel of 1851, *The House of the Seven Gables*. The author knew the ancient structure well as it was the home of his cousin, and as he was born nearby. Initially built in 1668 with only four gables, it acquired three more around 1690. Visitors are taken on a guided tour that wonderfully weaves together the factual history of the 17th-century house, gracious living, and Hawthorne's Gothic tale of sin and redemption.

The same waterfront complex includes period **gardens** and some other historic houses. **Hawthorne's Birthplace**, a house from about 1750, was moved here from nearby Union Street and is included on the tour. The **Hooper-Hathaway House** of 1682 has beams believed to have been from the 1630s home of the colony's first governor, while the **Counting House** of 1820 is set up as a period captain's office. The oldest house, the **Retire Becket House** of 1655, now contains the Museum Shop.

Follow the map to **Salem Common** (3), a.k.a. Washington Square. Lined with the dignified homes of prosperous 19th-century citizens, this has been common land since 1685. Quartered in an old stone church in its northwest corner is the **Salem Witch Museum** (4), where the supernatural hysteria of 1692 is brought to life through multimedia reenactments. ☎ *(508) 744-1692. Open daily 10–5, closing at 7 in July–Aug. Closed Thanksgiving, Christmas, and New Year's. Adults $4, seniors (62+) $3.50, children (6–14) $2.50.* ♿.

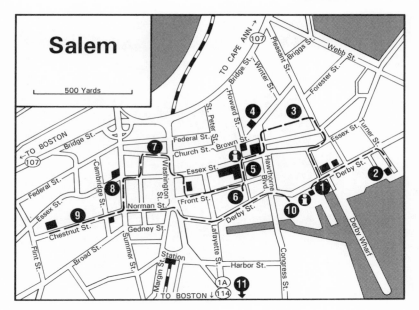

Continue around to the:

*PEABODY ESSEX MUSEUM (5), East India Sq., Salem, MA 01970, ☎ (508) 745-1876, taped information (508) 745-9500 and (800) 745-4054, FAX 9508) 744-6776. *Open Mon. (Tues. from Nov.–late May)–Sat. 10–5 (Thurs. till 8), Sun. noon–5. Closed Mon. from Nov.–late May, Thanksgiving, Christmas, New Year's. Adults $7, seniors (62+) and students $6, children (6–18) $4, families $18. Shops.* 📷. ♿.

America's oldest continuously-operating museum was founded in 1799 and later became known as the Peabody Museum of Salem, while the nation's fourth-oldest historical society began in 1821 as the Essex Institute. In 1992 these neighbors got together to form the Peabody Essex Museum, surely the most significant attraction in Salem, and one that is absolutely not to be missed. Nearly half a million objects collected over two centuries fill 30 galleries and 11 historic homes on either side of Liberty Street. Don't worry—you don't have to see them all to thoroughly enjoy this place.

The focus here is on Salem's long maritime history, decorative arts and artifacts from Asia and the Pacific, New England history, art, and architecture, historic homes, natural history, and more. Among its treasures are centuries of figureheads, ship models and navigational devices, scrimshaw, porcelains and elaborate furnishings from the Far East, an Hawaiian feather cape, stuffed exotic birds, and a great many paintings, especially of maritime subjects. Several of the historic houses on the property may be visited on

House of the Seven Gables

guided tours, for which reservations are suggested. These include the **John Ward House** of 1684, the Georgian **Crowninshield-Bentley House** of 1727, and the elegant ***Gardner-Pingree Mansion** of 1804.

Head south a block to the **Burying Point** (6), the oldest cemetery in Salem. The graves here date back as far as 1637, and include the only known original tombstone of a *Mayflower* passenger, and the remains of a witch-craft trial judge. Closeby is the **Salem Witch Trials Memorial**, a modern place for quiet contemplation. Also nearby is the **Salem Wax Museum of Witches and Seafarers**, a commercial multimedia presentation of the whole witchcraft thing as well as life on the high seas. *288 Derby St.,* ☎ *(508) 740-2929. Adults $4, seniors $3.50, under 14 $2.50.*

Follow the map past the **Old Town Hall**, perhaps stopping at another commercial attraction, the **Witch Dungeon Museum** (7). A live reenactment of an actual 1692 witch trial is performed by actors, and there's a tour of a re-created dungeon. *16 Lynde St.,* ☎ *(508) 741-3570. Open Apr.–Nov. daily 10–5. Adults $4, seniors $3.50, children (6–14) $2.50.* The subject is further explored at the nearby **Witch House** (8), a restored home of one of the actual judges, and the supposed venue of pretrial examinations of the accused. Built in 1642, this large dwelling has period furnishings and, for the sensi-tive, a suitably ominous atmosphere. *310½ Essex St.,* ☎ *(508) 744-0180. Open mid-March through Oct., daily 10–4:40 (6 in summer). Adults $5, children (5–16) $1.50.*

Goods stored in the Bonded Warehouse

Stroll down to ***Chestnut Street** (9), a broad, aristocratic thoroughfare lined with elegant Georgian, Federal, and Greek Revival mansions. **Hamilton Hall**, at number 9, was named for a frequent guest, Alexander Hamilton, and was also visited by Lafayette. ☎ *(508) 744-0805. Open weekdays 10–2. Free.* A bit farther down the street is the renowned ***Stephen Phillips Memorial Trust House** of 1804, moved here from Danvers in the mid-19th century. Its interior is decorated with furnishings gathered from around the world by Salem sea captains, and the carriage house features antique automobiles. *34 Chestnut St.,* ☎ *(508) 744-0440. Open Memorial Day weekend to mid-Oct., Mon.–Sat. 10–4:30. Adults $2, under 12 $1.*

Your tour is essentially finished, so why not head over to **Pickering Wharf** (10) for refreshments, shopping, a meal, or even a cruise?

If time permits, you might want to drive south on Lafayette Street (MA-1A) for about a mile and a half to Forest River Park and the intriguing **Pioneer Village—Salem 1630** (11). This living replica of 17th-century Salem features costumed "Puritans" going about their everyday life, practicing the skills of yesterday. Period buildings, from the governor's house to thatched cottages, from workshops to wigwams, were faithfully re-created in 1930 and recently restored. ☎ *(508) 745-0525. Open Memorial Day weekend–Oct., Mon.– Sat. 10–5, Sun. and holidays noon–5. Adults $4.50, seniors (62+) and youths (13–17) $3.50, children (6–12) $2.50.*

Trip 8

*Cape Ann

Boston's "other cape" is much closer and in many ways just as appealing as Cape Cod. Only 35 miles northeast of the city and easily reached by car or commuter train, Cape Ann offers an intimate experience punctuated with several first-class attractions.

First charted as Cap aux Isles by Samuel de Champlain in 1604, this rocky peninsula was renamed for James I's consort, Queen Anne, the mother of Charles I. A fishing industry has thrived here since 1623, with Gloucester its port. Still a major fishing center, Gloucester gets its catch both locally and from as far away as Iceland and Scandinavia, processing it for a widespread market. There's a lot to see around the working harbor, two artists' colonies to explore, a "medieval" castle and a decorator's mansion to visit, and numerous sights to enjoy—both the strange and the picturesque.

If you have the time for a longer stay, why not combine this trip with the one to Saugus, Lynn, and Marblehead; or with Salem; or to Essex, Ipswich, and Newbury?

GETTING THERE:

By car, the scenic way is to take routes **MA-1A** and **MA-127** via Salem and Beverly. Otherwise, pick up **MA-128** from its intersection with I-95 or US-1 and head east to Exit 16. There you connect with MA-127, heading east toward Gloucester.

Parking in Rockport can be difficult; better to use the town lot and its shuttle bus.

Commuter trains operated by **MBTA** connect Boston's North Station with both Gloucester and Rockport. Service is fairly frequent on weekdays, less so on Saturdays, and limited on Sundays. ☎ (617) 722-3200 for schedules. Local bus service around Cape Ann is operated by **CATA**, ☎ (508) 283-7916.

PRACTICALITIES:

Summer is the best time to visit Cape Ann; that's when everything is open. Several of the sights have complex spring and fall schedules, so check the individual listings carefully. Very few places operate during the winter months.

Whale-watching cruises are a big attraction here. Usually lasting several hours, they should be arranged in advance. Some firms in Gloucester are: **Cape Ann Whale Watch,** ☎ (508) 283-5110 or (800) 877-5110; **Capt. Bill's Whale Watching,** ☎ (508) 283-6995 or (800) 33-WHALE; **Seven Seas Whale Watching,** ☎ (508) 283-1776 or (800) 238-1776; and **Yankee Whale Watch,** (508) 283-0313 or (800) WHALING. Dress warmly, bring sunglasses and sunscreen lotion.

For further information contact the **Cape Ann Chamber of Commerce Visitor Information Center,** 33 Commercial St., Gloucester, MA 01930, ☎ (508) 283-1601 or (800) 321-0133. Also handy is the **Gloucester Visitors Welcoming Center** by the intersection of MA-127 and MA-133 at the west end of Gloucester, ☎ (800) 649-6839. In Rockport, check the **Rockport Chamber of Commerce** on Upper Main Street (MA-127), ☎ (508) 546-6575.

FOOD AND DRINK:

Of course, seafood predominates on Cape Ann, but a thriving tourist industry insures that landlubbers won't go hungry.

Rockport has been a dry town since 1856, although you can bring your own drinks from elsewhere. Most restaurants provide setups.

Evie's Rudder (73 Rocky Neck Ave. in Gloucester) Housed in an ancient fish-packing shed on the waterfront, right in the middle of the art colony, this fun place has been serving imaginative dishes—both seafaring and landlubber—for decades. An experience! ☎ (508) 283-7967. X: winter. $$

Peg Leg Restaurant (2 King St. at Beach St. in Rockport) Lobster, fish, clam chowder—plus meat and veggie dishes, all in a homey setting. A local favorite. ☎ (508) 546-3038. X: Nov.–March. BYOB. $$

Cameron's (206 Main St. in Gloucester) A good value in local seafood and meat dishes. ☎ (508) 281-1331. X: Sun. lunch. $ and $$

Ellen's Harborside (T-Wharf, Dock Sq., in Rockport) Excellent seafood at modest prices. ☎ (508) 546-2512. X: Dec.–March. $ and $$

Portside Chowder House (Bearskin Neck, Dock Sq., in Rockport) This tiny restaurant offers chowders, seafood, burgers, sandwiches, and salads—all at low prices. ☎ (508) 546-7045. $

LOCAL ATTRACTIONS:

Numbers in parentheses correspond to numbers on the map.

*HAMMOND CASTLE MUSEUM (1), 80 Hesperus Ave. (follow signs south from MA-127), Gloucester, MA 01930, ☎ (508) 283-2080. *Open June–Aug., daily 10–5; May and Sept.–Oct., Wed.–Sun. 10–5; rest of year, weekends 10–5. Closed Thanksgiving, Christmas, New Year's. Adults $6, seniors $5, children (4–12) $4. Guided tours.*

Dr. John Hays Hammond, Jr. (1888–1965) was an electronics engineer who pioneered the concept of remote control and developed various tele-communications devices. He obviously did well at this; well enough during the Roaring Twenties to build himself a huge medieval-style castle in a dramatic setting overlooking the sea. For his very own Xanadu, Hammond combed Europe for artifacts ranging from the ancient Roman to the Renais-sance, topping them off with a 13th-century-style ***Great Hall** complete with the world's largest ***organ** in a private residence. To this place came the most illustrious guests of the era; all anxious to experience Dr. Hammond's weird eccentricities. You can take it all in, too, and marvel at the ***view** of **Norman's Woe**, a rocky reef described in Henry Wadsworth Longfellow's poem *The Wreck of the Hesperus.*

Continuing along MA-127 soon brings you into **Gloucester**, whose **Visitors Welcoming Center** is at Stage Fort Park, near the intersection of MA-127 and MA-133. Cross the East Coast's busiest drawbridge, first built around 1643, and continue to the ***Fishermen's Memorial Statue** (2) of *The Man at the Wheel,* honoring "They That Go Down To The Sea In Ships," the more-than-ten-thousand Gloucester fishermen lost at sea since 1623. Sculpted in 1923 by Leonard Craske, this image is surely the quintessential icon of New England's coast.

Gloucester, America's oldest seaport, has always looked to the sea for its livelihood. Today, much of the catch comes from foreign waters, but this is still the major seafood processing center. Park your car near **Harbor Cove** (3) for a close look at all the activity, soaking up the atmosphere of over 350 years of continuous fishing. A few blocks inland are several historic homes and churches, among them the **Sargent-Murray-Gilman-Hough House** (4) of 1782. Now restored and open as a museum, it was built in the Georgian style for Judith Sargent Murray, an influential writer and wife of the Univer-salist Church leader John Murray. Their descendants included two governors and the painter, John Singer Sargent. *49 Middle St.,* ☎ *(508) 281-2432. Open June–Columbus Day, Sat.–Mon. noon–4. Adults $3, seniors $2.* Just a few blocks east is the:

CAPE ANN HISTORICAL MUSEUM (5), 27 Pleasant St., Gloucester, MA 01930, ☎ (508) 283-0455. *Open Tues.–Sat., 10–5. Adults $3.50, seniors $3, students with ID $2.* ♿.

Gloucester's long and colorful history comes to life in this superb mu-seum devoted to Cape Ann's past. Exhibits include the largest collection anywhere of 19th-century ***seascapes** by noted artist Fitz Hugh Lane, as well as others by Maurice Prendergast and John Sloan. Two boats used in solo crossings of the Atlantic are here: the dory *Centennial* of 1876 and the sloop *Great Republic* of 1900. Examining them and the other maritime artifacts recalls Rudyard Kipling's marvelous tale of Gloucester fishermen, *Captains Courageous.* There's a lot more, plus a restored 1804 sea captain's house.

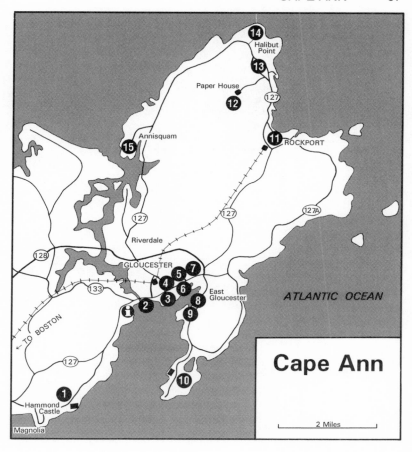

Cape Ann

2 Miles

Head back to the waterfront and turn south along the **Harbor Loop** (6), passing a Coast Guard station and a waterside park with an interesting view. Nearby is an industrial building in which Clarence Birdseye developed his method of freezing food in 1925, a process that was to prove a boon to the local fish-packing business and eventually to busy people everywhere. Maritime artist Fitz Hugh Lane (1804–65) lived in the seven-gabled stone house overlooking the harbor. Gloucester was once famous for its schooners, and one of these, **The Adventure**, has returned as a living museum to the great age of sail. You can board her when she's in port. ☎ *(508) 281-8079. Admission $3.*

Head east on Main Street (MA-127). Rising above the town on Prospect Street are the two bell-shaped towers of **Our Lady of Good Voyage** (7), a

The Fishermen's Memorial Statue in Gloucester

Portuguese church of 1915 noted for having the first modern carillon in America, installed in 1922. Inside are models of ships that sailed from Gloucester; the statue of the Virgin holds an infant Jesus in one hand and a Gloucester schooner in the other. ☎ *(508) 283-1490. Open Mon.–Fri. 10–4. Free.*

It's a little out of the way, but you might want to turn south on East Main Street in East Gloucester in the direction of Rocky Neck and Beauport. Along the way you'll come to the **North Shore Arts Association** (8), where local artists display their works. *197 East Main St.,* ☎ *(508) 283-1857. Open June–Sept., Mon.–Sat. 10–5, Sun. 1–5.* **Rocky Neck** (9) is home to America's oldest continuously operating ***art colony**, established in the 19th century and still going strong. Park your car in the public lot and take a stroll among the ancient, weathered fishing buildings that now serve as studios, galleries, shops, restaurants, and the like.

Continuing south from Rocky Neck soon brings you to:

*BEAUPORT (10), 75 Eastern Point Blvd., Gloucester, MA 01930, ☎ (508) 283-0800. *Open mid-May to mid-Sept., Mon.–Fri. 10–4.; mid-Sept. to mid-Oct., Mon.–Fri. 10–4, weekends 1–4. Closed holidays. Adults $5, seniors $4.50, children (6–12) $2.50.* ♿.

Rockport Harbor and Motif No. 1

Interior designer Henry Davis Sleeper (1873–1934) indulged his every passion in this rambling, strange home with 22 different roof levels and some 40 rooms. Secret passages, doors to nowhere, fake windows, and all manner of theatrical tricks abound. Along the tour are antique-strewn chambers honoring the Founding Fathers, a China Trade Room, a Byron Room, an Indian Room, and much more; all the product of a wild imagination. This is definitely not your ordinary restored-house tour.

Continue along the shore route (MA-127A) to the sublimely picturesque village of ***Rockport** (11), a fishing port that became an artists' colony that doubles as a tourist haunt—at least in summer. Despite its enormous popularity, Rockport remains a very attractive place, pleasing nearly all who visit there. If you can't find a place to park, head out to the town lot on inland route MA-127 and take the bus back. Rockport is also served directly by commuter rail from Boston's North Station.

Long before it was discovered by tourists or artists, Rockport's main business was, well, rocks. Granite was quarried here since the 1820s, and shipped from its port, hence the name. The rugged, natural beauty of its coastline attracted painters, craftsmen, photographers, and tourists since the late 19th century, and still does. **Bearskin Neck**, a small promontory jutting out into the harbor, is lined with old fishing sheds that today house studios, boutiques, cafés, and the like. From it you get a good view of *Motif No. 1, a red fishing shack that inspired many a painting.

Back in town, the 18th-century clapboard house at 35 Mt. Pleasant Street (MA-127A) was once the home of Hannah Jumper, the woman who in 1856 rid Rockport of demon rum by leading a vigilante group on a bottle-smashing crusade. It is still a dry town. Nearby, at 12 Main Street, is the **Rockport Art Association**, with its changing exhibitions of paintings, graphics, sculptures, and photographs. ☎ (508) 546-6604. Open Mon.–Sat. 10–5, Sun. noon–5. If you want to learn something about local history, just head out toward the train station, stopping at the **Sandy Bay Historical Society and Museum** at 40 King Street. Built in 1832 by a quarry owner, this granite house features Early American and Victorian room settings, exhibits on the Atlantic Cable, fishing, the granite industry, and lots of local artifacts. ☎ (508) 546-9533. Open July–Labor Day, daily 2–5; by appointment at other times. Adults $3, seniors $2, under 13 free; includes the Old Castle, below.

Continuing around the cape on MA-127, you can make a little detour at Pigeon Cove via Curtis and Pigeon Hill streets to a most unusual sight. A triumph of recycling, the **Paper House** (12) was built by the Elis F. Stenman family over a period of 20 years, from 1922 until 1942. Its walls are con-structed of layer upon layer of newspapers, as is the furniture. All shellacked together, they are still readable and recount such headline stories as Lind-bergh's historic flight. Some 100,000 newspapers—mostly from Boston— were used in the project. ☎ (508) 546-2629. Open July–Aug., daily 10–5, and by appointment. Adults $1, children (6–14) 50¢.

Another weird sight, the **Old Castle** (13), is nearby. Not exactly much of a stronghold, this lonely saltbox of 1715 might have looked that way to hallucinating fishermen out to sea too long. Still, it's a fine example of an early 18th-century home and shop, and it's filled with interesting artifacts and period furniture. ☎ (508) 546-9533. Open July–Labor Day, daily 2–5. Adults $3, seniors $2, under 13 free; includes the Sandy Bay Historical Museum, above.

Halibut Point State Park (14), at the northeastern extremity of Cape Ann, offers walking trails, abandoned granite quarries, bird watching, an old submarine-spotting tower from World War II, picnicking, and magnificent *views extending as far as Maine. ☎ (508) 546-2997. Open daily. $5 parking fee from late May to Columbus Day, otherwise free.

Return to Gloucester via MA-127 through **Annisquam** (15), a remote village that was settled in 1631 as Planter's Neck. This is a lovely place, well worth probing if you have the time.

Essex, Ipswich, and Newburyport

This easygoing daytrip north of Boston has no "must-see" sights, no cultural highlights demanding your full attention—only a nice selection of low-key attractions scattered about a scenic shoreline. Not only is it relaxing, it is also cheap. Several of the sites are free; others have only modest admissions. Even the restaurants are good buys.

There are more minor attractions here than you can possibly see in one day, so you'll have to pick and choose according to your interests. By staying overnight, this trip could be combined with the three previous ones to form a mini vacation.

GETTING THERE:

By car, take routes **I-93** or **US-1** north from Boston to **MA-128**, then head east to Exit 15. From here go north to Essex, turning left on **MA-133** (Main Street). This takes you to the shipbuilding museum, beyond which a right onto Spring Street and another right on Dodge Street leads to the marina and the river cruises.

Continue north towards Ipswich. For the Crane Memorial Reservation turn right on Argilla Road. The Whipple and Heard houses are at Main Street (MA-133/MA-1A) and County Road. Continue north through Rowley, bearing right on **MA-1A** where it separates from MA-133, and heading north towards Newbury.

For Plum Island and the Parker River Wildlife Refuge, turn right on Rolfe's Lane in Newbury, then right again on Water Street. The Coffin House is back on MA-1A, here called High Road, just before Newburyport. This becomes High Street. Turn right on State Street to the Custom House Maritime Museum.

Heading west on High Street soon brings you to both routes US-1 and I-95 for the return drive. All told, the total round-trip distance from Boston is roughly about 100 miles.

PRACTICALITIES:

This trip is best made between mid-May and mid-October, when most of the attractions are open. If possible, avoid Mondays through Wednesdays. For more information, contact the **North of Boston Convention & Visitors**

Bureau, 48 Cabot St., Box 642, Beverly, MA 01915, ☎ (508) 921-4990 or (800) 742-5306, FAX (508) 921-4956. In Newburyport, you can try the seasonal Information Kiosk on Merrimac St., ☎ (508) 462-6680.

FOOD AND DRINK:

Scandia (25 State St. in Newburyport) Creative French and American cuisine in a small, dimly lit, romantic setting. Reservations suggested, ☎ (508) 462-6271. $$ and $$$

Jerry Pelonzi's Hearthside (109 Eastern Ave., MA-133, in Essex, just south of the town center) Seafood, steak, and the like, in a cozy, centuries-old rustic farmhouse. ☎ (508) 766-6002. $$

Captain's Quarters (Boardwalk at Merrimac St. in Newburyport) An exceptional value in seafood and steak. ☎ (508) 462-3397. $ and $$

Woodman's Lobster Pool (121 Main St., MA-133, in Essex) Home of the fried clam since 1914, this "eat-in-the-rough" joint is highly regarded throughout New England. ☎ (508) 768-3642. $

Spud's Restaurant and Pub (US-1, ¼ mile north of junction with MA-133, north of Ipswich) A rustic, friendly eatery that's locally popular. ☎ (508) 948-7551. $

LOCAL ATTRACTIONS:

Numbers in parentheses correspond to numbers on the map. The old village of **Essex** (1) has been harvesting clams and building ships since 1634, and it's still at it. Locals claim to have launched more two-masted boats than any other town in the world, once reaching a production rate of roughly one vessel a week. Today Essex is more noted as a major antiques center, with more than 60 dealers attracting customers from all over. About a dozen seafood restaurants in all price ranges are another draw. Much of the town's colorful past is preserved in the **Essex Shipbuilding Museum**, where you can see how wooden vessels were built by visiting an old shipyard, handling the actual tools, and experiencing other hands-on exhibits. There are also artifacts, scale models, photos, a video, and the 83-foot Essex-built schooner *Evelina M. Goulart* of 1927. *28 Main St., ☎ (508) 768-7541. Open mid-May to mid-Oct., Thurs.–Sun., 11–4. Adults $3, seniors $2.50, under 12 free.*

While thinking about boats, why not take a ride in one? **Essex River Cruises** (2) offers narrated scenic river cruises lasting about 90 minutes. *35 Dodge St., ☎ (508) 768-6981 or (800) 748-3706. Operates daily, May to Oct. Departures at 9, 11, 1, 3, 5, and 7. Adults $14, seniors $12 (Mon.–Fri.), children under 12 $7.*

Head north to **Ipswich**. A right turn on Argilla Road leads in a few miles to the **Richard T. Crane Memorial Reservation** (3), a public beach and nature preserve surrounding a mansion built in 1927 for the Crane family of plumbing fame. The 59-room "summer cottage," called **Castle Hill**, is used for

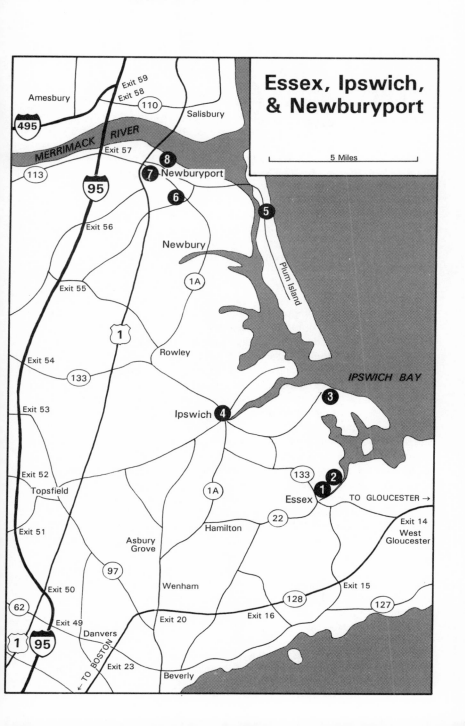

Essex, Ipswich, & Newburyport

5 Miles

Amesbury

Exit 59
Exit 58
110
Salisbury

495

MERRIMACK RIVER

Exit 57

113

95

8

7 Newburyport

6

5

Exit 56

Newbury

1A

Exit 55

Plum Island

1

Exit 54

133

Rowley

IPSWICH BAY

Exit 53

3

Ipswich 4

Exit 52

Topsfield

1A

133

2

1

Essex

TO GLOUCESTER →

22

Exit 14
West
Gloucester

Exit 51

Hamilton

Asbury
Grove

97

Wenham

128

Exit 15

127

Exit 50

62

Exit 49

Danvers

Exit 20

Exit 16

← TO BOSTON

1 95

Exit 23

Beverly

concerts and other cultural events, but is sometimes open for tours. *290 Argilla Rd.,* ☎ *(508) 356-4351.* ♿. Visitors are usually welcome to stroll the lovely grounds, admiring the statuary-lined *Grand Allée* that slopes down to the sea. If you do get into the mansion on a tour, you can see an entire library brought over from a castle in England, exotic bathrooms, and other trappings of the super rich. ***Crane Beach**, once part of the estate, is among New England's best and stretches on for some four miles. A walk along **Pine Hollow Trail** from the parking lot offers great views. ☎ *(508) 356-4354. Open daily 8–dusk. Parking fee varies. Bathhouses, lifeguards, picnicking.* ♿ ♿.

Back in Ipswich, you can enjoy a stroll through the delightful old town that calls itself "The Birthplace of American Independence." How's that? Not Boston? Well, it seems that back in 1687 a local clergyman named John Wise led a protest against a property tax levied by the British governor, more or less coining the phrase "no taxation without representation." His writings were republished in 1772 to strengthen the cause of resistance. Ipswich also claims to have more 17th-century buildings than any other place in America; over 40 of its houses that remain in use today date from before 1725. One of these, the **John Whipple House** (4) of 1655, has been preserved with 17th- and 18th-century furnishings. Its herb garden grows authentic medicinal plants common in the 17th century. Admission to this also includes the nearby **John Heard House**, a Federal home of 1795 noted for its China Trade and Early American furnishings. Antique carriages are also featured here. *Whipple House, 53 South Main St.,* ☎ *(508) 356-2811; Heard House. 40 South Main St.,* ☎ *(508) 356-2641. Both open May to mid-Oct., Wed.–Sat. 10–4, Sun. 1–4. Adults $5, under 13 free.*

Head north through Rowley and Newbury. Those wishing to visit Plum Island and the ***Parker River National Wildlife Refuge** (5) should turn right on Rolfe's Lane, then right again on Water Street, which becomes the Plum Island Turnpike in a few miles. Birders will love this waterfowl haven, as will anyone who just appreciates good coastal scenery. Visitors can hike, bike, swim, fish, study nature, pick berries, and even go cross-country skiing in winter. ☎ *(508) 465-5753. Open daily dawn to dusk, beach closed Apr.– Aug. to protect nesting birds. Headquarters open Mon.–Fri. 8–4:30. Closes when parking lots are full. $5 per private car, or $2 per pedestrian or bicyclist.* ♿.

Back on High Road (MA-1A) stands the **Tristram Coffin House** (6), begun around 1654 and expanded several times since. Eight generations of Coffins have lived here, and all left treasures behind to mark the evolution of domestic life in New England. Of special interest are the 17th- and 18th-century kitchens, the buttery, and the 19th-century parlor decorations. *14 High Rd.,* ☎ *(508) 463-2057. Open June to mid-Oct., Wed.–Sun., noon–4. Adults $4, seniors $3.50, children (6–12) $2.*

Continue into **Newburyport** (7), the birthplace of the U.S. Coast Guard

An antiques shop in Essex

and home to many a clipper ship in the heyday of the China Trade. **High Street** (MA-1A) and some of the adjoining streets are a veritable museum of American Federal architecture, a wonderful place to stroll around taking in the sights. Visits can be made to the **Cushing House**, home of the Historical Society of Old Newbury. Built in 1808, the 21-room Federal-style mansion was the residence of Caleb Cushing, an important politician, confidant of presidents, and the first ambassador to China. It features an outstanding collection of period furnishings and artwork, along with an 1840s garden with rare roses. *98 High St., ☎ (508) 462-2681. Open May–Oct., Tues.–Sat. 10–3. Adults $3, students $1.50.*

Down by the waterfront is the **Custom House Maritime Museum** (8), housed in a Classic Revival custom house of 1835. Over three centuries of local maritime history are covered here, including shipbuilding from 1639 on, the birth of the U.S. Coast Guard in 1790, and the glorious days of the China trade and the clipper ships. *25 Water St., ☎ (508) 462-8681. Open April to mid-Dec., Mon.–Sat. 10–4, Sun. 1–4. Adults $3, seniors $2, children $1.50.*

Trip 10

Lexington and the Minute Man National Historical Park

No one knows which side fired that first shot on April 19, 1775, but it was the opening act of the American Revolution, and it happened right here in Lexington. Seventy-seven Colonial militiamen, forewarned of the approach of British troops by Paul Revere on his Midnight Ride, stood their ground on Lexington Green. It was meant to be a simple display of defiance before dispersing in face of an overwhelming force of Redcoats, but somehow a trigger got pulled against orders and a battle ensued. In the end, eight Americans lay dead and ten more were wounded. The British then moved on to Concord, where they suffered losses and retreated under heavy fire to Boston.

The events of that day can be best understood by following the route from Lexington to Concord, stopping at sites along the way. Over half of this trail lies within the Minute Man National Historical Park, so most of the attractions are free, courtesy of the American taxpayers. A few outside the park have a modest admission charge, but overall this is a very inexpensive daytrip—so perhaps you can splurge for lunch.

Concord is also the focus of the next daytrip (see page 82), which concerns itself with later events, especially those of a literary and cultural nature. By staying overnight, both trips could be combined with those to Lowell and Andover, or with Fruitlands and Harvard.

GETTING THERE:

By car, Lexington is about 12 miles northwest of downtown Boston. Take Route **MA-2** to the intersection with **MA-4/MA-225** and head north about 1½ miles to the Heritage Museum, then another mile to Lexington Green.

Go west on Massachusetts Avenue about 2½ miles to the Battle Road Visitor Center, then 7 miles west on **MA-2A** through Concord to the North Bridge Visitor Center.

By public transportation, you can get to either Lexington or Concord easily enough, but not from one to the other or to the sites in between. For Lexington, take the Red Line "T" subway to Alewife in Cambridge, then an MBTA bus. Concord is served by commuter train from Boston's North Station, on the Fitchburg line. A more practical possibility is to take one of the several guided bus tours offered.

The Minute Man Statue at North Bridge

PRACTICALITIES:

While this trip can be made at any time, you'll find a lot more open from April through October. **Patriots' Day**, the Monday nearest April 19th, is celebrated with battle reenactments in both Lexington and Concord.

For further information contact the **Merrimack Valley Convention & Visitors Bureau**, 22 Shattuck St., Lowell, MA 01852, ☎ (508) 459-6150 or (800) 443-3332, FAX (508) 459-4595, Web Site: www.lowell.org. Local information is available at the **Lexington Visitor Center**, 1875 Massachusetts Ave., Lexington, MA 02173, ☎ (617) 862-1450, and at the **Concord Chamber of Commerce Visitor Kiosk**, Heywood St., Concord, MA 01742, ☎ (508) 369-3120.

FOOD AND DRINK:

You'll find plenty of chain restaurants in and around Lexington and Concord; for finer dining consider:

> **Hartwell House** (94 Hartwell Ave., Lexington, north of Battle Rd. Visitor Center via Airport Rd., then right) Inspired American cuisine, reservations recommended. ☎ (617) 862-5111. X: Sat. lunch, Sun. $$$

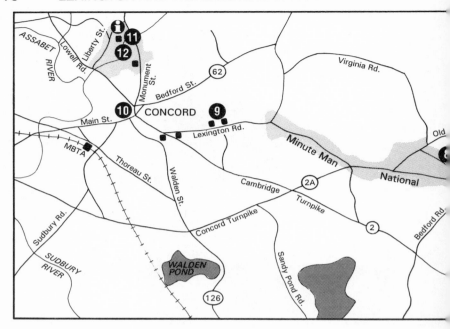

Colonial Inn (48 Monument Sq., on the Green in Concord at MA-2A and MA-62) Traditional New England cuisine in an historic 1716 inn. Reservations suggested. ☎ (508) 369-9200. $$ and $$$

Peking Garden (27 Waltham St., just south of Lexington Green) Excellent Chinese meals, including buffets and dim sums. ☎ (617) 862-1051. $$

Walden Station (24 Walden St., south of Monument Sq. in Concord) Good American food at reasonable prices. ☎ (508) 371-2233. $ and $$

SUGGESTED TOUR:

Numbers in parentheses correspond to numbers on the map. As good a place to begin as any, especially since it's the closest to Boston, is the **Museum of Our National Heritage** (1). Founded by the Scottish Rite Masons, this thoroughly modern museum presents changing exhibitions on American history and popular culture from Colonial times to the present. There is, of course, a special focus on Lexington and the American Revolution. *33 Marrett Rd. (MA-2A),* ☎ *(617) 861-6559. Open Mon.–Sat. 10–5, Sun. noon–5. Closed Thanksgiving, Dec. 24–25, New Year's. Free. Gift shop.* &.

Go north on Massachusetts Avenue (MA-4/MA-225) to the **Munroe Tavern** (2). This restored 1695 structure served as the British headquarters and

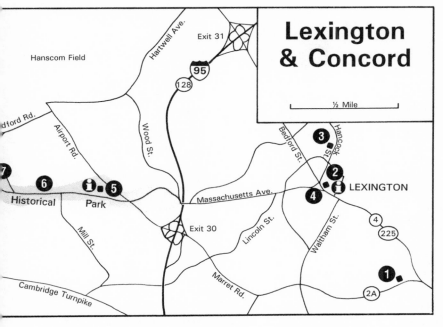

field hospital during the bloody retreat from Concord back to Boston, throughout which the Redcoats were subjected to heavy sniper fire and suffered great losses. George Washington dined here in 1789; you can still see his table along with a number of artifacts. *1332 Massachusetts Ave.,* ☎ *(617) 647-9238. Open Apr.–Oct., Mon.–Sat. 10–5, Sun. 1–5. Adults $3, children (6–16) $1. Combination tickets with other Lexington houses available.*

Continue north past Lexington Green and turn right on Hancock Street to the **Hancock-Clarke House** (3). This was the destination of Paul Revere's famous Midnight Ride, where he informed John Hancock and Samuel Adams that "The Regulars are out." He *did not* shout "The British are coming," as legend would have you believe—after all, the Colonials thought of themselves as British and were angry with the king, not with Great Britain. Originally built in 1698 and later enlarged, the house was the ancestral home of John Hancock and at the time of the battle belonged to the Reverend Jonas Clarke, a strong supporter of the rebels. Hancock and Adams were hiding there from the British, who considered them to be dangerous rabble-rousers. Now restored, the house contains period furnishings and artifacts from the battle. *36 Hancock St.,* ☎ *(617) 861-0928. Open Apr.– Oct., Mon.–Sat. 10–5, Sun. 1–5. Adults $3, children (6–16) $1. Combination ticket with other houses available.*

Return to *Lexington Battle Green (4), where the first conflict of the Revolution took place early in the morning of April 19. The local militiamen, led by Captain John Parker, had gathered around 2 a.m. to discuss strategy, then waited for the British at *Buckman Tavern, just across the street. Here they probably warmed themselves on "flip," a popular drink made of beer, rum, molasses, and eggs. A quart of this cost three pence. Today's visitors will have to do without the flip, but they can tour the original taproom, kitchen, and the rest of the restored 1709 inn. *1 Bedford St., ☎ (617) 862-5598. Open Apr.–Oct., Mon.–Sat. 10–5, Sun. 1–5. Last tours at 4:30. Adults $3, children (6–16) $1. Combination tickets available.* The Lexington Visitor Center, where you can get free local information, is right behind this. On the Battle Green itself you'll find a Minuteman statue (not the famous one), representing Captain Parker as he appeared on that morning when he uttered the immortal words: "Stand your ground. Don't fire unless fired upon. But if they mean to have a war, let it begin here!" Several of the militiamen killed in the conflict are buried beneath the Revolutionary Monument on the Green, dedicated in 1799 and probably the first such memorial to the war. Captain Parker and some other notables lie in rest across the street in the Old Burying Ground, whose oldest stone dates from 1690.

Drive west along Massachusetts Avenue and into the Minute Man National Historical Park, stopping first at the Battle Road Visitor Center (5) to watch a 22-minute film of the events that led to war, see the exhibits, and pick up a free map. *Airport Rd., just off Massachusetts Ave. (MA-2A), ☎ (617) 862-7753. Open mid-April through Oct., daily 9–5:30. Free. &.* A short distance west of this is the Paul Revere Capture Site (6), where the patriot was apprehended by the British around 2 a.m. on April 19, after he had informed Hancock, Adams, and others in Lexington and was on his way to Concord to warn the militia there. Fortunately, the message was also carried by William Dawes and Dr. Samuel Prescott. Dawes escaped and returned to Lexington; Prescott evaded the Brits and got through to Concord. Revere was soon released and made it back to Lexington in time to hear the first shots.

Some other historic structures along the route are the Captain William Smith House (7), home of the leader of the Lincoln Minute Men, and the Hartwell Tavern (8), a typical 18th-century country inn. Both are restored and may be seen. The Wayside (9) was home to Samuel Whitney, the muster master of Concord's militia in 1775. In the next century it became, at various times, the home of the Bronson Alcott family, Margaret Sidney, and Nathaniel Hawthorne; all part of the literary life that gathered around Concord in the mid-1800s. ☎ *(508) 369-6975. Open mid-Apr. through Oct., tours Fri.–Tues. 10:30–4. Admission $3.*

Continue on through Concord (10), a quiet old town renowned as the site of the first real battle of the Revolutionary War, and also for its 19th-century literary associations—described in the daytrip beginning on page 82. Turn

North Bridge

right on Monument Street to the **North Bridge Visitor Center** (11) of the Minute Man National Historic Park. Here you can get a good introduction to the "shot heard 'round the world," the armed militia resistance that sent the British Redcoats fleeing back to Boston on the afternoon of April 19, 1775. Located in a house built in 1911 by a descendant of Concord's militia leader, the center has interesting exhibits, artifacts, and a short film on the battle. *174 Liberty St.,* ☎ *(508) 369-6993. Open daily 9–5:30, with reduced hours in winter. Closed Thanksgiving, Christmas, and New Year's. Free.* ♿.

Walk down the path to the famous ***Minute Man Statue**, sculpted in 1873 by Daniel Chester French, who also created the statue of John Harvard in Cambridge and the one of Lincoln at Washington's Lincoln Memorial. The term "Minute Man" refers to a member of a local militia, who was always ready on a minute's notice to defend his town against Indians or, as it happened, against the king. Just steps away is the ***North Bridge** (12), a 1956 replica of the one that inspired Ralph Waldo Emerson to write: "By the rude bridge that arched the flood. / Their flag to April's breeze unfurled; / Here once the embattled farmers stood, / And fired the shot heard 'round the world." This is where patriot militiamen first shot back at the British, sending them into retreat and pursuing them with unrelenting fire all the way to Boston. In all, 73 Redcoats died, 174 were wounded, and 26 were missing. American losses amounted to 49 dead, 40 wounded, and 5 missing. Total war had become inevitable.

Concord Town, Walden Pond, and Lincoln

Historically speaking, Concord is doubly blessed. Not only was it the site of the Revolutionary War's first real battle, but it later became a center of literature and intellect. Within a few blocks of each other lived the major figures of the mid-19th-century transcendentalist movement: Ralph Waldo Emerson, the Alcotts, Henry David Thoreau, and others. Several of their homes are preserved today and may be visited, as can their graves.

While Concord attracts throngs of tourists in season, and Walden Pond no longer has quite the solitude that Thoreau experienced, Lincoln remains refreshingly undiscovered by all but the knowledgeable few. This trip combines easily with the previous one to Lexington and the Minute Man National Historical Park, and by staying overnight, with the following ones to Lowell and Andover, or with Fruitlands and Harvard.

GETTING THERE:

By car, you can follow the route of the previous trip, or take a faster route via **MA-2** (Concord Turnpike). Concord is about 20 miles northwest of downtown Boston.

Head south from Concord on Walden Pond Road, **MA-126**, to Walden Pond, then continue south. The Codman House is on Codman Road, a quarter-mile east of MA-126. Just north of it, Baker Bridge Road goes past the Gropius House, continuing on Sandy Pond Road to the DeCordova Museum.

By train, it's a 40-minute ride from Boston's North Station to Concord. Take the MBTA Fitchburg Line. All of the sites in town are within walking distance of the Concord station, but Walden Pond is about a two-mile trek away. The Codman and Gropius houses, and the DeCordova Museum, are even farther.

PRACTICALITIES:

Most of the attractions on this trip are open from mid-April through October, but often closed on holidays, Mondays, Tuesdays, or even Wednesdays. Note that the Codman and Gropius houses are open from June until mid-October only. Check the individual listings, and phone ahead if any particular sight is crucially important to you.

For further information contact the **Merrimack Valley Convention & Visitors Bureau**, 22 Shattuck St., Lowell, MA 01852, ☎ (508) 459-6150 or (800) 443-3332, FAX (508) 459-4595, Web Site: www.lowell.org. A more local source is the **Concord Chamber of Commerce Visitor Kiosk**, Heywood St., Concord, MA 01742, ☎ (508) 369-3120.

FOOD AND DRINK:

See the listings for the previous trip, Lexington and the Minute Man National Historical Park, on page 76. To this can be added:

> **Longfellow's Wayside Inn** (Wayside Inn Rd., Sudbury; go south on MA-126, then west on US-20 and follow signs) This historic inn has been serving wayfarers since 1716, making it the oldest operating inn in America. It's filled with antiques, the staff wear Colonial costumes, and the cuisine is regional New England. A working gristmill grinds the flour for the homemade bread. Reservations are suggested, ☎ (508) 443-1776. $$ and $$$

LOCAL ATTRACTIONS:

Numbers in parentheses correspond to numbers on the map. Ralph Waldo Emerson's grandfather built the **Old Manse** (1) around 1770, and stood guard below it on April 19, 1775, as his family watched the first battle of the Revolutionary War from the upstairs windows. The great poet himself lived here as a child in 1813, and again in 1834 as he wrote his first book of essays, called *Nature*. From 1842 to 1845 the house was occupied by another literary figure, Nathaniel Hawthorne, whose collection of stories entitled *Mosses from an Old Manse* gave the place its name. Emerson's ancestral family, the Ripleys, lived here for about 170 years, and it is mostly their furnishings that visitors see today, along with mementos of Emerson and Hawthorne. ☎ *(508) 369-3909. Open mid-Apr. through Oct., Mon. and Wed.–Sat. 10–5, Sun. and holidays 1–5. Closed Tues. Last tour at 4:30. Adults $4.50, seniors (62+) and students $3.50, children (6–12) $2.50.*

Close to the Old Manse, on Bedford Road (MA-62), is the **Sleepy Hollow Cemetery** (2). Ralph Waldo Emerson, Nathaniel Hawthorne, Henry David Thoreau, the Alcotts, and other literary greats are buried here on Authors' Ridge; Emerson's grave has a particularly appropriate marker. Another permanent resident is sculptor Daniel Chester French, whose work *Mourning Victory* graces the place. ☎ *(508) 371-6299. Open daily, 7–dusk. Free.* ♿.

Just a few blocks to the south stands the **Ralph Waldo Emerson House** (3), where the poet lived most of his life, from 1835 until his death in 1882. The bulk of his work was written here. Nearly all of the furnishings are original and belonged to the Emersons, as did the mementos and artifacts. *28 Cambridge Tpk.,* ☎ *(508) 369-2236. Open for tours mid-Apr. to late Oct., Thurs.–Sat. 10–4:30, Sun. and holidays 2–4:30. Adults $4.50, children (7–17) $3.*

Head out Lexington Road (MA-2A) to **The Wayside** (4), which figures in both the events of April 19, 1775, and in the literary renaissance of the 19th century. In 1775, this was the home of the roll caller, or muster master, of the Concord militia that fought so well in the opening battle of the Revolutionary War. Bronson Alcott (1799–1888), the transcendentalist philosopher and educator, lived here for three years with his wife and four daughters: Anna, the author Louisa May, Elizabeth, and Abba May. This was also home, at other times, to authors Nathaniel Hawthorne and Margaret Sidney. *455 Lexington Rd.,* ☎ *(508) 369-6975. Open mid-Apr. through Oct. Tours on Fri.–Tues., 10:30–4. Adults $3, under 16 free.* East of the home are the original Concord grapevines, where the prolific Concord grape was developed in the mid-19th century. This particular variety launched the commercial growing of table grapes in America; it yields good jelly and juice, and awful wine.

Just west of The Wayside is the **Orchard House** (5), home of the Alcotts from 1858 until 1877. This is where Louisa May Alcott wrote *Little Women* in 1868, and where her father, Bronson, established his School of Philosophy in another small building on the property. Until Louisa May's success as an author, the Alcott family was in chronic need of money as the father involved himself in disastrous utopian schemes such as Fruitlands (see page 93). He was also a vegetarian, an abolitionist, and an early advocate of women's rights. Concord, home of transcendentalism, was the perfect place for them. *399 Lexington Rd.,* ☎ *(508) 369-4118. Open Apr.–Oct., Mon.– Sat. 10–4:30, Sun. 1–4:30; rest of year, Mon.–Fri. 11–3, Sat. 1-4:30, Sun. 1– 4:30. Closed early Jan., Easter, Thanksgiving, Christmas. Adults $5.50, seniors (62+) $4.50, children (6–12) $3.50.*

Return on Lexington Road. Across the street is the:

*CONCORD MUSEUM (6), 200 Lexington Rd., Concord, MA 01742, ☎ (508) 369-9763. *Open Apr.–Dec., Mon.–Sat. 9–5, Sun. noon–5; rest of year, Mon.–Sat. 11–4, Sun. 1–4. Closed New Year's, Easter, Thanksgiving, Christmas. Adults $6, seniors (62+) $5, students $3. Museum shop.* ⟶.

Emerson's study, Thoreau's personal belongings from Walden Pond, even one of the lanterns hung from Boston's Old North Church on the night of Paul Revere's Midnight Ride—it's all here amid artifacts of local history, period room settings, and American decorative arts from the 17th to the 19th centuries.

Concord has two more attractions, both within easy walking distance. Across the street and slightly to the west is the **Concord Art Association** (7) with its changing exhibitions of American arts and crafts. The house itself, built around 1750, has a secret room where weapons were hidden during the Revolutionary War; this was later used by the Underground Railway to shelter fugitive slaves. *37 Lexington Rd.,* ☎ *(508) 369-2578. Call for open-*

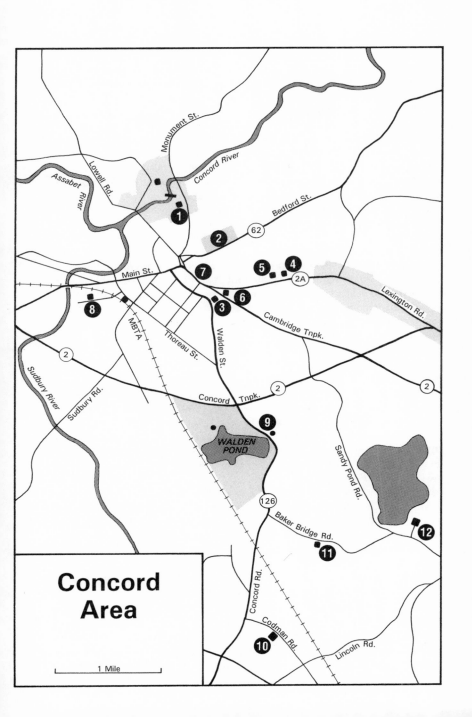

Concord
Area

1 Mile

ing times. Another site, the **Thoreau Lyceum** (8) is near the train station. It's filled with Thoreau memorabilia, and there's a replica of his Walden Pond cabin. *156 Belknap St.,* ☎ *(508) 369-5912. Call for opening times. Nominal admission.*

Walden Road leads south to the:

*WALDEN POND STATE RESERVATION (9), Route 126, Concord, MA 01742, ☎ (508) 369-3254. *Open daily 5 a.m. to sunset. Lifeguards on duty Memorial Day to Labor Day. Hiking, swimming, canoeing and rowing, picnicking, fishing, cross-country skiing. Parking fee in season. A maximum of 1,000 visitors are allowed at a time; after that it closes.*

Pick up a map of the reservation at the parking lot, examine the replica of Thoreau's cabin there, then cross the road and walk down to the pond. A woodland path to the right leads to the actual site of the cabin where Henry David Thoreau (1817–62) lived from 1845 to 1847, and where he was inspired to write his seminal work, *Walden.* A pile of stones marks the spot, along with a sign bearing the quotation: "I went to the woods because I wished to live deliberately, to front only the essential facts of life. And see if I could not learn what it had to teach and not, when I came to die, discover that I had not lived." Walden Pond is still a peaceful place, especially when you get away from the beach and into the woods.

Continuing south on MA-126 and then turning left on Codman Road brings you into Lincoln, and to the gorgeous old **Codman House** (10). Built around 1749 and later transformed into a English-style country estate, it remained in the Codman family for over two centuries. Architectural styles here run the gamut from Georgian to Federal to Victorian to Colonial Revival and, for good measure, include a romantic Italianate garden. This is a real treat, and not too many people know about it. Yet. ☎ *(617) 259-8843. Open June through mid-Oct., Wed.–Sun. noon–5. Last tour at 4. Adults $4, seniors 64+ $3.50, children (6–12) $2.*

Nearby, the **Gropius House** (11) is as different architecturally as can be. Walter Gropius (1883–1969) was the founder of the famed Bauhaus school of design in Germany in 1919; in 1937 he fled the Nazis and moved to America to head Harvard's School of Architecture. Gropius built this home for himself in 1938, using native New England materials in ways that reflect Bauhaus teachings. Inside, there is original furniture by Marcel Breuer, and artworks by such friends as Josef Albers and Henry Moore. *68 Baker Bridge Rd.,* ☎ *(617) 259-8843. Open June to mid-Oct., Wed.–Sun., noon–5; rest of year on the first Sat. & Sun. of each month, noon–5. Last tour at 4. Adults $5, seniors 64+ $4.50, children (6–12) $2.50.*

One last attraction in the area, and an unusual one, is the ***DeCordova Museum and Sculpture Park** (12). After his death in 1945, industrialist and art collector Julian de Cordova left his hilltop 1880 mansion to the town of

A wooden carving of Thoreau and a replica of his cabin at Walden Pond

Lincoln to use as a museum. Noting that Boston, and Massachusetts in general, has few outlets for contemporary art, the directors decided to focus on living American artists, especially those working in New England. Thirty-five acres of the lovely lakeside estate are set aside for changing exhibitions of sculpture, and there are outdoor concerts in summer. *51 Sandy Pond Rd., ☎ (617) 259-8355. Museum open Tues.–Fri. 10–5, Sat.–Sun. noon–5, closed holidays. Park open daily 8 a.m. to 10 p.m. Adults $4, seniors (60+), students, and children (6–12) $3. Park is free.*

Trip 12

Lowell and Andover

One of America's first planned industrial cities, Lowell in the mid-19th century was the very model of progressive urbanization. Its textile factories began harnessing the plentiful power of the Merrimack River in 1822 and soon evolved as the "Manchester of America," with 25 factories by 1827. In another decade it was producing some 40 million yards of cloth a year. What was more remarkable was an almost paternalistic attitude towards employees. Charles Dickens, that most severe critic of English sweatshops, visited Lowell in 1842 and remarked that "no face there bore an unhealthy or unhappy look." A bit overstated perhaps, but working conditions here were quite good for that era.

Alas, times changed. An influx of immigrant labor willing to work for less, competition from states with lower wages, and the development of more efficient power sources led to social unrest—and disaster for Lowell's economy. By the 1950s the city hit rock bottom. Since then, the establishment of new high-tech industries brought a measure of prosperity, and in 1978 the old industrial core was restored as the Lowell National Historical Park. Several historic textile mills, over five miles of canals, operating gatehouses, worker housing, and even turn-of-the-century trolley cars have been preserved as a monument to America's Industrial Revolution. Thousands of visitors from all over come to learn about this rich heritage, and to have fun taking boat tours and riding the old streetcars.

From Lowell it's only a short drive to the lovely Colonial town of Andover, home of the Phillips Academy since 1778. Its 450-acre campus has several historic buildings, a noted gallery of American art, an archaeological museum, and an inn that's a fine place for dinner. By staying overnight, this trip combines well with the previous ones to Lexington and Concord, or with the following one to Fruitlands and Harvard.

GETTING THERE:

By car, Lowell is about 33 miles northwest of Boston. Take Route **US-3** to Exit 30N, then the Lowell Connector to Exit 5N, Thorndike St. Follow signs to the free parking lot at the Visitor Center. Those coming via **I-495** should get off at Exit 36.

To get to Andover via Route I-495, get off at Exit 41 and go south on **MA-28** (Main St.) to the Phillips Academy. Return to Boston via Route **I-93**.

PRACTICALITIES:

The Lowell National Historical Park is open daily from July through Labor Day, but closed on Mondays and Tuesdays the rest of the year. The Quilt Museum is closed on Mondays from November through April; the Whistler Museum on Mondays and Tuesdays all year round, and every day in January and February. In Andover, the Addison Gallery of American Art is closed on Mondays, and also in August.

For further information contact the **Merrimack Valley Convention & Visitors Bureau**, 22 Shattuck St., Lowell, MA 01852, ☎ (508) 459-6150 or (800) 443-3332, FAX (508) 459-4595, Web Site: www.lowell.org.

FOOD AND DRINK:

Andover Inn (Phillips Academy campus, Chapel Ave., in Andover) International cuisine in a formal setting. On Sunday evenings the inn features an authentic Indonesian rijsttafel. Dress well and reserve. ☎ (508) 475-5903. X: Sun. lunch in summer. $$$

Speare House (525 Pawtucket Blvd., 2 miles west of Lowell on MA-113) The "Castle on the Merrimack" features traditional American cuisine in a princely setting. ☎ (508) 452-8903. $$

Athenian Corner (207 Market St., near the Visitor Center on Lowell) Shish kebab and other classic Greek dishes. ☎ (508) 458-7052. $ and $$

Dubliner (197 Market St., near the Visitor Center in Lowell) An Irish pub with steaks, seafood, and sandwiches. X: Sun. ☎ (508) 459-9831. $

Club Diner (145 Dutton St., near the Visitor Center in Lowell) This classic old diner treats its patrons to real home cooking. ☎ (508) 452-1679. $

LOCAL ATTRACTIONS:

Numbers in parentheses correspond to numbers on the map.

*LOWELL NATIONAL HISTORICAL PARK (1), 246 Market St., Lowell, MA 01852, ☎ (508) 970-5000. *Open July to early Sept., daily 10–5; rest of year Wed.–Sun. 10–5. Visitor Center opens at 8:30. Closed Thanksgiving, Christmas, New Year's. Free; modest fee for some activities and sites. Reservations suggested for boat and trolley tours.* ❶. ♿.

Begin at the **Visitor Center**, where you can get a free map of the many sites spread around the historic core area. You can also find out about various ***ranger-guided tours**, some on foot and others by boat and/or trolley car. Boats operate in summer; the replica 1901 electric trolleys (some open-sided!) run daily from March through late November. *Boat and/or trolley tours are $3 for adults, $2 for seniors over 61, and $1 for children (6–16).* While at the Visitor Center you can also watch the introductory multimedia show, and view exhibits.

For many, the park's leading attraction is the ***Boott Cotton Mills Museum**, located about a half-mile northeast of the Visitor Center, between the Eastern Canal and the Merrimack River. Housed in an old brick cotton mill of 1873, the museum features some 88 noisy, operating looms, some of which are busy weaving cloth towels to be sold at the gift shop. These same looms had once migrated south where labor was cheaper, but were later returned as part of the Historical Park. When the mills first opened in the 1830s each weaver tended only two looms, but a century later had to take care of twenty! Exhibits upstairs cover such subjects as the transition into an industrial society, labor, production processes, and the rise, fall, and rebirth of Lowell. *Open Mon.–Fri. 9:30–4, Sat., Sun., and holidays 10–5. Adults $3, seniors $2, children $1.* &. While there, you might want to check out the **Tsongas Industrial History Center Family Programs**. These hands-on workshops allow participants to weave on the looms, work on an assembly line, and engage in other kinds of labor.

Nearby, the **Working People Exhibit** is housed in an old Boott Mills boardinghouse, where "mill girls" of the mid-19th century once lived in comparative comfort, and later immigrants eked out an existence. There are several other sites scattered around the area, some operated by the **Lowell Heritage State Park** in conjunction with the Lowell National Historical Park, but all described in the brochure you'll get at the Visitor Center. While in the neighborhood, you can also visit the:

NEW ENGLAND QUILT MUSEUM (2), 18 Shattuck St., Lowell, MA 01852, ☎ (508) 452-4207. *Open May–Oct., Mon.–Sat. 10–4 and Sun. noon–4; rest of year Tues.–Sat. 10–4 and Sun. noon–4. Closed major holidays. Adults $3, seniors (60+) and children (7–17) $2. Gift shop.* &.

American quilting, past and present, is explored in changing exhibitions of beautiful and sometimes unusual examples of the art.

About two blocks west of the Visitor Center is the:

WHISTLER HOUSE MUSEUM OF ART (3), 243 Worthen St., Lowell, MA 01852, ☎ (508) 452-7641. *Open March–Dec., Wed.–Sat. 11–4 and Sun. 1–4; also on Tues. 11–4 from June–Aug. Closed major holidays. Admission $2, reserve ahead.* &.

James Abbott McNeill Whistler, the renowned painter, was born here in 1834 but left at the age of three. His entire adult life was spent in Europe, where he died in 1903. The museum showcases 19th- and early-20th-century works by American artists.

A few blocks south of here is the new:

AMERICAN TEXTILE MUSEUM (4), 491 Dutton St., Lowell, MA 01852, ☎ (508) 441-0400. *Scheduled to open in late 1996; call for times and admission fees.*

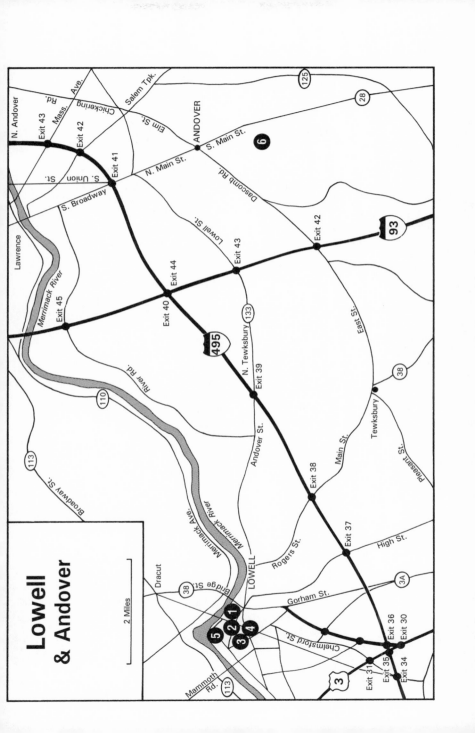

Lowell
& Andover

2 Miles

Housed in an historic mill building, the museum traces the history of American cloth-making with an operating woolen mill and weave room, tools, machinery, artifacts, and illustrations.

While in Lowell, try to take a short drive north to **Pawtucket Falls** (5), where the mighty Merrimack River drops some 32 feet. It was this release of energy that powered the looms of Lowell, and it's still an impressive sight when viewed from the Pawtucket Canal Gatehouse on School Street.

If time permits, you could drive east to **Andover** and the historic **Phillips Academy** (6). Founded in 1778, this co-ed residential school for grades nine through twelve has a lovely 450-acre campus rivaling that of many a university. Visitors are especially drawn to the **Addison Gallery of American Art**, noted for its fine collection of paintings, sculpture, drawings, and photographs by American masters. Don't miss the ***ship models** in the basement; they trace maritime history from sail to steam engine. *Phillips Academy, Chapel Ave., Andover,* ☎ *(508) 749-4015. Open Sept.–July, Tues.–Sat. 10–5 and Sun. 1–5. Closed major holidays. Free.* ♿. Another attraction is the **Robert S. Peabody Foundation for Archaeology** with its exhibits on North American prehistoric archaeology and Native American cultures. *Phillips Academy, Phillips and Main streets, Andover,* ☎ *(508) 749-4490. Open early Sept to July, Tues.–Fri. noon–5, Sat. 10–1. Closed major holidays. Free.*

Also on Main Street in Andover is the **Andover Historical Society**, featuring period rooms, furniture, and artifacts in an 1819 house and barn. *97 Main St.,* ☎ *(508) 475-2236. Open Mon.–Fri. 1–3 and Sat. 9–5. Closed major holidays. Adults $2, seniors and children $1.*

Fruitlands and the Harvard Area

Twice in its history, the little town of Harvard became Utopia—once for over a century and a second time for only a brief moment. An idealistic group of Shakers settled here in 1791 and stayed until 1919, leaving behind the structures and artifacts of a most engaging community. In the middle of this time span, the transcendentalists descended with their impossible dreams and wholly impractical notions of a "New Eden." The heritage of both movements can be experienced today at the wonderful Fruitlands Museums, a complex of old farm buildings spread over a 200-acre site with woodland paths and lovely vistas. Other remnants of the Shaker village can be seen just to the north.

Children, and the truly young-at-heart, will enjoy the Toy Cupboard Theater and Museum in nearby South Lancaster; grown-ups will undoubtedly prefer the unusual winery at Bolton. For those with more than a day to spend, this excursion combines well with the one to Concord (page 82), or with the one to Worcester (page 138).

GETTING THERE:

By car, Harvard is about 35 miles northwest of downtown Boston. Take Route **MA-2** to Exit 38A, then go south briefly on **MA-110**, quickly turning right onto Old Shirley Road. Follow this and Prospect Hill Road for a bit over two miles to Fruitlands.

For the old Shaker village, head north of MA-2 on MA-110, turning right on South Shaker Road, then left (north) on Shaker Road.

For South Lancaster, go south on MA-110, then right into the town. Bolton is on **MA-117**, just west of the intersection with **I-495**.

PRACTICALITIES:

The focus of this daytrip, the Fruitlands Museums, are open from mid-May through mid-October, but never on Mondays except when they're a holiday. You can call the museum complex directly at (508) 456-3924. For general information, contact the **Worcester County Convention & Visitors Bureau**, 33 Waldo St., Worcester, MA 01608, ☎ (508) 753-2920, FAX (508) 754-8460. Purely local information about the Shaker village and the Holy Hill Conservation Area can be had from the Harvard Town Clerk, ☎ (508) 456-3607.

FOOD AND DRINK:
You might pack a picnic lunch to enjoy outdoors at Fruitlands; otherwise try the:

Fruitlands Tea Room (at the Fruitlands Museum) An unusually attractive place for light lunches with a panoramic view, indoors or out. ☎ (508) 456-3924. X: Mon., winter. $ and $$

LOCAL ATTRACTIONS:
Numbers in parentheses correspond to numbers on the map.

*FRUITLANDS MUSEUMS (1), 102 Prospect Hill Rd., Harvard, MA 01451, ☎ (508) 456-3924. *Open mid-May to mid-Oct., Tues.–Sun. 10–5. Also open on holiday Mondays. Grounds open daily. Adults $6, seniors (60+) $5, students $3.50, children (4–17) $2.50. Gift shop.* X.

Amos Bronson Alcott, the philosopher, educator, and father of Louisa May Alcott, founded his hopelessly idealistic society in an early-18th-century farmhouse here in 1843. He and his transcendentalist followers practiced a narrow version of vegetarianism, consuming only veggies that reached toward the sky and eschewing those that were earthbound, such as potatoes and carrots. In opposition to slavery and animal cruelty, they wore neither cotton nor wool, but clad themselves in linen from humanely-grown flax. They also spent their days thinking, while their women folk plowed the fields and minded the house. Not a bad life, perhaps, but it didn't last long. In less than a year they were all out of here. Today the original ***Fruitlands Farmhouse** is a museum of the transcendentalist movement, with mementos of the Alcotts, Ralph Waldo Emerson, Henry David Thoreau, and others.

Nearby stands the **Shaker House** of 1794, moved here from the former Shaker village just north of Harvard, which was disbanded in 1919. The Shakers were a fascinating group of people, very talented and hard working. Their story is more thoroughly explored at the Hancock Shaker Village, an element of the Northern Berkshires daytrip, described on page 175. You might want to check this out. In the meantime, this small museum displays a wonderful collection of Shaker furniture, crafts, and industries, including a chair that belonged to Mother Ann, the sect's founder. Fruitlands also has an **Indian Museum**, featuring Native American artifacts and cultural exhibits. The **Picture Gallery** contains portraits by early-19th-century itinerant artists along with landscapes by followers of the Hudson River School, including works by Thomas Cole, Albert Bierstadt, and Frederick Church. Besides the museums, there are also beautiful grounds to explore, hiking trails with panoramic views extending into New Hampshire, picnic facilities, various events, a gift shop, and a tea room.

Harvard's Shaker community was disbanded in 1919, but some of its simple but quite attractive houses remain in what is now the town's **Shaker**

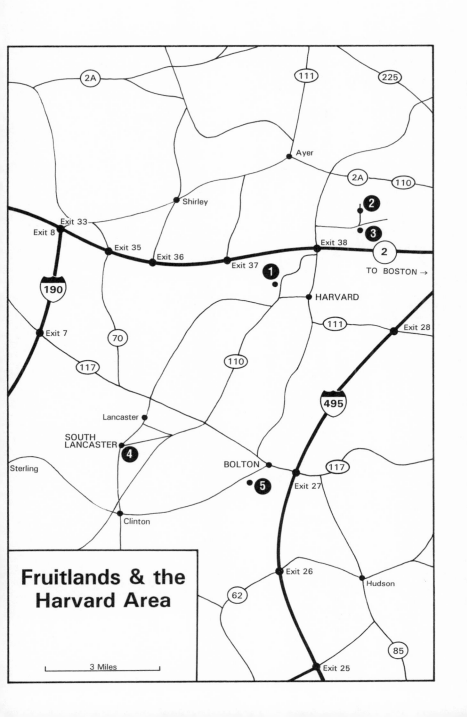

Fruitlands & the Harvard Area

2A
111
225
Ayer
2A
110
Shirley
Exit 33
Exit 8
Exit 35
Exit 36
Exit 38
Exit 37
2
TO BOSTON →
190
HARVARD
111
Exit 28
Exit 7
70
110
117
495
Lancaster
SOUTH LANCASTER
BOLTON
117
Sterling
Exit 27
Clinton
Exit 26
Hudson
62
85
Exit 25

3 Miles

Historic District (2). These can be seen by driving north on MA-110 past the intersection with MA-2, then turning right onto South Shaker Road, and left on Shaker Road. Near this last intersection is the **Holy Hill Conservation Area** (3). Once used by the Shakers for outdoor worship, the Holy Hill is about a half-mile trek up a trail, and still has a Shaker cemetery and some foundations of their buildings.

Less than ten miles to the southwest of Harvard is a little-known attraction that's a special treat for small children:

TOY CUPBOARD PUPPET THEATER AND MUSEUM (4), 57 East George Hill Rd., South Lancaster, MA 01561, ☎ (508) 365-9519. *Open Apr.–Oct., call ahead for dates and times. Admission $3.* ♿.

For over 50 years this miniscule theater has been entertaining small children, their parents, and their grandparents, with classic tales charmingly enacted by puppets. The adjacent museum of toys was once the home of John Greene Chandler, an early author of children's books.

Another way to end the day is at the:

NASHOBA VALLEY WINERY (5), 100 Wattaquadoc Hill Rd., Bolton, MA 01740, ☎ (508) 779-5521. *Open daily 11–6. Nominal charge for tours.*

Unlike most other wineries, Nashoba crafts its wines from the juice of fruits and berries: apples, peaches, blueberries, strawberries, elderberries, and the like. The results are not only unusual, they are also surprisingly dry, well-balanced, and refreshing. Besides tasting the wines, visitors can pick their own fruit in season, explore the orchards, picnic, tour the winery, and perhaps purchase some wine to take home.

Quincy

Only one town in America can lay claim to two U.S. presidents. Both John Adams and his son, John Quincy Adams, were born in Quincy (then called Braintree), as was John Hancock, the first president of the congress, first signer of the Declaration of Independence, and first governor of the State of Massachusetts. George Bush, the 41st president, was born in the adjoining town of Milton. All of this would be of merely academic interest if there were not much to show for it; happily there is.

Quincy, pronounced KWIN-zee, was settled in 1625. Two years later it was taken over by one Thomas Norton, an English adventurer given to mad frivolities and drunken orgies, for which the Puritans soon sent him packing. A quiet farming community until the development of granite quarries in 1750, Quincy acquired its name in 1792 from that of a prominent local family. Its shipbuilding industry developed in the 19th century, producing the only seven-master schooner ever built, the world's first nuclear surface ship, and many major naval vessels such as the USS *Salem,* which you can visit. In recent times the town has turned to more modern pursuits, but has preserved enough of its past to make this an unusual destination.

Quincy is barely outside of Boston and could easily be combined with the in-town daytrips described in Section II, or explored on the way to Plymouth or Cape Cod (pages 102-121).

GETTING THERE:

By car, Quincy is about eight miles south of downtown Boston. Take Route **I-93** (Southeast Expressway) to Exit 12, then **MA-3A** to the sites. Going to Hingham adds four miles to the journey; to Hull another five.

By subway, take the Red Line "T" subway bound for Braintree to the Quincy Center stop, a short walk from the historic sites. The USS *Salem* can be reached from here via the number 220 or 221 bus—or walk two miles. Continuing on to Weymouth, Hingham, and Hull by public transportation is impractical.

PRACTICALITIES:

The houses of the Adams National Historic Site are open for tours daily from mid-April until mid-November, although the Visitor Center remains open all year round except on Thanksgiving, Christmas, and New Year's Day. Other sites in Quincy, Weymouth, Hingham, and Hull follow their own schedules, but are usually closed in the off-season. Check the individual listings. The USS *Salem* is open daily all year round.

For further information, contact the **South Shore Chamber of Commerce**, 36 Miller Stile Rd., PO Box 488, Quincy, MA 02269, ☎ (617) 479-1111.

FOOD AND DRINK:

Whiton House (1217 Main St. in Hingham, MA-228 at MA-53) Dining on American cuisine in a country mansion. ☎ (617) 749-5325. $$

Saporito's Florence Club Café (11 Rockland Circle in Hull, between Washington Blvd. and MA-228) Open for dinner only, Saporito's isn't much to look at but has wonderful Italian cuisine. ☎ (617) 925-3023. X: lunch, Mon., Tues., major holidays. $$

The British Relief (152 North St. in Hingham, near the Old Ordinary) A local favorite for inexpensive home cooking in a homey setting. ☎ (617) 749-7713. $

LOCAL ATTRACTIONS:

Numbers in parentheses correspond to numbers on the map.

*ADAMS NATIONAL HISTORIC SITE (1), Visitor Center at 1250 Hancock St., Quincy, MA 02169, ☎ (617) 770-1175. *Visitor Center open daily all year, except Thanksgiving, Christmas, and New Year's. Houses open April 19 to Nov. 10, daily 9–5. Visitor Center free. All three houses $2, under 16 free, church $1 extra. Fee includes "trolley" bus to historic houses.* &.

It is hard to overestimate the role that the Adams family played in American history, both in terms of political and intellectual contributions. Originally from Somerset, England, they settled on the South Shore of Massachusetts Bay in the 17th century and continued on in Quincy well into the 20th. Three of their homes have been preserved as a National Historic Site. Purchase your ticket at the Visitor Center (1), then take the free bus to **The Old House** (2) at 135 Adams Street. Built in 1731, it was purchased in 1787 by John Adams and remained in the family until 1927, being deeded to the nation in 1946. Both presidents lived here, as did several generations of their descendants. Many of the original furnishings are still in place, along with memorabilia and the 18th-century formal gardens.

Continue on by bus, car, or on foot about a mile or so to the **Birthplaces of John Adams and John Quincy Adams** (3). John Adams, the first Vice-President and second President of the United States, was born in this 1681 saltbox-style farmhouse at 133 Franklin Street on October 30, 1735. It was from here that he left for Harvard to begin his long career, and to the adjacent property that he returned in 1764 with his wife, Abigail. This second, even older (circa 1646) house at 141 Franklin Street, was the birthplace of his son, John Quincy Adams, on July 11, 1767. The family lived here for twenty years before moving on to the "Old House" described above.

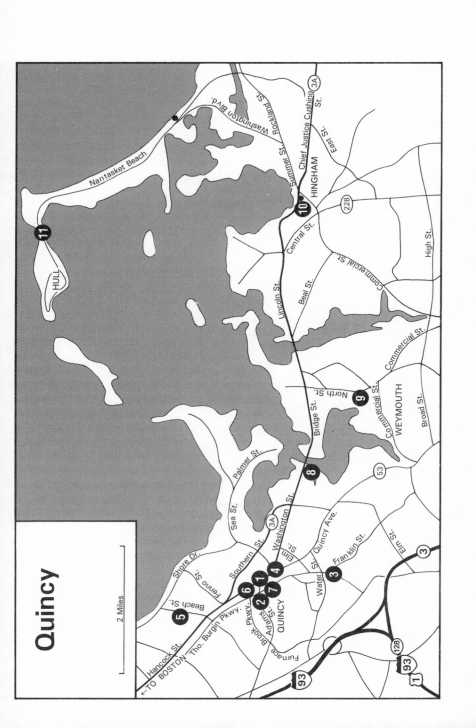

Quincy

2 Miles

Both presidents, and their wives, are buried at the **United First Parish Church** (4) of 1828. Located at 1306 Hancock Street, near the Visitor Center, this granite Greek Revival structure has a magnificent interior with a small museum and a crypt containing the tombs. ☎ *(617) 773-1290. Open for visitors Apr. 19 through Nov. 10, daily. Adults $1.*

While in town, you might want to check out some sites associated with the leading family, the Quincys. In the northern part of town, a few blocks west of Merrymount Park, stands the **Colonel Josiah Quincy House** (5) of 1770. Six successive Josiah Quincys lived here; wealthy merchants, political and social leaders all. One was a president of Harvard, three were mayors of Boston. You can learn all about them, and see their family heirlooms, in this elegant Georgian mansion. *20 Muirhead St.,* ☎ *(617) 227-3956. Open June to mid-Oct., tours on Tues., Thurs., Sat., and Sun. at noon, 1, 2, 3, and 4. Adults $2, under 17 free.*

Earlier generations of Quincys lived at the **Quincy Homestead** (6), originally built around 1685 by Edmund Quincy and enlarged to its present size by the third Edmund Quincy in 1706. His son, the fourth Edmund, had a daughter named Dorothy who married John Hancock, another local lad who did well. The house is furnished with 17th- and 18th-century antiques, and there's a herb garden. *1010 Hancock St., entrance on Butler Rd.* ☎ *(617) 472-5117. Open May–Oct., tours Wed.–Sun., noon–4, or by appt. Adults $3, under 12 $1.* ♿.

The **Quincy Historical Society** (7) occupies the former home of the **Adams Academy**, a school founded by John Adams to provide the classical education needed for college entrance. Exhibits here relate to local history, including artifacts of the nation's first commercial railway, granite quarrying, and shipbuilding. *8 Adams St.,* ☎ *(617) 773-1144. Open Mon.–Fri. 9–4, Sat. 1–4. Donation.*

And now for a real maritime treat:

*U.S. NAVAL SHIPBUILDING MUSEUM (8), Fore River Shipyard, Quincy, MA 02169, ☎ (617) 479-7900. *Open daily, 10–7. Adults $6, seniors (60+) and children (4–12) $4, 3 and under free. Ship's store.* ☕. *Partially* ♿, *video available.*

The cruiser **USS *Salem***, longer than many a battleship, was launched here in 1949 and served valiantly throughout the Cold War. She was the flagship of the Sixth Fleet in the Mediterranean, carried a crew of 1,600, and could steam at more than 30 knots. Visitors can take escorted tours or explore the ship on their own. Either way, they can visit the bridge and the admiral's cabin, climb inside the gun turrets, and experience what life was like below decks.

There are several other attractions south of Quincy, beginning with the

Abigail Adams Birthplace (9) in Weymouth. Built in 1685 and restored to its mid-18th-century condition, this old parsonage was the birthplace in 1744 of Abigail Smith, who married John Adams in 1764 after three years of courtship. It is furnished with period pieces, some of which belonged to the Smith family. *180 Norton St., take North St. south from MA-3A, in Weymouth.* ☎ *(617) 335-1067. Open July through Labor Day, Tues.–Sun. 1–4, and by appt. in June and Sept. to mid-Oct. Adults $1, children 25¢.*

Hingham (10) is the next town down MA-3A. Follow Lincoln Street to **The Old Ordinary** of 1680, which in 1702 became a tavern licensed to sell "strong water" provided the customers were sent home at reasonable hours "with ability to keep their legs." Extensive additions were made in the 1740s, and the place is now a 14-room museum of regional history, filled with unique treasures. *21 Lincoln St., Hingham,* ☎ *(617) 749-0013. Open mid-June to mid-Sept., Tues.–Sat., 1:30–4:30. Adults $3, under 12 $1.* While in Hingham, you might want to visit the **Old Ship Church**, considered to be the oldest wooden church in continuous use in America. It was built in 1681; the pews and pulpit date from 1755, and the Victorian decorations are from the mid-19th century. *90 Main. St., Hingham,* ☎ *(617) 749-1679. Open July– Aug., daily noon–4; by appt. the rest of the year. Donation.*

Hull (11) juts out on a narrow peninsula into Boston Bay, offering fabulous panoramic ***views** refreshed by sea breezes. Just after leaving the mainland, stop at the **Carousel Under the Clock** on Nantasket Beach. The sole survivor of a one-time amusement park, this 1928 merry-go-round has 66 antique horses and a wonderful Wurlitzer organ. ☎ *(617) 925-0472. Operates Memorial Day to Labor Day, daily; April to late May and Sept. to mid-Nov., weekends. $1.50 per ride.* Continue on to the **Lifesaving Museum** in Hull, housed in an 1889 lifesaving station that later served as a Coast Guard station. Dramatic rescues are recounted here, as are Boston harbor shipwrecks. There's a lookout tower, a radio room, lifesaving equipment, a surf boat, lighthouse artifacts, and an activity room for children. *1117 Nantasket Ave.,* ☎ *(617) 925-5433. Open from late June–Labor Day, Wed.–Sun., noon–5; rest of year, weekends, school holidays, and Mon. holidays, noon– 5. Closed Thanksgiving, Christmas, New Year's. Adults $3, seniors $2, children (5–17) $1.50.* ♿.

Trip 15

*Plymouth

New England's first permanent European settlement began right here in December, 1620, when some 102 Pilgrims arrived aboard the *Mayflower* in search of religious freedom. Today it's tourists—another kind of pilgrim, really—who come by the thousands to relive one of the most precious moments in American history. They won't be disappointed.

The story begins in England at the dawn of the 17th century, when a small group of Puritans broke away from the Church of England in a dispute over Biblical interpretation. Persecuted, they fled to Amsterdam, and later Leiden, remaining in Holland for nearly 12 years. In 1617, unable to get along with the Dutch, a group of them elected to emigrate to the New World. A small ship, the *Speedwell*, carried them to Southampton to join another group of settlers from England. After many delays, the voyagers finally departed from Plymouth, England, aboard the 180-ton *Mayflower* on September 16, 1620.

They were ostensibly headed for Virginia, where they had been granted territory, but wound up on Cape Cod instead. Dropping anchor at Province-town after a terrible 65-day voyage, 41 of the men drew up the "Mayflower Compact," establishing a *de facto* government intended to head off mutiny from those who wanted to go to Virginia. After scouting the territory, a suitable piece of land was found on December 21, 1620, and the 102 colonists landed at Plymouth a few days later. Half of them perished that winter.

For today's visitors, the whole epic history is brought back to life at a number of sites. You won't be able to visit all of them in one day, but you will be able to get a good understanding of the events—and have fun doing it. Those with more time at their disposal may want to combine this trip with ones to Quincy, Cape Cod, Martha's Vineyard, New Bedford, or Fall River.

GETTING THERE:

By car, Plymouth is about 40 miles southeast of Boston via Route **MA-3**. If you're starting your visit at Plimoth Plantation, get off at Exit 4 and follow signs. For downtown Plymouth use Exit 6. You might prefer to leave your car parked in one place and use the Plymouth Rock Trolley service (below) to get around, or walk.

Buses operated by the **Plymouth & Brockton Street Railway** provide service from Boston, Logan Airport, and Hyannis on Cape Cod. Be sure to board a bus that's going to downtown Plymouth/Plimoth Plantation, not just the out-of-town Plymouth Bus Terminal. ☎ (508) 746-0378 for information.

PRACTICALITIES:

There's much more to see in Plymouth than can be done in a single day, so you'll have to pick and choose carefully. If your plans include the wonderful Plimoth Plantation, begin your tour south of the town; otherwise start at the southern end of the Historic District. Most of the sights in town can be reached on foot, or you might want to use the convenient **Plymouth Rock Trolley**. This fancy tourist bus provides frequent service between most of the sights, using an all-day, unlimited-rides boarding pass that costs $6 for adults, $3 for children (3–12). It operates daily from Memorial Day through October, and on weekends in November. ☎ (508) 747-3419 for details.

Plymouth is really a warm-weather place, whose major attractions operate from April through November only. Most are open daily, while a few follow a more complex schedule—check the individual listings. You'll be on your feet a lot, so wear comfortable shoes.

For further information, contact **Plymouth Visitor Information**, P.O. Box ROCK, Plymouth, MA 02361, ☎ (508) 746-6668 or (800) USA-1620. Their Internet address is http://media3.com/800-USA-1620. Another Web site is http://www.plymouth1620.com/users/pcdc.

FOOD AND DRINK:

Isaac's (114 Water St., by the harbor) Seafood in a smart contemporary setting, with a grand view of the harbor. Reservations advised, ☎ (508) 830-0001. $$ and $$$

Hearth & Kettle (25 Summer St. at the John Carver Inn, near the Sparrow House) Cape Cod specialties in a Colonial setting, served by staff in period costume. ☎ (508) 746-7100. $$

McGrath's (Water St., at the Town Wharf) Family dining by the harbor; seafood specialties. ☎ (508) 746-9751. $$

Mamma Mia's (122 Water St., by the harbor) A popular waterfront place for Italian dishes, pizza, and sandwiches. ☎ (508) 747-4670. $ and $$

Lobster Hut (Town Wharf) Self-service seafood, with some landlubber items offered. Indoor or outdoor seating. ☎ (508) 746-2270. $

LOCAL ATTRACTIONS:

Numbers in parentheses correspond to numbers on the map.

*PLIMOTH PLANTATION (1), Warren Ave. (MA-3A), 2½ miles south of Plymouth, P.O. Box 1620, Plymouth, MA 02362, ☎ (508) 746-1622, Fax (508) 746-4978. *Open Apr.–Nov., daily 9–5. Admission including May-flower II, adults $18.50, children (5–12) $11; Plantation only, adults $15, children $9. Gift shop. ✗. Limited &.*

Following a brief orientation, visitors can wander back in time to the year 1627 in this marvelous re-creation of the original ***Pilgrim Village** at

Plymouth. Costumed "interpreters," speaking in period dialects and portraying specific people, go about the daily life of the colonists—and you're free to join them, or just take it all in. For a quite different experience, stroll along a path to ***Hobbamock's Homesite**, a re-created Native American settlement peopled with Native interpreters in authentic period costumes. Another attraction is the **Carriage house Crafts Center**, where artisans use period tools and materials to reproduce the material goods of 17th-century Plymouth. All-in-all, a most enjoyable—and informative—visit!

The rest of the attractions are in the Historic District of Plymouth, where the actual original settlement of 1620 was located, about 2½ miles to the north. The first one you'll come to is the **Harlow Old Fort House** (2) of 1677. Actually, its timbers date from an earlier fort that stood on Burial Hill until being dismantled in 1676. They were then given to Sergeant William Harlow as a reward for service. Harlow's descendants and relatives lived here until 1920, when it was restored as a house museum depicting the lives of ordinary folk here in the late 17th century. *119 Sandwich St. (MA-3A),* ☎ *(508) 746-0012. Open July–Labor Day, Tues.–Sun. noon–4:30; June and Labor Day–Columbus Day, Wed.–Sat. noon–4:30. Adults $2.50, children (6–16) 50¢.*

A bit farther down the street stands the **Howland House** (3) of 1667, the only surviving house in Plymouth in which a passenger on the *Mayflower* lived. The earliest part of the structure is restored to its 1667 condition, with period furnishings and a few items thought to have belonged to the original inhabitants, while later additions are set around 1700 and 1750. *33 Sandwich St.,* ☎ *(508) 746-9590. Open Memorial Day weekend to Columbus Day, daily 10–4:30; Thanksgiving Day and its weekend, 10–3. Adults $2.50, children (6–12) 50¢.*

Bearing left through Brewster Gardens soon brings you to the **Richard Sparrow House** (4), the left side of which dates from 1640 and is the oldest house left standing in Plymouth. Since 1932, the right side (1690) has been home to a pottery and craft shop, while the original portion is restored and open to visitors. *42 Summer St.,* ☎ *(508) 747-1240. Open Memorial Day weekend–Dec. 24, Thurs.–Tues. 10–5. Admission $1.* Closeby is the **Jenney Grist Mill** (5), a 1971 re-creation of an original mill of 1636 that operated for some 212 years. Grain is still ground, and there's a pleasant public park. *6 Spring Lane,* ☎ *(508) 747-3715. Free.*

A block north on Market Street stands the **1749 Court House** (6), the oldest wooden courthouse in America. Actually, its timbers were once part of an earlier court section added to an existing public structure around 1670. Today it's open as a museum, complete with a restoration of the original courtroom. *Town Square,* ☎ *(508) 830-4075. Open seasonally. Free.* &.

Closeby is the **First Parish Church**, built in 1899, whose congregation dates all the way back to the Puritans in England who in 1606 broke with the

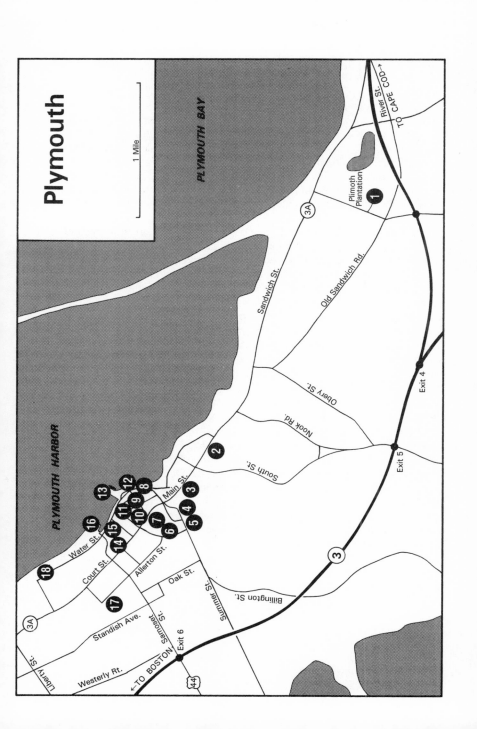

established Church, moved to Holland, and then became the Pilgrims of 1620. The nearby **Church of the Pilgrimage**, built around 1840, has maintained the original Congregational faith of the Pilgrim Fathers ever since the First Parish Church became Unitarian in 1802.

Burial Hill (7) rises west of the Town Square. An early fort, with guns from the *Mayflower*, was built here around 1622, and a watchtower added in 1643. Since 1637 the hill has been a cemetery, the final resting place of several notable Americans. Visitors can examine a replica of the powder house, and there's a good view. Every Friday in August, and on Thanksgiving Day, locals get to dress up as Pilgrims and walk from Plymouth Rock to Burial Hill to re-enact the religious service of the 51 survivors of that first winter.

Leyden Street has the distinction of being the first street in New England. Recalling the old name of the town in Holland from which the Pilgrims came, this was their original dirt lane of 1621. Yankees maintain that the first Thanksgiving was held hereabouts, although Virginians claim to have celebrated it as early as 1619. Whether turkey was actually on the menu is not known. Follow the street east to **Cole's Hill** (8). This is where the Pilgrims secretly buried their dead during that terrible winter of 1620–21; secretly so that the Native Americans would not discover their losses.

Located on the hill is the **Plymouth National Wax Museum** (9), where the whole story of the Pilgrims is told in some 26 life-size dioramas enhanced with light, sound, and animation. *16 Carver St.,* ☎ *(508) 746-6468. Open mid-Feb. through Nov., daily 9–5. Adults $5, children (5–12) $2.* Just behind this, on North Street, the mid-18th-century **Spooner House** (10) offers glimpses into the daily life of a local family over a period of two centuries. Handed down from generation to generation of the Spooner family and filled with their furnishings, it became a museum in 1954. *27 North St.,* ☎ *(508) 746-0012. Open July–Aug. Tues.–Sun. noon–4:30; June and Sept.– Columbus Day, Wed.–Sat. noon–4:30. Adults $2.50, children (6–12) 50¢.*

Step around the corner to the **Mayflower Society Museum** in the **Edward Winslow House** (11) of 1754. Winslow's great-grandfather, also named Edward, was a passenger on the *Mayflower* who became governor, wrote several books on the colonies, and later captured Jamaica for England's ruler, Oliver Cromwell. Changing hands during the Revolutionary War as a result of the Winslow Family's Tory sympathies, the house was greatly enlarged in the Victorian style during the late 19th century. Its marvelous flying staircase, seeming to defy gravity, links the two sections together. Furnished with period antiques, the house is also noted for its genealogical library and formal gardens. *4 Winslow St.,* ☎ *(508) 746-2590. Open July–Aug., daily 10–5; Memorial Day weekend–June and Sept.–mid-Oct., Fri.–Sun. 10–5; also Thanksgiving Day weekend. Adults $2.50, children (6–12) 25¢.*

Down by the water is the famous **Plymouth Rock** (12), or what's left of it. Whether the Pilgrims actually stood on it, or even noticed it, is conjectural,

Baking demonstration at Plimoth Plantation

although legend says it was their stepping stone off the boat. In earlier times, tourists chipped away pieces of it for souvenirs, greatly reducing its size. That practice is frowned upon today. Out on a nearby pier is the:

*MAYFLOWER II (13), State pier, Plymouth, MA 02360, ☎ (508) 746-1622. *Open April–Nov., daily 9–5, remaining open until 7 in July–Aug. Adults $5.75, children (5–12) $3.75; combination ticket with Plimoth Plantation available.*

No one knows exactly what the original *Mayflower* looked like, but general information about merchant ships of her era and tonnage led to the construction of this English replica in 1957. It is probably pretty accurate. In any case, she is not something you'd want to be at sea on for 66 grueling days—especially not on the North Atlantic in winter! And not with over a hundred fellow passengers in such cramped quarters.

Costumed guides speaking in period dialect portray the original passengers and crew, recounting experiences of the 1620 voyage for the enlightenment of today's visitors. Don't miss this special treat!

For a closer connection with the real Pilgrims, stroll a few blocks inland to Court Street and the:

PILGRIM HALL MUSEUM (14), 75 Court St. (MA-3A), Plymouth, MA 02360, ☎ (508) 746-1620. *Open Feb.–Dec., daily 9:30–4:30; closed Jan. and Christmas. Adults $5, seniors (64+) $4, children (6–12) $2.50.*

Visitors to this, one of America's oldest public museums (1824), are treated to the most extensive collection of actual Pilgrim artifacts anywhere. Not reproductions or replicas, but the real things. Nowhere else can you see such treasures as the only actual painting from life of a *Mayflower* passenger, Bibles belonging to John Alden and William Bradford, the swords of Myles Standish and John Carver, furniture, decorative arts, tools, and remains of a ship of 1626 that was similar to the *Mayflower*. There are also models of Pilgrim buildings, graphic presentations of their story, and a video to watch.

Down by the waterfront stands the **Hedge House** (15). A young merchant shipowner, one Major William Hammatt, built this highly unusual home in 1809. Purchased by another merchant named Thomas Hedge in 1830, it remained in the family for nearly a century until the Antiquarian Society acquired it in 1919. Today it's filled with 19th-century furniture, china, costumes, toys, and the like. *126 Water St., ☎ (508) 746-0012. Open June–Columbus Day, days and hours vary. Nominal admission.*

Closeby is the **Town Wharf** (16), where fishing boats still off-load their catch. There are also tour boats, docking facilities for private craft, and good restaurants nearby. Overlooking the scene is the **National Forefathers' Monument** (17), an 81-foot-high solid granite monument begun in 1859 and not finished until 1889. On it, Faith is surrounded by Liberty, Law, Education, and Morality; the latter clutching the Ten Commandments and the Scroll of Revelation. A bas-relief recalls the story of the Pilgrims.

A nice place to end your visit is at the:

CRANBERRY WORLD VISITORS CENTER (18), 225 Water St., Plymouth, MA, 02360, ☎ (508) 747-2350. *Open May–Nov., daily 9:30–5. Free.* ♿.

Cranberries have grown here for time immemorial, and are still a major crop. The Ocean Spray people invite you to learn all about them, see an actual bog, watch a cooking demonstration, and enjoy free cranberry refreshments.

*Cape Cod I
The Upper Cape and
the Mid-Cape

One or two daytrips can hardly do justice to Cape Cod, but even a short probe of this remarkable spit of land will help you discover the spot that's just right for a longer vacation. It can be a lot of fun, too, especially if you avoid the summer crowds. Overall, the Cape is so enticing that you'll easily forgive any aggravation caused by its popularity.

Shaped like a fishhook and named for its catch, this 70-mile-long peninsula is not only one of the loveliest places in America; it is also exceptionally rich in history. Back in 1620, the Pilgrims made their initial landfall here before going on to Plymouth. The first local Indian trading post opened in 1627, and the first town in these parts developed only ten years later. The Cape flourished on fishing, whaling, and merchant shipping. Now it's best known for its relaxed lifestyles, sunny beaches, nature preserves, quaint villages, art colonies—and tourists. The year-round population of about 175,000 more than doubles as the summer folks arrive.

This excursion covers the Upper Cape (nearest the mainland) and the Mid-Cape, while the following one explores the Outer Cape. If time permits, why not stay overnight (make reservations!) and combine the two, possibly even including a daytrip to Martha's Vineyard (see page 122) on a third day? Those with even more time at their disposal might want to combine it with the trips to Quincy, Plymouth, New Bedford, and Fall River.

GETTING THERE:

By car, it's about 60 miles from downtown Boston to the beginning of Cape Cod, Sagamore. Take Route **MA-3** all the way. Visiting all of the stops described on this trip will add a circular route of about 90 miles, in addition to your return journey.

Buses operated by the **Plymouth & Brockton Street Railway Co.** (☎ 508-775-5524) provide convenient service from Boston to Hyannis, and from there to Provincetown, making stops along the way. **Bonanza Bus Lines** (☎ 800-556-3815) runs frequent buses from Boston to Bourne, Falmouth, and Woods Hole; and from New York to Hyannis and Woods Hole. For other than a few major sights in the towns, however, you'll still need wheels to get around the Cape. Bicycle rentals are offered in the major tourist towns, and the terrain is flat enough to make them practical. Ask at the local tourist offices for current details.

PRACTICALITIES:

Late spring and early fall are the best times to visit Cape Cod, before or after it becomes inundated with tourists. If you do come in summer, at least try to avoid weekends. Those returning on a Sunday in the high season will face horrendous traffic; better to have dinner on the Cape and make the return journey later in the evening.

For further information, contact the **Cape Cod Chamber of Commerce** at US-6 and MA-132, Hyannis, MA 02601, ☎ (508) 362-3225, FAX (508) 362-3698. Phone numbers for local information are: Brewster (508) 255-7045; Canal Region (508) 759-3122; Dennis (508) 398-3568; Falmouth (508) 548-8500; Harwich (508) 432-1600; Hyannis (508) 362-5230; Mashpee (508) 477-0792; Yarmouth (508) 778-1008.

FOOD AND DRINK:

Here are a few choices from the vast selection of eateries in all price ranges:

Dan'l Webster Inn (149 Main St. in Sandwich) A lovely place for American and Continental cuisine in a light-filled conservatory, or the Colonial or Victorian dining rooms. Reservations advised, ☎ (508) 888-3623. $$ and $$$

Abbicci (43 Main St. in Yarmouth Port) Sophisticated Italian cuisine in an elegant, contemporary setting. Reservations advised, ☎ (508) 362-3501. $$ and $$$

Horizons (98 Town Neck Rd. in Sandwich, a mile north of the Heritage Plantation) Casual indoor/outdoor dining overlooking the bay; seafood, steaks, and the like. ☎ (508) 888-6166. X: Nov.–Apr. $$

Tower House (2671 Main St., MA-6A, in Brewster) Seafood, beef, chicken and more, indoors or out. ☎ (508) 896-2671. $$

Captain's Chair (166 Bayview St. in Hyannis) This family-owned harborfront restaurant has been a local favorite for decades. ☎ (508) 775-5021. $$

Starbuck's (645 MA-132 in Hyannis) An eclectic mixture of ethnic dishes, exotic drinks, and unusual decor makes this a fun place to dine. ☎ (508) 778-6767. $$

Up the Creek (36 Old Colony Rd. in Hyannis) Great values in seafood, meat, and chicken dishes; a local favorite. Reservations are helpful. ☎ (508) 771-7866. $ and $$

Sandy Neck Restaurant (679 MA-6A, 5 miles east of Sandwich) Sandwiches, salads, and light lunches. ☎ (508) 362-2943. $

LOCAL ATTRACTIONS:

Numbers in parentheses correspond to numbers on the map.

Although it may look like a peninsula, Cape Cod is technically an island, separated from the mainland by a wide canal. Join Route US-6 and cross the **Sagamore Bridge** (1), a beautiful span offering great views of the Cape. Beneath it is the 500-foot-wide **Cape Cod Canal**, a 17-mile-long ditch first proposed in the 17th century and completed in 1914 by the Army Corps of Engineers. At the Cape end, next to the bridge, is the **Pairpoint Glass Works**, reputedly the oldest in America. Visitors can watch as skilled glassblowers carry on the ancient art, long a local specialty. *851 Route MA-6A, ☎ (508) 888-2344. Open Mon.–Fri. 9–6. Free.*

Leave the main highway and continue east on scenic MA-6A, turning south on MA-130 to the:

*HERITAGE PLANTATION (2), Grove and Pine streets, Sandwich, MA 02563, ☎ (508) 888-3300. *Open mid-May until late Oct., daily 10–5. Last admission 4:15. Adults $8, seniors (60+) $7, children (6–18) $4. ♨. &.*

All manner of Americana, from Currier and Ives prints to automobiles of the 1930s, from Colonial firearms to a 1912 Looff carousel, are gloriously displayed in replica buildings spread throughout a manicured 76-acre park. Once the estate of the horticulturist Charles Dexter, famed for his rhodo-dendrons, Heritage Plantation is especially lovely in the late spring. Some 36 antique and classic cars are exhibited in a reproduction of the Round Barn at Hancock Shaker Village (see page 177); visitors may even sit in the Model T Ford of 1913. They may also ride the wonderful carousel while discovering a whole world of American arts and crafts. The Military Museum, itself a reconstruction of an historic Revolutionary War structure, houses firearms from the Colonial period through the Spanish American War, along with over 2,000 hand-painted miniatures depicting American military history from 1620 to 1900. To top it all off, there's an old windmill from 1800, transplanted from elsewhere on the Cape.

Return north on MA-130 to the town of **Sandwich** (3), the oldest settlement on Cape Cod. Founded in 1637 and still relatively unspoiled, Sandwich later became famous for its mass-produced pressed glass. Examples of this can be seen at the **Sandwich Glass Museum**, whose extensive collection of pieces produced here between 1825 and 1888 is renowned by collectors around the world. *129 Main St., ☎ (508) 888-0251. Open Apr.–Oct., daily 9:30–4:30; Nov.–Dec. and Feb.–Mar., Wed.–Sun. 9:30–4. Adults $3.50, children $1. &.*

Also in Sandwich is the restored 17th-century **Hoxie House**, a saltbox with period furnishings, and **Dexter's Gristmill**, where grains are still ground as they have been since the 1650s. *Main and Water streets, ☎ (508) 888-1173. Open daily, mid-June to early Oct. Combination ticket $2.50.*

Other interesting attractions in town include the **Thornton W. Burgess Museum**, the **Green Briar Nature Center & Jam Kitchen**, the **Wing Fort House**, and the **Yesteryears Doll and Miniature Museum**.

You obviously won't have time for all of these, so plan on coming back and then head east along picturesque MA-6A to the village of **Barnstable** (4), from whose harbor depart whale-watching excursions in season. While there, you might want to visit the **Donald G. Trayser Museum** in the Old Custom House of 1856. Maritime artifacts, ship models, Indian relics, scrimshaw, antique tools, paintings, and an old wooden jail make up the exhibits. ☎ *(508) 362-2092. Open mid-June through Columbus Day, Tues.– Sun. 1:30–4:30. Donation.* ♿.

Continue on to **Yarmouth Port** (5). Here you'll pass the **Winslow Crocker House**, a Georgian structure from around 1780. It's filled with 17th-, 18th-, and 19th-century furnishings including furniture, hooked rugs, ceramics, pewter, and the like. *250 MA-6A,* ☎ *(508) 362-4385. Open June to mid-Oct., Tues., Thurs., Sat., and Sun., noon–4. Adults $4, seniors $3.50, children $2.*

Next along the route is **Dennis** (6), home to the commercial cultivation of cranberries and the Cape Playhouse, a famous summer theater. Just beyond the cemetery, turn right on Old Bass River Road, then left on Scargo Hill Road to the **Scargo Hill Tower**. A short climb to its top will reward you with a fabulous ***view** of the entire Cape, from Plymouth to Provincetown.

Brewster (7) is next, and as far east as this daytrip goes. If you're planning on combining this with the next trip by staying overnight, you might want to modify both trips a bit to avoid any duplication of the routes. A right turn on Stoney Brook Road, as you first enter the town, leads in about a mile or so to the **Stoney Brook Mill**. This working replica of an early gristmill still grinds the corn in July and August, and there's a small museum upstairs. Outside is a herring run, where fish surge upstream from the ocean to spawn from mid-April until early May.

Return to MA-6A (Main Street) and turn right. Nearby is the **Cape Cod Museum of Natural History** with its 80 acres of nature trails, cranberry bogs, marshes, and an unspoiled beach—all alive with native flora and fauna. There are also indoor exhibits and various activities. ☎ *(508) 896-3867. Open Mon.–Sat. 9:30–4:30, Sun. 12:30–4:30. Closed some major holidays. Adults $4, children (6–14) $2.* Continue east on Main Street a short distance to the:

*NEW ENGLAND FIRE AND HISTORY MUSEUM (8), 1439 Main St. (MA-6A), Brewster, MA 02631, ☎ (508) 896-5711. *Open Memorial Day to Labor Day, daily 10–4; day after Labor Day to Columbus Day, Sat.–Sun. noon–4. Adults $4.75, seniors $4.25, children (5–12) $2.50.* ♿.

Firefighting through the ages is the theme here, and it's well covered with a superb collection of equipment and memorabilia from Revolutionary

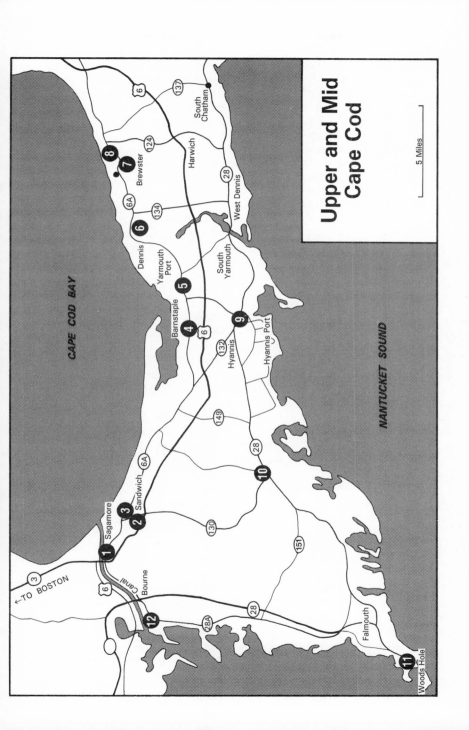

Upper and Mid
Cape Cod

5 Miles

CAPE COD BAY

NANTUCKET SOUND

←TO BOSTON

Canal

Bourne

Sagamore

Sandwich

Barnstaple

Dennis

Yarmouth Port

South Yarmouth

Hyannis

Hyannis Port

Brewster

Harwich

West Dennis

South Chatham

Falmouth

Woods Hole

3

6

6A

130

151

28

28A

149

132

6

134

6A

124

28

137

times to the 1930s, along with an lively animated diorama of the Great Chicago Fire of 1871. There's a reproduction of Benjamin Franklin's Union Fire House, the only 1929 Mercedes-Benz fire engine in existence, and the late Arthur Fiedler's vast collection of fire hats. The museum, spread among six buildings on a three-acre site, also features an 1890s apothecary shop, a blacksmith's, a herb garden, and more.

Turn south on MA-124 in the direction of Harwich. A left turn on Tubman Road brings you to the **Bassett Wild Animal Farm**, a wonderful spot for children. Both domestic and exotic animals live here in natural surroundings, and there's a petting zoo, pony and hay rides, a picnic area, and the like. *620 Tubman Rd., ☎ (508) 896-3224. Open mid-May to mid-Sept., daily 10–5. Adults $5.75, children (2–11) $4. Rides 75¢.* ♿.

Continue south, turning west on MA-39 and then again on MA-28, the main road of the south shore. The route leads through West Harwich, West Dennis, South Yarmouth, and West Yarmouth, then into **Hyannis**, departure point of the:

CAPE COD SCENIC RAILROAD (9), 252 Main St., Hyannis, MA 02601, ☎ (508) 771-3788. *Operates June–Oct., Tues.–Sun. plus Mon. holidays; also weekends and holidays in May, and special Christmas trains mid-Nov. to mid-Dec. Dinner trains Tues.–Sun. summer and fall, weekends winter and spring except Jan. Excursions depart Hyannis at 10, 12:30, and 3. Dinner trains at 6:30 require advance reservations and proper attire. Excursion round trips: Adults $11.50, seniors (65+) $10.50, children (3–12) $7.50. Special price for dinner trains.* ✘. ☕.

These scenic two-hour excursions aboard vintage diesel-hauled trains provide a wonderfully nostalgic way to see another side of Cape Cod. Stopovers are possible at Sandwich, where you can explore the sights before taking a later train back to Hyannis. The route goes as far west as the Cape Cod Canal, and a running commentary full of history and folklore is provided. The three-hour dinner trains, returning to Hyannis at 9:30 P.M., are a delightful way to end your daytrip.

Travelers of a certain age will recall those days in the early 1960s when Hyannis was a part of the magical Camelot. Although the Kennedy compound cannot be seen, there is a memorial to the late president on Ocean Street in adjacent Hyannisport. More memories can be stirred at the **John F. Kennedy Hyannis Museum**, where photos, memorabilia, and a video celebrate JFK's ties to the town. *397 Main St., Hyannis, ☎ (508) 790-3077. Open Feb.–Dec., Mon.–Sat. and holidays 10–4, Sun. 1–4. Adults $3, under 16 free.* ♿.

Continue west on MA-28. In a few miles, you'll come to the exquisite **Cahoon Museum of American Art** (10). Whimsical, naïve paintings are the specialty here, transporting visitors into a never-never world of mermaids cavorting in outlandish maritime settings. There are also landscapes of the Hudson River School, masterful renderings of sailing ships, American Impressionists, and primitive portraits. All are displayed in a one-time tavern and inn built in 1775, purchased in 1945 by artists Ralph and Martha Cahoon as their home and studio. *4676 Falmouth Ave. (MA-28), just east of MA-130, Cotuit, ☎ (508) 428-7581. Open Tues.–Sat. 10–4, closed major holidays. Donation.*

Route 28 continues west into the lovely old town of **Falmouth,** just a hop away from **Woods Hole** (11). The latter is both a major port for ferries to Martha's Vineyard (see page 122) and Nantucket, and one of the world's leading centers for marine and oceanographic research. *Parking here is difficult in season; you will be better off leaving your car in Falmouth and taking the bus to Woods Hole (☎ 800-352-7155, operates June to September, stops at Falmouth Mall and other places).* What's there to see in Woods Hole? For starters, there's the **Woods Hole Oceanographic Institution's Exhibit Center**, where the research carried on by WHOI is explained with an introductory video, displays, and a mock-up of their famous submersible, *Alvin. 15 School St., ☎ (508) 289-2663. Open May–Oct., Tues.–Sat. 10–4:30, Sun. noon–4:30; Mar.–Apr. and Nov.–Dec., Fri.–Sat. 10–4:30, Sun. noon–4:30. Donation.* On a related subject, the **National Marine Fisheries Aquarium** is a federal research center operated in conjunction with the National Oceanic and Atmospheric Administration. Visitors are welcome to see the fish and exhibits about them. *Water and Albatross sts., ☎ (508) 548-7684. Open mid-June to mid-Sept., daily 10–4; rest of year, Mon.–Fri. 10–4. Free.* Visits to the famous **Marine Biological Laboratory** are possible but must be arranged for at least two weeks in advance, *☎ (508) 548-3705, ext. 623. Free.*

Return to Falmouth and head north on MA-28 or, if time permits, the slower-but-more-scenic MA-28A. Up near the Bourne Bridge is one last major sight, the **Aptucxet Trading Post Museum** (12). Reputed to be the first trading post in English-speaking North America, this primitive building was first erected in 1627 by the Pilgrims. What you see today is, of course, a reproduction, but it's a good one and it's on the original foundations. Inside, there are samples of the sort of goods that were traded to both the Native Americans and the Dutch, as well as period artifacts. One of the treasures is a rune stone thought by some to be proof of visits by ancient Phoenicians around 400 B.C. There's also a replica of an 18th-century saltworks, a windmill, and President Grover Cleveland's private railroad station—his summer White House was nearby. *24 Aptucxet Rd., a mile west of Bourne Bridge via Shore Rd., ☎ (508) 759-9487. Open July–Aug., Mon.–Sat. 10–5, Sun. 2–5; May–June and Sept. to mid-Oct., Tues.–Sat. 10–5, Sun. 2–5. Nominal admission. Picnic facilities. ♿.*

If you're heading back towards Boston, you might find it better to take the Bourne Bridge, then I-495 and MA-24.

Trip 17

*Cape Cod II The Outer Cape and Provincetown

Things get wilder and more natural as you travel farther out the Cape, where the landscape remains much as it did when the Pilgrims first arrived here in 1620. Most of this land is protected against development by the federal and state governments; you have only to wander a short way off the main road to discover an unspoiled paradise of beaches, dunes, marshes, and the like. The few towns along the way are for the most part appealing and offer a variety of unusual, low-key attractions. And then there is Provincetown, well worth the daytrip in itself. This art colony *cum* tourist mecca thrives on alternative lifestyles, sophistication, and hedonistic audacity; a real treat for people-watchers. You won't find anything else quite like it in New England.

GETTING THERE:

By car, Provincetown, the farthest point on this trip, is 112 miles southeast of downtown Boston. Take Route **MA-3** to the Sagamore Bridge, then **US-6** to Exit 11 for Chatham.

Buses operated by the **Plymouth & Brockton Street Railway Co.** (☎ 508-775-5524) provide convenient service from Boston all the way to Provincetown, with stops along the way. This is practical if you're seeing only one or two places.

Boats are another option if you're headed only for Provincetown. **Bay State Cruises** (☎ 617-723-7800) offers regular summer service from Boston, a trip of about three hours.

PRACTICALITIES:

Late spring and early fall are the best times to visit the Outer Cape, before or after it becomes overrun with tourists. Those coming in summer should at least try to avoid weekends. Returning on a Sunday in high season pits you against horrible traffic; better plan on having dinner on the Cape and making a late return.

Don't forget the sunscreen lotion, bug repellent, sunglasses, and other beach essentials! And if you go for a walk in the woods, be sure you know what poison ivy looks like.

For further information, contact the **Cape Cod Chamber of Commerce** at US-6 and MA-132, Hyannis, MA 02601, ☎ (508) 362-3225, FAX (508) 362-3698. Local sources of information are: **Chatham Information Booth**, 533 Main St. in Chatham, ☎ (508) 945-5199; **Wellfleet Information Booth**, off US-6 in South Wellfleet, ☎ (508) 349-2510; and the **Provincetown Chamber of Commerce**, 307 Commercial St. in Provincetown, ☎ (508) 487-3424.

FOOD AND DRINK:

Where there are tourists there are restaurants; you won't go hungry. Some of the better choices are:

The Impudent Oyster (15 Chatham Bars Ave., off Main St., east of the rotary in Chatham) A wide and varied menu of international dishes for every taste, with an emphasis on seafood. Reservations suggested, ☎ (508) 945-3545. $$ and $$$

Ciro & Sal's (4 Kiley Ct., behind 430 Commercial St. in Provincetown) It's open for dinner only, and you'll probably need reservations, but this is a great place to end the day before heading home. The quintessential Provincetown eatery specializes in Northern Italian cuisine. ☎ (508) 487-0049. X: Mon.–Thurs. off season. $$ and $$$

Lobster Claw (MA-6A at MA-28 in Orleans) Touristy but fun, this popular family restaurant specializes in lobster, seafood, and steaks. ☎ (508) 255-1800. X: Dec.–Mar. $$

Old Jailhouse Restaurant (28 West Rd., off MA-6A at Skaket Corners in Orleans) Healthy American dishes in an old jailhouse. ☎ (508) 255-5245. $$

Bayside Lobster Hutt (Commercial St. in Wellfleet) An old oyster shack with a dory on its roof, Bayside is as informal as can be. Lobster, clams, fish, and corn-on-the-cob are featured. ☎ (508) 349-6333. X: Oct.–May. $ and $$

The Moors (5 Bradford St., near jct. of MA-6A in Provincetown) Portuguese and American specialties, mostly from the sea. ☎ (508) 487-0840. X: Nov.–Mar. $ and $$

Café Blasé (328 Commercial St. in Provincetown) An outdoor café in the middle of the action; offers burgers, sandwiches, salads, pizza, and the like. ☎ (508) 487-9465. X: Oct. to Memorial Day. $

LOCAL ATTRACTIONS:

Numbers in parentheses correspond to numbers on the map.

The delightful little port of ***Chatham** (1) is a good place to begin the day's exploration. Get off US-6 at Exit 11 and follow MA-137 south to the intersection with MA-28, then turn left and head east into town. Continue on Main Street and turn south (right) on Shore Road to the **Chatham Lighthouse** for a marvelous view. From here, Bridge Street will take you west to Stage Harbor

Road and the **Old Atwood House Museum**. Built around 1752 by a local sea captain, this two-story house remained in the Atwood family for five generations. It is now restored and furnished with pieces from several periods. There is a portrait gallery of Chatham sea captains, historic photos of the town, maritime artifacts, and sea shells. One of the outbuildings shelters some marvelous murals of local folk in fantasized religious settings. Also on the grounds is an old lighthouse turret and a herb garden. *347 Stage Harbor Rd.,* ☎ *(508) 945-2493. Open mid-June through Sept., Tues.–Fri. 1–4. Adults $3, under 12 $1.*

Head north on Stage Harbor Road, crossing Main Street, and turn left on Depot Road to the **Chatham Railroad Museum**, housed in the former station of 1887. While the collection is small, it does include a fully restored 1910 wooden caboose from the old New York Central, along with scale models and railroad memorabilia. ☎ *(508) 945-5199. Open mid-June to mid-Sept., Tues.–Sat. 10–4. Donation.*

Continue north on MA-28 to **Orleans** (2), named in 1797 for a visiting French duke who fled the revolution in his native land, thus saving his neck. Another French connection was made in the late 19th century when a transatlantic cable was laid from here to Brest, France, to facilitate telegraphic communication. Although it ceased operations in the 1950s, it's still here and open to the public as the **French Cable Station Museum.** You can see the original equipment and get an explanation of how it worked. Interestingly, the news of Lindbergh's 1927 landing in Paris arrived here first, before being flashed across the nation. *MA-28 at Cove Rd.,* ☎ *(508) 240-1735. Open July–Labor Day, Tues.–Sat., 2–4. Nominal admission.*

The road soon joins US-6 heading for Eastham, more or less the southern end of the:

*CAPE COD NATIONAL SEASHORE (3), South Wellfleet, MA 02663, ☎ (508) 349-3785. *Open daily all year. Free, $5 parking fee at beaches in summer. Swimming, hiking, bicycle trails, nature trails, bridle paths, picnic areas, visitor centers, historic sites, interpretive programs.* ♿.

Extending from a bit south of here to the very tip of the Cape, the National Seashore covers some 44,600 acres and has about 40 miles of sandy beaches. It was established in 1961 to protect the fragile environment from commercial exploitation, and to provide the public with some of the nicest beaches on the East Coast. Unlike most parts of the National Park Service, this National Seashore is intermixed with commercially developed land and small towns that have been there for centuries.

Begin at the **Salt Pond Visitor Center** (4), where you can pick up a detailed map of the park and find out about current activities. Better yet, you can gain a good understanding of the area and its fragile environment from the audiovisual program, exhibits of the Cape's history, and hands-on nature displays. *US-6 at Eastham,* ☎ *(508) 255-3421. Open daily Mar. through Dec., weekends Jan.–Feb. Closed Christmas. Free.* ♿.

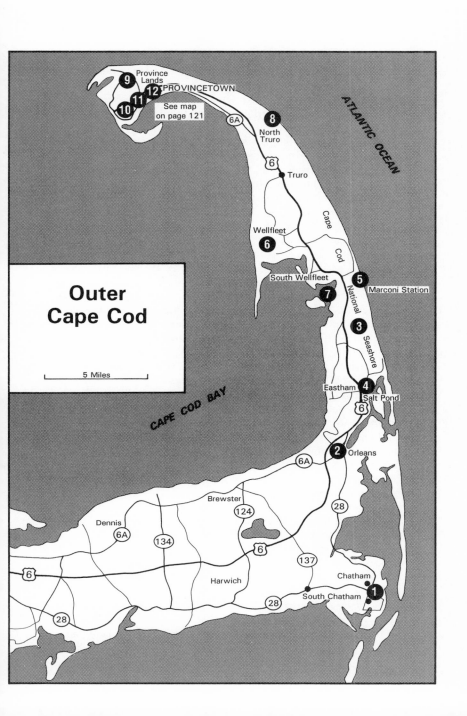

Outer
Cape Cod

5 Miles

ATLANTIC OCEAN

Province
Lands

PROVINCETOWN

9

12

11

10

See map
on page 121

6A

8

North
Truro

6

Truro

Wellfleet

6

Cape

Cod

South Wellfleet

5

Marconi Station

7

National

3

Seashore

Eastham

4

Salt Pond

6

CAPE COD BAY

2

Orleans

6A

Brewster

124

Dennis

28

6A

134

6

6

137

6

Harwich

Chatham

28

South Chatham

1

28

Feel like taking a walk? The **Nauset Marsh Trail** begins at the Visitor Center and winds around for about a mile with wonderful views of the marshes and bay. The quarter-mile-long **Buttonbush Trail** is designed for the visually-impaired, with markers in large type and braille. Visitors can also head out to the nearby **Coast Guard Beach** or **Nauset Light Beach**, the latter of which is particularly attractive.

A bit farther north on US-6, the **Marconi Station Area** (5) has its own beach, is home to the park's headquarters, and features remnants of a unique historical site. It was from here, in 1903, that Guglielmo Marconi sent the first wireless communication to Europe, a message from President Theodore Roosevelt to King Edward VII. The station was abandoned after World War I and little remains of it, but there is an interpretive shelter recounting its history, along with a scale model. The *Atlantic White Cedar Swamp Trail begins here, leading for a mile and a quarter through an amazing variety of vegetation, from lush forest to swamps to dunes.

In the middle of all this is the little old town of **Wellfleet** (6), once a whaling port and once the oyster capital of New England. Today it's a low-key summer resort with more than its share of art galleries. Some of its past can be seen at the **Wellfleet Historical Society Museum**, which features maritime artifacts, primitive paintings, photos, and Marconi memorabilia. *Main St.,* ☎ *(508) 349-9157. Open late June to early Sept., Tues.–Sat. 2–5. Adults $1, under 12 free.* Also in the neighborhood is the **Wellfleet Bay Wildlife Sanctuary** (7), a nature preserve run by the Massachusetts Audubon Society. For the ambitious, there are some five miles of hiking trails through woods and fields, heathland and beach. *US-6, South Wellfleet,* ☎ *(508) 349-2615. Open daily all year, closed Mon. off season. Adults $3, seniors and children $2.* ♿.

Continue north on US-6, turning right in North Truro to the **Highland Lighthouse** (8). Also known as the Cape Cod Light, it was built in 1857 as the third lighthouse on this location since 1797 and is still operated by the Coast Guard. Its enormously powerful beam can be seen far out to sea, alerting mariners to the dangerous waters nearby. Although you can't go inside, it does make a spectacular sight.

For a last fling with nature before descending on Provincetown, remain on US-6 and turn right on Race Point Road to the National Seashore's **Province Lands Visitor Center** (9). As at the Salt Pond Visitor Center, you can get maps and all sorts of information here, watch an excellent audiovisual program, and look at the nature exhibits. There's a wonderful panoramic *view from the observation deck. ☎ *(508) 487-1256. Open mid-April through Nov., daily 9–5 or 6. Free.* ♿. Nearby, the **Beech Forest Trail** offers a mile-and-a-half-long stroll through an evolving environment. Also in the area is scenic **Race Point Beach** and **Herring Cove Beach**, the latter facing right into the setting sun.

So much for nature—now it's off to the sinful delights of **Provincetown**. Sin was probably not what the Pilgrims had in mind when they made their first landfall in the New World here in 1620, following that long, arduous journey. They didn't stay long. The whole story is told at the ***Pilgrim Monument and Museum** (10), which also covers a lot of local history. The monument itself is fantastic—a 252-foot-high granite tower that looks for all the world like the 14th-century Torre del Mangia in Siena, Italy. There is no elevator, so you'll have to climb it on foot if you wish to experience the magnificent ***view** from its top, a sweeping panorama of the entire Cape. Down below, in the museum, are displays on the Pilgrim's visit, items salvaged from shipwrecks, marine artifacts, antique firefighting equipment, arctic matters, and a host of other subjects. ☎ *(508) 487-1310 or (800) 247-1620. Open July–Aug., daily 9–7; Apr.–June and Sept.–Nov., daily 9– 5. Adults $5, children (4–12) $3. Partially* ♿.

Wander down past the tourist information office and **MacMillan Wharf**, the departure point for several whale-watching and excursion cruises. **Commercial Street**, the main drag and a great place for people-watching, leads to the **Provincetown Heritage Museum** (11). P-town's colorful past is celebrated with re-created interiors, artifacts from the fishing industry, art, and a half-scale model of a Grand Banks fishing schooner. *356 Commercial St.,* ☎ *(508) 487-7098. Open mid-June to Sept., daily 10–6. Adults $3.* The **Provincetown Art Association** (12), at 460 Commercial Street, is the best place to see works by artists associated with Provincetown, along with special exhibitions. ☎ *(508) 487-1750. Open late May–Oct., daily; rest of year at various times. Hours vary. Adults $2, seniors and children $1.*

As to those sinful aspects of P-town, you're on your own.

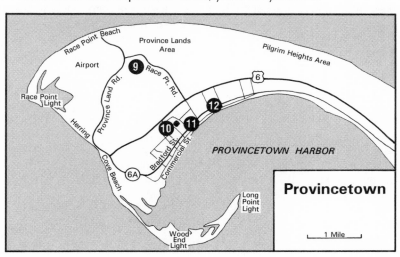

Trip 18

Martha's Vineyard

Taking a daytrip to Martha's Vineyard may seem a bit ridiculous, but it's entirely possible and is actually a great way to discover just the right spot for a longer stay. Or perhaps you are curious about this fabled island and have only a day to sample it. Either way, it's a nice excursion if you avoid peak travel periods.

Martha's Vineyard was named by the English explorer Bartholomew Gosnold in 1602 after his daughter, Martha, and the abundance of wild grapes that grew here. At least that's the legend. Another legend concerns the Norsemen, who may have visited these parts around A.D.1000. In 1524 the Florentine navigator Verrazzano sailed by and called it Louisa; earlier than that the Indians named it No-epe. Native Americans have lived here for millennia, and much of the island is still home to the Wampanoag Tribe. The latter have their own tribal government at Gay Head, officially recognized by the U.S. Government.

A visit to Martha's Vineyard should be a relaxing experience; you needn't dash around looking for famous sights. Just being here is enough as long as you venture beyond the main villages. However, should you feel so inclined, there are several small museums and historic homes to keep you busy. This trip combines well with the two previous ones to Cape Cod.

GETTING THERE:

By car, your best bet is to go to Woods Hole on Cape Cod, park your car there, and take the passenger ferry (see below) to Vineyard Haven on Martha's Vineyard. There is no practical way of taking a car over to the Vineyard for a daytrip. Woods Hole is about 85 miles southeast of Boston via routes **MA-3** to Sagamore and **US-6** to the Bourne Bridge. Cross the bridge and take **MA-28** to Falmouth and, if necessary, Woods Hole Road to the ferry. There are three parking lots for the ferry; two of these are in Falmouth and have a shuttle bus, and the other one is by the ferry in Woods Hole. Signs along MA-28 will direct you to a lot that's not filled, and you can get parking information by tuning your radio to 1610 AM. Parking costs $7.50 per calendar day.

Buses operated by **Bonanza Bus Lines** provide service from Boston and other towns to Woods Hole, ☎ (800) 556-3815. From there take the ferry as below.

Ferries operated by the **Steamship Authority** provide convenient year-round service between Woods Hole and Vineyard Haven, and also summer service to Oak Bluffs. Each crossing takes about 45 minutes. No reservations are needed for passengers. Bicycles may be brought on board for a small extra charge. For information and/or auto reservations ☎ (508) 477-8600, TDD (508) 540-1394. ☕. ♿.

Other seasonal ferry services include: Falmouth to Oak Bluffs (35 minutes), ☎ (508) 548-4800; Hyannis to Oak Bluffs (1 hour 45 minutes), ☎ (508) 778-2600; Falmouth to Edgartown (1 hour), ☎ (508) 548-9400; New Bedford to Vineyard Haven (90 minutes), ☎ (508) 997-1688; and Oak Bluffs to Nantucket (2 hours 15 minutes), ☎ (508) 693-0112.

By air: Those with deep pockets can save time and traffic by flying. Contact **Cape Air**, ☎ (800) 352-0714, or **USAir Express**, ☎ (800) 428-4322.

GETTING AROUND:

You don't need a car to explore Martha's Vineyard, but you will need wheels of some kind:

Shuttle Buses operate from May through October, connecting Vineyard Haven, Oak Bluffs, and Edgartown every 15 or 30 minutes. An Up-Island service is provided from late June to early September, going to Chilmark, West Tisbury, Gay Head, and the airport. ☎ (508) 693-1589 or 693-0058.

Bus Tours are another option, providing a narrated 2½-hour run to all six towns and Gay Head Cliffs. They meet the ferries from spring to fall. Contact: **Gay Head Sightseeing**, ☎ (508) 693-1555; **Island Transport**, ☎ (508) 693-0058, or **M.V. Sightseeing**, ☎ (508) 627-8687.

Bicycle and Moped Rentals are a practical way to get around. There are many miles of dedicated bike paths, and the roads are pretty level except for the climb to Gay Head. Rental firms abound in Vineyard Haven, Oak Bluffs, and Edgartown. Reservations are not necessary. You may, of course, bring your own bicycle on the ferry.

Car Rentals are offered by numerous firms, some of which specialize in Jeeps, vans, and off-road vehicles. Ask the local tourist office for details. Be aware that driving, and especially parking, can be difficult in season.

PRACTICALITIES:

Martha's Vineyard is at its loveliest in spring and fall, and most crowded in summer. If possible, avoid coming in July and August, especially on a weekend. Be sure to pack suncreen lotion, sunglasses, and insect repellant.

For further information, contact the **Martha's Vineyard Chamber of Commerce**, P.O. Box 1698, Beach Road, Vineyard Haven, MA 02568, ☎ (508) 693-0085. For instant, updated printed information, use the phone on your FAX machine to call (508) 696-0433.

FOOD AND DRINK:

There are plenty of good eateries on the Vineyard. Many are open for dinner only, and some are in "dry" towns where you can bring your own drinks—these are indicated as BYOB. Some choices that are also open for lunch are:

The Navigator (2 Lower Main St. in Edgartown) Hearty New England fare, specializing in seafood. Indoor/outdoor dining overlooking the harbor. ☎ (508) 627-4320. X: Nov.–Apr. $$ and $$$

Black Dog Tavern (by the harbor in Vineyard Haven) Everyone eats at the Black Dog, a rustic seaside place overlooking the harbor. They serve all kinds of food with a creative touch. Join the crowds, buy a T shirt, and BYOB. No reservations. ☎ (508) 693-9223. $$

David Ryan's (11 N. Water St. in Edgartown) Cheerful, lively, and contemporary, with creative American cuisine from sandwiches to seafood. ☎ (508) 627-4100. X: Jan. $$

The Wharf Pub (Lower Main St. in Edgartown) A great value in pub grub, especially from the sea. ☎ (508) 627-9966. $ and $$

Aquinnah (Gay Head Cliffs) This family-style restaurant is owned by Native Americans and offers fabulous views along with seafood, burgers, and the like. BYOB. ☎ (508) 645-9654. X: off season. $ and $$

Papa's Pizza (Circuit Ave. in Oak Bluffs) Big, bustling, and full of atmosphere. ☎ (508) 693-1400. $

LOCAL ATTRACTIONS:

Numbers in parentheses correspond to numbers on the map. Your tour will probably begin in **Vineyard Haven** (1), where most of the ferries dock. Those coming via Oak Bluffs or Edgartown, or landing at the airport, can make simple adjustments. While in town, if time permits, you might wander around the docks before heading east for about four miles to **Oak Bluffs** (2). Near the docks here is the **Flying Horses Carousel**, billed as the nation's oldest operating merry-go-round. The horses were carved around 1876, have real horsehair and stirrups, and still feature brass rings that earn you free rides. Join the fun! *Oak Bluffs and Circuit avenues.* ☎ *(508) 693-9481. Operates Easter Sat. to mid-May, weekends only; mid-May to Columbus Day, daily. Hours vary. Rides $1.*

Oak Bluffs began in 1835 as a venue for Methodist camp meetings, where thousands of worshippers gathered on the groves and pastures to sing and hear sermons. In time, the communal tents gave way to family tents, and then to the brightly-painted ***Gingerbread Cottages** that remain in use today. There are several hundred of these, each a filigreed triumph of the jigsawers' art, all arranged around the central **Tabernacle** where services are held. Visitors are welcome to stroll through this remarkable sight, and to visit the **Cottage Museum** at 1 Trinity Park in the Camp Ground. Here, one of the

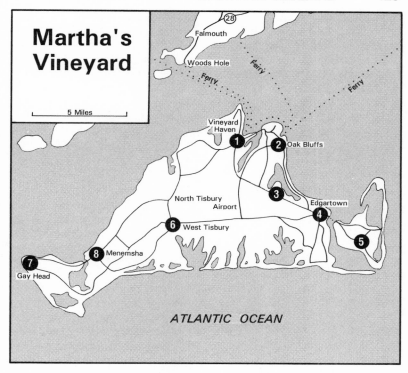

Martha's Vineyard

5 Miles

Falmouth

Woods Hole

Ferry

Ferry

Ferry

Vineyard
Haven

1

2 Oak Bluffs

3

North Tisbury
Airport

Edgartown

4

6 West Tisbury

5

8 Menemsha

7
Gay Head

ATLANTIC OCEAN

cottages has been restored to its late-19th-century appearance, with furniture, artifacts, and memorabilia from the Camp Ground's heyday. ☎ *(508) 693-0525. Open mid-June to mid-Sept. Nominal admission.*

Nature lovers may want to stop at the **Felix Neck Wildlife Sanctuary** (3), encompassing some 350 acres of marshlands, beaches, fields, and woodlands. There are several miles of self-guided trails to enjoy, a nature center, and plenty of native waterfowl and nesting ospreys to watch. *Edgartown-Vineyard Haven Rd., ☎ (508) 627-4850. Open July–Aug., daily 8–4:30; rest of year Tues.–Sun. 9–4. Grounds open daily all year, 8–7. Adults $3, seniors $1, children $2.* ♿.

Edgartown (4), six miles from Oak Bluffs, was the island's first Colonial settlement, and has been the county seat since 1642. During the early 1800s it prospered mightily on the whaling industry, so many a sea captain built his stately white home here. The area near the docks is especially rich in these elegant structures. Amble around the old streets to take in the sights, perhaps stopping at the **Vincent House** of 1672. Considered to be the oldest house on the island, it is maintained in a way that shows how homes were built over three centuries ago. *Main and Church streets, ☎ (508) 627-8017. Open*

Memorial Day–Columbus Day, daily 10:30–3. Another interesting structure is the Thomas Cooke House of 1765, now part of the **Vineyard Museum**. During the summer, visitors can take docent-led tours through 12 rooms filled with antique furniture, scrimshaw, ship models, plus whaling and farming artifacts. The rest of the museum, in adjacent buildings, is open all year round and features many unusual Vineyard items. Foremost among these is the enormous Fresnel lens that cast its beam from the Gay Head Lighthouse from 1856 until 1952. Along with its machinery, it's housed in a replica watch tower. There's a herb garden, and a carriage shed containing a whaleboat, a mid-19th-century fire engine, a peddlar's wagon, and much more. Treasures collected worldwide by Vineyard seafarers are displayed in the Maritime Gallery, while Native American artifacts and mementos of Vineyard history are shown in another old house. *59 School St.,* ☎ *(508) 627-4441. Open July 5–Labor Day, Mon.–Sat. 10–4:30, Sun. noon–4:30; spring and fall Tues.–Sat. 10–4:30; winter Wed.–Fri. 1–4, Sat. 10–4. Closed some major holidays. Adults $5, seniors and youths (12–17) $4, under 12 free; reduced rates off season.*

Edgartown is also the jumping-off point for **Chappaquiddick Island** (5), reached by the famous "On Time" ferry, whose name belies its schedule. ☎ *(508) 627-9427. Operates daily, year round. Round-trip fares: individuals $1, moped/motorcycle & rider $3.50, bicycle & rider $2.50, car & driver $4.50.* Time permitting, you might want to go over for a look at some practically unspoiled natural areas.

Those with suitable wheels can explore the more remote parts of Martha's Vineyard, known locally as "Up-Island." The term is of nautical origin; as you travel west you are moving "up" in degrees longitude. This can be a difficult trip by bicycle as it is deceptively long and sometimes hilly, and is even a problem for those on mopeds. A limited shuttle bus service is offered in summer, but be sure to confirm this lest you get stuck. From Edgartown, West Tisbury Road leads west about nine miles to **West Tisbury** (6), site of **Chicama Vineyards**. Vinifera grapes are cultivated here, made into varietal wines, and sold on the spot. Tours are offered. *Stoney Hill Rd.,* ☎ *(508) 693-0309. Open June–Oct., daily except major holidays. Free.*

*Gay Head (7), best approached via Beetlebung Corner, South Road, Menemsha Pond, and Moshup Trail, is the most spectacular sight on the Vineyard. The 60-foot-high, brilliantly-hued cliffs mark the westernmost extent of Martha's Vineyard, a dramatic backdrop for the red-brick lighthouse at its end. The land around here belongs to the Wampanoag Indian Tribe, who also operate the visitor facilities.

Return via Lighthouse Road and **Menemsha** (8), a picturesque, working fishing village of great charm. From here, North Road and State Road will bring you back to Vineyard Haven.

New Bedford

New Bedford calls itself "New England's *Real* Seaport," and with justification. Once the whaling capital of the world, it is still a major fishing port alive with the smell of the sea, a working place not excessively gussied up for tourists. Yet it does have attractions for visitors, not the least of which are the memories of Herman Melville. The famed author stayed here in 1840 just before setting out on his world adventures; parts of his *Moby-Dick* are set in New Bedford. The city's classic Whaling Museum is arguably the best of its kind anywhere, and provides the key to understanding so much of coastal New England. Then there are the cobblestoned streets of the waterfront to explore, perhaps boarding an historic schooner or taking a passenger ferry to an offshore island, several interesting museums and a magnificent mansion to visit, and plenty of opportunities for unusual dining and shopping experiences.

One of the few really sheltered harbors in New England, New Bedford was first settled in 1640 by a group of Quakers. Its whaling industry began in 1765 and brought great prosperity until the discovery of oil in Pennsylvania in 1859, which did away with the need for whale oil. A textile industry flourished from around 1880 until the 1920s, since eclipsed by other manufacturing industries. Fishing is still a major occupation, and supports the largest fleet in the nation. New Bedford is noted for its large Portuguese population.

For those able to stay longer than a day, this trip combines well with Cape Cod, Martha's Vineyard, Plymouth, or Fall River; as well as with Newport, Bristol, Providence, or the Blackstone Valley in Rhode Island.

GETTING THERE:

By car, New Bedford is about 58 miles south of Boston. Take Route **I-93** (Southwest Expressway) south to Exit 4, then **MA-24** south to Exit 12 at East Taunton. Continue south on **MA-140**, then **MA-18** into the Downtown New Bedford Historic District. Parking is available near the Whaling Museum.

Buses operated by American Eagle, ☎ (508) 993-5040 or (800) 453-5040, link New Bedford with Boston.

PRACTICALITIES:

New Bedford's major attraction, the Whaling Museum, is open daily (except Thanksgiving, Christmas, and New Year's), but some of the other sights may be closed on Mondays or may follow a more complex schedule. Check the individual listings for those that interest you.

For further information contact the **New Bedford Office of Tourism**, 47 N. 2nd St., New Bedford, MA 02740, ☎ (508) 991-6200, or their **Waterfront Visitor Center** at Pier 3, ☎ (508) 979-1745 or (800) 508-5353.

FOOD AND DRINK:

Freestone's (41 William St., near the Whaling Museum) A wide range of American dishes, served in the unusual setting of a 19th-century bank. ☎ (508) 993-7477. $$

Lisboa Antiga (1 Merrill's Wharf, just south of State Pier) Delicious Portuguese cuisine right on the waterfront. ☎ (508) 999-4495. $$

Café Mimo (1528 Acushnet Ave., north of I-195 and Brooklawn Park) Located up in the North End, this cozy neighborhood restaurant offers traditional Portuguese cuisine. ☎ (508) 996-9443. $$

Thad's Steak & Seafood (1313 Ashley Blvd., MA-18, a mile or so north of I-195 Exit 15) Great-value meals in the North End of town. ☎ (508) 995-4646. X: Tues. $ and $$

Phoebe's (7 South 6th St., near Union St.) A popular neighborhood spot for breakfast and lunch. ☎ (508) 999-5486. $

LOCAL ATTRACTIONS:
Numbers in parentheses correspond to numbers on the map.

*NEW BEDFORD WHALING MUSEUM (1), 18 Johnny Cake Hill, New Bedford, MA 02740, ☎ (508) 997-0046. *Open Mon.–Sat. 9–5, Sun. 1–5, Sun. in July–Aug. 11–5. Closed Thanksgiving, Christmas, New Year's. Adults $4.50, seniors (59+) $3.50, children (6–14) $3. Museum shop.*

The whole wonderful saga of American whaling comes gloriously to life here in the foremost museum of its kind. New Bedford thrived on whaling from the late 18th century until the middle of the 19th, when an enormous catch in 1857 caused prices to tumble. The end was marked by the discovery of oil in Pennsylvania, by which time the number of whales in the Atlantic had diminished and New Bedford whalers were forced to venture as far away as the Arctic and Indian oceans. Losses in the Civil War reduced the fleet considerably, so that by the 1880s the industry died out and the town turned to fishing and manufacturing for its livelihood. But it was great while it lasted, and that's what this museum celebrates.

Visitors are invited to board the half-scale replica **Lagonda*, the world's largest ship model, based on a fully-rigged mid-19th-century whaling bark. The American art of **scrimshaw** is well represented, and there are figureheads, sailmakers' gear, paintings, and photographs galore. Upstairs are sail and rigging lofts, a cooperage, and the like. A visit here is essential to understanding the maritime trade that once sustained coastal New England.

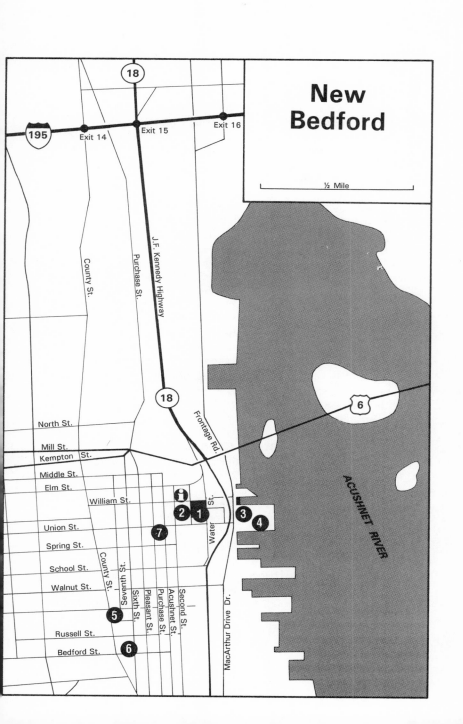

Just across the street is the **Seamen's Bethel** (2), an 1832 non-denominational chapel dedicated to the moral guidance of sailors, some of whom surely needed it. Herman Melville worshipped here in 1840, and immortalized the place in his classic novel *Moby-Dick*. Visitors can sit in his pew and examine the unusual bowsprit-shaped pulpit, then go downstairs to the Salt Box meeting room with its cenotaphs inscribed with the names of fishermen lost at sea. ☎ *(508) 992-3295. Open June–Oct., daily 10–4; rest of year Sat. 10–4, Sun. 1–4. Donation requested.* Next door is the **Mariner's Home** of 1790, still used as a lodging for itinerant seamen and not open to the public.

Stroll down William and Rodman streets, using the pedestrian overpass to reach the waterfront and the new **Visitors Center**, which offers free guided and self-guided walking tours. Although you can't board it, the lightship *New Bedford* is anchored next to the **Coast Guard Exhibit** at the **State Pier** (3). You can, however, board a ferry nearby for the hour-long cruise to isolated, tiny **Cuttyhunk Island**, an unspoiled place of great natural beauty and few inhabitants. *Pier 3,* ☎ *(508) 992-1432 for schedules and reservations.* There is also seasonal passenger ferry service direct from New Bedford to Martha's Vineyard, *Cape Island Express,* ☎ *(508) 997-1688.*

Another vessel you can board, at least when it's in port, is the two-masted schooner ***Ernestina*** (4). Built in 1894, she fished the Grand Banks for decades, explored the Arctic, and sailed the Atlantic in the packet trade. Restored as the state's official "Tall Ship," she is now used for special cruises and educational programs. ☎ *(508) 992-4900.*

From here on south are other colorful working wharfs, all well worth exploring. Returning to the town proper, you might want to see:

THE ROTCH-JONES-DUFF HOUSE & GARDEN MUSEUM (5), 396 County St., New Bedford, MA 02740, ☎ (508) 997-1401. *Open Tues.–Sat. 10–4, Sun. 1–4. Adults $3, seniors (65+) $2, students w/ ID $1, under 12 free. Museum store. Partially ♻, call ahead.*

Great fortunes were made in the heyday of whaling, at least by the merchants. Nowhere is this better reflected than in the magnificent Greek Revival mansion built in 1834 for William Rotch, Jr., one of the finest examples of that style. Herman Melville may well have had this place in mind when he wrote ". . . all those brave houses and flowery gardens . . . were harpooned and dragged hither from the bottom of the sea." in Chapter VI of *Moby-Dick*. Fully restored to reflect the lifestyles of the three families who lived here from 1834 until 1981, the house also features marvelous gardens with a wildflower walk, a dogwood *allée,* and a boxwood parterre.

The nearby **New Bedford Fire Museum** (6), located in what was the oldest continuously working fire station in the country until being decommissioned in 1979, makes an interesting stop when it's open. Along with historic engines and artifacts, there are various activities for visitors to have

By the waterfront in New Bedford

fun with. *51 Bedford St. at 6th St.,* ☎ *(508) 992-2162. Open July–Aug., daily 9–4. Nominal fee.* On your way back, be sure to pass the **Zeiterion Theatre** (7) at 684 Purchase Street. Built in 1923 as a house for vaudeville and silent flicks, it has been restored as an unusually elegant performing arts center that today features classical music, dance, jazz, movies, theater, and all sorts of attractions. ☎ *(508) 997-5664 for information.* ♿.

Trip 20
Fall River

Motorists passing by the old industrial port of Fall River on Route I-195 can gaze down on a proud sight. There, nestled beneath the highway bridge, is the battleship USS *Massachusetts* of World War II fame. And berthed next to it is a destroyer, a submarine, and various other naval craft; all of which—along with the battleship—can be thoroughly explored from stem to stern. Anyone who loves the sea should definitely not miss this magnificent experience.

As an additional treat, within easy strolling distance of the ships is the fascinating Marine Museum, the Old Colony & Fall River Railroad Museum, an historic carousel, the Fall River Heritage State Park, and an exact replica of HMS *Bounty*—which can also be boarded. The Fall River Historical Society's museum, nearby, has exhibits on one of America's most infamous murder mysteries, and the city also offers a famous religious shrine.

For bargain hunters, an equally compelling attraction is the city's reputation as the factory outlet center of New England. Many of the old granite mills that once made Fall River the "Textile Capital of the World" now house scores of brand-name factory outlets where shoppers can save significant amounts on clothing, accessories, gifts, home furnishings, jewelry, and the like. The savings may be even greater since Massachusetts has no sales tax on clothes!

By staying overnight, this trip can easily be combined with the one to New Bedford; or with Newport, Bristol, Providence, or the Blackstone River Valley in Rhode Island.

GETTING THERE:

By car, Fall River is about 55 miles south of Boston. Take Route **I-93** (Southeast Expressway) south to Exit 4, then **MA-24** south to Exit 7 at Fall River. Continue south on **MA-79** a short distance and follow signs to Battleship Cove.

Those arriving via Route **I-195** from other points in New England should get off at Exit 5 and follow signs.

Most of the factory outlets are south of Exit 8A off I-195. From the Battleship Cove area you can get to them directly by making a left onto Anawan Street, which becomes Pocasset Street. Bear left past Government Center and make the first right onto Pleasant Street. Go south and turn right onto Quarry Street in the heart of the shopping district.

By bus, Fall River is connected with Boston and some other points in New England by **Bonanza Bus Lines**, ☎ (617) 423-5810 or (800) 556-3815. You'll probably need a taxi to get to Battleship Cove.

The USS Massachusetts

PRACTICALITIES:

The main attraction, Battleship Cove, is open daily all year round (except Thanksgiving, Christmas, and New Year's), as are the factory outlets. Other sights are either seasonal or close on Mondays and/or Tuesdays in the off-season.

Be aware that probing inside the warships requires some degree of physical agility—especially in the submarine.

For further information contact the **Bristol County Convention & Visitors Bureau**, 70 North Second St., PO Box 976, New Bedford, MA 02741, ☎ (508) 997-1250 or (800) 288-6263, FAX (508) 997-9090. Information is also available at the Fall River Heritage State Park, next to Battleship Cove.

FOOD AND DRINK:

Some suggestions for lunch:

Leone's (4 Davol St., near Battleship Cove) Seafood, steak, and other dishes, overlooking the bay. ☎ (508) 679-8158. $$

McGovern's (310 Shore St., off MA-138, south of Battleship Cove) A popular family restaurant offering a wide variety of dishes at reasonable prices. ☎ (508) 679-5010. X: Mon. $ and $$

Officer's Wardroom (aboard the battleship *Massachusetts*) Decent lunches at budget prices, self-service. $

LOCAL ATTRACTIONS:

Numbers in parentheses correspond to numbers on the map.

*BATTLESHIP MASSACHUSETTS (1), Battleship Cove, Fall River, MA 02721, ☎ (508) 678-1100 or (800) 533-3194, FAX (508) 674-5597. *Open daily except Thanksgiving, Christmas, and New Year's, 9–5. Adults $8, seniors (65+) $6, children (6–14) $4. Admission includes battleship, destroyer, submarine, landing craft, exhibits of PT boats, aircraft, and more. Gift shop.* ✕. ♨.

The main attraction here is the 35,000-ton, 680-foot-long battleship ***USS *Massachusetts***, a formidable warship if ever there was one. Launched in 1941, she saw combat from North Africa to the shores of Japan, firing in anger both the first and the last 16-inch shells of World War II. The ship was deactivated in 1946, and ordered sold for scrap in 1962. Fortunately, she was saved by her wartime crew, who raised money to buy her and then found a fitting home for "Big Mamie" in Fall River.

Visitors may tour all nine decks of this floating city, where some 2,300 men once lived, worked, and fought. Like them, you can climb inside the big gun turrets, elevate the smaller guns on the main deck, check out the bridge, probe through the engine room, try a Navy bunk, or even go to the brig. There are three color-coded routes that may be followed, but you're free to explore pretty much wherever you please.

Floating next to the battleship is the ***USS *Lionfish***, a World War II submarine with all of her equipment still intact. Visitors are invited to tour every part, from the conning tower to the torpedo rooms, experiencing the incredibly cramped quarters from which 76 men of the "Silent Service" once defended their nation.

The destroyer **USS *Joseph P. Kennedy, Jr.***, named for President Kennedy's older brother who was killed in World War II, saw action in both Korea and Vietnam. Interestingly, she intercepted a Soviet freighter carrying missiles to Cuba during the Cuban Missile Crisis of the Kennedy administration. Again, you are free to explore the ship from stem to stern.

The only two **P.T. Boats** on display anywhere in the world are both here, housed in a protective building. Although you cannot board them, openings in the sides permit inspection of the interiors. Other exhibits feature a World War II LCM landing craft, a Japanese suicide attack boat, a Huey helicopter, and a T-28 trainer plane of the Vietnam era.

Just down the road, a bit beyond the highway bridge, is the:

MARINE MUSEUM AT FALL RIVER (2), 70 Water St., Fall River, MA 02721, ☎ (508) 674-3533. *Open May–Oct., Mon.–Fri. 9–5, weekends noon–5; Nov.–Apr., Tues.–Fri. 9–5, weekends noon–5. Adults $3.50, children (6–12) $2.50. Gift shop.* ♿.

Luxury passenger ships of the old Fall River Line (1847–1937) once plied

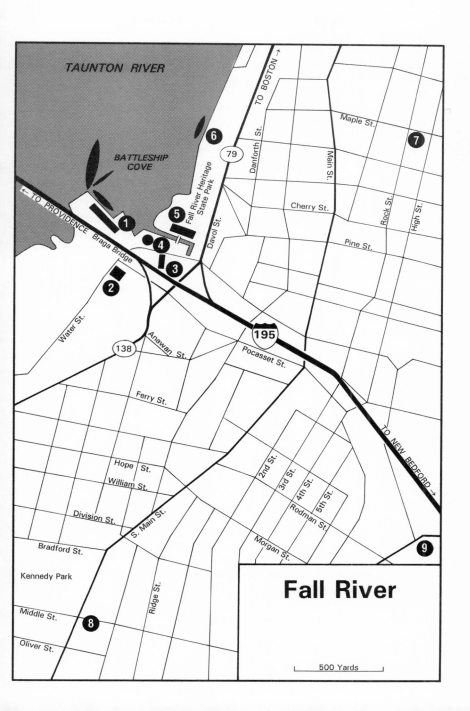

Fall River

TAUNTON RIVER

BATTLESHIP
COVE

← TO PROVIDENCE Braga Bridge

TO BOSTON →

Danforth St.

Maple St.

Main St.

Cherry St.

Rock St.

High St.

Pine St.

79

Fall River Heritage State Park

Davol St.

195

138

Anawan St.

Pocasset St.

Water St.

Ferry St.

TO NEW BEDFORD →

Hope St.

William St.

2nd St.

3rd St.

4th St.

5th St.

Rodman St.

Division St.

S. Main St.

Morgan St.

Bradford St.

Kennedy Park

Ridge St.

Middle St.

Oliver St.

500 Yards

the waters from New York City to New England, making Fall River their home port. Those days are, alas, long gone, but their heritage lives on in this splendid museum. Here you can see models, photos, artifacts, and all sorts of memorabilia from the floating palaces. Another fascinating item on display is the huge one-ton, 28-foot **model of the *Titanic***, made for the 1952 movie about that 1912 tragedy. Around this is gathered the largest exhibit of *Titanic* artifacts and memorabilia in the United States, with a recorded account by a survivor, many photos, and a video on the sunken vessel's discovery. There is also a marvelous 12-foot scale model of the HMS *Bounty*, created for the 1962 movie "Mutiny on the Bounty."

Return to Battleship Cove, opposite which is the:

OLD COLONY & FALL RIVER RAILROAD MUSEUM (3), Central and Water streets, Fall River, MA 02722, ☎ (508) 674-9340. *Open daily from July to Labor Day, Sun.–Fri. noon–5, Sat. 10–5. From mid-Apr. through June and Labor Day to early Dec. it is open on weekends and holidays, 10–4. Adults $1.50, seniors and children (5–12) 75¢. Gift shop.*

Housed in several railroad cars, this small museum presents a history of railroading in the Fall River area. Along with a collection of artifacts, there's a model railroad you can run and videos to watch.

Across the street is the:

FALL RIVER CAROUSEL (4), 1 Central St., Fall River, MA 02720, ☎ (508) 324-4300. *Open daily from Memorial Day to Labor Day. Rides $1.*

The Philadelphia Toboggan Company built this delightful hand-carved, hand-painted carousel in 1920; now it's been restored for a new generation to enjoy. Have fun!

Stroll over to the:

FALL RIVER HERITAGE STATE PARK (5), 200 Davol St. West, Fall River, MA 02720, ☎ (508) 675-5759. *Open daily from Memorial Day to Labor Day, 9–8; remainder of year Wed.–Sun. 9–4. Free. Picnic facilities.* ❶. *Partially* ♿.

Exhibits at the Visitors' Center include a multimedia show on the rich ethnic heritage of the people who made Fall River the major textile-producing center of the Western Hemisphere, old looms, historic photos on child labor in the mills, and the like. You can also climb the bell tower for a **view**, go for a sail (if qualified), or play in a paddleboat.

Outside, stroll along the waterfront park to **HMS *Bounty*** (6), a full-size replica of the famous ship made for the movie. Visitors can go aboard in the summer season for a narrated tour. ☎ *(508) 673-3886, admission charged.*

About a half-mile or so to the northeast is the:

FALL RIVER HISTORICAL SOCIETY MUSEUM (7), 451 Rock St., Fall River, MA 02720, ☎ (508) 679-1071. *Open June through Sept., Tues.–Fri. 9–4:30*

HMS Bounty, *USS* Massachusetts, *and the I-195 bridge*

and weekends 1–5; Apr.–May and Oct.–Dec., Tues.–Fri. 9–4:30. Adults $3.50, children (6–14) $1.50. Gift shop.

Located in a 19th-century mill owner's mansion, this elegant museum concentrates on local history. Of greater interest to visitors, however, is the ***collection of artifacts** relating to one of America's most notorious murder cases. "Lizzie Borden took an ax / And gave her mother forty whacks / And when she saw what she had done / She gave her father forty-one!" goes the old rhyme immortalizing the public's utter disbelief at Lizzie's acquittal in 1893. Did she do it? The evidence, including the hatchet itself, is all here to help you decide.

About a mile south of Battleship Cove, by the corner of South Main and Middle streets opposite Kennedy Park, stands **St. Anne's Church and Shrine** (8), attracting tourists and pilgrims from afar. It is regarded as one of the most inspiring in the nation. The church, of unusual design, was built by French-Canadian immigrants in 1906 and features lovely stained-glass windows from Rennes in France. There is also a noted organ and handsome ceiling ornamentation. ☎ *(508) 674-5651.*

For many visitors, Fall River's greatest attraction is its many factory outlet stores. This area, in fact, claims to have invented outlet shopping back in the late 1950s when clothing manufacturers began direct sales to the public. The concept spread, and today most of the shops are conveniently gathered together into a few huge former industrial buildings. Bargain hunters should head for the **Fall River Factory Outlet District** (9) just south of Exit 8A of Route I-195. See "Getting There" for directions from Battleship Cove.

Trip 21

Worcester

Poor Worcester. Perhaps the second-largest city in New England is just too close to Boston to get noticed, yet it does have some really first-rate attractions that are all too often overlooked. Located right smack in the center of things, it couldn't be easier to reach. This comfortable daytrip features a world-class art museum with major collections, a museum of European arms and armor in a mock medieval castle, a fascinating science center, and an 18th-century clockshop filled with ticking antiques. There are also historic homes and exhibitions, and a dramatic chasm of great natural beauty.

For those with more than a day at their disposal, this excursion could easily be combined with one to Sturbridge or Springfield; or with the Blackstone River Valley or Providence in Rhode Island.

GETTING THERE:

By car, Worcester is about 42 miles west of Boston. Take Route **I-90** (Massachusetts Turnpike) to Exit 11, then **MA-122** (Grafton St.) into the city center. Parking is available near all of the sites.

Trains operated by **Amtrak** provide limited service from Boston or Springfield, with connections to some other New England towns. ☎ (800) USA-RAIL for schedules.

Buses operated by **Peter Pan Bus Lines**, ☎ (800) 237-8747, and **Greyhound**, ☎ (800) 231-2222, provide service to Worcester from Boston and other points in New England. The Worcester Bus Terminal, ☎ (508) 754-4600, is downtown within local bus or walking distance of most of the attractions.

PRACTICALITIES:

Avoid coming to Worcester on a Monday or major holiday, when most of the attractions are closed. On Sundays they do not open until noon or 1 p.m.

For further information contact the **Worcester County Convention & Visitors Bureau**, 33 Waldo St., Worcester, MA 01608, ☎ (508) 753-2920, FAX (508) 754-8460.

FOOD AND DRINK:

> **The Castle** (1230 Main St., MA-9, in Leicester, 5 miles west of Worcester) Dine on Continental fare in a replica 16th-century castle overlooking Lake Sargent. Reserve. ☎ (508) 892-9090. X: Sun. lunch, Mon. $$ and $$$

In the Higgins Armory Museum

Maxwell Silverman's Toolhouse (25 Union St. at Lincoln Sq., near the Art Museum) American cuisine in a smartly renovated factory building. Reserve. ☎ (508) 755-1200. X: Sun. lunch. $$

Arturo's (411 Chandler St., MA-122, 2 miles northwest of I-290 Exit 13) Northern Italian cuisine in a casual setting. ☎ (508) 755-5640. X: Sat. lunch, Sun. lunch. $$

Museum Café (in the Worcester Art Museum) An unusually pleasant place for good light lunches. X: Sun., Mon. $

Boulevard Diner (155 Shrewsbury St., a bit east of City Hall, beyond I-290) Worcester is the spiritual home of diners; this 1930s example is a real find. ☎ (508) 791-4535. $

LOCAL ATTRACTIONS:

Numbers in parentheses correspond to numbers on the map.

Worcester's **City Hall** (1) faces an attractive common, across from which is a vast complex of over 100 discount outlet stores under one roof. Before snapping up the bargains, however, you should explore a bit of the downtown area. Just a few blocks to the northeast is the **Worcester Historical Museum** (2), where the city's colorful past is celebrated. Among the many artifacts are patent models of the sort of sometimes-strange 19th-century inventions that brought about early industrial prosperity. Lunch wagons, a local specialty around the turn of the century and the forerunners of diners, are also well represented. *30 Elm St., ☎ (508) 753-8278. Open Tues.–Sat. 10–4, Sun. 1–4. Adults $2, under 18 free.* ♿.

Back on Main Street, **Mechanics Hall** (3) is a grandiose auditorium of 1857 that is still used for cultural events. A few blocks to the north stands what is to many the city's prime attraction, the:

*WORCESTER ART MUSEUM (4), 55 Salisbury St., Worcester, MA 01609, ☎ (508) 799-4406. *Open Wed.–Fri. 11–3, Sat. 10–5, Sun. 11–5. Closed Jan. to mid-Feb., Easter, July 4, Thanksgiving, Christmas. Adults $5, seniors & students $3, under 12 free. Museum shop.* ✗. ♿.

Ranging from ancient Egypt to present-day America, the Worcester Art Museum's treasures span some five millennia of worldwide creativity. And major works they are, including mosaics from 6th-century Antioch, a 13th-century *Last Supper* fresco from Italy, Far Eastern antiquities, pre-Columbian finds, El Greco's *Repentant Magdalen*, and Gauguin's **Brooding Woman*. Among the American paintings are works by John Copley, James McNeill Whistler, Winslow Homer, John Singer Sargent, Mary Cassat, Childe Hassam, Albert Ryder, and Samuel F.B. Morse. While enjoying them, you might want to visit the unusually good Museum Café for a snack or lunch.

Practically next door to the art museum is the magnificent **Salisbury Mansion** (5) of 1772. Fully restored to its 1830s appearance, the Georgian-style house has period furnishings and carefully re-created wall and floor treatments based on actual inventories. *40 Highland St., ☎ (508) 753-8278. Open Thurs.–Sun. 1–4. Adults $2, under 18 free.* ♿.

A few blocks to the northwest, out along Salisbury Street, is the home of the **American Antiquarian Society** (6). Founded in 1812, this independent research library has the largest collection of source materials pertaining to the first centuries of American history, the period from around 1640 until 1877. Visitors are welcome to see their exhibits. *185 Salisbury St., ☎ (508) 755-5221. Open Mon.–Fri. 9–5. Free.*

Besides the art museum, Worcester's other really major attraction is located about two miles to the north. Don't miss the:

*HIGGINS ARMORY MUSEUM (7), 100 Barber Ave., Worcester, MA 01606, ☎ (508) 853-6015. *Open Tues.–Sat. 10–4, Sun. noon–4, closed holidays. Adults $4.75, seniors (60+) $4, children (6–16) $3.75.* ♿.

Step inside the re-created Great Hall of an 11th-century castle to see the largest on-display collection of medieval and Renaissance armor in the Western Hemisphere. John Woodman Higgins, a local industrialist, collected these suits of armor along with antique weapons during his trips around the world. In the early 1930s he built this impressive museum inside

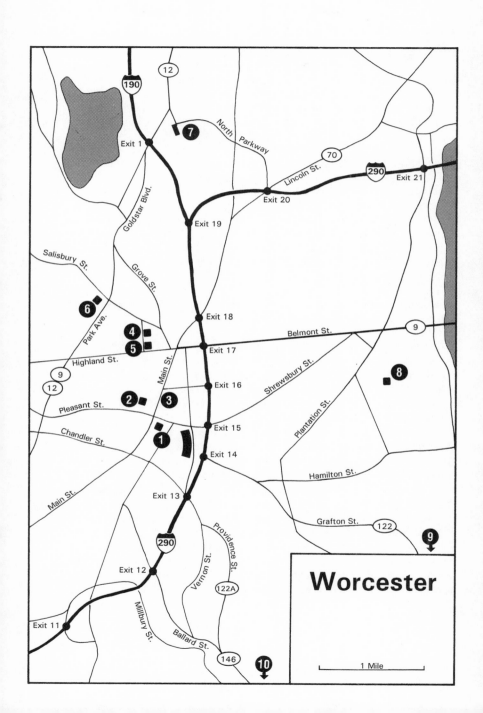

Worcester

1 Mile

an old factory building to house some 5,000 pieces, dating from prehistoric to more recent times, in a suitable setting. Some are true works of art, finely crafted and beautifully engraved. There's a sound-and-light show, interactive displays, weapons demonstrations, and even replica armor that visitors can dress up in. Kids love this place!

Children, and adults too, can also enjoy a visit to the:

NEW ENGLAND SCIENCE CENTER (8), 222 Harrington Way, south of MA-9, about 1½ miles east of downtown, Worcester, MA 01605, ☎ (508) 791-9211. *Open Mon.–Sat. 10–5, Sun. noon–5, closed some holidays. Adults $6, seniors (65+) and children (3–16) $4. Planetarium $2. Train ride $1. &.*

Spread across some 59 acres, the Center features a natural science museum, interactive exhibits, a wildlife center with daily shows, an aquarium, an observatory, a planetarium, an African communities room, and much more. Tying it all together is a narrow-gauge railroad offering scenic train journeys to visitors.

Heading south of the Turnpike on MA-122 and MA-140 brings you to the village of Grafton, where you'll find the:

WILLARD HOUSE AND CLOCK MUSEUM (9), 11 Willard St., Grafton, MA 01519, ☎ (508) 839-3500. *Open Tues.–Sat. 10–4, Sun. 1–5, closed Thanksgiving, Christmas, New Year's. Visit by guided tours only, 1½ hours. Adults $3, children (6–12) $1.*

The Willard brothers, all four of them, were famous clockmakers who lived in this 1718 homestead during the late 18th and early 19th centuries. Simon Willard (1753–1848), the most renowned of them, invented the Willard Patent Timepiece in 1802, which is today known to collectors as the "banjo" clock. Other creations include the tall case clocks commonly called "grandfather" clocks. Some 73 of these and other ticking timepieces are displayed in period settings in the original house and clockshop, along with family memorabilia.

After all these man-made sights, you might want to finish your day with an amble through nature's splendor. A great place to do this locally is at the **Purgatory Chasm State Reservation** (10) on Purgatory Road off MA-146 a few miles south of the turnpike. A dramatic rocky ravine cuts a gash some 80 feet deep into the earth, through which runs a half-mile-long trail, passing caves along the way. For the less ambitious, there are picnic tables and a playground. ☎ *(505) 278-6486. Closed in winter.*

*Sturbridge

You'll need the better part of a day—at least four hours—to savor Old Sturbridge Village, a re-created New England rural community set in the 1830s. Like Plimoth Plantation, Mystic Seaport, or even Colonial Williamsburg in Virginia, OSV (as it's referred to) is brought to life by costumed "villagers" acting out the daily routines of a cherished past. The era it celebrates was a time of transition as traditional farming began to make way for an emerging Industrial Revolution. Along with agriculture, visitors can witness early rural industries, businesses, trades, and crafts.

OSV was founded in 1938 as a historic re-creation on some 150 acres of farmland along the Quinebaug River. Most of the buildings, along with their furnishings, are authentic and were brought here from other parts of New England. Begun by the brothers Albert and J. Cheney Wells, two wealthy businessmen and antique collectors from nearby Southbridge, the project was slow to materialize, but finally opened to the public in 1946. OSV now features more than 40 carefully restored structures on over 200 acres of gorgeous land. As a non-profit educational institution, it is supported by admission fees, memberships, sales, and donations. What is most remarkable about the place is just how well everything is done, and how enjoyable a visit here is!

Quite apart from OSV, the adjacent town of Sturbridge is an interesting destination in itself. By staying overnight you could combine this trip with nearby Worcester, Springfield, or the Pioneer Valley.

GETTING THERE:

By car, Sturbridge is about 60 miles southwest of Boston. Take Route **I-90** (Massachusetts Turnpike) to Exit 9, then **I-84** south to Exit 3. Follow **MA-20** (Main St.) west into Sturbridge and the Old Sturbridge Village entrance on the left, opposite the tourist office.

By bus, **Peter Pan Bus Lines** offers service from Boston and elsewhere to Old Sturbridge Village at times convenient for a daytrip. ☎ (413) 381-2900 or (800) 237-8747 for schedules.

PRACTICALITIES:

Every season has its joys at OSV, but it's perhaps best in the late spring and early fall, when there are fewer visitors and the weather's still fine. From April through October the Village is open daily, 9–5; during the rest of the year it's open on Tuesdays through Sundays, 10–4, but closed on some holidays. From Jan. through mid-Feb. it is open on weekends only. Check first if you're coming in the off-season.

Admission to the Village is valid for two consecutive days and costs $15 for adults. Seniors (65+) pay $13.50, youths (6–15) $7.50, and children under 6 are free. Group rates are available by advance reservation.

Because of the authenticity of each building, **wheelchair access** varies. Structures that are generally accessible are indicated on the map you'll receive. A number of access services, including wheelchair loans, are provided. A sign-language interpreter is available on the third Saturday of each month.

Frequent **special events** are held all year round. Ask at the Visitor Center about these, or call ahead for a free printed schedule. Some events require advance registration and/or extra fee.

For further information call Old Sturbridge Village direct, ☎ (508) 347-3362, TDD/TTY (508) 347-5383, FAX (508) 347-5375, Web Site: www.osv.org. Regional information can be had from the **Sturbridge Information Center**, 380 Main Street, Sturbridge, MA 01566 (on MA-20 opposite the OSV entrance), ☎ (508) 347-7594 or (800) 628-8379.

FOOD AND DRINK:

There are plenty of places to eat in Sturbridge, including two within OSV. Some choices are:

Publick House (on The Common, MA-131, 2 miles east of the Village) Bountiful New England fare at a 1771 inn. Several dining rooms with differing menus. ☎ (508) 347-3313. $$ and $$$

Whistling Swan (502 Main St., west of the Village entrance) Choose between an elegant, intimate dining room or a casual loft upstairs. Continental and American specialties. ☎ (508) 347-2321. $$ and $$$

Bullard Tavern (in OSV) Enjoy a buffet lunch of seasonal New England specialties. $$

Tavern Cafeteria (in OSV) Located behind the Bullard Tavern, with indoor/outdoor tables. Light meals, sandwiches, salads and the like. $

Rom's (on MA-131, 2½ miles east of the Village) A huge, old establishment offering good Italian-American dishes at very reasonable prices. ☎ (508) 347-3349. $

SUGGESTED TOUR:

You might prefer to just wander around on your own, but here's a route that covers nearly everything in about 1½ miles. *Numbers in parentheses correspond to numbers on the map.*

Begin at the **Visitor Center** (1), where you can watch an introductory video, helpful in understanding the time period you're about to enter.

The Center Meetinghouse

Stroll up the lane to the **Friends Meetinghouse** (2). Although a small minority in rural 19th-century New England, Quakers (formally known as the Society of Friends) maintained a way of life noted for its simplicity and honest integrity. This unadorned structure was their place of worship.

Another church, this one typical of New England towns, is now known as the **Center Meetinghouse** (3) although it began life in 1832 as a Baptist church in the town of Sturbridge. Beautifully sited at the end of the Common, this elegant Greek Revival building is noted for its box pews. In those days, New England churches often served as venues for town meetings, elections, lectures, concerts, celebrations, and political events, as well as for religious services.

New England villages are typically built around an open tract of public land called a "common," where sheep often grazed. Walk along OSV's **Common** to the **Fenno House** (4), the oldest residence in the Village. Built in 1704 and depicted as the residence of an elderly widow and her spinster daughter, both the house and most of its furnishings were already out of style by the 1830s. Next to it is the **Fitch House** (5) of 1737, originally sited in Connecticut. Home to a prosperous family, it was expanded over the years and is presented as it would have appeared in 1830, complete with a rather elegant parlor and fashionable flower garden.

Along the same side of the Common stands the **Thompson Bank** (6), an 1830's financial institution from Connecticut. Its imposing Greek columns, granite vault, and stylish interior instilled confidence in the bank's own notes, issued before a national system of currency was adopted. Ask the banker about monetary systems in an age long before ATMs. Just beyond the bank is the Grant Store, where you can use today's cash to purchase souvenirs, gifts, snacks, and the like.

The ***Salem Towne House** (7), at the far end of the Common, is an unusually luxurious home for its time and place. Built in 1796 in nearby Charlton, Massachusetts, it was the residence of one Salem Towne Jr. and family, who inherited the property in 1825. Mr. Towne was both a businessman and a farmer, and was active in local politics and social life. The large, early Federal-style house was clearly built to impress—in its architecture, its furnishings, and especially in its lovely ***garden setting**. The adjacent farmyard is a model of progressive 1830s agricultural practice.

If you're thinking about lunch, you might want to check out the nearby Bullard Tavern facing the Common, and perhaps make a reservation for their New England buffet. Behind it is a lower-price cafeteria, with atmospheric interior dining rooms as well as outdoor picnic tables.

Leave the Common behind and stroll down a country lane, crossing a picturesque **covered bridge** separating the mill pond from the Quinebaug River. The water here powers three working mills, all superb examples of early rural industry. The first of these, the ***Sawmill** (8), is actually a reproduction dating only from 1984, but it's on the site of a real one that disappeared long ago, a victim of changing technology. Typically, these mills served a local clientele and operated only in late winter and early spring, when water was abundant. Demonstrations here, however, are performed throughout the year.

Another millstream furnishes power to the **Gristmill** (9), a reproduction built in 1939 on the site of a 19th-century mill. Old timbers were used in its construction, and both the millstones and the machinery are authentic antiques. Next door to it is the **Carding Mill**, an original structure from Maine. Its machinery dates from as far back as the 1820s, and is based on designs that the British attempted to keep secret but which were illegally brought to America by emigrating mechanics.

Visitors can watch as skilled hands toil in the **Blacksmith Shop** (10), where iron and steel is fashioned into useful wares. This shop was built of granite shortly after 1802, and moved to the Village in 1957. A real blacksmith lived in the nearby **Bixby House** (11) of about 1800, and his descendants continued to live there until it was moved to OSV in 1986.

Turn up the dirt road into the real countryside, stopping at the ***Freeman Farm** (12) for a glimpse of rural life in the 1830s. The house, barns, and smokehouse all date from that period, and along with the fields represent a typical small New England farm of the era. Today, the activities are carried on by costumed "farmers" just as they were then. Traditional varieties of crops are grown, and even the livestock have been bred to look like their

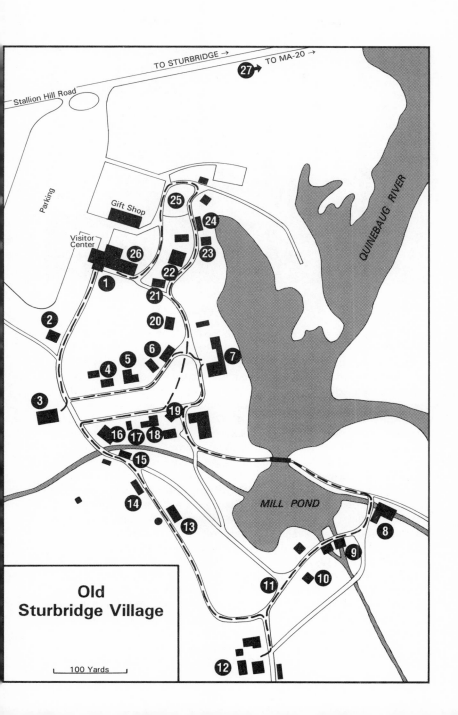

TO STURBRIDGE →

TO MA-20 →

Stallion Hill Road

Parking

Gift Shop

Visitor Center

QUINEBAUG RIVER

MILL POND

Old Sturbridge Village

100 Yards

In the Blacksmith Shop

early 19th-century counterparts. Next to the farm is the small **Cooper Shop**, where the making of barrels, buckets, and pails is demonstrated.

On the way back to the village you'll pass an active **Pottery** (13) that dates from around 1819 but was originally located in Goshen, Connecticut, where it produced traditional redware until 1864. The **District School** (14), down the road a piece, is a typical one-room schoolhouse from New Hampshire, dating from around 1800. During the 1830s, schools such as this were undergoing radical reforms, such as actually training teachers and requiring children to attend.

Visitors can watch footwear being made at the early 19th-century **Shoe Shop** (15), from which it was often exported to faraway markets as part of a thriving industry. Note that in the 1830s they apparently had not yet discovered the difference between right and left feet. Cross the small bridge to the **Asa Knight Store** (16), built around 1810 in Vermont. A source of wondrous merchandise from around the world as well from domestic factories, the store is now "stocked" with reproduction goods that look as fresh as the real stock did in the 1830s.

Back on the Common, turn right to the small Connecticut **Law Office** (17) of 1796. Most early 19th-century lawyers learned their trade by apprenticeship, but formal law schools were beginning to change the system. Next door is the **Richardson Parsonage** (18), a mid-18th-century "lean-to" house painted white to harmonize with the more elegant structures on the Common. Ministers' salaries were never very high, and until 1833 were (in Massachusetts) often paid out of town taxes. To make ends meet, they and their families commonly engaged in light farming and gardening. Step over to the adjacent **Tin Shop** (19) to watch the tinsmiths at work, turning out containers that would eventually put the potters out of business.

Cross the Common and follow the map to the **Printing Office** (20), built in Worcester, Massachusetts, in 1780 and equipped as it would have been in 1830. Across the road from it is the Cider Mill, where the popular beverage was made.

You are now leaving the Village and entering an area of special exhibits and demonstrations. The **Glass Exhibit** (21) features an excellent collection of 19th-century New England glass products. Close to it is the large **Firearms, Spinning, and Weaving Exhibit** (22), where the history of New England militias unfolds with a fine collection of period arms. Demonstrations of spinning and weaving are also given. The **Brick Theatre** (23) offers various events throughout the day (see your schedule), while brooms—an important rural industry—are made in a shop across the street.

Don't miss the **Lighting Exhibit** (24) with its illuminating collection of lamps from prehistoric times through the 19th century. Closeby, you can watch baskets being made and wool being dyed. The **Herb Garden** (25) cultivates plants used by early New Englanders for medicinal, culinary, and household uses.

One last sight—and one that should definitely not be missed—is the renowned ***J. Cheney Wells Clock Gallery** (26) behind the Visitor Center. This is one of the major collections of timepieces made in New England between 1750 and 1840, and it is beautifully presented in a most engrossing manner. Before leaving OSV, be sure to visit the well-stocked Gift Shop and Bookstore, located just outside the Visitor Center.

The town of Sturbridge itself has a number of antiques, crafts, and specialty shops that you might want to visit. The nearby **Mellea Winery**, a few miles to the east off CT-131 in Dudley, offers free tours and tastings. ☎ *(508) 943-5166. Open Memorial Day weekend through Oct., Wed.–Sun., noon–5; weekends in Nov.–Dec.* Another worthwhile attraction, about a mile west of the OSV entrance on MA-20, is the:

SAINT ANNE SHRINE (27), 16 Church St., Fiskdale, MA 01518, ☎ (508) 347-7338. *Open Mon.–Fri. 10–4, Sat.–Sun. 10–6. Gift shop. Free, donations accepted.*

Many believe that a miracle took place at Saint Anne's Church in 1887, and have flocked there ever since, embellishing the grounds with monuments of their devotion. Among the points of interest are Stations of the Cross, a Pietà, and a Grotto of Lourdes. Whether this moves you or not, you might very well be fascinated by the marvelous ***Assumptionist Exhibit of Russian Icons**. Brought here in 1971, this is one of the foremost collections or rare icons in the world.

Trip 23
Springfield

Springfield is not exactly a major tourist destination, but it does offer a surprisingly broad range of unique attractions that just might compel a visit. Basketball fans can shoot their own hoops at the Naismith Hall of Fame, firearms fanciers can relish one of the largest collections of military arms in the world, and motorcycle enthusiasts can drool over a vast assemblage of historic cycles. On a more general note, the Museum Quadrangle features two choice art museums, a local history museum, and a science museum. West Springfield, just across the river, offers a restored Colonial village that predates Sturbridge; while nearby Holyoke has a noted Victorian mansion and a state park celebrating local industrial history.

GETTING THERE:

By car, Springfield is about 90 miles southwest of Boston. Take Route **I-90** (Massachusetts Turnpike) to Exit 6, then **I-291** south to **I-91**. Continue south on this a very short distance to Exit 6 in the center of the city. Head north on **State Street** to the Springfield Armory National Historic Site, whose entrance is on Federal St., to the left.

Return south on State St. a few blocks to the Museum Quadrangle, on the right. Court Square is below this, at Court and Main streets.

Go under the I-91 highway and turn left on **West Columbus Ave.** a few blocks to the Basketball Hall of Fame.

The rest of the sites are scattered north of downtown, in West Springfield, and in nearby Holyoke. See the site descriptions for locations.

By train, Springfield is about 90 minutes southwest of Boston's South Station via **Amtrak**, ☎ (800) USA-RAIL for schedules and fares. Service is also provided from New Haven and other towns in Connecticut. The station in Springfield is about a mile from the major attractions; local buses and cabs are available.

By bus, Springfield is connected to Boston and elsewhere by **Peter Pan Bus Lines**, ☎ (413) 781-2900 or (800) 237-8747. It's a good mile or so from the terminal at Main and Liberty streets to the nearest attractions.

PRACTICALITIES:

Springfield is best visited late in the week or on a weekend, when more of its attractions are open. The two major ones—the Armory and the Basketball Hall of Fame—operate daily (Armory closes Mondays during the off-season)

150

Springfield Armory

except on Thanksgiving, Christmas, and New Year's. Parking is generally available at or near each of the sites.

For further information contact the **Greater Springfield Convention & Visitors Bureau**, 34 Boland Way, Springfield, MA 01103, ☎ (413) 787-1548 or (800) 723-1548, FAX (413) 781-4607.

FOOD AND DRINK:

Student Prince and Fort (8 Fort St., 5 blocks northwest of Court Sq.) An old favorite serving German/American classics since 1935. ☎ (413) 734-7475. $$

Old Storrowton Tavern (1305 Memorial Ave., in Old Storrowton Village, West Springfield) Continental/American cuisine in a Colonial setting. ☎ (413) 732-4188. X: Sun. $$

Tavern Inn (91 W. Gardner at W. Columbus Ave., 2 blocks south of the Basketball Hall of Fame) A good value for Italian/American dishes. ☎ (413) 736-0456. X: Sun. lunch. $

Pizzeria Uno (1 Columbus Center at E. Columbus Ave. and Bridge St., 3 blocks northwest of Court Sq.) A chain restaurant with excellent pizzas and the like. ☎ (413) 733-1300. $

LOCAL ATTRACTIONS:

Numbers in parentheses correspond to numbers on the map.

SPRINGFIELD ARMORY NATIONAL HISTORIC SITE (1), 1 Armory Sq., Federal & State streets, Springfield, MA 01105, ☎ (413) 734-8551. *Open daily, Memorial Day through Labor Day, 10–5; Tues.–Sun. 10–5 the rest of the year. Closed Thanksgiving, Christmas, New Year's. Free.* ♿.

Springfield has long been famous for its small military arms, and here's where you'll find one of the best gun collections in the world. Located in the original 1850 Main Arsenal, in the middle of what is now a college campus, the museum exhibits include rare weapons from as far back as the 17th century, along with the famous Springfields, M-1 Garands, Remingtons, Colts, and others. One outstanding item is the "***Organ of Guns**," celebrated in Longfellow's poem *The Arsenal at Springfield.* Other displays are concerned with gun manufacturing, inventions, and related personalities.The Springfield Armory was founded in 1777 and was the main source of shoulder arms for the U.S. military from 1794 until deactivation in 1968.

Head down State Street to the:

SPRINGFIELD MUSEUM QUADRANGLE (2), Springfield Library and Museums Association, 220 State St., Springfield, MA 01103, ☎ (413) 739-3871. *Museums open Thurs.–Sun., noon–4. Adults $4, children 6–18 $1, includes all four museums.*

Four museums, along with the main library, are conveniently grouped together around a tree-shaded green in the center of town. Foremost among them is the **George Walter Vincent Smith Art Museum**, which houses a vast collection of Oriental armor and arms, the largest assortment of Chinese cloisonné in the Western world, Islamic rugs, an elaborate Shinto shrine, jade, bronzes, textiles, and ceramics. There is also a wonderful collection of 19th-century American paintings including a major work by Frederic Church. Impressionist, Expressionist, and early modern European paintings are featured at the **Museum of Fine Arts**, along with earlier works by both European and American masters. Among the contemporaries you'll find outstanding art by such names as George Bellows, Charles Sheeler, Georgia O'Keefe, Lyonel Feininger, and Alexander Calder.

Children, especially, will enjoy a visit to the **Springfield Science Museum**. Between the life-size Tyrannosaurus Rex model, the new Monsanto Eco-Center with its exotic living creatures, the Exploration Center, the African Hall, and the planetarium, both you and the kids should have a wonderful time. There are also man-made wonders ranging from Native American artifacts to early aircraft.

Local lore and traditions are preserved at the **Connecticut Valley Historical Museum**, where you'll find period room settings, antique furniture, pewter and silver wares, decorative art, and the like.

Just two blocks south of the Museum Quadrangle is **Court Square**, a revitalized civic center that includes a lovely grouping of early 19th-century buildings along with the early 20th-century City Hall, Symphony Hall, and a 300-foot-high Italianate campanile.

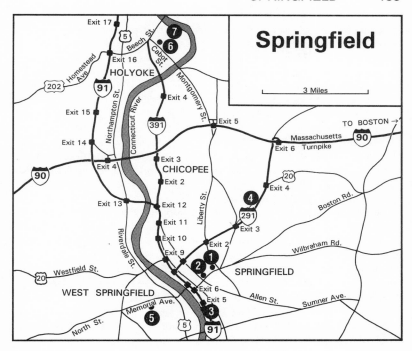

Go under the Interstate highway and head south on West Columbus Avenue to the:

*NAISMITH MEMORIAL BASKETBALL HALL OF FAME (3), 1150 W. Columbus Ave., Springfield, MA 01101, ☎ (413) 781-6500. *Open daily, 9–6, closing at 5 from Sept.–June. Closed Thanksgiving, Christmas, New Year's. Adults $8, seniors and children (7–15) $5, under 7 free. Gift shop.* ♿.

Basketball was invented in Springfield in 1891 by Dr. James Naismith of the Y.M.C.A., so it's entirely fitting that its major shrine should be located here. More than just a collection of old uniforms, this state-of-the-art, 11.5-million-dollar facility really captures the essence of the game. Participatory (shoot your own hoops!) and interactive virtual-reality exhibits combine with artifacts, lockerroom re-creations, and the like for hours of great fun.

North of the city center, near Exit 4 off I-291, is the:

INDIAN MOTORCYCLE MUSEUM AND HALL OF FAME (4), 33 Hendee St., Springfield, MA 01139, ☎ (413) 737-2624. *Open daily 10–5, closed major holidays. Adults $3, children $1.* ♿.

Indian motorcycles, the first to be powered by gas, were produced here in Springfield from 1901 until 1953. Now a part of history, they are still prized for their quality and beauty. At various times, the company also manufactured aircraft engines, cars, snowmobiles, outboard motors, and bicycles. You can see a vast collection of these, along with other American-made machines, toys, and memorabilia, in a part of the original factory.

Just across the river from downtown Springfield, in the Eastern States Exposition grounds in West Springfield, is the:

STORROWTON VILLAGE MUSEUM (5), 1305 Memorial Ave., West Springfield, MA 01089, ☎ (413) 787-0136. *Open mid-June through Labor Day, Mon.–Sat. 11–3:30; all day during Big E Exposition (mid- to late Sept.). Also Mon.–Fri. by appointment the rest of the year. Closed major holidays. Adults $5, children (6–16) $3. Tours. Gift shop.* ✗.

Although much smaller than Old Sturbridge Village, and not nearly as famous, Storrowton is considerably older. Early American buildings were brought here in the 1920s from all over New England, restored, and arranged into a typical village scene. Along with a church and meetinghouse, there is a school, a blacksmith's, a tavern, and a variety of homes.

A few miles north of Springfield, reached via I-391 to US-202 (Beech St.), then east a few blocks and south on Cabot St., is the:

WISTARIAHURST MUSEUM (6), 238 Cabot St., Holyoke, MA 01040, ☎ (413) 534-2216. *Open Wed., Sat., Sun. 1–5. Nominal admission.*

This lavish Victorian mansion was once home to a wealthy silk manufacturer named William Skinner, who stuffed its interior with incredible decorations, art, and furniture of the period. Outside, there are richly landscaped gardens and a carriage house with Native American and natural history exhibits.

Nearby is the:

HOLYOKE HERITAGE STATE PARK (7), 221 Appleton St., Holyoke, MA 01040, ☎ (413) 534-1723. *Various attractions open at varying times, call ahead. Park free, nominal charges for attractions.*

Located down by the canals, this park celebrates Holyoke's industrial heritage in an atmospheric setting of old factory buildings. There's an exhibition of papermaking, and of the town's gritty history. With luck, the **Heritage Park Railroad** might be running, taking visitors on a 10-mile ride in vintage cars. The park also features a noted **Children's Museum**, a restored merry-go-round, a crafts shop, and the **Volleyball Hall of Fame**—right here in the town where the game was invented in 1895.

The Pioneer Valley

Stretching from Canada south to Long Island Sound, the 407-mile-long Connecticut River cuts a dramatic path right down the middle of New England. Not the least of its attractions is the length through western Massachusetts, especially in the Five-College Area north of industrial Springfield. This is a land of mountains, lakes, and farms—and of sophisticated college towns. The latter form the cultural highlights of today's excursion, while the natural features offer gorgeous views. It's this mixture of academia and rural bliss that gives the valley its special flavor.

For those with more than a day at their disposal, this trip could easily be combined with the previous one to Springfield, and with the following one to Deerfield.

GETTING THERE:

By car, the farthest point on this trip, Northampton, is about 105 miles west of Boston. Take Route **I-90** (Massachusetts Turnpike) to Exit 4, West Springfield/Holyoke. Head north on **I-91** to Exit 17, then on **MA-141** to the Mt. Tom State Reservation.

Take East Street and **US-5** north into Main Street, Northampton.

Cross the river on **MA-9** and follow it east into Amherst. **MA-47** leads south to South Hadley via the J.A. Skinner State Park; otherwise take **MA-116** past the Nash Dinosaur Tracks.

From South Hadley go east to Granby, then take **US-202** into Belchertown, where you pick up **MA-9** going past the Quabbin Reservoir. This eventually leads to Worcester, where you can get on the Massachusetts Turnpike for the return journey.

PRACTICALITIES:

This is primarily a scenic drive, but you might want to check the individual listings for the college museums and other cultural offerings. For further information contact the **Greater Springfield Convention & Visitors Bureau**, 34 Boland Way, Springfield, MA 01103, ☎ (413) 787-1548 or (800) 723-1548, FAX (413) 781-4607.

FOOD AND DRINK:

The three college towns offer an amazing variety of good eateries. Here's a sampling:

In Northampton:

Eastside Grill (19 Strong Ave., Northampton) Seafood, steaks, and Cajun specialties with a New Orleans touch. ☎ (413) 586-3347. X: Sun. lunch. $$ and $$$

Paul & Elizabeth's (150 Main St., Northampton) Wholesome natural food, vegetarian and otherwise; plus wine and beer. ☎ (413) 584-4832. $$

Northampton Brewery (11 Brewer Court) Microbrews, steaks, seafood, burgers, sandwiches, pizza—served indoors or out. ☎ (413) 584-9903. $

Miss Florence Diner (99 N. Main St., MA-9, west of Northampton) It's worth the 3-mile drive to sample a real old-time diner with great food at low prices. ☎ (413) 584-3179. $

In Amherst:

Lord Jeffery Inn (30 Boltwood Ave., Amherst) Contemporary American cuisine in a Colonial setting. Reservations advised. ☎ (413) 253-2576. $$ and $$$

Judie's (51 N. Pleasant St., Amherst) A local favorite for its cheery decor and inventive American cuisine. No reservations. ☎ (413) 253-3491. $$

The Pub (15 E. Pleasant St., Amherst) A typical student hangout, with all manner of food and drink. ☎ (413) 549-1200. $

In South Hadley:

Windows on the Common (25 College St., Village Commons) An elegant, contemporary place with a large, eclectic menu. ☎ (413) 534-8222. $$

Woodbridge's (South Hadley Common) Full meals, burgers, and sandwiches in a casual setting. ☎ (413) 536-7341. $

LOCAL ATTRACTIONS:

Numbers in parentheses correspond to numbers on the map. How better to begin a scenic trip than with a scenic overview? The **Mount Tom State Reservation** (1) provides spectacular *vistas from a perch high above a tight bend in the Connecticut River. Below you lies the scene that inspired Thomas Cole to paint his masterpiece, *The Ox-Bow,* in 1836. ☎ *(413) 527-4805. Admission $2 per car Memorial Day to Labor Day, weekends, and holidays. Hiking, picnicking, fishing, canoeing, cross-country skiing.* ♿. The nearby **Mt. Tom Ski Area & SummerSide** offers water fun in summer, downhill skiing in winter. ☎ *(413) 536-0416.*

Northampton (2), settled in 1654, is the home of **Smith College**. With some 2,700 students, this is the largest private liberal arts school for women

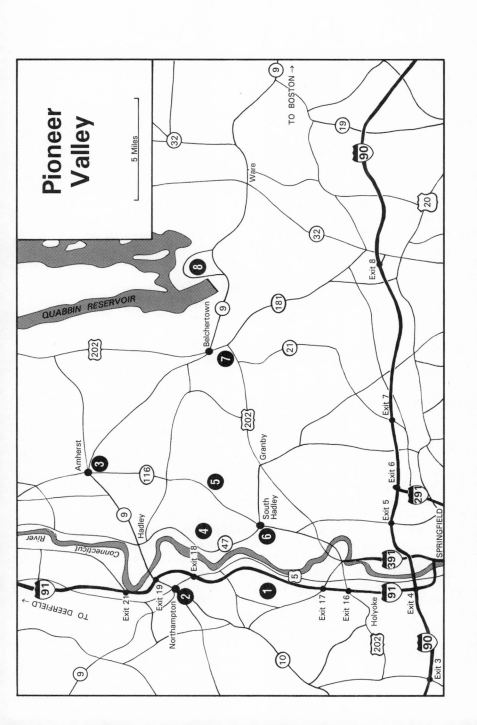

in America. Visitors come primarily to enjoy its superb **Museum of Art**, which specializes in works by 19th- and 20th-century European and American painters such as Picasso, Degas, Winslow Homer, and James McNeill Whistler. *Elm St. (MA-9).* ☎ *(413) 585-2760. Open during the academic year, Tues. & Fri.–Sat. 9:30–4, Wed.–Thurs. & Sun. noon–4. Times may vary. Free.* ♿.

Another local site that might interest you is the **Coolidge Memorial Room** in the **Forbes Library** at 20 West St. (MA-66). Calvin Coolidge (1872–1933), the 30th President of the United States, had his law practice in Northampton and became the town's mayor for two terms before serving as Governor of Massachusetts. Personal mementos and family photos on display here bring out the human side of "Silent Cal," a man few people knew well. Among the items shown is the infamous Indian headdress that he occasionally donned in public, to the amusement of friends and enemies alike. ☎ *(413) 584-8399. Open Mon.–Tues. 1–5, Wed. 2–4, and by appt. Closed holidays. Free.* ♿.

Northampton's utterly delightful ***Words & Pictures Museum** explores the wonderful world of sequential art, from cave drawings to hieroglyphics to the cartoon art of today. Founded by the creator of those outrageous Teenage Mutant Ninja Turtles, the museum has four floors of exhibits, including an interactive zone themed like the pages of a comic book. *140 Main St.,* ☎ *(413) 586-8545. Open Tues., Wed., Fri. & Sun. noon–5, Thurs. noon–9, Sat. noon–6. Adults $3, seniors & students $2, children (under 18) $1.* ♿.

Amherst (3) is home to the prestigious college of the same name, as well as to the giant University of Massachusetts and tiny, innovative Hampshire College. Together, they support an academic life that belies its rural setting. This is a youthful place, one that's fun to explore on foot—starting at the Town Common right in the center of things. The most unusual site in town is the **Emily Dickinson Homestead**, where the reclusive poet was born and where she lived most of her life (1830–86). Today, her second-floor bedroom has been restored to the way it was when she penned her best verses; the sleigh bed and her white dress are still there, as is the garden she tended. The house is owned by Amherst College and used as a residence, but visitors may make an appointment to see selected rooms. *280 Main St.,* ☎ *(413) 542-8161. Visits by appointment; May–Oct. Wed.–Sat. afternoon; spring and late fall Wed. and Sat. afternoon. Admission $3.*

While at Amherst College, you might want to visit their excellent **Pratt Museum of Natural History.** Wonderfully old-fashioned in its displays, the museum boasts some of the finest collections of dinosaur tracks, skeletons of extinct creatures, minerals, fossils, meteorites, and the like—even an early human skull. *Amherst College campus at the Quadrangle,* ☎ *(413) 542-2165. Open Sept. to mid-June, Mon.–Fri. 9–3:30, Sat. 10–4, Sun. noon–5; rest of year Sat. 10–4, Sun. noon–5. Closed major holidays. Donation.*

From Amherst you can head south on either of routes MA-47 or MA-116. Both lead to South Hadley. Going by way of MA-47 allows you to stop at **Skinner State Park** (4) for wonderful *****views** from the top of Mount Holyoke that stretch as far as 70 miles. Follow signs for the **Summit House**, one of the oldest mountaintop inns in New England. ☎ *(413) 586-0350. Park open April to mid-Nov., weather permitting, Mon.–Thurs. 8–6, Fri.–Sun. 10–6. Parking $2 per car from Fri.–Sun. Hiking, picnicking, historic site.* ♿.

The other route, MA-116, takes you past the **Nash Dinosaur Tracks** (5), an admittedly commercial enterprise, but for some an interesting one. Dinosaur footprints from around 200 million years ago were found on the site here in 1802; today's visitors can see them, and even purchase some. ☎ *(413) 467-9566. Open Apr.–Christmas. Nominal fee.* ♿.

Mount Holyoke College, founded in 1837, is the nation's oldest institute of higher learning for women. Its 800-acre campus in **South Hadley** (6), home to nearly two thousand students, was beautifully designed by the firm of Frederick Law Olmsted. Among its attractions is the **Mount Holyoke College Art Museum**, a superb collection of works ranging from ancient times to the 20th century. ☎ *(413) 538-2245. Open Tues.–Fri. 10–5, Sat.–Sun. 1–5, closed holidays and school vacations during the academic year. Free.* ♿.

Head east to Granby, then follow US-202 into **Belchertown** (7). The **Stone House Museum** here makes an interesting stop before visiting the vast Quabbin Reservoir. Period 18th- and 19th-century American furniture, decorative arts, and toys are on display, along with carriages, stagecoaches, sleighs, and the like. *20 Maple St.,* ☎ *(413) 323-6573. Open May–Oct., Wed. & Sat., 2–5. Nominal charge.*

Quabbin Reservoir (8), the quencher of Boston's thirst, gets its name from an Indian word meaning "a lot of water." And that it certainly has. Holding some 412 billion gallons, Quabbin was first proposed around 1900, but lawsuits from those about to be inundated, and from the State of Connecticut, held up excavations until 1926. After completion in 1939, it took the Swift River about seven years to fill it up and completely drown the four "lost towns" that lie beneath its surface. Today, its banks form a wonderful nature preserve, teeming with rare species. Visitors can get a great *****view** of it all from the observation tower near Winsor Dam, two miles east of Belchertown. Just follow the signs for Quabbin Hill. ☎ *(413) 323-7221. Visitor Center open daily. Hiking trails, picnicking, shore drives, fishing. No swimming, no hunting, no pets.*

Trip 25

*Historic Deerfield

Perhaps more than any other place in New England, Deerfield blends the preserved past with the living present so perfectly that visitors may think they've stepped into a tranquil dream, awakened only by occasional cars along the main street. Unlike Sturbridge, Mystic, or Plimoth Plantation, Deerfield is not a re-creation, nor do its people dress in period costumes or carry on the ancient crafts. But they do welcome you into the restored historic homes and regale you with tales of a colorful past, some of which are quite amazing. Nearly all of the homes are on their original site, where they were built in the 18th and 19th centuries.

Deerfield was not always a peaceful village. First settled by Europeans in 1669 on land inhabited by Native Americans for at least 8,000 years, it was the scene of violent massacres in 1675, the 1690s, and finally in 1704, after which the site was abandoned. Rebuilt in 1707 with better defenses, and later with a peace treaty, it prospered as an agricultural center during the 19th century. Today it is best known for its educational institutions— especially the world-renowned Deerfield Academy, a co-ed boarding school for grades nine to twelve that is located in the center of the old village.

GETTING THERE:

By car, Deerfield is about 88 miles west of Boston. Take Route **MA-2** west to Greenfield, then **US-5/MA-10** south towards Deerfield. Bear right into Historic Deerfield and park in the lot behind the Information Center.

Those coming from elsewhere in New England can use Route **I-91**, getting off at exits 24N or 25S (from the south), or Exit 26 (from the north).

PRACTICALITIES:

Anytime is a good time to visit Historic Deerfield, as its preserved houses are open every day except Thanksgiving, Christmas Eve, and Christmas Day, from 9:30 a.m. to 4:30 p.m. The Memorial Hall Museum is open from May through October, daily from 10 a.m. to 4 p.m. Admission to all of the Historic Deerfield properties, valid for two days and including two walking tours, is: Adults $10, children (6–17) $5. Admission to the Memorial Hall Museum is: Adults $5, children $2, under 6 free.

Wheelchair access to the various buildings varies, and is indicated on the map you'll receive. Please call in advance for special assistance.

The Wells-Thorn House

Special events are held throughout the year. For further information or to arrange special Tours-by-Appointment, contact **Historic Deerfield Inc.**, Box 321, Deerfield, MA 01342, ☎ (413) 774-5581, FAX (413) 773-7415.

FOOD AND DRINK:

Deerfield Inn (The Street, across from the Information Center) Fine cuisine in elegant Colonial surroundings since 1884. Reservations recommended. ☎ (413) 774-5587 or (800) 926-3865. $$ and $$$
Coffee Shop (in the Deerfield Inn, across from the Information Center) Light lunches served in the downstairs cafeteria or the Tavern. ☎ (413) 774-5587. $

LOCAL ATTRACTIONS:

Numbers in parentheses correspond to numbers on the map.
    Begin your visit at the **Hall Tavern & Information Center** (1), where you can park, purchase your ticket, and watch a short orientation program. The ticket, valid for two consecutive days, entitles you to visit any of the twelve restored buildings operated by Historic Deerfield Inc., a non-profit organization founded in 1952. Most of the houses have tours at stated times; a few can be entered whenever they are open. The houses are located along a shady, quiet, mile-long main street known simply as "The Street."
    While at the Information Center, you might want to visit the adjacent **Hall**

Tavern of 1760, an active museum of early tavern life. This is one of the few buildings moved here from elsewhere in the region.

The **tour sequence** described below involves the least amount of walking needed to see everything, but check it against the schedule of opening times you'll receive. You may have to make some modifications.

The mid-18th-century **Frary House** (2), just down The Street, was an early part of Deerfield's restoration when it was rescued from ruinous condition in 1890 by Miss C. Alice Baker, a teacher, antiquarian, and eccentric character. You'll hear more about her in the 1795 extension of her home, known as the ***Barnard Tavern**. Once the center of village life, the building preserves its barroom, kitchen, and grand ballroom. Be sure to examine the unusual photos of costume parties in the late 19th century, and to visit the delightful ***fiddlers' gallery**.

Deerfield's early days are best illustrated in the ***Wells-Thorn House** (3), begun around 1720, extended in 1751, and completed in the 1850s. Tours begin in the earliest section and follow the development of the local economy, domestic life, and tastes in the Connecticut Valley from the 1720s through the mid-19th century.

Across The Street and a block to the south stands the **Dwight House** (4), originally built circa 1725 in Springfield MA, some 35 miles to the south. About to be demolished in 1950, it was brought to Deerfield as one of the few historic buildings not standing on its original site. The beautifully-carved ornamental doorway lends a striking appearance, while the interior is filled with elegant Boston and Connecticut Valley furniture.

Strolling east on Memorial Street brings you to the venerable **Memorial Hall Museum** (5), housed in the original Deerfield Academy building since 1880. Not part of Historic Deerfield Inc., it is operated by the Pocumtuck Valley Memorial Association, one of the nation's oldest preservation societies. The highly eclectic collections of artifacts, both Native American and Colonial, began as early as 1797! The first permanent period rooms in America are here, crammed with items dating from the 18th century to the 20th, often displayed the way they would have been a century ago. Pride of place goes to the ***Old Indian House Door** of 1698, a rare survivor from the French and Indian War attack in 1704 that demolished the village. The invaders chopped a hole in it with their hatchets, then fired into the defenders. ☎ *(413) 774-7476. Open May through October, daily 10–4:30. Adults $5, children $2, under 6 free.* &.

Return to the **Town Common** (6), graced by a church of 1824 and an unusual post office, the latter a replica of the village's 1696 meeting house. Next to it is the **Museum Store** with its stock of crafts, reproductions, and books; all housed in the original 19th-century village store. The **Deerfield Inn** of 1884 makes a welcome stop in the event of hunger or thirst.

Cross The Street to the **Stebbins House** (7), Deerfield's first brick residence. Built in 1810, it has particularly fine furnishings of the Federal era as

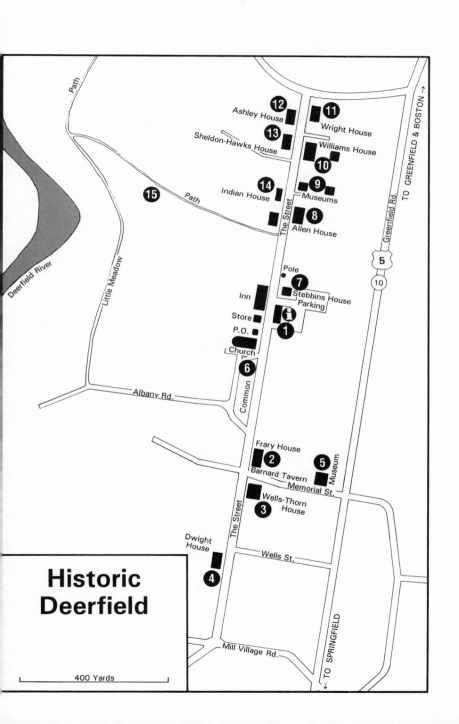

Historic
Deerfield

400 Yards

well as 19th-century French wallpaper depicting the voyages of Captain Cook. Next to it is a re-creation of the **Liberty Pole**, first erected in 1774 to protest the king's attitude toward his colonists. Tory Loyalists chopped it down under cover of darkness, but another was put up in its place. Today it serves as a reminder of the bitter conflict that tore families and communities apart during the Revolutionary years.

The ***Allen House** (8) should not be missed. Dating from about 1720, this simple structure was until recent times the home of Henry Needham Flynt (1893–1970) and his wife Helen Geier Flynt (1895–1986), who did so much to lovingly restore Historic Deerfield. Looking as though the Flynts just stepped out for a moment, the house is beautifully furnished with early American furniture and decorative arts. More of the Flynt's treasures can be seen at the nearby **Silver and Metalwork Collection** (9) as well as at the **Textile Museum**, just behind it.

Continue on to the **Hinsdale and Anna Williams House** (10), a mid-18th-century home converted to the fashionable Federal style in 1817. It is now furnished as it would have been in the 1820s and 30s, with some of the French scenic wallpaper surviving from that time. The barn behind it has a good collection of carriages.

At the northern end of The Street stands the **Wright House** (11) of 1824, noted for its ***George Alfred Cluett Collection of American Furniture and Clocks**. Especially rich in items of the Chippendale and Federal periods, it also displays many pieces of superb Chinese porcelains collected by the Flynts.

One of the more interesting dwellings in Deerfield is the ***Ashley House** (12) of about 1730. Home to the Reverend Jonathan Ashley, at Tory sympathizer who remained loyal to the crown until his death in 1780, it reflects the rich lifestyle of a member of the ruling elite.

The **Sheldon-Hawks House** (13) of 1743 remained in the same family until 1946. One of its owners, George Sheldon, was an early collector of local artifacts and a founder of the Memorial Hall Museum in the late 19th century. Today the house serves as an exhibition of high-quality American antiques and English ceramics.

The **Indian House Memorial** (14) is a replica of the Old Indian House of 1698, a survivor of the French and Indian attack of 1704 that was demolished in 1847. Of the original structure, only the hatchet-scarred door remains, and it's in the Memorial Hall Museum. This reincarnation is not a part of Historic Deerfield, but it may be visited when open.

A nice way to end your visit is to take a **country walk** (15) following the footpath to the Deerfield River.

Southern Berkshires

For over a century, city folk have been fleeing to the Berkshires to escape the pressures of urban life, bringing to these lovely hills just enough sophistication to create a heady mix of lifestyles. Best known for its music festivals, theater, and arts as well as its bucolic scenery, the area is also rich in historic attractions and outdoor recreations.

Although they rise over a hundred miles west of Boston, the Berkshire hills are well worth the drive. You can't possibly cover everything in just one day, so here they're divided into two daytrips that could be taken consecutively or broken down into smaller excursions. The first concentrates on the best sights south of the Massachusetts Turnpike, while the following one explores the fertile areas to the north. If you have the time, why not stay overnight (or longer), and trace these routes at a more leisurely pace? Otherwise, pick and choose carefully from the numerous attractions offered.

GETTING THERE:

By car, Stockbridge, the first stop, is about 125 miles west of Boston. Take Route **I-90** (Massachusetts Turnpike) to Exit 2 at Lee, then **MA-102** west into Stockbridge.

Continue west about 2 miles on MA-102 (Main St.) to the junction of **MA-183**, turning left (south) there for about a half-mile to the Norman Rockwell Museum.

For Chesterwood, continue south on MA-183 a very short distance, then turn right on Williamsville Road.

For the Botanical Gardens, go back (north) on MA-183 to the junction of MA-102 and follow signs. West Stockbridge is just a few miles west on MA-102.

Return to Stockbridge. For Naumkeag, turn north at the intersection of Main and Pine streets, opposite the Red Lion Inn. Bear left on Prospect Hill Road.

Follow **US-7** south past Monument Mountain and into Great Barrington and the Albert Schweitzer Center.

Bash Bish Falls is reached by taking **MA-23/MA-41** west to South Egremont, then turning right on Mount Washington Road. Follow signs for Mount Washington State Forest, and then for the falls.

For Bartholomew's Cobble, return to Great Barrington and take US-7 south.

For the Bidwell House and Gingerbread House, return to Great Barrington and follow MA-23 east, then head north on local roads.

Continue north to Exit 2 of I-90, the Massachusetts Turnpike.

PRACTICALITIES:

You'll need good weather for this scenic drive. Although every season has its charms, perhaps the most attractive time to tour the Berkshires is during the fall foliage season.

Consider staying overnight and combining this trip with the next one, or breaking up the trip into shorter sections and spending several nights in the area.

For further information, especially about overnight accommodations, contact the **Berkshire Visitors Bureau**, Berkshire Common, Pittsfield, MA 01201, ☎ (413) 443-9186 or (800) 237-5747, FAX: (413) 443-1970. Web Site: http://berkcon.com/tbc/nfp/nfp013/nfp013.html.

FOOD AND DRINK:

Red Lion Inn (Main St. in Stockbridge) THE place to dine in Stockbridge features New England cuisine. Choose between a formal dining room, an informal tavern, or a casual pub. Dress well and reserve for the main dining room. ☎ (413) 298-5545. $$ and $$$

La Tomate Bistro (293 Main St. in Great Barrington) Fine cuisine from the south of France. Reservations recommended. ☎ (413) 528-3003. X: Mon. $$

Michael's (Elm St. in Stockbridge, a block southeast of the Visitor Center) Fancy burgers, soups, salads, Italian dishes, vegetarian specialties, and the like. ☎ (413) 298-3530. $ and $$

Ali's (The Mews, behind Main St. in Stockbridge) A favorite lunch stop. ☎ (413) 298-3550. $

Martin's (49 Railroad St. in Great Barrington) A great informal place for light lunches. ☎ (413) 528-5455. $

LOCAL ATTRACTIONS:

Numbers in parentheses correspond to numbers on the map.

Begin your tour in ***Stockbridge** (1), surely one of the most attractive small towns in New England. Founded in 1734 as a mission bringing Christianity to the Indians, it was soon settled by Europeans who drove the Native Americans out by 1785. They wound up in Wisconsin. Artists and writers have been drawn here since the early 1800s, and wealthy industrialists since the Civil War.

You may recognize **Main Street** (Routes 7 and 102) as the subject of a famous painting by Norman Rockwell, who lived here from 1953 until his death in 1978. Park near the Visitors Center to pick up some brochures, then wander along the delightful tree-lined street. At the corner of South Street is the immense **Red Lion Inn** of 1773. Farther east, at Sergeant Street, stands the original **Mission House** of 1739, moved here from nearby Eden Hill in the 1920s. Now a museum of Colonial life in the Berkshires, it is furnished with authentic period pieces and has a small Indian museum. ☎ *(413) 298-3239.*

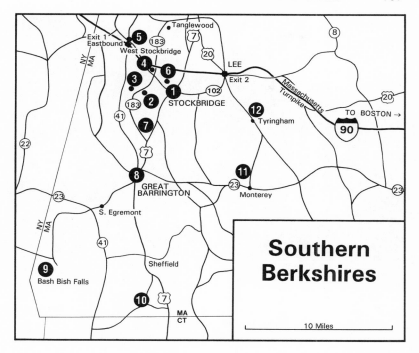

Southern
Berkshires

10 Miles

*Open Memorial Day through Columbus Day, Tues.–Sun. and holidays, 11–
4. Adults $5, children (6–12) $2.*

Continue down Main Street to the old **Village Green** and **Town Hall**, site
of the annual Town Meeting, a local tradition for over two centuries. Next to
it is the 160-year-old red-brick Congregational Church and the Children's
Chime Tower of 1878, rung each evening from "apple blossom time until
frost." Heading back, you'll soon pass the **Merwin House**, a.k.a. "Tran-
quility." Built in the 1820s in the Federal style, it contains both European and
American decorative arts and furnishings from the late 19th and early 20th
centuries. ☎ *(413) 298-4703. Open June through mid-Oct., Tues., Thurs.,
and weekends, noon–5. Admission $4.*

Return to your car and drive west on MA-102 (Main Street) towards the
next three attractions (see GETTING THERE for directions):

*THE NORMAN ROCKWELL MUSEUM AT STOCKBRIDGE (2), Rte. 183,
Stockbridge, MA 01262, ☎ (413) 298-4100, TTY (413) 298-4137. *Open
daily 10–5, except Thanksgiving, Christmas, New Year's. Adults $8, chil-
dren (5–17) $2. Studio open May–Oct. Gift shop.* &.

Norman Rockwell's Studio

Nearly everyone loves the easily-accessible work of Norman Rockwell (1894–1978), except perhaps a few diehard cultural snobs. He preferred to call himself an illustrator, not an artist, but his highly evocative renderings of the American scene may cause you to redefine just what "art" is. This is the largest collection of Rockwell originals in the world, and includes all 321 of his *Saturday Evening Post* covers, as well as some pieces that might surprise you. Special galleries, downstairs, present changing exhibitions of other artists whose works relate to Rockwell's.

Situated on a 36-acre estate with magnificent views, and housed in a stunning new building, the Rockwell Museum was recently moved here from the center of Stockbridge. Also moved here is **Rockwell's *Studio**, a charming and very personal place that's open to visitors from May through October. Don't miss it.

Nearby is:

CHESTERWOOD (3), 4 Williamsville Rd., Stockbridge, MA 01262, ☎ (413) 298-3579. *Open May through Oct., daily 10–5. Adults $6.50, children (13–18) $3.50, children (6–12) $1.50. Gift shop. Gardens. Trails. Picnic facilities. ⚹, call ahead.*

Another gifted American artist working in the popular vein, Daniel Chester French (1850–1931) spent his summers living and creating sculptures here from 1897 until the end of his life. Everyone is familiar with his work, which includes the statue of *Abraham Lincoln* at the Lincoln Memorial in Washington, and the *Minute Man* in Concord, Massachusetts.

D.C. French built his studio here in 1898, and his lovely Colonial Revival residence in 1901. Today, the estate is maintained by the National Trust for Historic Preservation. Covering some 160 acres, the grounds feature country gardens and a woodland trail with extensive views. Visits usually begin in the **Barn Gallery** with a review of his life, along with an exhibition of sculptural models. The **House**, furnished as it was in his time, reveals much about the man. The real treat at Chesterwood is the ***Studio**, complete with railroad tracks that enabled French to wheel his large sculptures out into the sunlight to examine the effects of natural lighting.

On the way back to Stockbridge, you might stop at the:

BERKSHIRE BOTANICAL GARDENS (4), Rts. 102 and 183, Stockbridge, MA 01262, ☎ (413) 298-3926. *Open May–Oct., daily 10–5. Adults $5, seniors $4, children under 12 free. Picnic facilities. Woodland trails. Garden shop. Special events.*

Stop at the visitor center for a map of the gardens, then set out to explore 15 acres of intimate landscapes, perennials, herbs, antique roses, and other beautiful sights. There's also a terraced vegetable garden, greenhouses, ponds, and a waterfalls. This is a delightful place to stretch your legs, or to have a picnic.

Another kind of a break could be made at nearby **West Stockbridge** (5), a separate and even smaller community. In recent years it's become a rather commercialized artists' colony, with all sorts of galleries, craft shops, boutiques, restaurants, and cafés, but it's still a lot of fun.

Return to Stockbridge. To the north, on Prospect Hill, is:

NAUMKEAG (6), Prospect Hill Rd., Stockbridge, MA 01262, ☎ (413) 298-3239. *Open Memorial Day weekend to Columbus Day, Tues.–Sun. and holidays, 10–4:15. Closed Tues. after a Mon. holiday. Adults $6.50 for house and gardens, $5 for gardens only. Children (6–12) $2.50.*

The renowned architect Stanford White designed this gracious mansion in 1885 for Joseph Choate, a prominent New York attorney and ambassador to Great Britain. Epitomizing the extravagance of the Gilded Age, Naumkeag is a strange assemblage of asymmetrical elements, with bay windows and turrets popping up in the most unusual places. Its furnishings are still in place, along with a magnificent collection of ***Chinese porcelains**, antiques, rugs, and tapestries. The formal ***Gardens** are considered to be among the finest in the country.

Leave Stockbridge and head south on US-7, passing the **Monument Mountain Reservation** (7) along the way. Nathaniel Hawthorne, Herman Melville, and Oliver Wendell Holmes climbed to the peak here one fine summer day in 1850, had a formal picnic, and gazed out across the striking landscape. So can you. Three miles of trails lead from the parking area to the summit for a glorious ***view**, or you can have a picnic without doing any climbing at all.

Great Barrington (8), population 7,725, is the largest community in the Southern Berkshires. Its citizens revolted against the British crown as early as 1774, and in 1886 its Main Street became the first thoroughfare in the world to be illuminated by alternating current, a rather odd distinction to be sure. Just outside the town is the **Albert Schweitzer Center**, where the great doctor, theologian, philosopher, and musician's life is celebrated at an old farm and wildlife sanctuary. ☎ *(413) 528-3124. 50 Hurlburt Rd., follow signs from Taconic Rd. off MA-23 in Great Barrington. Donation.*

A nice side trip to make from here is to ***Bash Bish Falls** (9), practically at the borders with New York State and Connecticut. Follow the directions under GETTING THERE (page 165) and use the second parking lot. Take the easy trail (not the steep one!) to the spot where Bash Bish Brook, flowing through a deep gorge, plunges 50 feet into a lovely pool. Legend has it that an Indian maiden, unhappy in love, jumped to her death here, and that the falling water still calls her name—Bash Bish, Bash Bish. This is a wonderful place to relax at the end of a busy day.

Another interesting side trip from Great Barrington is to follow US-7 and MA-7A south past Sheffield to Ashley Falls and **Bartholomew's Cobble** (10). This unusual rocky outcropping, a National Natural Landmark, is renowned for its vast variety of ferns and wildflowers. Trails lead to marvelous views of the Housatonic River Valley, extending deep into nearby Connecticut. There's also a small natural history museum with Indian relics, bird watching, and picnicking. ☎ *(413) 229-8600. Open daily in season, 9–5. Adults $3, children $1.* Near the entrance stands the **Colonel John Ashley House** of 1735, where the Sheffield Declaration of grievances against English rule was drafted in 1773. Today it houses an extensive collection of redware and early industrial tools, along with period furnishings. ☎ *(413) 229-8600. Open May–Oct.; call for dates. Adults $5, children (6–12) $2.*

Returning from Great Barrington to the Massachusetts Turnpike, head east on MA-23 to Monterey and there turn north on Tyringham Road. To the left off this beyond Lake Garfield, on Art School Road, is the **Bidwell House** (11). Built around 1750 and elegantly restored, this white Georgian parsonage features beautiful interiors filled with antiques. ☎ *(413) 528-6888. Open Memorial Day weekend to Columbus Day, Tues.–Sun., 11–4. Adults $5, seniors and students $4, children $3.*

Passing through the delightful village of Tyringham brings you to the highly picturesque ***Gingerbread House** (12), today occupied by the Tyringham Art Galleries. Once the home of sculptor Henry Kitson, this thatched-roof cottage is a magical scene right out of a fairy tale, and has an even more unusual interior. ☎ *(413) 243-3260. Memorial Day to Labor Day, daily, 10–5. Adults $1, under 12 free.*

*Northern Berkshires

The Berkshires remain just as lovely north of the Massachusetts Turnpike as they are to the south, but here they offer even more attractions—a little something for everyone. Literary buffs can tour the homes of Edith Wharton and Herman Melville. Art lovers may be surprised at the amazingly rich holdings of Williamstown's two museums, and may also visit the Berkshire Museum. If music is your thing, why not take a look at Tanglewood, summer home of the Boston Symphony? Just about everyone, including children, will enjoy a stop at Hancock Shaker Village, a preserved agricultural complex of enormous social interest, where oxen still pull the plows.

Perhaps you'd just like to wallow in natural splendor. There's plenty of it at the Pleasant Valley Sanctuary, atop Mount Greylock, along the Mohawk Trail, and at Natural Bridge and Shelburne Falls. Railfans can indulge their passion at the Berkshire Scenic Railway or the Hoosac Tunnel exhibition.

Now, you can't possibly see all of this in just one day, so you'll have to pick and choose carefully. If your interests cover a broad range of subjects, and you have the time, consider staying overnight (or longer!) at one of the many inns, B&Bs, or motels—or just come back again for a return visit.

GETTING THERE:

By car, Lenox, the first stop, is about 125 miles west of Boston. Take Route **I-90** (Massachusetts Turnpike) to Exit 2 at Lee, then **US-20** north towards Lenox.

For The Mount, turn left on Plunkett St. just south of the junction of US-20 and US-7 at Lenox.

For the Berkshire Scenic Railway, turn right off US-20/US-7 and onto Housatonic Street, taking it east to Willow Creek Road.

For Tanglewood, go into Historic Lenox Village and continue west on **MA-183**.

Continue north on **US-7**. For the Pleasant Valley Sanctuary, turn left on West Dugway Road just north of Lenox, following signs to West Mountain Road.

For Arrowhead, continue north on US-7 almost into Pittsfield, then turn right onto Holmes Road.

The Berkshire Museum is on US-7 near the center of Pittsfield.

Turn left (west) on **US-20** at Pittsfield for the Hancock Shaker Village.

Turn right (east) on **MA-9** at Pittsfield to Dalton for the Crane Museum.

Continue north on US-7 for Mount Greylock, on the right.

Continue north to Williamstown for the art museums.

Turn right (east) at Williamstown onto **MA-2** for North Adams, Natural Bridge, and the Mohawk Trail, following it to Shelburne Falls, then continuing on MA-2 back to Boston.

PRACTICALITIES:

Good weather is essential for this scenic excursion, best taken between April and late November. The area is at its most attractive during the fall foliage season, but expect crowds then. Many of the attractions are closed in winter. In general, the museums are closed on Mondays.

Be sure to allow ample time (at least three hours) for the Hancock Shaker Village if you intend a visit there.

Consider staying overnight and combining this trip with the previous one, or with the one to Historic Deerfield. You might also break the tour up into shorter sections by spending several nights in the area.

For further information, especially about overnight accommodations, contact the **Berkshire Visitors Bureau**, Berkshire Common, Pittsfield, MA 01201, ☎ (413) 443-9186 or (800) 237-5747, FAX (413) 443-1970, Web Site: http://berkcon.com/tbc/nfp/nfp013/nfp013.html.

FOOD AND DRINK:

Along with the usual chain restaurants, you might try:

Church Street Café (65 Church St., Lenox Village, just west of US-7) Regional American specialties, served indoors or out. Reservations suggested. ☎ (413) 637-2745. $$ and $$$

The Springs (US-7, 12 miles north of Pittsfield in New Ashford) Fine Continental and American cuisine since 1930. ☎ (413) 458-3465. $$

Village Café (Visitors Center, Hancock Shaker Village) Healthy, Shaker-inspired light lunches in pleasant surroundings. $

Cobble Café (27 Spring St. in Williamstown) Creative dishes in an offbeat setting. ☎ (413) 458-5930. $

LOCAL ATTRACTIONS:

Numbers in parentheses correspond to numbers on the map.

THE MOUNT—EDITH WHARTON RESTORATION (1), Plunkett St., Lenox, MA 01240, ☎ (413) 637-1899, FAX (413) 637-0619. *Open early May to late May, weekends 10–3; late May through Oct., Tues.–Sun. 9–3. Last tour at 2. Also open Mon. in July and Aug., noon–3, last tour at 3. Also open Memorial Day, Labor Day, Columbus Day, last tour at 2. Adults $6, seniors $5.50, youths (13–18) $4.50, children under 12 free. Book and gift shop.*

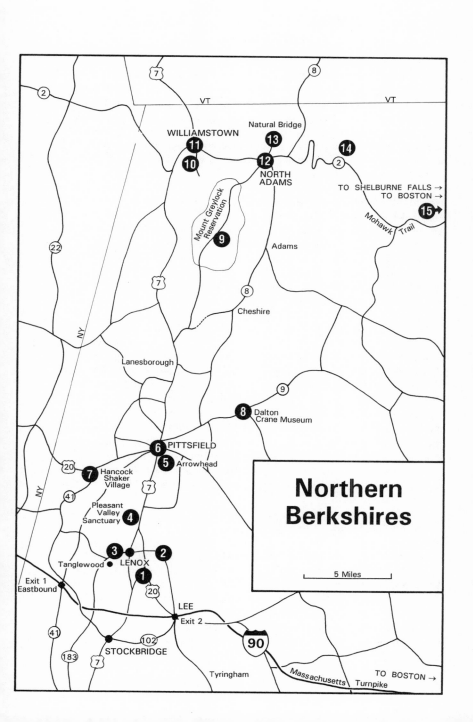

Northern Berkshires

5 Miles

Edith Wharton (1862–1937), renowned author of such classics as *The Age of Innocence*, created this magnificent summer home and its gardens in 1902. In it she expressed the ideas espoused in her first book, *The Decoration of Houses*. Today it is undergoing an extensive long-term restoration, and at the same time serves as home to Shakespeare & Company, a theatrical group devoted to The Bard, Wharton, and others. This affords an unusually good opportunity to witness a restoration-in-progress and to gain a more literary insight into the life of one of America's great authors.

Not far from here is the:

BERKSHIRE SCENIC RAILWAY MUSEUM (2), Willow Creek Rd., Lenox, MA 01240, ☎ (413) 637-2210. *Open Memorial Day weekend through Oct., weekends and holidays only, 10–4. Museum free. Short rides: Adults $1.50, seniors and children $1. Gift shop. Special events.* ♿.

An all-volunteer, not-for-profit group has restored the old 1902 Lenox Station and opened it as a museum of local railroading, with operating model trains as a special treat. Some interesting pieces of rolling stock reside outside, and short train rides are offered.

Historic **Lenox Village** lies just west of US-7/US-20. Once a summer hideaway for the very rich, it is now the center of cultural activities in western Massachusetts. Stroll or drive around its streets, admiring the stately old mansions, then continue west on MA-183 (West Street) to **Tanglewood** (3). This 210-acre estate has been the summer home of the Boston Symphony Orchestra since 1936, with performances from late June to early September. Besides the BSO concerts, there are chamber groups, soloists, and even pop, folk, and jazz offerings. Seats should be arranged well in advance, but last-minute outdoor "lawn" tickets are often available on the spot. And, even if there is no performance while you're there, you might want to just look around the lovely site. *For program and ticket information* ☎ *(413) 637-5165, during the off-season call Symphony Hall in Boston,* ☎ *(617) 266-1492.* ♿.

Just north of Lenox is the:

PLEASANT VALLEY WILDLIFE SANCTUARY (4), 472 West Mountain Rd., Lenox, MA 01240 ☎ (413) 637-0320. *Open Tues.–Sun., dawn to dusk. Adults $3, children $2.*

Seven miles of nature trails lead through meadows and woodlands, offering the chance to watch busy beavers building their dams, humming-birds flying about, and other marvels of nature. There's also a wildflower walk, a limestone cobble, a hemlock gorge, and (in summer) a natural history museum.

To the north, just below Pittsfield, is:

ARROWHEAD (5), 780 Holmes Rd., Pittsfield, MA 01201, ☎ (413) 442-1793. *Open Memorial Day–Labor Day, daily 10–5; day after Labor Day–Oct., Fri.–Mon. 10–5. Adults $5, children (6–16) $3.50. Tours. Video show. Gift shop. Nature trail.*

Herman Melville (1819–91) lived in this 18th-century farmhouse from 1850 until 1863, when the lack of commercial success as a writer forced him to sell and take up gainful employment elsewhere. It was here that he wrote his masterpiece, *Moby-Dick*, perhaps while staring out the window at whale-shaped Mount Greylock. Today, restored to its mid-19th-century appearance and furnished with Melville memorabilia, it's home to the Berkshire County Historical Society.

Continue into Pittsfield, home of:

THE BERKSHIRE MUSEUM (6), 39 South St. (US-7, just north of intersection with US-20, on the right), Pittsfield, MA 01201, ☎ (413) 443-7171. *Tues.– Sat. 10–5, Sun. 1–5, also Mon. in July & Aug. Closed some holidays. Adults $3, seniors & students $2, children (12–18) $1. Museum shop. Lectures, concerts, films. ♿.*

There's a little something for everyone at the Berkshire Museum, whose exhibits range from art to live fish. The galleries house permanent collections of 19th-century American paintings—especially those of the Hudson River School—along with European and 20th-century art. There are also artifacts from ancient civilizations, exhibitions of local history, a natural science section, and an aquarium with over a hundred different living species.

While in Pittsfield, you might also stop at the **Berkshire Athenaeum** for a look at their Herman Melville Memorial Room, an excellent collection of Melville memorabilia. ☎ *(413) 499-9486. 1 Wendell Ave., across the square from the museum and one block east on East St.*

Head west on US-20 to:

*HANCOCK SHAKER VILLAGE (7), Junction US-20 & MA-41, Pittsfield, MA 01202, ☎ (413) 443-0188, FAX (413) 447-9357. *Open Apr. through Nov., daily 9:30–5 (10–3 before Memorial Day and from late Oct. through Nov.; tours only at these times). Tours by appt. Dec.–Mar. Adults $10, children (6– 17) $5, families $25. Special events. Videos. Museum shop. ✕ (seasonal). Picnicking facilities. Partially ♿.*

Whatever else you do on this trip, don't miss the northern Berkshire's premier attraction. And allow plenty of time for it. Hancock Shaker Village, the third of 19 Shaker communities in the eastern United States, was home to members of an unusually creative religious sect from 1790 until 1960. They called it "The City of Peace." After the last of their numbers retired, the village was sold to a non-profit group for preservation as a living museum.

Who were the Shakers, and why are some aspects of their lifestyle so fascinating today? First emerging in England in 1747 as dissident members of

The Round Stone Barn and the Brick Dwelling

the Quaker faith, they believed that God was both male and female; and that their leader, Mother Ann Lee (1736–84), was the incarnation of the female divine principle, as Jesus had been the incarnation of the male. Correctly known as the United Society of Believers in Christ's Second Appearing, the group was popularly known as "Shakers" because of the ecstatic song and dance that accompanied their worship. After being persecuted in England, Mother Ann and eight followers emigrated to America in 1774 and settled near Albany, NY. By 1850, when the movement reached its height, there were some 6,000 Shakers in the Northeast and Midwest. They practiced equality of the sexes, open confession of sins, communal ownership of property, pacifism, and celibacy; perpetuating themselves by conversions and the adoption of orphans. An industrious (and relatively prosperous) people, they were also highly aesthetic, a trait for which they are best remembered today. Shaker furniture, architecture, and artifacts represent levels of design purity that have never been surpassed.

Take a look at the day's schedule of events, which you'll receive along with a map, and plan your visit around it. A simple sequence for a walking tour takes you first to the **Garden Tool Shed** of 1922 and the adjacent **Herb Garden**, where medicinal and culinary herbs were grown for the Shakers' own use and for sale to the outside "World." Close to this is the brick **Poultry House** of 1878. The chickens have left the coop, and are replaced with an exhibition and a short **orientation video** about "The City of Peace."

Inside the Brick Dwelling

The very symbol of Hancock is its marvelous ***Round Stone Barn** of 1826, rebuilt and enlarged over the years. Be sure to take a guided tour of this fascinating structure, a triumph of functionalism and ingenious simplicity. Round barns are not unique to Shakers, but precious few of them have ever been built anywhere due to the initial cost of construction. They are, however, extremely efficient, allowing just one person to feed an entire herd.

Take a look at the surrounding fields, where you might see oxen pulling plows. The adjacent **Barn Complex**, dating from 1910 to 1939, reminds visitors that the village was primarily a farm community. Today, parts of it house a video theater with continuous short presentations, the Good Room serving light snacks, and a Discovery Room where you can enjoy hands-on activities.

Closeby is the heated **Brick Garage** where the Shakers' early Cadillac and other automobiles were kept from freezing from about 1915 on. The **Ice House** provided cold storage for meats and vegetables until refrigeration was introduced around 1927. One of the older structures, the **Tan House** of 1835, was originally used for tanning leather, but when this proved unprofitable was converted to other industrial purposes. A working forge and cabinetmaker's shop can be seen there today.

Seeming very much out of place in this world of simplicity is the **Trustees' Office and Store**, first built in 1813 but thoroughly Victorianized in 1895. By this time the Shakers were trying to project a more contemporary image in an effort to attract new converts. That effort failed, and this comfortable structure became the last in the village to be occupied.

Cross the highway at the crosswalk. Behind the Cemetery, with its single monument, is Mount Sinai, once the site of intense spiritual activities. Its restoration is planned as part of a long-term project. The **Schoolhouse** was first built around 1820; what you see today is a 1976 replica. Pass the Horse Barn of 1850 and visit the **Ministry Shop**, which served as headquarters for the local bisophric. If time permits, you might want to settle into its video theater to view a wonderful hour-long film by Ken Burns entitled "***Hands to Work, Hearts to God**," which runs continuously. The **Meetinghouse**, next door, is where Sunday services were held. In keeping with the rule of celibacy, there are separate entrances for brethren and sisters.

Recross the highway, stopping at the workshops where Shakers once practiced crafts and trades. Demonstrations of these traditional activities are given to interested visitors. Hancock's main building is the large ***Brick Dwelling House**, built in 1830 to house about one hundred brethren and sisters in separate-but-equal quarters, each to their own side of the central aisle and each with their own stairway and door. Besides communal living quarters, there are cooking and dining facilities, meeting rooms, sewing rooms, an infirmary, and a pharmacy. Both kitchen demonstrations and talks on Shaker daily life are given here. One last building that should not be missed is the **Laundry and Machine Shop**, begun as early as 1790 and added to over the next 80 years. Combining a machine shop with a laundry is not so strange when you consider that the water feeding the overshot wheels to drive the machines could then be used for washing. Today there are exhibitions inside.

Return to Pittsfield. From there you might want to head east about five miles on MA-9 to Dalton and the:

CRANE MUSEUM (8), Housatonic St., Dalton, MA 01226, ☎ (413) 684-2600. *Open June to mid-Oct., weekdays, 2–5. Free.*

Crane & Company of Dalton makes paper, in particular the paper used for American currency, as well as other fine specialty papers. They've been doing this since 1801, and now they've put the whole fascinating history of American papermaking on display in this intriguing little museum. Housed in a former old stone mill of 1844, the exhibits include historic currencies and samples of other quality papers from the past.

Heading north from Pittsfield on US-7 soon brings you to the:

MOUNT GREYLOCK STATE RESERVATION (9), Rockwell Rd., Lanesborough, MA 01327, ☎ (413) 499-4262. *Visitor Center open daily except Thanksgiving and Christmas. Hiking trails. Picnicking. Cross-country skiing. Fishing. Hunting.* ✗.

At 3,491 feet, **Mount Greylock** is the highest point in Massachusetts, with magnificent **views* extending across five states. And you don't even have to climb it as the road goes right to the summit. Turn right off US-7 onto Rockwell Road about a mile north of Lanesborough, and follow it for about two miles to the Visitor Center. Here you can get information, trail maps, and view environmental displays. Another eight miles brings you to the summit, marked with the strange 90-foot granite **War Memorial Tower** from which you'll get the best views. Also at the summit is the rustic **Bascom Lodge** operated by the Appalachian Mountain Club (AMC), offering meals and lodging. ☎ *(413) 743-1591. Open mid-May to late Oct.*

From here it is possible to take Notch Road directly to North Adams (12) and the Mohawk Trail (MA-2), or return on Rockwell Road to US-7 and head north to Williamstown, home of the:

*STERLING AND FRANCINE CLARK ART INSTITUTE (10), 225 South St., Williamstown, MA 01267, ☎ (413) 458-9545. *Open Tues.–Sun. 10–5, also Mon. in July & Aug. Free.* &.

Turn east on Main Street (MA-2) for a short distance, then south on South Street for less than a mile to one of the Berkshire's greatest surprises. Here, hidden away in the self-styled "Village Beautiful," is an amazing, world-class art museum. Robert Sterling Clark (1877–1956) and his French wife Francine spent four decades collecting major works ranging from the Italian Renaissance to the American Impressionists, and built a lovely marble temple to house them far away from any urban area. Among the varied talents represented are Piero della Francesca, Memling, Fragonard, Gainsborough, Turner, Goya, Corot, Degas, Monet, Toulouse-Lautrec, Cassatt, Remington, Homer, and Sargent. There are more than 30 pieces by Renoir alone. If you love art, you can't possibly afford to miss this treat—especially since it's free!

And if that's not enough, Williamstown has another excellent art museum:

WILLIAMS COLLEGE MUSEUM OF ART (11), Main St. between Spring and Water streets, Williamstown, MA 01267, ☎ (413) 597-2429. *Open Tues.– Sat. 10–5 and Sun. 1–5; closed Mon. except Memorial Day, Labor Day, and Columbus Day. Also closed Thanksgiving, Christmas, New Year's. Free. Museum shop.* &.

Centrally located on the beautiful Williams College campus, this is one of the nation's finer college art museums, enabling students to benefit from first-hand knowledge of the works of art. Although the collections cover an exceptionally broad span of art history, they focus on American art from the 18th century to the present, contemporary and modern works, and non-Western art. There is an active program of changing exhibitions.

Head back toward Boston on MA-2, perhaps stopping at nearby North Adams to visit the:

WESTERN GATEWAY HERITAGE STATE PARK (12), Furnace St. off MA-8, behind City Hall, North Adams, MA 01247, ☎ (413) 663-6312. *Open daily year-round 10–5. Closed some major holidays. Free. Partially* ♿.

Historical exhibitions here celebrate the building of the Hoosac Tunnel, one of the greatest railroad engineering triumphs of the 19th century. Dug at the cost of nearly 200 lives, and almost five miles long, the tunnel took 25 years to complete. When opened in 1875, it linked Massachusetts with the West and made North Adams into a bustling industrial center. The old freight yard has been restored and made into an urban historic park, with a cluster of original wooden railroad buildings now housing a Visitor Center, exhibitions, shops, and restaurants.

Just north of North Adams, on MA-8, is the:

NATURAL BRIDGE STATE PARK (13), Rte. 8, North Adams, MA 01247, ☎ (413) 663-6392. *Open mid-May to mid-Oct., weekdays 10–6, weekends 10–8. $3 per car. Picnic facilities. Hiking trails. Cross-country skiing.*

Spanning a deep, narrow chasm some 475 feet long, this natural water-eroded bridge is the only example of its type in North America. It was formed some 550 million years ago, and is surrounded by unusual rock formations, flora, and fauna.

This scenic section of Route MA-2 has been known as the ***Mohawk Trail** (14) since 1914, when it became one of the first designated tourist routes in the country. Its history, however, goes back to a time long before automobiles were ever dreamt of. Native Americans used this route for hundreds of years, and their footpath was widened by 17th-century European settlers to accommodate first the horse, and then wheeled vehicles. Despite occasional heavy traffic—especially in the fall foliage season—it offers a fabulous driving experience that ranks among the most enjoyable in New England. And the shortest route back to Boston.

If time permits, make a stop at **Shelburne Falls** (15) to admire the town's famous **Bridge of Flowers**, an abandoned 1908 trolley bridge that was recycled as a 400-foot-long flower garden, blossoming from spring to fall. Signs lead the way to Salmon Falls, where you can examine glacial potholes from the last Ice Age.

Section IV

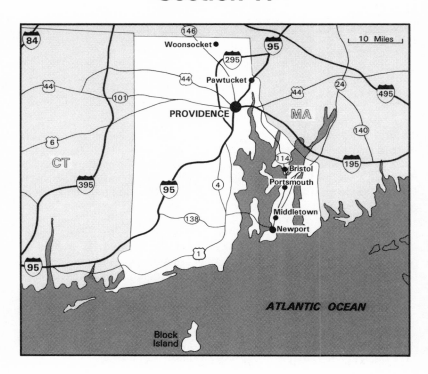

DAYTRIPS TO
RHODE ISLAND

America's smallest state has the curious distinction of possessing the longest name: The State of Rhode Island and Providence Plantations. Historically, it might be better known as the Reluctant State as it was the last of the original colonies to join the Union—and then practically at gunpoint. Rhode Islanders are nothing if not independent; stubborn might be a better word. Home to outcasts from puritanical Massachusetts, pirates, rumrunners, and America's wealthiest families, Rhode Island's colorful past has left a legacy every bit as compelling as any other New England state.

Whether your travels take you to Providence, Newport, Pawtucket and the Blackstone Valley, or Bristol and Portsmouth, you're always within easy daytrip range of Boston and most other bases in New England.

Trip 28

Providence

You won't find many New England cities that are quite as attractive as Providence. Or as easy to explore. This walking tour leads you through one of America's best-preserved Colonial neighborhoods; visits an Ivy League university, several historic buildings, and a world-class art museum; then crosses the river to Rhode Island's impressive State House. From there it ambles through a revitalized downtown business district, stopping by the early-19th-century forerunner of all shopping malls.

Providence, and indeed all of Rhode Island, was founded by an extraordinary man. Roger Williams (1603–83) left England around 1631 to become a Puritan minister in Salem, Massachusetts, but his unpopular opinions soon aroused controversy. He insisted that the land rightfully belonged to the Indians, and that government should be separate from religion. In 1635 Williams was expelled from the colony and fled south with a few of his followers. There he purchased land from the Narragansett Indians, and named his new settlement in honor of God's Providence. Offering broad religious tolerance, the town quickly grew and was granted a royal charter in 1663 by King Charles II that confirmed its liberal institutions.

For those who can stay overnight, this trip combines well with the ones to the Blackstone Valley, Bristol and Portsmouth, or Newport; or with Fall River or New Bedford in nearby Massachusetts.

GETTING THERE:

By car, Providence is about 50 miles southwest of Boston via Route **I-95**. Street parking is difficult, although you might be lucky in the College Hill area, where the walk begins. To try this, get off I-95 at Exit 23 and head southeast. Commercial parking lots are plentiful near the State House and downtown districts, reached from exits 23 or 22 off I-95.

Those coming via Route **I-195** from elsewhere in New England should get off at Exit 2 and follow South Main St. into the College Hill or downtown areas.

By train, Providence is less than an hour from Boston's South or Back Bay stations via **Amtrak**, ☎ (800) USA-RAIL for schedules and fares. The station is right on the walking route. Economical rush-hour commuter service is provided by **MBTA**, ☎ (617) 722-3200 or (800) 392-6100.

By bus, frequent service is provided by **Bonanza Bus Lines** to and from

Boston, a 45-minute ride. The Bonanza terminal in Providence is at Exit 25 off I-95; there is a shuttle bus to downtown. For information ☎ (617) 720-4110, (401) 751-8800 or (800) 556-3815. Additional service is offered by **Greyhound**, ☎ (401) 454-0790 or (800) 231-2222.

PRACTICALITIES:

Providence is best visited on a normal weekday, when more of its attractions are open and the streets are alive with activity. The superb RISD Museum of Art is closed on Mondays and major holidays, and also on Sundays and Tuesdays from July through Labor Day. Another major sight, The John Brown House, closes on Mondays and holidays, and also from January through February. The State House (Capitol) is closed on weekends.

The suggested walking tour (about three miles in length) includes a few fairly steep climbs, so wear comfortable shoes.

If you parked downtown, or came by train or bus, you can pick up the circular walking route there instead of at Prospect Terrace, and continue around to your starting point.

For further information contact the **Greater Providence Convention & Visitors Bureau**, 30 Exchange Terrace, Providence, RI 02903, ☎ (401) 274-1636 or (800) 233-1636. Information is also available at the **Roger Williams National Memorial Park** along the walking route.

FOOD AND DRINK:

Rhode Island's capital is famous for its high culinary standards. Some good places for lunch along (or near) the walking route are:

Rue de l'Espoir (99 Hope St., 8 blocks southeast of Brown University, near Williams St.) Unusual and varied cuisine; eclectic, ethnic, and avant-garde. ☎ (401) 751-8890. X: Sun., Mon. $$ and $$$

Hemmenway's Seafood Grill & Oyster Bar (1 Old Stone Sq., on the river, 2 blocks south of RISD) Terrific seafood with a view of the river. ☎ (401) 351-8570. $$ and $$$

Pot au Feu (44 Custom House St., 2 blocks northeast of the Arcade) Classic French cuisine; formal upstairs, casual bistro down below. ☎ (401) 273-8953. $$ and $$$

Union Station Brewery (36 Exchange Terrace at Kennedy Plaza, south of Water Place) Home-brewed beers and unusual pub dishes. ☎ (401) 274-2739. X: weekends. $$

Wyatt's Rotisserie (165 Benefit St., 3 blocks north of RISD) Specializes in spit-grilled chicken. ☎ (401) 751-7900. X: lunch on weekends. $

Downcity Diner (151 Weybosset St., 3 blocks southwest of the Arcade) Fine, upscale dishes at down-to-earth prices. Weekend brunches. ☎ (401) 331-9217. $

Several nice ethnic fast-food places for a quick lunch, or a snack, can be found in the **Arcade** (11), along with a familiar burger outlet. All are priced $.

SUGGESTED TOUR:

This walk begins on College Hill, but if you've parked downtown (or came by train or bus) you should pick up the route there and follow it around. *Numbers in parentheses correspond to numbers on the map.*

The best ***view** of Providence is from **Prospect Terrace** (1), perched high on College Hill. Roger Williams is buried here, and there's a somewhat stiff monument of him gazing across the panoramic skyline. That dazzling white dome straight ahead is the State House (9), the seat of Rhode Island's government, which you'll be visiting later.

Follow the map to:

BROWN UNIVERSITY (2), 45 Prospect St., Providence, RI 02912, ☎ (401) 863-2378. *Guided tours start at the College Admissions Office, Corliss-Brackett House, at Prospect and Angell streets. Tours Mon.–Fri. at 10, 11, 1, 3, & 4 (11 & 3 only during Christmas & spring vacations); and on Sat. at 10, 11, & noon from mid-Sept. to mid-Nov. Information for self-guided tour at same office. Free. Partially* ♿.

Whether you take a guided tour or just stroll around on your own, Brown is a highly worthwhile stop. Established in 1764, it is the seventh-oldest college in the United States and, like Harvard and Yale, a member of the Ivy League. Its ceremonial entrance on Prospect Street, the wrought-iron **Van Wickle Gates**, is opened only twice a year; outward for the graduating class and inward to welcome new freshmen. Just east of it is **University Hall**, dating from 1770 and the oldest building on campus. Wander around, then head south on Brown Street, turning right on Power Street to the:

*JOHN BROWN HOUSE (3), 52 Power St., Providence, RI 02906, ☎ (401) 331-8575. *Open March–Dec., Tues.–Sat. 11–4 and Sun. 1–4; Jan. & Feb, Sat. 11–4, Sun. 1–4, weekdays by appt. for groups only. Closed holidays. Adults $5, seniors $3, children (7–17) $2.*

John Brown was a merchant and shipbuilder who opened commerce with China after failing at the slave trade, and a member of a large family that brought wealth and fame to Providence in the late 18th and early 19th centuries. His home, completed in 1788, was called "the most magnificent and elegant mansion I have ever seen on this continent" by John Quincy Adams. Among the other famous guests entertained here was George Washington.

Now maintained as a museum, the three-story Georgian mansion contains a marvelous collection of furniture and decorative arts in period room settings. Of the original Brown family pieces, the nine-shell ***secretary** is regarded as one of the finest examples of American Colonial furniture anywhere. John Brown's chariot, built in 1782, is supposedly the earliest American vehicle of its type still extant.

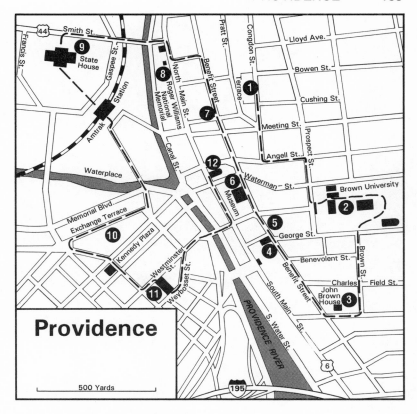

Providence

500 Yards

Turn right onto ***Benefit Street**, a mile-long thoroughfare lined with beautifully restored Colonial, Federal, and Victorian houses. This is considered by many to be the most impressive concentration of original Colonial homes in America, especially in its northern reaches. On your left, at Hopkins Street, is the **Governor Stephen Hopkins House** (4) of 1707. Stephen Hopkins (1707–85) was a signer of the Declaration of Independence, the first chancellor of Brown University, a Chief Justice of the Superior Court, and ten times governor of Rhode Island during Colonial times. George Washington stayed here twice, in 1776 and again in 1781. You can visit, too, if it's open. ☎ *(401) 751-7067. Open Apr.–mid-Dec., Wed. & Sat., 1–4., and by appt.*

The **Providence Athenaeum** (5) is one of America's oldest libraries and cultural centers. According to legend, Edgar Allan Poe courted Sarah Whitman here, although their engagement was broken owing to Poe's capacity for booze. On display inside the granite Greek Revival building of

Governor Stephen Hopkins House

1838 is a remarkable collection of original Audubon illustrations, rare books, and a few decorative art treasures. ☎ *(401) 421-6970. Open Mon.– Fri. 8:30–5:30, and Sat. 9:30–5:30 except in summer. Free.*

Brown University is not the only institution of higher learning on College Hill. The **Rhode Island School of Design**, called RISD or *Riz-dee* for short, is one of the nation's premier art, architecture, and design schools. Anyone with even the slightest interest in art should not fail to visit its:

*MUSEUM OF ART, RHODE ISLAND SCHOOL OF DESIGN (6), 224 Bene-fit St., Providence, RI 02903, ☎ (401) 454-6500. *Open mid-June through Aug., Tues.–Sat., noon–5; and Sept. to mid-June, Tues., Wed., Fri., Sat. 10:30–5, Thurs. noon–8, Sun. & holidays 2–5. Closed Mon., Thanksgiving, Christmas, New Year's July 4. Adults $2, seniors $1, children (5–18) 50¢, under 5 free. Gift shop.* &.

Although not excessively large, this world-class museum has a fabulous collection covering nearly the entire scope of art from Classical times to the present. Many of its works are absolutely first rate. Upstairs, a huge **Japanese Buddha** from the 12th century occupies its own room, an **Egyptian mummy** from around 300 B.C. resides nearby, and between them are galleries filled with African, Pre-Columbian, Indian, Chinese, and Japanese objects. On the main level, the entire history of Western art unfolds in rooms devoted to

Greek, Roman, and Etruscan antiquities; medieval treasures including a 12th-century sculpture from the great abbey at Cluny in France; and high-lights of Renaissance art. Among the 19th- and 20th-century works are masterpieces by Poussin, Delacroix, Corot, Cézanne, Rodin, Matisse, and Picasso. Manet's *Repose* and Monet's *Bassin d'Argenteuil* are especially noteworthy.

*Pendleton House, a separate building connected internally, features an extraordinary collection of American furniture and decorative arts of the Colonial period, all beautifully displayed in period room settings.

Continue down lovely Benefit Street to the **Old State House** (7) of 1762 where, on May 4, 1776, Rhode Island declared its independence from Great Britain two full months before the folks gathered in Philadelphia agreed on the same course of action. ☎ *(401) 277-2678. Open Mon.–Fri., 8:30–4:30. Closed holidays. Free.*

Follow the map, turning downhill to the **Roger Williams National Memorial** (8). Located on the site of the first Providence colony, this 4.5-acre park includes a Visitor Center in the northeast corner with exhibits on Williams' life and times. This is also a good place to get tourist information about Providence. ☎ *(401) 521-7266 Visitor Center open daily, 8–4:30. Closed Thanksgiving, Christmas, New Year's. Short-term parking. Free.* ❶. ♿.

Cross the river and head uphill to the dazzling white:

RHODE ISLAND STATE HOUSE (9), 82 Smith St., Providence, RI 02900, ☎ 277-2357. *Open Mon.–Fri., 8:30–4:30. Closed holidays. Free. Self-guided tours during business hours, guided tours by appt.* ♿.

Rhode Island's capitol building, the State House of 1900, is among the most beautiful in the nation. Designed by the famous architectural firm of McKim, Mead, and White, it is built of sparkling white Georgia marble and boasts one of the largest self-supporting domes on Earth. Step inside and go upstairs to examine several important treasures, including Rhode Island's original royal ***charter**, signed in 1663 by King Charles II. In the Governor's Reception Room, which you're free to enter, hangs a familiar sight—the famed full-length ***portrait of George Washington** by Rhode Island native Gilbert Stuart. There are also mementos of another Rhode Islander, General Nathanael Greene (1742–86), a hero of the Revolutionary War. The Civil War is represented by a portrait of General Ambrose Burnside (1824–81), a resident of Providence, one-time governor of the state, U.S. senator, and trend-setter in tonsorial fashion.

Exit from the south side of the State House and stroll down past the impressive railroad station to **Waterplace**, a lovely new urban park that makes exceptionally good use of its riverside location. Cross the Woonas-quatucket River and turn right into **Exchange Terrace** (10) and the adjacent

Kennedy Plaza and City Hall Park. There's an equestrian statue of General Burnside here, and a City Hall of 1878 designed after the Louvre in Paris. Providence's tourist information office, the Convention & Visitors Bureau, is located at number 30 Exchange Terrace.

Follow the map south to Westminster Mall, a pedestrianized shopping street. To the left it becomes Westminster Street, where you'll find the sole surviving granddaddy of all the indoor shopping malls in America. Built in 1828, the **Arcade** (11) houses three floors of shops around an open gallery running from Westminster to Weybosset streets. Its two end façades are quite different as two separate architects were used, each insisting on his own design. Thoroughly refurbished, the Arcade has a number of interesting, eclectic shops, and several inexpensive restaurants—a nice place for lunch or a snack. ☎ *(401) 272-2340. Open Mon.–Sat. 10–6, longer hours during Christmas season.* ⎋.

Follow the map through Providence's thriving business district and cross the river, returning to College Hill where the walk began. One last attraction, on North Main Street, is the **Meeting House of the First Baptist Church in America** (12). The congregation was founded in 1638 by none other than Roger Williams himself, although he soon left it to become a Seeker opposed to all sects. The present wooden structure dates from 1775 and was built by ships' carpenters, which accounts for the fact that the 185-foot-tall steeple has enough give in it to have survived fierce hurricanes. A magnificent chandelier of Waterford crystal graces the simple interior, as do the massive Ionic columns. ☎ *(401) 454-3418. Open Mon.–Fri., 9:30–3:30, guided tours available; also tours on Sun. at 10:45 (July–Aug.) or 12:15 (Sept.–Jun.). Closed Sat. and holidays. Free, donation accepted.*

The Blackstone River Valley

America's Industrial Revolution began in the late 18th century in Pawtucket, Rhode Island, the "place by the waterfalls" where the Blackstone River drops into the Seekonk. Those first mills are still there, still making cloth, only now it's for the enlightenment of visitors. From here north to Woonsocket (and extending well into Massachusetts) are reminders of a rich heritage that once fueled the nation's economy. All along the way, too, are spots of natural beauty along with interesting historic sites. Being a bit off the beaten path, the Blackstone River Valley is refreshingly free of tourist hordes. For those who can stay a little longer, this trip combines well with nearby Providence, and also with Fall River or Worcester in Massachusetts.

GETTING THERE:

By car, Pawtucket is about 47 miles southwest of Boston via Route **I-95**. Take Exit 27 and follow signs to the Slater Mill. From there, follow the map and text directions to the other sites.

PRACTICALITIES:

The most important attraction on this trip, the Slater Mill, is open on Tuesdays through Sundays from June through Labor Day, and on weekends only from March through May and Labor Day until late December. It is closed on most holidays. A few of the other sites have complex schedules; be sure to check those that particularly interest you.

Narrated **riverboat tours** are offered at various locations along the route from May through October. Ask the tourist office, below, for current schedules.

For further information, contact the **Blackstone Valley Tourism Council**, P.O. Box 7663, Cumberland, RI 02864, ☎ (401) 334-0837, Fax (401) 334-0566.

FOOD AND DRINK:

Some good places for lunch are:

The Peppermill (636 Central Ave. in Pawtucket, a mile northeast of the Children's Museum) American cuisine in a century-old firehouse. ☎ (401) 728-7474. $$

Chan's (267 Main St. in Woonsocket, at the junction of RI-126 and RI-122, Railroad St.) A long-time favorite for traditional Chinese cuisine in various styles. ☎ (401) 765-1900. $$

Modern Diner (364 East Ave. in Pawtucket, a mile south of the Slater Mill) An old, classic diner with classic diner food. ☎ (401) 726-8390. $

Moon's Landing (4077 Mendon Rd., RI-122, in Cumberland, a mile north of RI-120, just south of Woonsocket) Real American cooking in a cozy little restaurant. ☎ (401) 658-0449. $

LOCAL ATTRACTIONS:

Numbers in parentheses correspond to numbers on the map.

*SLATER MILL HISTORIC SITE (1), 727 Roosevelt Ave., Pawtucket, RI 02862, ☎ (401) 725-8638, Fax (401) 722-3040. *Open June through Oct., Tues.–Sat. 10–5 and Sun. 1–5, closed Mon. and holidays; March through May and Nov. to 3rd Sun. in Dec., weekends 1–5, closed holidays except Columbus Day and Veterans' Day. Adults $5.50, seniors $4.50, children (6–12) $3.50. Museum shop.*

Samuel Slater (1768–1835), an ambitious young lad from Derbyshire, England, was possessed of a fine memory and a good sense of business. Defying British laws prohibiting the exportation of industrial secrets, he disguised himself as a farm boy and sailed for the New World to make his fortune. In 1790 Slater contracted with Moses Brown of Providence to stealthily reproduce the best of English cotton machinery and build America's first successful factory by the waterfalls in Pawtucket. This was the real beginning of the Industrial Revolution that transformed the infant nation from an agricultural backwater into a manufacturing giant.

The whole fascinating story is explored right here in the restored original **Slater Mill** of 1793; the **Sylvanus Brown House** of 1758, where preindustrial methods are demonstrated; and the **Wilkinson Mill** of 1810, an operating 19th-century machine shop. A 16,000-pound waterwheel still powers the machinery as it did in the days before steam took over. A multimedia show is offered, there are special programs on the subject, and temporary exhibitions in the Wilkinson Gallery.

Just across the river is the **Children's Museum of Rhode Island** (2), a hands-on experience for kids from 2 to 11 years of age. Housed in an 1840 mansion, the museum features Great-Grandmother's Kitchen where young visitors can pretend to cook in the old manner, a room-sized relief map of the state, and other activities that are both fun and educational. *58 Walcott St., Pawtucket,* ☎ *(401) 726-2590. Open year round, Tues.–Sat. 9:30–5 and Sun. 1–5. Closed first two weeks after Labor Day. Admission $3.50.*

While in Pawtucket, you might want to make a little side trip to the **Slater Memorial Park** (3), a 200-acre site with full recreational facilities including the famed ***Looff Carousel** of 1894. This is the earliest existing work by the woodcarver Charles Looff, who also created the carousel at New York's

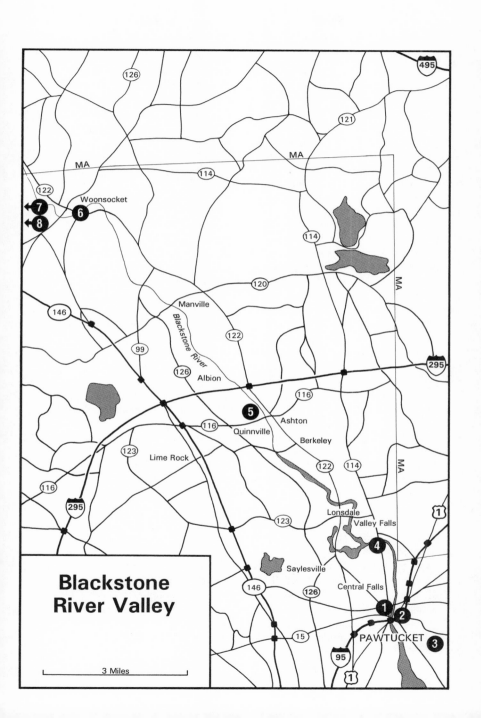

Blackstone
River Valley

3 Miles

Coney Island. Installed here in 1910 and restored in 1978, the merry-go-round operates daily in July and August, and on weekends from Easter to June and September to Columbus Day. *Newport Ave. (US-1A), south of RI-15,* ☎ *(401) 728-0500, ext. 252. Park open daily, free.* Also in the park is the **Daggett House**, a gable-roofed structure of 1685 containing outstanding antiques and historic artifacts. ☎ *(401) 333-1268 or 722-2631. Open June–Sept., weekends 2–5, and by appt. Nominal fee.*

Return to the west bank of the Blackstone River and turn right onto Broad Street (RI-114), following it north into **Valley Falls**. Down by the river, near the foot of Elm Street, is the **Valley Falls Heritage Park** (4). Ruins of a former mill stand next to a waterfall, with explanatory signs telling its story. ☎ *(401) 728-2400. Open daily, sunrise to sunset. Free. Picnic facilities.* ♿.

Head west across the river on RI-123, turning north on Old River Road. After a mile or so, bear right onto River Road, following it north to the **Blackstone River State Park** (5). Well hidden between the river and a restored section of its canal, this little bit of greenery masks noise from nearby Route I-295 with the sounds of a waterfall. Visitors can walk along the towpath to seek out remnants of early industry. ☎ *(401) 334-7773. Open daily, dawn to dusk. Free.* ♿.

Route RI-126 leads north to **Woonsocket** (6), an old town founded in 1666 at a spot called Miswoosakit by Native Americans. Originally agricultural, the settlement turned to industry in the early 19th century by exploiting the river's plentiful water power. With a predominantly Eastern European, Russian, and French-Canadian immigrant population, Woonsocket was quite a colorful place in its heyday. Reminders of that past can be seen in the **Harris Block** at 169 Main Street. Built in 1856 as a school and assembly hall for mill workers, the historic structure is now the City Hall. Abraham Lincoln gave a campaign speech here in 1860. ☎ *(401) 762-6400. Open Mon.–Fri. 8:30–4. Free.* ♿. The nearby **Train Station** of 1882 replaced an earlier one of 1847, and is now used by the National Park Service.

If time permits, you might follow the map west a few miles to **Slatersville** (7), near the intersection of RI-102 and RI-5. One of America's oldest mill villages, it was founded by Samuel Slater and his partners as a paternalistic company town; albeit an attractive one with a pretty village green. See if you can tell the difference between the workers' and owners' houses along Greene Street.

Want to see a little more? Just continue west beyond the Blackstone River Valley, taking routes RI-102 and RI-107 into **Harrisville** (8). Built around the Stillwater Worsted Mill of 1857, this hamlet was thoroughly renovated by the mill owner during the 1930s, making it into what he considered a typical New England Village. New pseudo-Colonial structures were added, others moved, and the remainder restored. It's still a picturesque place today, and is on the National Historic Register.

Historic Newport

There's so much to see and do in Newport that it really requires at least two daytrips, which could be combined by staying overnight or taken as separate excursions. The first explores the historic town and its magnificent Ocean Drive; the second (beginning on page 202) wanders through the legendary palaces of the Gilded Age.

"America's First Resort" thrives on tourism, but it's no tourist trap. With over three-and-a-half centuries of living history to offer its visitors, Newport abounds in perfectly preserved buildings of the 17th, 18th, and 19th centuries. Its colorful docks are still alive with seafaring activity, its harbor with the naval ships of today.

Although legend has it—on exceedingly scanty evidence—that the town was first settled by Norsemen around A.D. 1000, Newport's earliest documented founding was in 1639. That was the year that religious dissidents fleeing puritanical Massachusetts followed the lead of Roger Williams (see Providence trip) and headed south in search of freedom. By 1646 the town was already a shipbuilding center, and a century later became wealthy on the unholy "Triangle Trade"—the exchange of African slaves for West Indian sugar to make Newport rum. Whatever its sins, the town did provide tolerance for other dissident minorities including Quakers, Jews, and Baptists.

Occupied by the British throughout most of the American Revolution, Newport suffered grave economic damage from which it did not recover until the mid-19th century. By then it had become the favorite summer resort of America's richest families, heralding the arrival of the extravagant "Gilded Age" of social ostentation. This fabled era lasted until the early 20th century, only to be done in by the income tax. Its fantastic opulence is explored on the next trip.

If you have more than a day or two to spend, why not combine a visit to Newport with ones to nearby Bristol, Providence, or the Blackstone Valley; or with Fall River or New Bedford in Massachusetts?

GETTING THERE:

By car, Newport is about 75 miles south of Boston. Take **MA-24** past Fall River and into Rhode Island. Continue south on **RI-114**, which merges with **RI-138** in Middleton. Once in Newport follow Broadway to Thames Street, then go around Brick Market Place to America's Cup Avenue and the **Gateway Center** (1). You can park in the pay lot there, visit the tourist office, take a walking tour, and retrieve your car later for the Ocean Drive.

From other parts of New England you might be better off using Route **I-95** and the Jamestown and Newport bridges.

By bus, Newport is served from Boston's Back Bay Station by **Bonanza Bus Lines**, ☎ (617) 720-4110, (401) 846-1820, or (800) 556-3815. They stop conveniently at Gateway Center (1), from which the historic area can be seen on foot. It's a fairly long walk to the mansions described on the next trip, but you can take a local bus or cab there. Ocean Drive is best explored on a bicycle, which can be rented in town.

PRACTICALITIES:

Newport is crowded in summer, but of course there's more to do then. Late spring and early fall are the most pleasant times for a visit, with many activities opening in May and remaining open through October. A few minor sights may be closed on Mondays and/or Tuesdays; check the individual listings for details.

Newporters tend to dress smartly; those following their lead may feel more at home in this stylish town. In general, the better restaurants require proper attire for dinner.

For further information contact the **Newport County Convention & Visitors Bureau** at 23 America's Cup Avenue, Newport, RI 02840, ☎ (401) 848-8048 or (800) 326-6030. Ask them about the many special events and festivals that may enhance or interfere with your plans. The **Newport Activity Line** is a free, 24-hour, year-round, menu-driven voice information service, reached by dialing (401) 848-2000 or (800) 263-INFO.

FOOD AND DRINK:

Sophisticated Newport has been dining well for a long time, so there's no need to resort to fast food or chain restaurants. Here are a few good choices on or near the walking route:

> **White Horse Tavern** (Marlborough St. & Farewell St., near Friends Meeting House) America's oldest operating tavern has provided traditional cuisine since the 1680s! The setting is absolutely authentic and the service flawless. Dress well and reserve. ☎ (401) 849-3600. X: Tues. lunch. $$$

> **La Forge Casino** (186 Bellevue Ave., next to the Casino) A casual pub, a sidewalk café, and a lovely dining room make up this old favorite, featuring steak and seafood specialties along with lighter lunches. ☎ (401) 847-0418. $$ and $$$

> **Black Pearl** (Bannister's Wharf) Both an informal tavern, an outdoor café, and a fancy dinner restaurant, this is where the yachting crowd comes to enjoy superb seafood and other dishes. Reservations and jacket needed for the Commodore Room only. ☎ (401) 846-5264. $$ and $$$

Brick Alley Pub (140 Thames St., south of the Brick Market) All kinds of American food—burgers, seafood, sandwiches, salads, and the like—indoors or out. ☎ (401) 849-6334. $ and $$

Mudville Pub (8 West Marlborough St., a block east of the Visitor Center) A great sports bar overlooking the ball park. Burgers, sandwiches, light lunches, and the like. ☎ (401) 849-1408. $

Franklin Spa (229 Spring St., 4 blocks south of Trinity Church) The locals have been eating here since 1840. Nothing fancy, just sound homemade luncheonette fare. ☎ (401) 847-3540. $

Pick Pockets Deli (7 Memorial Blvd., a block north of the Casino) Light Middle Eastern, vegetarian, and other healthy meals to take out or eat there. ☎ (401) 846-2226. $

SUGGESTED TOUR:

Numbers in parentheses correspond to numbers on the map.

Luckily, the best place to begin a walking tour of old Newport is also the best place to park your car. Besides parking facilities, **Gateway Center** (1) also houses the bus station, various shops, and Newport's friendly **Visitor Center**—one of the best tourist information offices anywhere.

At this time, or perhaps at the end of your walk, you might want to make a little side trip into a nearby neighborhood called **The Point**. Among the many authentically restored Colonial houses in this quiet residential area is the:

*HUNTER HOUSE (2), 54 Washington St., Newport, RI 02840, ☎ (401) 847-1000. *Open May through Sept., daily 10–5; also weekends in Apr. and Oct., 10–5. Adults $6.50, children (6–11) $3.*

One of the few large Colonial residences to have escaped destruction by the British during the Revolution, Hunter House was built in 1748 and belonged to staunch Tories at the time of the conflict. Toward the end of the war it served as the headquarters of Admiral de Ternay, commander of the French naval forces, and is today recognized as a prime example of mid-18th-century domestic architecture. The **carved pineapple** above its doorway is a symbol of hospitality dating from the time when returning sea captains announced their safe arrival from the West Indies by placing the fruit in front of their homes. You'll see this symbol all over town.

Beautifully restored and furnished with authentic pieces made in 18th-century Newport, the house also has a lovely period **garden** overlooking Narragansett Bay.

Return to Gateway Center (1) and stroll over past the old ball park of 1908, still hosting semi-pro baseball games on summer evenings. The **Brick Market** was built in 1762; today it's surrounded by a variety of interesting shops. The original 18th-century building, nicely restored, now houses the:

MUSEUM OF NEWPORT HISTORY (3), Thames St. at Long Wharf, Newport, RI 02840, ☎ (401) 841-8770. *Open Mon. and Wed.–Sat. 10–5, Sun. 1–5. Closed Tues. and holidays. Adults $5, seniors $4, children (6–18) $3, under 6 free.*

This is a good place to get your bearings before exploring historic Newport, whose colorful past is re-created through the use of interactive computers, audiovisuals, graphics, artifacts, and the whole panoply of contemporary museum presentation.

Stroll east into **Washington Square**, the center of town in Colonial days. At its end is the **Old Colony House** (4) of 1741, once the seat of Rhode Island's government. It was from the balcony here that the first Declaration of Independence by a colony was announced on May 4, 1776, two months before the one representing all the colonies was proclaimed in Philadelphia. This is also where George Washington conferred with Count Rochambeau in 1781 to plan the Battle of Yorktown, the last significant engagement of the Revolutionary War. Other famous guests included Jefferson, Lafayette, Jackson, and Eisenhower. The interior is decorated with fine period furniture and a full-length portrait of Washington by Gilbert Stuart. ☎ *(401) 846-2980. Open by appointment.*

Stroll up Farewell Street to the **Friends Meeting House** (5), one of the first such structures in the country. Begun in 1699, the building was enlarged over the years and remained home to the New England Yearly Meeting of the Society of Friends until 1905. Quakers played a dominant role in Newport's early history, although their pacifist attitudes towards the British were hardly welcome. The recently-restored building is noted for its elegant simplicity and ingenious design. ☎ *(401) 846-0813. Open by appointment.*

The oldest restored house in Newport is just a few steps away. Built around 1675, the **Wanton-Lyman-Hazard House** (6) was home to Colonial governors and Tory tax collectors, the last of whom fled for his life during the Stamp Act Riot of 1765. Tours through the house and its lovely garden give a good idea of everyday life in Colonial Newport. ☎ *(401) 846-0813. Open mid-June to early July, Fri. & Sat. 10–4; and early July through late Sept., Thurs.–Sun. 10–4, other times by appt. Adults $4, children under 12 free.*

Quakers were not the only group to find religious tolerance in Newport. America's oldest Jewish house of worship, the ***Touro Synagogue** (7), dates from 1763 and was designed in a classical style after Sephardic temples in Portugal and Holland. Newport has had a Jewish community since 1658, when Sephardim first arrived from Europe, followed by Ashkenazim. On display in the richly-decorated interior is the oldest torah in North America, and a 1790 letter from George Washington proclaiming "May the children of the stock of Abraham . . . continue to enjoy the goodwill of the other inhabitants; while everyone shall sit in safety under his own vine and fig tree." ☎ *(401) 847-4794. Guided tours from July 4th weekend until Labor Day, Sun.–Fri. 10–4; shorter hours or by appointment the rest of the year. Closed Sat. and during services.*

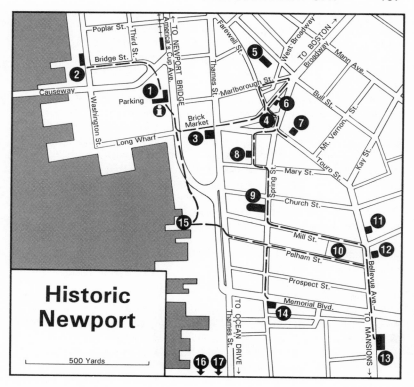

Historic Newport

500 Yards

Follow the map down Clarke Street, possibly stopping at the **Artillery Company of Newport Armory and Military Museum** (8). America's oldest militia organization with continuous service was founded in 1741, and built this Greek Revival style armory in 1836. Inside, you'll find both American and foreign weapons, artifacts, and lots of uniforms from Colonial to modern times. Over one hundred nations from around the world are represented. ☎ *(401) 846-8488. Open June through Sept., Wed.–Sat. & Mon., 10–4; and Sun. noon–4. Adults $2, children $1.50.* ♿.

Trinity Church (9), on nearby Spring Street, was built in 1726 to a design based on Sir Christopher Wren's London churches. George Washington worshipped here (pew 81), as did Bishop George Berkeley—who donated the organ, which was supposedly tested by George Frederick Handel himself before being shipped to America. The Perry Bothers, Oliver Hazard and Matthew Calbraith, were both baptized here, and both became renowned naval heroes of the 19th century. Because of its English ties, the church escaped damage during the Revolution. This connection to the mother country was restated in 1976 with visits by both Queen Elizabeth II and the Archbishop of Canterbury. The ***interior**, with its three-tiered pulpit, box pews, great clock, and Tiffany windows is well worth seeing. ☎ *(401) 846-0660. Open daily; May and early Sept. to mid-Oct. 1–4, mid-June to Labor Day 10–4, rest of year 10–1. Episcopal services on Sun. 8 & 11, 8 & 10 in summer.* ♿.

Turn east on Mill Street to the **Old Stone Tower** (10) in Touro Park. Its origin is unknown, giving rise to numerous colorful theories—the most unlikely of which is that it was built by Norsemen around A.D. 1000! Other possible builders include Native Americans, Portuguese sailors, the Irish, and English colonists. Although its design is indeed unusual, the most plausible story is that it was a windmill erected around 1660 by the first governor of the colony, one Benedict Arnold, a distant ancestor of the traitor.

Just north on Bellevue Avenue stands the **Redwood Library and Athenaeum** (11). Peter Harrison, regarded as America's first great architect, built this structure—the oldest library building in the United States—in the pure Palladian style in 1748. Today's visitors can step inside to admire the collection of rare books and early American paintings by Gilbert Stuart and others. ☎ *(401) 847-0292. Open Mon.–Sat. 9:30–5:30, closed holidays. Donation.* ♿.

Also nearby is the:

NEWPORT ART MUSEUM (11), 76 Bellevue Ave., Newport, RI 02840, ☎ (401) 848-8200. *Open Memorial Day to Labor Day, daily 10–5; rest of year Tues.–Sat. 10–4 and Sun. noon–4. Adults $6, seniors & students $4, 12 and under free, reduced prices in winter.* ♿.

Newport's art museum is partly housed in the former ***Griswold mansion** of 1864, a magnificent example of the "stick style" so popular in the 19th century. Designed by Richard Morris Hunt, the architect of several grand mansions in Newport as well as other famous structures throughout the Northeast, it is used exclusively for the museum's superb changing exhibitions. A highly-regarded permanent collection of American art resides in the adjacent Cushing Memorial Gallery, a Beaux Arts structure of 1919.

Tennis anyone? If the sport excites you, be sure to stroll down the avenue to the:

INTERNATIONAL TENNIS HALL OF FAME (13), Newport Casino, 194 Bellevue Ave., Newport, RI 02840, ☎ 849-3990. *Open daily 10–5. Closed Thanksgiving and Christmas. Admission limited during tournaments. Adults $6, seniors $3.50, children under 16 $3, families $12. Gift shop.*

The world's largest tennis museum occupies the magnificent **Newport Casino** of 1880, once an exclusive country club of the Gilded Age. The shingle-style buildings were designed by Stanford White, probably the most

The Old Stone Tower

famous American architect of the 19th century. They were commissioned by two rowdy playboys whose antics did not amuse the then-leading social club, and quickly became a favorite gathering place for the more fun-loving members of society. National lawn-tennis championships were held here until 1915, and the tradition continues with professional tournaments today. The 13 historic **grass courts** are open to visitors for a fee; arrangements should be made in advance. Interactive video displays test visitors' tennis skills in the **museum** rooms, which also feature historical artifacts, trophies, art, memorabilia, and halls where the legendary greats are honored.

Along the way to the next attraction, you might want to make a little detour to **St. Mary's Roman Catholic Church** (14) at the corner of Memorial Boulevard and Spring Street. Those old enough to remember the days of Camelot will want to step inside to see the spot where President (then Senator) John F. Kennedy and Jacqueline Bouvier were married on September 12, 1953—ten years before his assassination ended an era. ☎ *(401) 847-0475. Open to visitors Mon.–Fri. 7:30–11 a.m.; services at posted times.* ♿.

*Bowen's Wharf (15) is the last stop in the historic district. A colorful place, it has a nice mixture of genuine seafaring atmosphere and attractive tourist amenities. A few commercial fishing boats still dock here, but mostly you'll see private pleasure craft. Numerous excursions ranging from an hour to a half-day in length are offered aboard schooners, sailboats, motorboats, and even a rumrunner from the Prohibition days of the 1920s. Departures are from Bowen's Wharf and the adjacent Bannister's Wharf. Besides the

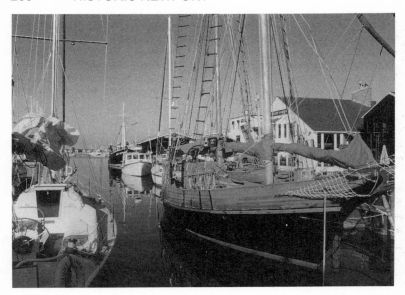

At Bowen's Wharf

boats, the area is thick with boutiques, crafts shops, restaurants, and cafés.

You could easily end the day right here, or retrieve your car (or rent a bike) and take a wonderful ride along **Ocean Drive**. To do this, just follow Thames Street south to Wellington Avenue, then turn right and continue along to:

FORT ADAMS STATE PARK (16), Ft. Adams Rd., Newport, RI 02840. ☎ *(401) 847-2400. Open daily year-round, dawn to dusk. Entry fee $4 per car for non-residents ($2 for seniors, free for handicapped) from Memorial Day through Labor Day, free rest of year. Picnicking, bathing beach, fishing piers, boat launching ramps, soccer and rugby fields.* &.

Erected in the early 19th century to protect Narragansett Bay and Newport Harbor, this massive fortress remained a command post for coastal batteries until 1945. Today, the fort itself is closed due to unsafe conditions, but the park around it offers a variety of activities along with a fabulous ***view** of Newport and its harbor. Both the Newport Folk Festival and the JVC Jazz Festival are held here each August, ☎ (401) 847-3700 for information.

Continue around to:

HAMMERSMITH FARM (17), Ocean Drive, Newport, RI 02840, ☎ 846-7346. *Open April through mid-Nov., daily 10–5, closing at 7 from Memorial Day through Labor Day, and at 4 during Standard Time. Also open weekends*

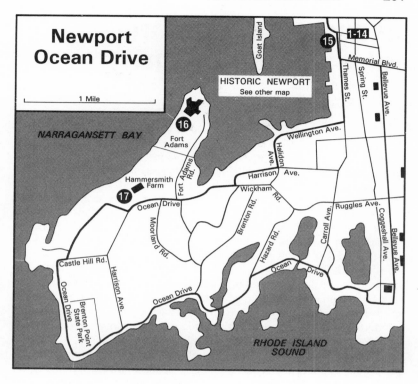

Newport
Ocean Drive

1 Mile

NARRAGANSETT BAY

HISTORIC NEWPORT
See other map

RHODE ISLAND
SOUND

from mid-March to April. Christmas tours in early Dec. Adults $7, children 6–12 $3. Guided tours. Gift shop.

Following their 1953 wedding at St. Mary's Church (14), the Kennedys had their reception at this lovely estate, a childhood home of Jacqueline Bouvier Kennedy. After becoming President, John F. Kennedy sometimes used it as his summer White House. Still the only working farm in Newport, Hammersmith dates back to 1640, although the mansion was built in 1887 by John Auchincloss, whose descendant Hugh married Mrs. Kennedy's mother. The gardens were created by Frederick Law Olmsted of Central Park fame, and of course there are great ***views**. Inside, the main house has been kept as it was during Jacqueline's childhood and during the Kennedy administration.

Continue along ***Ocean Drive**, a winding road that follows the coast and offers spectacular vistas, especially around sunset. You might want to make a rest stop at **Brenton Point State Park** (18), where the views are best, the parking free, and picnic tables are available. The drive eventually connects with Bellevue Avenue—the focus of the next daytrip.

Trip 31

*Newport Mansions of the Gilded Age

Long ago, in a fabled time well before income taxes, guilt trips, or air conditioning, the wealthiest families in America flocked to Newport to escape the summer heat. There they built their so-called "cottages," shamelessly ostentatious mansions that rival even the great palaces of Europe. Beginning in the mid-19th century and peaking early in the 20th, Newport's "Gilded Age" was the most opulent era in American history. An instant aristocracy of robber barons, flush with riches from the nation's booming industries, took pleasure in the lavish spending of fortunes.

Alas, it could not last. Taxes, the Great Depression, and a shortage of servants brought about the end of a fabulous period and left behind a string of "white elephants" that no one could afford to maintain. Nearly demolished to make way for subdivisions, the most flamboyant of the houses were saved from the wreckers' ball and are today Newport's number one tourist attraction. No visitor should fail to see at least one of them.

The best of the mansions open to the public are conveniently lined up along (or near) Bellevue Avenue, forming a strip of sumptuous wealth nearly two miles long. All but two are owned and operated by the Preservation Society of Newport County, a non-profit organization dedicated to saving the county's heritage. They offer a variety of combination tickets that can save you money if you plan to visit two or more buildings.

Along with man-made splendor, this trip also offers a chance to explore the marvelous Cliff Walk, a public pathway separating the mansions from the sea and offering magnificent vistas all along the way.

GETTING THERE:

By car, Newport is about 75 miles south of Boston. Take **MA-24** past Fall River and into Rhode Island. Continue south on **RI-138**, then turn south on **RI-138A** (Aquidneck Ave.), entering Newport on Memorial Blvd. A left turn onto Bellevue Ave. takes you to the mansions, each of which has free parking for visitors.

By bus, Newport is served from Boston's Back Bay Station by **Bonanza Bus Lines**, ☎ (401) 846-1820 or (800) 556-3815. Get off at Gateway Center and the tourist office, from which you can get a local bus or cab to the mansions.

PRACTICALITIES:

FOOD AND DRINK:

See the appropriate entries on pages 194 and 195.

LOCAL ATTRACTIONS:

You won't be able to see everything in a day, so pick and choose according to your interests. Allow at least an hour for each mansion. *Numbers in parentheses correspond to numbers on the map.*

KINGSCOTE (1), Bellevue Ave. at the corner of Bowery St., Newport, RI 02840, ☎ (401) 847-1000. *Open May–Sept., daily, 10–5; Apr. & Oct., weekends, 10–5. Adults $6.50, children (6–11) $3. Discount combo ticket with other properties available.*

One of the first of the "cottages," Kingscote was built in 1839 as a summer residence for George Noble Jones, a wealthy plantation owner from Savannah, Georgia. It was designed in the Gothic Revival style by the noted architect Richard Upjohn, with a later addition by McKim, Mead and White. Quite different from the other mansions, this rather unpretentious Victorian structure could actually be called charming. Since it is probably the least visited of the properties, you can enjoy an unhurried tour without crowding. The ***dining room**, added in 1881, is famous for its Tiffany glass wall. Other highlights include the cork ceilings, believed to be the first use of cork to control sound, Chinese art and porcelains, parquet floors, and early Rhode Island furniture by Goddard and Townsend.

Just a short distance south is:

THE ELMS (2), Bellevue Ave. at Dixon St., Newport, RI 02840, ☎ (401) 847-1000. *Open May–Oct., daily, 10–5; rest of year, weekends, 10–4. Adults $7.50, children (6–11) $3. Discount combo ticket with other properties available. Museum store.*

Saved from destruction in 1962, this 56-room classic French château is renowned for its magnificent ***sunken gardens** and 14 acres of beautifully-landscaped grounds complete with statuary, fountains, and marble gazebos. The "cottage" itself, completed in 1901, is a near copy of the 18th-century Château d'Asnières near Paris. It was built for Pennsylvania coal baron Edward J. Berwind, who amassed a great fortune selling coal to the U.S. Navy, and was designed by Philadelphia architect Horace Trumbauer. Mr. Berwind's sister continued to live here until her death in 1961, albeit often in the stables—which were considerably less expensive to heat. Beautifully restored, the enormous interior rooms reflect a refined French taste in the manner of Louis XV and Louis XVI.

Continue south to:

CHÂTEAU-SUR-MER (3), Bellevue Ave. at Shepard Ave., Newport, RI 02840, ☎ (401) 847-1000. *Open May–Sept., daily, 10–5; rest of year* *weekends and some holidays only, 10–5, closing at 4 in the off-season. Adults $6.50, children (6–11) $3. Discount combo ticket with other properties available.*

Despite its French name, this richly-appointed "cottage" is designed very much in the Victorian style. Its dark, heavy interior blends Turkish, Oriental, European, and American elements into an agreeable, almost cozy environment. When first built in 1852, it overlooked the sea, hence the name. Hemmed in by other mansions since then, it was rebuilt in 1872 by Richard Morris Hunt, a famous architect who went on to greater glories here in Newport. Many of the original furnishings are still in place, and there's a wonderful ***collection of Victorian toys** and dollhouses upstairs. Don't miss the distinctive **Chinese moon gate** on the south wall that once framed a view of the sea.

Head left towards the ocean and Newport's star attraction:

*THE BREAKERS (4), Ochre Point Ave., Newport, RI 02840, ☎ (401) 847-1000. *Open April–Oct., daily 10–5, also weekends in Nov. 10–4 and Holiday special in Dec. Adults $10, children (6–11) $3.50; price includes Breakers Stable. Discount combo ticket with other properties available. Museum store. Partially ♿.*

Cornelius Vanderbilt II (1843–99), son of William "The public be damned!" Vanderbilt and grandson of the Commodore, was regarded as the most parsimonious of men. You'd never know it from this place. Perhaps his wife had something to do with it, or maybe the great philanthropist had two sides to his personality, but in any case The Breakers is surely the most unabashedly grandiose "cottage" in all of Newport, if not in the entire Western Hemisphere. Conspicuous consumption takes on a whole new meaning for the ordinary folks who are ushered through on guided tours.

Whatever his motives, in 1893 Cornelius II engaged the great architect Richard Morris Hunt to build a replacement for their more modest mansion on the same property, which burned down in 1892. Resembling a 16th-century Genovese *palazzo* of the Italian Renaissance, The Breakers was completed in only two years—just in time for the debut of the Vanderbilt's eldest daughter, Gertrude. Needless to say, it was completely fireproof. Alas, Cornelius II had little time to enjoy the house as he suffered a stroke the next year and died in 1899.

The Breakers has a mere 70 rooms (after all, this was just a *summer* cottage), but some of them are pretty impressive. The ***Great Hall** soars 45 feet to a glorious, gilded *trompe-l'oeil* ceiling, from which hang four enormous chandeliers. To the side is the **Library** with its symbols of Vanderbilt wealth: cherubs holding a locomotive and a steamboat. The utterly fantastic ***fireplace** comes from 16th-century France. Nearby, the **Billiards Room** evokes images from a long-ago past, when gentlemen of leisure whiled away their time puffing on expensive cigars. Many social events took place in the

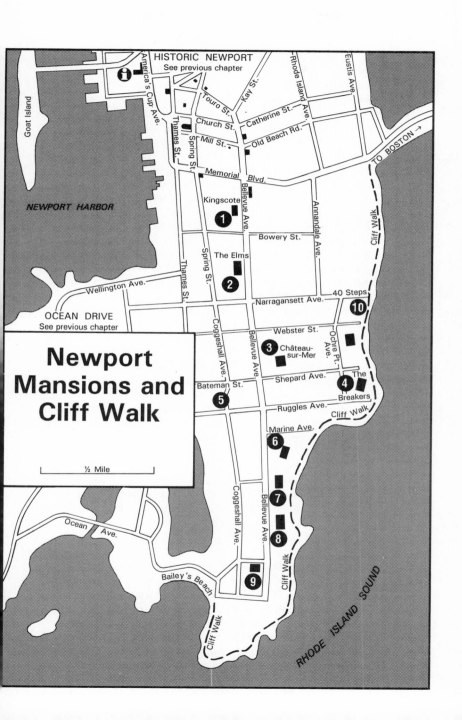

Newport Mansions and Cliff Walk

½ Mile

HISTORIC NEWPORT
See previous chapter

Goat Island

America's Cup Ave.

NEWPORT HARBOR

TO BOSTON →

Touro St.

Kay St.

Rhode Island Ave.

Eustis Ave.

Church St.

Catherine St.

Old Beach Rd.

Mill St.

Thames St.

Spring St.

Memorial Blvd.

Bellevue Ave.

Annandale Ave.

Kingscote

❶

Bowery St.

Cliff Walk

Spring St.

The Elms

❷

Thames St.

Wellington Ave.

OCEAN DRIVE
See previous chapter

Narragansett Ave.

40 Steps

❿

Coggeshall Ave.

Webster St.

Ochre Pt. Ave.

❸ Château-
sur-Mer

Bellevue Ave.

Shepard Ave.

❹ The
Breakers

Bateman St.

❺

Ruggles Ave.

Cliff Walk

Marine Ave.

❻

Coggeshall Ave.

❼

Bellevue Ave.

❽

Ocean Ave.

Bailey's Beach

❾

Cliff Walk

Cliff Walk

RHODE ISLAND SOUND

Grand Salon, or Music Room, built and furnished in France and shipped over in pieces. Perhaps the most spectacular of the rooms, however, is the 2,400-square-foot ***Formal Dining Room** with its Baccarat crystal chandeliers and 16th-century-style dining table seating 34 guests cushioned on hand-loomed damask. Somehow it's nice to know that the Vanderbilts usually took their meals in the simpler Breakfast Room.

As you stroll around the grounds outside, be sure to visit the delightful ***Children's Cottage**, a miniature version of the original mansion that burned down in 1892. It was here that the Vanderbilt girls learned the arts of gracious living by holding tea parties for their friends.

During the summer season, admission to The Breakers includes a visit to:

THE BREAKERS STABLE (5), Coggeshall Ave. at Bateman St., Newport, RI 02840, ☎ (401) 847-1000. *Open late May to early Sept., daily 10–5. Adults $3.50, children (6–11) $2, free for visitors to The Breakers.*

The horses may have departed to an equine Heaven, but otherwise the stables and carriage house remain much as they were some 80 years ago. Built in 1895 by Richard Morris Hunt, the same architect who created The Breakers (and much of Newport), this impressive structure features some 30 vehicles including the famous Vanderbilt "Venture" coach.

Nearby, and also overlooking the sea, is:

*ROSECLIFF (6), Bellevue Ave., Newport, RI 02840, ☎ (401) 847-1000. *Open April–Oct., daily 10–5. Adults $6.50, children (6–11) $3. Discount combo ticket with other properties available.*

If you've ever been to Versailles in France you'll know where the inspiration for this nifty château came from. Loosely based on Louis XIV's Grand Trianon by the famed architect Stanford White, Rosecliff was built in 1902 as a summer "cottage" for the Hermann Oelrichses of New York. Not only is its ***ballroom** the largest in Newport, it is also the loveliest. A grand heart-shaped ***staircase** lends a romantic touch, as does the rose garden. Some of the most outlandishly lavish social events in Newport's history took place here. Rosecliff has been used several times as a movie location, specifically for *The Great Gatsby* in 1974 and *True Lies* in 1994.

Practically next door is:

THE ASTORS' BEECHWOOD (7), 580 Bellevue Ave., Newport, RI 02840, ☎ (401) 846-3772. *Open Feb.–mid-May, Fri., Sat., Sun. 10–4; mid-May–Oct., daily 10–5; Nov.–mid-Dec., daily 10–4. Times may vary for private functions. Adults $7.75, seniors (65+) and children (6–12) $6. Special events, tea dances, and murder mysteries.*

A visit to the independently-owned Beechwood is really a ***theatrical event**, quite unlike anything else in Newport. Mrs. Caroline Schermerhorn Astor was the undisputed Queen of American Society in the late 19th

The Breakers

century, and set the standards by which the Old Rich were distinguished from the merely filthy rich. Today, the Astor family, friends, and servants are impersonated by actors who will greet you at the door and make you feel as though you were really a member of "The 400." Step back into the 1890s as you experience the upstairs/downstairs world of *the* Mrs. Astor, all the while having a lot of fun.

It's only a short stroll back into the decidedly less proper milieu of the *Nouveau Riche* at:

*MARBLE HOUSE (8), Bellevue Ave., Newport, RI 02840, ☎ (401) 847-1000. *Open April–Oct., daily 10–5; Jan.–March, weekends and holidays, 10–4. Adults $6.50, children (6–11) $3. Discount combo ticket with other properties available. Museum store. Partially ಹ.*

Millions of dollars' worth of imported marble were used to construct this elegant pile. Completed in 1892 for yachtsman William K. Vanderbilt, brother of Cornelius II (see The Breakers, above), Marble House was designed by Richard Morris Hunt. Unlike his dour brother, William thoroughly enjoyed the indulgences of the super rich, and lived accordingly.

Enter through the ten-ton gate and admire the Gobelin tapestries in the entrance hall. The extravagant ***Gold Room**, Newport's most lavish ballroom, is of course richly gilded in the real stuff. All of the furnishings, here and throughout the mansion, are original. Medieval art objects are displayed in the restored **Gothic Room**, while the **Dining Room** is furnished with bronze chairs so heavy that each guest required the services of a footman in order to sit down.

Stepping outside, be certain to visit the ***Chinese Teahouse** overlooking the sea *(open May–Oct.).* Added in 1913 by craftsmen brought over from China for the project, it is perfect in every way—except that there is no provision for making tea! This slight oversight was remedied by the addition of a miniature railway from the main house, on which rode footmen holding aloft silver trays while passing through the shrubbery. You'll have to walk there, however.

There's one more mansion to see, and it's not far away:

BELCOURT CASTLE (9), 627 Bellevue Ave., Newport, RI 02840, ☎ (401) 846-0669. *Open Feb.–Mar., daily 10–4; April–Memorial Day, daily 10–5 with tours at 11, 1, & 2; Memorial Day–mid-Oct., daily 9–5 with tours hourly; mid-Oct.–Nov., daily 10–4 with tours at 11, 1, & 2; special Christmas season tours daily in Dec. Adults $6.50, seniors & college ID $5, students (13–18) $4, children (6–12) $2. Scheduled guided tours are $1 extra. Private, ghost, and French history tours extra, reserve. Partially ♿ on request.*

Privately owned and still occupied, Belcourt was erected in 1893 for Oliver Hazard Perry Belmont, heir to the American Rothschild fortune. Architect Richard Morris Hunt based his design on French King Louis XIII's 17th-century hunting lodge. In 1896 Mr. Belmont married Alva, the divorced wife of his neighbor, William K. Vanderbilt (see Marble House, above). Surviving the gossip, she became a leading hostess in Newport society, and (after the death of Mr. Belmont) a (gasp!) suffragette, artist, and champion of the poor.

Following the death of Mrs. Belmont in 1933, the mansion changed hands several times, and for a short time around 1955 was the site of the Newport Jazz Festival. Neighbors soon put a stop to that, after which it was sold to the Harold B. Tinney family, who live there and operate it as a museum.

The 60-room ***interior**, furnished with priceless antiques, is every bit as splendid as you would expect. Of particular note is the ***Gold Coronation Coach**, a fabulous 1969 replica of an 18th-century Portuguese original.

After all this opulence, it's a relief to do something that costs nothing. Like many of the best things in life, the ***Cliff Walk** (10) is free. Extending some three miles from Memorial Boulevard south to Bailey's Beach, the path follows the rocky shoreline between the water's edge and the "cottages" of the super rich. The ***views** are quite wonderful, even if the trail is a bit rough in spots. Sometimes it even tunnels under private property. Although it can be accessed from several spots, the best place to get on it is at the Forty Steps, at the eastern end of Narragansett Avenue. Street parking is usually possible there.

Bristol and Portsmouth

Easy to access, yet a bit off the beaten path, the eastern shore of Narragansett Bay between Newport and Providence offers a wealth of unusual attractions that are all too often overlooked. Newport may have its ostentatious mansions; Bristol is blessed with more subtle affairs. Blithewold remains a supreme example of gracious living at the turn of the century, while the golden age of yachting is celebrated at the Herreshoff Marine Museum. Brown University's Haffenreffer Museum of Anthropology explores local Native American life before the first Europeans arrived, and the Coggeshall Farm Museum demonstrates agriculture in the 1700s. Children, gardeners, and just about anyone else will savor a visit to the Green Animals Topiary Garden. Two more historic Colonial structures, Prescott Farm and Whitehall, can be visited before returning home.

Much of this area was originally inhabited by the Wampanoag Indians, who got along well with the first white settlers. All of this changed in 1675, when the Indian leader known as King Philip began his bloody war against the Pilgrims. In the end, the conflict spread across much of New England, with the Native Americans the losers. The victorious colonists prospered, first from farming and later from shipbuilding. It was shipping, and in particular the slave trade, that brought great wealth to Bristol, reflected today in the surviving homes along Hope Street.

There is far more here than can be seen in one day, so you'll have to pick and choose carefully. Those able to stay overnight can enjoy more of the sights, or perhaps combine this trip with one to nearby Newport, Providence, or Fall River in Massachusetts.

GETTING THERE:

By car, Bristol is about 67 miles south of Boston. Take Route **MA-24** past Fall River and into Rhode Island. Get off at the Mount Hope Bridge exit and cross the toll bridge into Bristol. From other points in New England you might come by way of Providence or Newport.

For Portsmouth and Middletown, recross the bridge and head south towards Newport, following the map to specific sites.

PRACTICALITIES:

Avoid making this trip on a Monday or during the winter season (November through March at the least), when several of the best attractions are closed. Check the individual listings for each place that interests you as their opening times vary considerably.

For further information about the Bristol sites contact the **Bristol County Chamber of Commerce** at 654 Metacom Ave., PO Box 250, Warren, RI 02885, ☎ (401) 245-0750. For those in Portsmouth and Middletown contact the **Newport County Convention & Visitors Bureau** at 23 America's Cup Ave., Newport, RI 02840, ☎ (401) 849-8098 or (800) 326-6030.

FOOD AND DRINK:

You'll find plenty of places to eat here, especially chain restaurants along the main roads. Some excellent choices for lunch are:

Seafare Inn (3352 East Main Rd. in Portsmouth, just off RI-138 near Island Park) Fabulous seafood in a 19th-century mansion. Dress nicely and make reservations. ☎ (401) 683-0577. X: Mon. $$$

The Lobster Pot (119 Hope St., RI-114, in Bristol) Serving seafood along the waterfront since 1929. Reservations suggested. ☎ (401) 253-9100. X: Mon. $$ and $$$

Rhea's Family Restaurant (120 West Main Rd., RI-114, in Middletown) Simple meat and seafood dishes, plus Italian and Greek specialties. ☎ (401) 841-5560. $ and $$

Sandbar (755 Hope St., RI-114, in Bristol) Seafood platters, fish & chips, chowders, pasta, and sandwiches—all are bargains at this unpretentious little eatery. ☎ (401) 253-5485. X: Mon. $

Golden Goose Deli (365 Hope St., RI-114, in Bristol) Sandwiches, salads, chowders, and healthy alternatives, plus sinful desserts. ☎ (401) 253-1414. $

Aidan's Pub (5 John St., by the ferry dock in Bristol) Traditional Irish pub fare in a friendly setting. ☎ (401) 254-1940. X: Mon. $

LOCAL ATTRACTIONS:

Numbers in parentheses correspond to numbers on the map.

*BLITHEWOLD MANSION & GARDENS (1), 101 Ferry Rd, Bristol, RI 02809-0716, ☎ (401) 253-2707, FAX (401) 253-0412. *Grounds open year-round, daily except Mon. and holidays, 10–5. Mansion open Apr.–Oct., daily except Mon. and holidays, 10–4. Guided tours Apr.–Oct. Grounds only: Adults $4, children $1. Tour of mansion and gardens: Adults $7.50, children $2.50. Gift shop. Special events.*

Blithewold means "Happy Woods" in Old English, and indeed there is something especially joyful about this place. Huge it certainly is, yet very much alive with the spirit of the people who lived here. Pennsylvania coal baron Augustus Van Wickle built the original mansion as a gift for his wife, Bessie, in the late 19th century. Unfortunately, Augustus was killed in a hunting accident just four years later. His widow, remarried to a Boston merchant, continued to live there until the house burned down in 1906. The present structure, built in the style of a 17th-century English manor, was

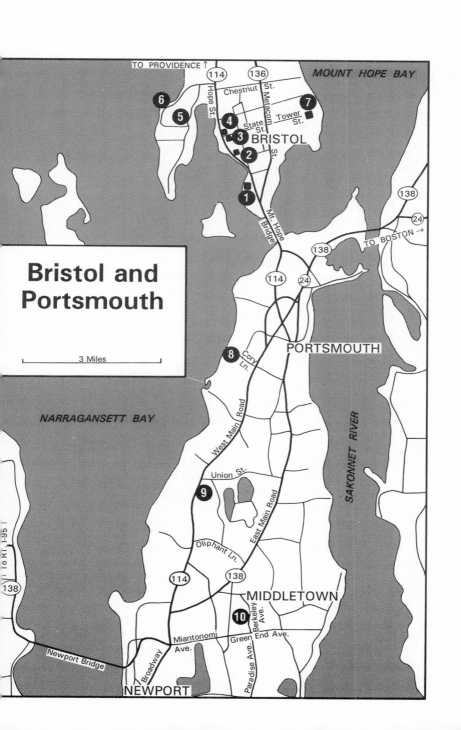

completed in 1908. Shown on an excellent *guided tour, it contains most of the original furnishings, which were saved from the flames. The Van Wickle's daughter Marjorie spent her summers here until passing away in 1976 at the age of 93, bequeathing the property to the Heritage Trust of Rhode Island for the enjoyment of future generations.

Every bit as appealing as the house, the delightful *gardens should not be missed. The best way to see them is on the guided tour, after which you can wander around on your own. Don't miss the giant 86-foot-tall sequoia, the exotic Oriental trees, the bamboo grove, the water garden, or the rock garden. Finish your tour off with a visit to the dock, where the Van Wickles parked their 72-foot-long Herreshoff yacht. If you'd like to see where these magnificent boats came from, you can drive north on RI-114 (Hope St.) just a short distance to the:

HERRESHOFF MARINE MUSEUM (2), 7 Burnside St., just east of Hope St., Bristol, RI 02809, ☎ (401) 253-5000. *Open May–Oct., Mon.–Fri. 1–4 and Sat.–Sun. 11–4. Adults $3, seniors $2, children (12–18) $1, under 12 free, families $5.* ⓗ.

From 1863 until 1945, the legendary Herreshoff Manufacturing Company, located right here, built some of the best yachts in the world, including eight successful America's Cup defenders and the first torpedo boats for the US Navy. Some 47 of the boats are on display at the museum, along with engines, fittings, photos, and memorabilia. The **Young Mariners' Discovery Center** demonstrates the fundamentals of marine science to school-age children, while the **America's Cup Hall of Fame** celebrates that most exciting of international competitions with models and videos.

Continue up Bristol's lovely *Hope Street, lined with historic homes and gardens dating from palmier days. The **Bristol Historical & Preservation Society Museum & Library** (3) is located in the old county jail, built in 1828 using stone ballast from Bristol sailing ships. All sorts of memorabilia are on display, including a few items owned or used by famous visitors. ☎ *(401) 253-7223. 48 Court St., just east of Hope St. Call for hours.* **Linden Place** (4) is the fanciest mansion in town, and once served as a backdrop for the 1974 movie *The Great Gatsby*. Well worth a visit, it was built in 1810 by General George DeWolf, a financial schemer and slave trader who lost his ill-gotten fortune in 1825. After he fled to Cuba in the middle of the night, creditors descended on the house and stripped it bare. Left to bankrupt relatives, it eventually became a boarding house, and then was mysteriously sold to the daughter of the original owner, who had inherited some of the Colt firearms fortune. Besides the restored mansion, the property includes an 18th-century summer house, a 19th-century carriage barn, and a ballroom building of 1906. ☎ *(401) 253-0390. 500 Hope St., near State St. Open Memorial Day–Columbus Day, Thurs.–Sun., 10–2, and by appt. Modest admission.* ⓗ.

Blithewold Mansion

Two smaller attractions lie on a peninsula just west of Bristol, reached by continuing north on Hope Street (RI-114), then turning left on Poppasquash Road. The **Coggeshall Farm Museum** (5) in Colt State Park re-creates agricultural life on an 18th-century Rhode Island coastal farm, complete with period chickens, sheep, cattle, and oxen. ☎ *(401) 253-9062. Open Tues.–Sun., 10–5 (4 in winter), closed Jan. Modest admission fee.* H. Just west of it is **Colt Drive** (6), a picturesque three-mile shoreline drive overlooking Narragansett Bay. Set on the former Colt family estate, the park provides picnic facilities, hiking trails, fishing, boating, and the like. *Colt State Park,* ☎ *(401) 253-7482. Open daily, dawn to dusk. Nominal charge per car.* ♿.

Another attraction in Bristol, reached by heading east on State Street, crossing Metacom Avenue (RI-136), and continuing east on Tower Road, is the:

HAFFENREFFER MUSEUM OF ANTHROPOLOGY (7), Tower Road, Bristol, RI 02809, ☎ (401) 243-8388. *Open June–Aug., Tues.–Sun. 11–5; and Sept.–May, weekends 11–5. Adults $2, children (4–12) $1.*

Long before the mansions and yachts, or even the Colonial farms, this land was home to Native Americans. The story of the Wampanoag Indians, along with other native peoples of North, Central, and South America,

Africa, and the Pacific islands, is documented here at Brown University's superb museum of anthropology. King Philip, the leader of the Wampanoag tribe, settled his people on this site during the 17th century, and it was here that he was killed in 1676, ending the bloody uprising known as King Philip's War.

From here you can return across the Mount Hope Bridge onto the original Rhode Island, a 15-mile-long island stretching south to Newport. Among the local attractions, the best known is:

GREEN ANIMALS TOPIARY GARDEN (8), 380 Cory's Lane (turn right off RI-114 about 3 miles south of the bridge), Portsmouth, RI 02871, ☎ (401) 683-1267. *Open end of April till end of Oct., daily 10–5. Adults $6.50, children (6–11) $3. Combination ticket with Newport mansions available. Toy museum. Gift shop.*

Small children love this whimsical place, and so do adults. Twenty-one *animals and birds are sculpted from living California privet and yew, including a camel, a giraffe, and a teddy bear. Begun in 1880, the topiary garden also contains some 60 trees and shrubs carved into geometric figures and ornamental designs, along with espaliered fruit trees, a rose arbor, and formal flower beds. The main house, overlooking the bay, has a wonderful **museum of Victorian toys**. For the horticulturally inclined there's a plant shop, along with a gift shop.

Continuing south on RI-114 soon brings you to the **Prescott Farm** (9), a restored Colonial complex with an operating windmill from around 1812. During the Revolutionary War, the farmhouse was occupied by British General William Prescott, who was captured here on July 9, 1777 in a daring raid and later traded for an American general. He was the highest-ranking prisoner taken during the conflict. Besides the farmhouse, there's a country store offering products of the farm and mill. ☎ *(401) 847-6230, 2009 West Main Rd. (RI-114), Middletown, RI. Open Apr.–Nov., Mon.–Fri. 10–4. Adults $2, children $1.* ♿.

Finally, almost in Newport, is the **Whitehall Museum House** (10) of 1729. To get there, continue south on RI-114. Shortly after it merges with RI-138, turn left on Miantonomi Avenue, which becomes Green End Avenue. Turn left again onto Berkeley Avenue in Middletown. The Irish philosopher and bishop, George Berkeley (1685–1753), built this hip-roofed country house during his three-year stay in America awaiting royal funds to establish a college in Bermuda. The money never came, so he returned to Ireland and left the property to Yale University for rental income. Now restored to its original condition, it is open to visitors in the summer. ☎ *(401) 846-3116. 311 Berkeley Ave., Middletown, RI. Open July–Labor Day, daily 10–5, and by appt. Adults $3, children $1.*

Section V

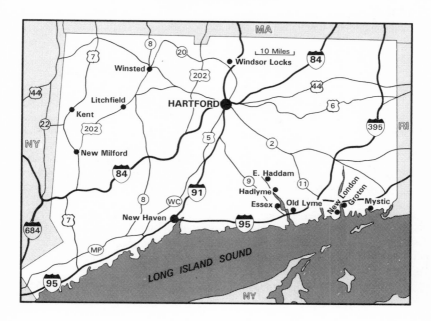

DAYTRIPS TO
CONNECTICUT

First explored by the Dutch in 1614, Connecticut quickly became an English colony populated by religious dissidents from Massachusetts. They adopted America's first written constitution as early as 1639, which is why it proudly calls itself the "Constitution State." More than 350 years of colorful history have packed the nation's third-smallest state with a remarkably wide range of attractions, from the wonderfully re-created seaport of Mystic to quirky little discoveries of the Tobacco Valley; from the stunning modern architecture of Hartford and New Haven to the pastoral delights of the Litchfield Hills.

All of the excursions in this section will take you about a hundred miles or so from Boston, or less from most other bases in New England. If time, money, and energy permit, why not combine several of these trips into one short vacation, taking advantage of the wonderful country inns and B&Bs that Connecticut is famous for?

Trip 33
*Mystic

If you visit only one place in Connecticut, make sure it's Mystic. This is easily one of the finest—and most enjoyable—restored villages in the United States, every bit as compelling in its way as Colonial Williamsburg or Old Sturbridge.

The Pequot Indians called the place "Missituk," meaning Great Tidal River, but their village was destroyed in a 1637 war with English settlers allied with other Native American tribes. For the next few centuries the area flourished as a shipbuilding and whaling center. Today, lovingly preserved, Mystic is Connecticut's leading year-round tourist destination.

For those able to stay another day or two, this trip combines well with the following ones to Groton/New London and the Connecticut River Valley.

GETTING THERE:

By car, Mystic is about 106 miles southwest of Boston via Route **I-95** to Exit 90 in Connecticut, where you turn south on **CT-27** for about a mile to Mystic Seaport.

For downtown Mystic, continue south on CT-27 (Greenmanville Ave.), taking the third right after the Seaport and crossing the drawbridge on Main St. (US-1).

For Stonington, go south on CT-27, then east on **US-1**. Continue south on Water St. (US-1A) past the Old Village Green to the Lighthouse Museum.

For the Denison Homestead and Pequotsepos Nature Center, return on US-1, turning north on Hewitt Rd. in Mystic, left on Mistuxet Ave., then right on Pequotsepos Rd.

The Mystic Aquarium is located just south of I-95 Exit 90 at CT-27, on Coogan Blvd. behind Olde Mistick Village.

The simplest way to Foxwoods is to take I-95 north to Exit 92, then CT-2 west past North Stonington to the reservation.

By train, Mystic is less than 2 hours southwest of Boston's South Station via **Amtrak**, ☎ 800-USA-RAIL for schedules and fares. The station is about a mile south of the Seaport; for the other sites you should take a cab.

PRACTICALITIES:

You won't be alone in Mystic, especially in the summer season. Actually, late spring and early fall are better times to visit. Allow an absolute minimum of three hours for the Seaport, even if you have to drop the other attractions, and try to get there as early in the day as possible to beat the crowds.

Mystic Seaport is open every day except Christmas; the Aquarium every day except Thanksgiving, Christmas, New Year's, and the last week of January. The Old Lighthouse Museum, Denison Homestead, and Pequot-sepos Nature Center follow a more complex schedule, generally being closed on Mondays or Tuesdays, and in winter.

For further information contact the **Southeastern Connecticut Tourism District**, 470 Bank St., New London, CT 06320, ☎ (860) 444-2206 or (800) TO-ENJOY; FAX (860) 442-4257; OR the **Mystic & Shoreline Visitor Information Center**, Bldg. 1D, Olde Mistick Village, Mystic, CT 06355, ☎ (860) 536-1641.

FOOD AND DRINK:

Mystic offers a vast selection of restaurants in every possible price range, from fast-food to the most elegant. A few good choices are:

Floodtide (Inn at Mystic, US-1 at CT-27, about a mile south of the Seaport) Continental and American cuisine in a splendid setting with a view. Indoor and outdoor dining. Sunday brunches. Reservations advised. ☎ (860) 536-8140. $$$

Seamen's Inne (105 Greenmanville Ave., at the north entrance of the Seaport) A lovely Colonial restaurant with classic New England cuisine. ☎ (860) 536-9649. $$

J.P. Daniel's (CT-184 in Old Mystic, about 2 miles north of I-95, just east of CT-27) Continental dishes in a friendly country setting. ☎ (860) 572-9564. $$

Two Sisters (4 Pearl St., off W. Main St., a few blocks west of the drawbridge) All manner of creative sandwiches, salads, and desserts. ☎ (860) 536-1244. $

Mystic Pizza (56 W. Main St., 4 blocks west of the drawbridge) The movie made it famous, and the food's still good. ☎ (860) 536-3737. $

LOCAL ATTRACTIONS:

Numbers in parentheses correspond to numbers on the map.

*MYSTIC SEAPORT (1), 75 Greenmanville Ave. (CT-27), Mystic, CT 06355, ☎ (860) 572-5315. *Open every day except Christmas: Spring & fall 9–5, summer 9–6, winter 10–4. Adults $16, children (6–15) $8, 5 and under free; second consecutive day free; group rates by advance reservation. Special events, crafts demonstrations, cruises (extra fee), shops, ✗, ☕. Partially ♿.*

One of New England's premier attractions, Mystic Seaport is an authentically re-created seafaring community of the 19th century; frozen in time and preserved for all to enjoy. With the decline of the shipbuilding industry following World War I, much of New England's maritime heritage was threatened. In 1929 several Mystic residents formed an association to save this legacy, which over the years grew into the non-profit Mystic Seaport Museum of today. A visit here, besides being educational, is also a lot of fun.

As you enter, you'll be given a map of the 17-acre site along with a schedule of the day's events. One of the major attractions is the only surviving American wooden sailing ship, the *Charles W. Morgan*. Built in 1841 and now a National Historic Landmark, she continued her trade until 1921, making some 37 voyages lasting up to four years. Climb aboard and go below deck to find out what life was like for those who sailed on her. Two other sailing vessels that may be boarded are the *Joseph Conrad*, a naval training ship of 1882, and the *L.A. Dunton*, a Gloucester fishing schooner of 1921. In season, for a modest additional charge, you can take a half-hour *excursion on the *Sabino* of 1908, the last coal-fired passenger steamboat still in operation in the U.S.A. Evening cruises lasting 1½ hours are also offered. Nearby is the **Henry B. DuPont Preservation Shipyard**, where you can observe restoration work being performed on vessels. More boat rides— sail, motor, or row-it-yourself— are offered in season (for an extra charge) at the Boathouse west of the *Sabino* Dock.

There's more to Mystic Seaport than just boats, of course. Covering much of the land area is a restored *maritime village** made up of authentic old buildings brought here from elsewhere. Nearly all of these are open to visitors, many are staffed with interpreters in period costume, and several feature demonstrations of old-time crafts and skills. Among them are houses, shops, a bank, a tavern, a school, a chapel, a ropewalk, a sail loft, a chandlery, and more. *Horse-and-carriage rides** through the village are available in season, for a small additional fee.

A museum area in the northern part of the Seaport includes the *Stillman Building**, whose exhibits trace local maritime history and include a wonderful collection of unusual scrimshaw along with ship models. Figureheads and decorative ship carvings fill the **Wendell Building**, while the North Boat Shed displays small boats and, adjacent, a marvelous ship's cabin from an 1883 "Down Easter." There's also a **Children's Museum** and a **Planetarium** with shows on navigation (extra fee).

Continue south on CT-27. If you'd like to visit **Downtown Mystic** (2), an attractive area of shops, art galleries, restaurants, and waterfront activity, just take the third right onto Holmes Street to Main Street (US-1), then turn right across the delightful old drawbridge.

Taking US-1 east a few miles, then US-1A south, brings you to the picturesque old town of **Stonington**, founded in 1649 and still a prosperous maritime place. Head down Water Street to **Cannon Square**, a lovely bit of green with two cannons that defended the town during the War of 1812. Continue almost to the water's edge, where you'll find the:

OLD LIGHTHOUSE MUSEUM (3), 7 Water St., Stonington Village, CT 06378, ☎ (860) 535-1440. *Open May–June and Sept.–Oct.,*

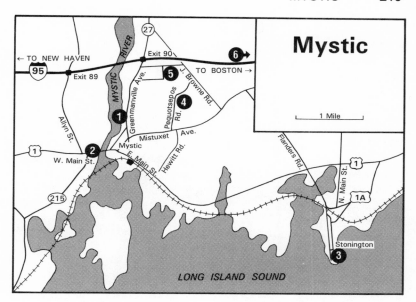

Tues.–Sun. 11–5; July & Aug. daily 11–5. Adults $3, children (6–12) $1.

Connecticut's first government-operated lighthouse, dating from 1823, today serves as a museum for whaling and fishing gear, arms, toys, articles from the Oriental trade, and other items of local history. There's also a ***great view** from the tower, extending across the Long Island Sound.

Back in Mystic, you can follow the map to the **Denison Homestead** and the **Denison Pequotsepos Nature Center** (4), both along Pequotsepos Road. The Homestead dates from 1717 and is furnished by descendants of the original settler, in the styles of five different eras: Colonial kitchen, Revolutionary bedroom, Federal parlor, Civil War bedroom, and a mid-20th-century living room. The nearby Nature Center covers some 125 acres and offers over seven miles of hiking trails through four distinctly different habitats. The Center also has a museum of native wildlife, an outdoor flight enclosure for raptors, and seasonal exhibits. *Homestead:* ☎ *(860) 536-9248. Open mid-May to mid-Oct., daily except Tues., 1–5. Adults $3, children $1. Nature Center:* ☎ *(860) 536-1216. Open Jan.–Apr., Tues.–Sat. 9–5; May–Dec. 25, Tues.–Sat. 9–5 and Sun. noon–5. Adults $3, children over 5 $1.*

Besides the seaport, Mystic's other great attraction is the:

*MYSTIC MARINELIFE AQUARIUM (5), 55 Coogan Blvd., Mystic, CT 06355, ☎ (860) 572-5955. *Open daily 9–5, closing at 6 in summer. Closed*

Mystic Seaport

Thanksgiving, Christmas, New Year's, and last full week in Jan. Adults $9.50, seniors $8.50, children (3–12) $6.50. Gift shop. ♿.

Thousands of sealife specimens from the world's oceans inhabit this vast indoor/outdoor complex, where a variety of natural habitats have been re-created. Daily demonstrations in the **Marine Theater** feature beluga whales and Atlantic bottlenosed dolphins, while sea lions and seals cavort on **Seal Island** and penguins have their own pavilion.

Practically next door to the Aquarium is **Olde Mistick Village**, a complete shopping center, almost a town, dressed up as an 18th-century village complete with a gristmill, meeting house, and bricked walks. You could easily end your day shopping here, or head up the road a few miles to have a fling with Lady Luck at **Foxwoods Casino** (6), the only such gaming facility in New England. Among the games offered are blackjack, craps, roulette, baccarat, poker, keno, slots, horse racing, or even "high stakes" bingo. There are also several restaurants, big-name entertainment, theaters, an arcade, and a resort hotel. *Route CT-2, Ledyard, CT 06339,* ☎ *(860) 885-3000 or (800) PLAY BIG. Open daily, 24 hours.*

Groton and New London

From exploring the inner depths of a nuclear submarine to climbing aboard a magnificent Tall Ship, from wandering through an historic seaport to relaxing at one of Connecticut's best beaches, there's a multitude of interesting things to do in the neighboring towns of Groton and New London.

Submarines are what Groton is all about, and you can relive their history at the U.S.S. *Nautilus* Submarine Force Library and Museum. Here you can also squeeze through the narrow passageways of the berthed *Nautilus*, the world's first nuclear sub. Memories of an earlier era, the Revolutionary War, are brought to life at the nearby Fort Griswold Battlefield State Park.

Just across the Thames River is the U.S. Coast Guard Academy, where a self-guided tour is offered to visitors. With luck, you'll arrive on a day when the U.S.C.G. Barque *Eagle*, "America's Tall Ship," is in port and you can go aboard.

Founded in 1646, the old town of New London was always a seafaring place. Much of its historic core near the City Pier survives and can be seen on an interesting walking tour. There is also an attractive art museum and an excellent beach with a small amusement park.

If you're able to stay overnight, this trip could easily be combined with the previous one to Mystic, or the following one to the Connecticut River Valley.

GETTING THERE:

By car, Groton is about 110 miles southwest of Boston via Route **I-95** to Exit 86 in Connecticut. Go north on **CT-12** about 1½ miles, then left on Crystal Lake Rd. to the Historic Ship *Nautilus* and its museum, located next to the U.S. Naval Submarine Base.

Return along the river on Military Highway and Thames St. to the National Submarine Memorial, just south of the I-95 bridge.

Head east a block, then south on Monument St. to the Fort Griswold Battlefield State Park.

Return to I-95 (South) and cross the big bridge over the Thames to New London. Get off at Exit 83 and follow signs north about a mile to the U.S. Coast Guard Academy. On the way back from the academy you'll pass the Lyman Allyn Museum.

Head south of I-95 into the town of New London, passing Ye Antientist Burial Ground along Huntington St. The Historic District centers on State St./Captain's Walk, the harbor, and Bank St. Follow signs to the Joshua

Hempsted House at the corner of Hempstead, Jay, and Truman streets.

Ocean Beach Park, about 3 miles to the south, is reached via Pequot or Ocean avenues.

By train, New London is a bit less than 2 hours southwest of Boston's South Station via **Amtrak**, ☎ 800-USA-RAIL for schedules and fares. You'll need to take local buses or taxis to the sites.

PRACTICALITIES:

Most of the sites are open daily, except that the *Nautilus* is closed on Tuesdays during the off-season and every day in early May and early December. The Lyman Allyn Museum is always closed on Mondays and major holidays. The Hempsted House and Monte Cristo Cottage have complex opening times that should be checked if you plan to visit them. Ocean Beach Park is closed from early September through mid-May.

When crossing the bridge over the Thames on I-95, look to the right to see if the Tall Ship *Eagle* is anchored there; this may help you to decide whether to visit the Coast Guard Academy.

For further information contact the **Southeastern Connecticut Tourism District**, 470 Bank St., P.O. Box 89, New London, CT 06320, ☎ (860) 444-2206 or (800) TO ENJOY; FAX (860) 442-4257. Ask about the 2½-hour **Oceanographic Cruises** (860-445-9007) offered in summer from Avery Point in Groton.

FOOD AND DRINK:

> **Lighthouse Inn** (6 Guthrie Place, overlooking the sea, on the way to Ocean Beach Park south of New London) Seafood with landlubber alternatives, in a Victorian setting. Sunday brunches. Dress well and reserve. ☎ (860) 443-8411. $$$

> **Ye Olde Tavern** (345 Bank St. in the historic section of downtown New London) Famous for steak, seafood, and the like. ☎ (860) 442-0353. X: Sun. lunch. $$

> **Recovery Room** (443 Ocean Ave./ Rte. 213, on the way to Ocean Beach Park south of New London) Excellent pizza. ☎ (860) 203-443. $

In addition, you'll find the usual run of chain and fast-food emporiums in both towns.

LOCAL ATTRACTIONS:

> *Numbers in parentheses correspond to numbers on the map.*

*U.S.S. *NAUTILUS* MEMORIAL / SUBMARINE FORCE LIBRARY & MU-SEUM (1), Crystal Lake Rd., Groton, CT 06349, ☎ (860) 449-3174 or (800) 343-0079. *Open April 15–Oct. 14: Wed.–Mon. 9–5, Tues. 1–5; Oct. 15– Apr. 14: Wed.–Mon. 9–4. Closed early May and early Dec. for mainte-*

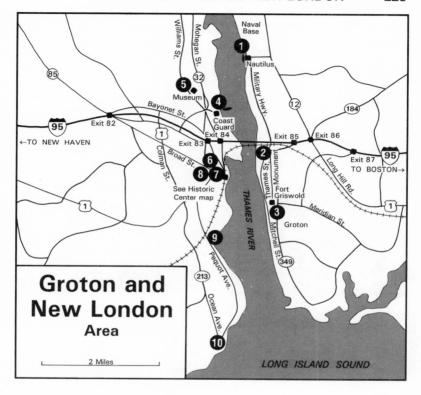

Groton and New London Area

2 Miles

nance, also Thanksgiving, Christmas, and New Year's. Free. Museum, video shows. Expect crowds during peak tourist season. ♿, *but not aboard submarine.*

You won't actually go for a dive, but a visit aboard the U.S.S. *Nautilus* offers at least a glimpse of life beneath the waves in the world's first nuclear submarine. Launched here in Groton in 1954, she has a glorious history of "impossible" adventures including the first trip by any ship to the North Pole. Eventually her technology was surpassed by newer nuclear submarines, and *Nautilus* was designated a National Historic Landmark in 1982. Still afloat, she receives visitors on self-guided audio ***tours** through the most interesting parts of the cramped interior.

Submarines are nothing new to the U.S. Navy. In the adjacent ***Museum** you can inspect a re-creation of the *Turtle*, an underwater craft that saw service in the Revolutionary War! There are plenty of other things to see in this thoroughly modern facility, and you can even peep through a working periscope while pretending to sink enemy ships.

The USS Nautilus

Turn right at the exit and follow south alongside the Thames River on Military Highway and Thames Street. After passing under the I-95 bridge you'll come to the **National Submarine Memorial** (2), built around the conning tower of the U.S.S. *Flasher* of World War II as a remembrance of the 52 U.S. submarines that perished during that conflict.

Head east a block, then go south on Monument Street to the:

FORT GRISWOLD BATTLEFIELD STATE PARK (3), Monument St. at Park Ave., Groton, CT 06340, ☎ (860) 445-1729. *Museum and tower open Memorial Day to Labor Day, daily 9–5; Labor Day to Columbus Day, weekends 10–5. Free.*

Benedict Arnold, an American whose very name means traitor, led British troops in a massacre of Colonial defenders here in 1781. The whole sad story is recalled in museum exhibits, and you can climb the 135-foot **Memorial Tower** for a sweeping ***view** of the Thames River estuary.

Return to I-95 South, cross the bridge to New London, and follow signs to the:

U.S. COAST GUARD ACADEMY (4), 15 Mohegan Ave., Rte. 32, New London, CT 06320, ☎ (860) 444-8270. *Open to visitors daily 9–5; Visitors Center open May–Oct., daily 10–5, and weekends in April 10–5. Tall Ship*

On board the USCG Barque Eagle

Eagle open when in port, ☎ *(860) 444-8595 for times. Free. Gift shop.* ✗. *Partially* ♿.

Begin your visit at the **Visitors Center**, where you can park, watch a video about the service, and obtain a map for a self-guided walking tour of the academy. The installation is rather hilly, so you may prefer to drive around instead. Among the attractions is the **Museum**, featuring historical arti-facts, ship models, and art. With luck, you'll be able to watch a dress parade of cadets; with even greater luck you can board the Tall Ship ***U.S.C.G. Barque *Eagle***. Built in 1936 in Hamburg, Germany and originally named the *Horst Wessel*, it was seized as a war reparation following World War II and still serves as a floating classroom, giving cadets their first taste of life at sea. With speeds up to 17 knots, *Eagle* regularly sails to Europe and the Carib-bean on training missions. It is the largest Tall Ship flying the American flag, the only square-rigger in government service, and a proud sight indeed.

On the way back to town you'll pass the:

LYMAN ALLYN ART MUSEUM (5), 625 Williams St., New London, CT 06320, ☎ (860) 443-2545, FAX (860) 442-1280. *Open July–Labor Day, Tues.–Sat. 10–5 and Sun. 1–5; Labor Day–June, Tues.–Sun. 1–5. Closed Mon. and major holidays. Adults $3, seniors & students $2, 12 and under free. Gift shop.* ♿.

Collections spanning five continents and five thousand years fill this small museum with art, antiques, toys, and all manner of interesting artifacts. The museum is especially noted for its paintings by Connecticut Impressionists, Hudson River School artists, early New England portraits, tribal arts from Africa, and decorative arts from Asia.

Continue south on Williams Street, passing I-95 and turning left onto Huntington Street to **Ye Antientist Burial Ground** (6) on the right. Established in 1653, this is the oldest graveyard in the county and features many fascinating tombstones of unusual design. It is said that the traitor Benedict Arnold rested here while helping the British burn New London in 1781, an act that must have caused more than a few bodies to turn in their graves.

You might want to park nearby and explore the **Historic Downtown** (7) section of New London on foot. Just down Huntington Street is **Whale Oil Row**, a group of 1832 Greek Revival houses built by leaders in the whale-oil business. Turn left on Captain's Walk/State Street past the Public Library of 1892 and the Soldiers & Sailors Monument of 1896. Just beyond is the **Union Railroad Station** of 1885, still used by Amtrak, the Waterfront Visitor Center, and the City Pier. From around here you can watch submarines, or catch a ferry to Block Island (RI) or Long Island (NY). Head south on Bank Street to the **U.S. Custom House**, built in 1833 of local granite. It houses a small museum of maritime artifacts. ☎ *(860) 447-2501. Open Mon., Wed., Fri., 1–4. Nominal fee.* ⟁. Two more blocks down Bank Street brings you to the **Shaw Mansion**, Connecticut's naval war office during the Revolutionary War and now a small museum of early New England history. ☎ *(860) 443-1209. Open May–Oct., Wed.–Fri. 1–4, Sat. 10–4, closed major holidays. Adults $3, seniors $2, children (5–12) $1.*

Also nearby, reached on foot or by car, are the:

HEMPSTED HOUSES (8), 11 Hempstead St., New London, CT 06320, ☎ (860) 443-7949. *Open mid-May to mid-Oct., Thurs.–Sun. noon–4. Adults $4, under 18 $1.*

The Joshua Hempsted House, New London's oldest surviving dwelling, dates from 1678 and is a showcase for early American furnishings. Of special interest is the Hempsted family diary, a rich source of information about everyday life in Colonial times. While there, you can also visit the Nathaniel Hempsted House of 1759, a rare example of cut-stone architecture of the era. Again, it's furnished with period pieces.

Back in your car, follow Bank and Howard streets followed by Pequot Avenue to the:

MONTE CRISTO COTTAGE (9), 325 Pequot Ave., New London, CT 06320, ☎ (860) 443-0051. *Open Memorial Day–Labor Day, Tues.–Sun. 10–5. Adults $4, under 13 free.*

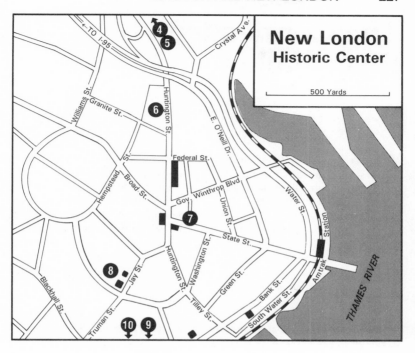

The playwright and Nobel prize winner Eugene O'Neill (1888–1953) spent his boyhood summers in this frame dwelling overlooking the Thames estuary. Now restored, the National Historic Landmark cottage was also the setting for two of his works: *Long Day's Journey Into Night* and *Ah, Wilderness!* Besides various memorabilia, visitors can also watch a multimedia presentation on his life.

To end the day, why not continue south on Pequot or Ocean Avenue to **Ocean Beach Park** (10), where you can take a dip in the Olympic-size pool or Long Island Sound, ride the triple waterslide, or just stroll the boardwalk? There's also miniature golf, arcade games, kiddie rides, food concessions, and the like. ☎ *(860) 447-3031 or (800) 962-0284. Open Memorial Day weekend through Labor Day, 8–midnight. Parking fee $2 per hour, maximum of $10 per day.*

Trip 35

The Connecticut River Valley

Whether your interests extend to history, art, scenic splendor, riding preserved steam trains and riverboats, or just enjoying the great outdoors, you'll find plenty of attractions along this lower section of the Connecticut River Valley. Settled since the early 17th century (and with many rich stories to tell), the region remains unspoiled by mass tourism. Its small Colonial villages, broad river, and thickly forested banks take the modest number of discriminating visitors back in time to a kinder, gentler era where they can experience some of the best qualities that New England has to offer.

Those able to stay overnight might consider combining this trip with the previous ones to nearby Mystic and Groton/New London.

GETTING THERE:

By car, Old Lyme ia about 123 miles southwest of Boston via Route **I-95** to Exit 70 in Connecticut. Follow signs to the museum, nearby.

Continue south on I-95 across the river to Exit 69 and take **CT-9** about 4 miles north to Exit 3, Essex. Follow signs to the attractions.

For the Gillette Castle continue north on CT-9 about 5 miles to Exit 6, then east on **CT-148** through Chester to the ferry. *If the ferry isn't running, take CT-154 north to East Haddam, then CT-82 south to the Gillette Castle.*

From the castle head north on **CT-82** about 6 miles to East Haddam. An alternative route back to Boston is to take CT-9 or CT-2 to Hartford, then I-84 and I-90.

PRACTICALITIES:

Check the opening times of each attraction carefully, as some are closed or operate on weekends only in the off-season. Museums in general are closed on Mondays. The valley is especially beautiful during the fall foliage season.

For further information contact the **Southeastern Connecticut Tourism District**, P.O. Box 89, New London CT 06320, ☎ (860) 444-2206 or (800) TO ENJOY, FAX (860) 442-4257 (for Old Lyme); OR the **Connecticut River Valley & Shoreline Visitors Council**, 393 Main St., Middletown, CT 06457, ☎ (860) 347-0028 or (800) 486-3346, FAX (860) 346-1043 (for the river valley).

FOOD AND DRINK:

Some recommended places for lunch are:

Old Lyme Inn (85 Lyme St., Old Lyme, near the Griswold Museum) Quality American cuisine in elegant surroundings. Reservations advised. ☎ (860) 434-2600. X: early Jan. $$$

Bee & Thistle Inn (100 Lyme St., Old Lyme, near the Griswold Museum) Contemporary American cuisine served in a romantic 1756 house. Noted for its Sunday brunch. Reservations advised. ☎ (860) 434-1667 or (800) 622-4946. X: Tues. $$ and $$$

Griswold Inn (36 Main St., Essex, near the River Museum) Serving traditional American cuisine since 1776. The Sunday Hunt Breakfast (11–2:30) is a great value. Reservations advised. ☎ (860) 767-1776. $$ and $$$

She Sells Sandwiches (Brewers Dauntless Shipyard, Essex, at the waterfront) Light breakfasts and creative lunches outdoors, overlooking the marina. ☎ (860) 767-3288. $

Additionally, there are a few chain restaurants near major exits along I-95. Better yet, pack a picnic lunch to enjoy at Gillette Castle, where sheltered tables are provided.

LOCAL ATTRACTIONS:

Numbers in parentheses correspond to numbers on the map.

FLORENCE GRISWOLD MUSEUM (1), 96 Lyme St., Old Lyme, CT 06371, ☎ (860) 434-5542, FAX (860) 434-6259. *Open June–Oct.: Tues.–Sat., 10–5, Sun. 1–5.; Nov.–May: Wed.–Sun. 1–5. Closed some major holidays. Adults $4, seniors $3, children under 12 free. Guided tours, video show. Gift shop.* ♿.

It is one thing to see significant art in a conventional museum; quite another to encounter it in the very surroundings in which it was created. The American Impressionist school of art flourished here around the turn of the century, when several noted New York painters took lodgings at Miss Florence's boarding house in Old Lyme, intent on capturing bucolic visions of an unspoiled land. Several of their works were painted right on the door panels of the house; others on canvas were given to Miss Florence. The best known of the artists was Childe Hassam (1859–1935), who trained in France and was deeply influenced by Monet.

The house itself, a late Georgian mansion built in 1817 as an extension of an earlier structure, is of great interest. Before falling on hard times, the Griswold family was quite prosperous, and the building has been restored to reflect this. Besides works of art by the various boarders, the galleries feature changing exhibitions of mostly local art. Don't miss the gardens, or the fully restored **studio** of William Chadwick, another noted American Impressionist.

While in the area, you might want to visit the nearby **Lyme Academy of Fine Arts**, an accredited art school located in a landmark 1817 house. Its galleries hold changing exhibitions of contemporary and traditional paintings and sculpture. *84 Lyme St.* ☎ *(860) 434-5232. Open Tues.–Sat. 10–4, Sun. 1–4. Donation.*

Return to I-95, cross the Connecticut River, and immediately take Exit 69. Follow Route CT-9 north for about 4 miles to Exit 3 and the:

ESSEX STEAM TRAIN & RIVERBOAT RIDE (2), Valley Railroad, Railroad Ave., Essex, CT 06426, ☎ (860) 767-0103. *Operates May through Oct. on varying days (daily in peak season), plus holiday specials in Nov., Dec., Feb., Mar., and Apr. Call for current schedules. Train & boat combination: Adults $14, children (3–11) $7. Train only: Adults $8.50, children $4.25. Senior discount. Children under 3 free. Parlor car extra. Other plans, group rates, and special events are offered. Diesel traction is sometimes substituted for steam.* ✗. *Gift shop.*

A vintage steam train uses some 3,000 gallons of water and three tons of coal to take you on an ***hour-long journey** into the past, whistling and chugging its way up the scenic Connecticut River from Essex to Deep River Landing. Here you can transfer to an old-fashioned riverboat for an additional hour's voyage farther upriver, passing green hills dotted with fine old houses and landmarks such as Gillette Castle and the Goodspeed Opera House, both of which are described below.

The train, powered by a classic steam-belching, bell-clanging locomotive, follows the route of the former Valley Railroad, which ran between Hartford and Old Saybrook from 1871 until it was gobbled up by J.P. Morgan's New York, New Haven & Hartford line.

Even if you don't have time for the train ride, at least stop by to examine the vintage equipment on display and perhaps watch some steam activity. Doing this costs nothing, and may lure you into taking the ride anyway.

Continue east to the village of Essex. Founded in 1648, Essex remains a wonderfully preserved river town whose prosperity derives from shipbuilding. Its past is fascinating, and can be best explored at the foot of Main Street in the:

CONNECTICUT RIVER MUSEUM (3), 67 Main St., Steamboat Dock, Essex, CT 06426, ☎ (860) 767-8269. *Open year round, Tues.–Sun. 10–5. Closed Mon. and major holidays. Adults $4, seniors $3, children (9–12) $2, under 9 free. Gift shop.* ♿.

Recently restored, this 1878 dockhouse features permanent and changing exhibitions celebrating the Connecticut River Valley's long and colorful history. Its prize possession is a replica of America's first submarine, the *Turtle*, launched in 1775 to blow up British ships, an endeavor at

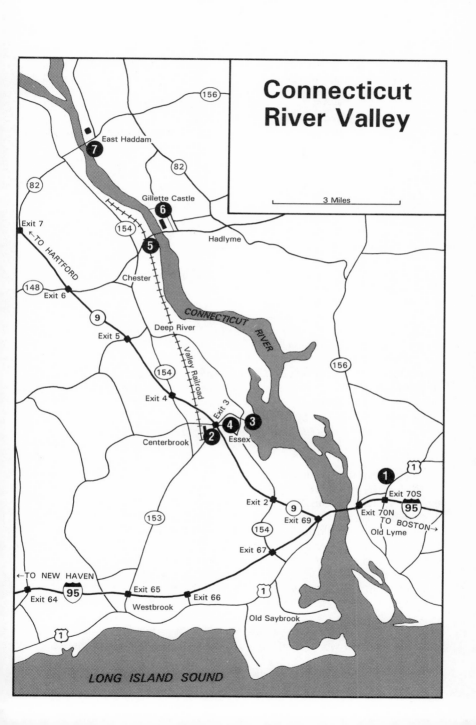

Connecticut River Valley

3 Miles

which it was none too successful. There are also ship models, navigation instruments, industrial artifacts, and a brass steamship bell that you can ring.

While in Essex, you might also want to visit the:

PRATT HOUSE (4), 19 West Ave., Essex, CT 06426, ☎ (860) 767-1191. *Open mid-June to Labor Day, Sat. & Sun. only, 1–4. Adults $2, children under 12 free.*

This two-story vernacular 1732 homestead, built by the locally famous Pratt family and owned by the Essex Historical Society, is furnished with artifacts of the 17th, 18th, and 19th centuries. There are fine collections of Connecticut redware, courting mirrors, and a herb garden.

Return to CT-9 and head north to Exit 6, then go east through picturesque Chester for a short voyage on the venerable:

CHESTER–HADLYME FERRY (5), ☎ (860) 566-7635. *Operates daily, April– mid-Dec., 7 a.m. to 6:45 p.m. Fares: Car & driver $2.25; additional pas- sengers, pedestrians, bikes, & mopeds 75¢.*

Follow signs to the state's second-oldest continuously operating ferry, in service since 1769 (but not with the same boat!). In a few waterborne minutes you'll be in Hadlyme, just under the magnificent:

*GILLETTE CASTLE STATE PARK (6), 67 River Rd., East Haddam, CT 06423 ☎ (860) 526-2336. *Grounds open all year daily 8–sunset; free. Castle open Memorial Day weekend to Columbus Day, daily 10–5; Columbus Day to last weekend before Christmas, Sat.–Sun. 10–4. Adults $4, children (6–11) $2, 5 and under free. Guided tours. Picnicking, hiking trails, fishing, ♨, gift shop. Leashed pets only, in picnic area only. Picnic shelter and ground floor of castle are ♿.*

High above the pastoral Connecticut River perches a bizarre dream ***castle** built by the great turn-of-the-century actor and portrayer of Sherlock Holmes, William Gillette (1853–1937). A native of Hartford, Gillette chose this site because of the superb ***view**. One of the first actors to hold that a characterization should be based on the performer's own strongest per- sonality traits, he applied the same principle to his castle, which he designed himself around 1914 and fitted out with strange mechanical devices of his own invention. He lived here from 1919 to 1937 with a supporting cast of up to 17 felines to whom he was greatly attached. The 24-room castle contains, among other things, a large collection of cat curios, along with scrapbooks, clippings, and other memorabilia of Gillette's stage career. There are also remnants of his private narrow-gauge railroad, a three-mile-long route over difficult terrain on which, playing engineer, he would terrify such house guests as Albert Einstein.

Today, Gillette's fieldstone creation is the centerpiece of a beautiful 184-

Gillette Castle

acre state park—a fact that reflects well on Connecticut in light of the stipulation in his will that the property should under no circumstances pass to "any blithering saphead who has no conception of where he is or with what surrounded."

Continue north on Route CT-82 to the riverside town of **East Haddam** (7), site of New England's longest remaining swing bridge and the venerable **Goodspeed Opera House**, a marvelously Victorian structure of 1876 located right at the bridge. Beautifully restored, the latter is famed for its productions of traditional musicals as well as new works, offered from April to December. ☎ *(860) 873-8668. Guided tours of the interior available in summer, call ahead.* Nearby, behind St. Stephen's Church, is the one-room **Nathan Hale Schoolhouse**, where the patriot taught in 1773. A few of his possessions are on display, along with artifacts of local history. ☎ (860) 873-9547. *Open on summer weekends, in the afternoon.*

Trip 36
New Haven

Museum fans will revel in this rewarding daytrip to New Haven, as will aficionados of fine architecture. From art to natural history, from musical instruments to old trolley cars, and from Colonial to Contemporary, you'll find quite a range of attractions on and near the lovely campus of Yale University.

New Haven began in 1638 when a group of Pilgrims laid out America's first planned city. Initially independent, it became part of Connecticut as early as 1662. An excellent harbor brought trade and, in 1716, the school that is still New Haven's greatest asset—Yale. Railroads, industry, factories, and immigrants followed in the 19th century, but by the mid-20th this boom turned to blight. Although much of the city has since been revitalized, some problems remain. Happily, the area of interest to tourists—the historic core and adjacent Yale campus—are as beautiful and welcoming as ever.

By staying overnight, this trip could easily be combined with the Connecticut River Valley, Hartford, or the Litchfield Hills.

GETTING THERE:

By car, New Haven is about 135 miles southwest of Boston. You have a choice of two fast routes. From center to center, the shortest way is via **I-90** (Massachusetts Turnpike) to Sturbridge, **I-84** to Hartford, then **I-91** into New Haven. Get off at Exit 3, Trumbull St. This route involves a toll road. Slightly longer, but free, is **I-93** south to Exit 1, then **I-95** via Providence and New London into New Haven. Go north on I-91 a short distance to Exit 3, Trumbull St., and head for The Green. There are several parking facilities in the area.

By train, service to New Haven from Boston's South or Back Bay stations, Providence, Mystic, or New London is provided by **Amtrak**, ☎ (800) USA-RAIL for schedules and fares. The ride from Boston takes upwards of three hours. New Haven's station is within walking distance of most of the sights, and there is a local bus.

PRACTICALITIES:

Avoid coming to New Haven on a Monday, when several major museums are closed. Hours of operation are reduced on Sundays. The University Art Gallery is also closed in August, and the Collection of Musical

Instruments on Mondays, Fridays, weekends, July, and August. Check times carefully to coincide with your interests. The best days to see the widest selection of museums are Tuesdays, Wednesdays, and Thursdays. For current details about the Yale University museums phone their Visitor Center at (203) 432-2300.

For further information contact the **Greater New Haven Convention & Visitors Bureau**, 1 Long Wharf Drive, New Haven, CT 06511, ☎ 777-8550 or (800) 332-7829.

FOOD AND DRINK:

There are plenty of good eateries around the Yale campus, especially in the lower price range. Some choices are:

Union League Café (1032 Chapel St., near the Center for British Art) French cuisine with creative touches, reservations suggested. ☎ (203) 562-4299. X: weekend lunch. $$ and $$$

Bruxelles (220 College St., a block southwest of The Green) Sophisticated contemporary cuisine in a lively setting. ☎ (203) 777-7752. $$

Louis' Lunch (261 Crown St., a block south of the Center for British Art) The great American hamburger was invented in this tiny diner about a century ago, and they still serve them their way. ☎ (203) 562-5507. X: Sun. $

Atticus Café (1082 Chapel St., next to the Center for British Art) Light lunches in a bookstore, very literary. ☎ (203) 776-4040. $

SUGGESTED TOUR AND LOCAL ATTRACTIONS:

Numbers in parentheses correspond to numbers on the map.

Nearly all of the attractions of New Haven are within comfortable walking distance of **The Green** (1), a 16-acre plot that has served as the town's common since 1638. In its center are three historic churches, whose present buildings date from around 1815. **Trinity Church**, near Chapel Street, is in the Gothic Revival style, while the **United Congregational Church** is a fine example of the Federal style. The latter contains America's first Hillebrand Tracker organ. Between them stands the **Center Church**, a Georgian beauty whose congregation first worshipped on this site in 1638. Built over an old burial ground, its crypt contains some 137 historic gravestones. *Tours offered Tues.–Sat., 10:30–3 and by appointment,* ☎ *(203) 787-0121.*

The **Yale University Visitor Center**, along the north side of The Green, offers maps and information for self-guided tours of the campus as well as student-led ***guided tours**. *149 Elm St.* ☎ *(203) 432-2300. Tours Mon.–Fri. at 10:30 and 2, Sat. & Sun. at 1:30. Free.*

For a short do-it-yourself tour that goes past the highlights and takes you to *all* of the university museums, begin at the **Phelps Gate** along the west side of The Green on College Street. Yale University was founded nearby in 1701 as the Collegiate School, but soon (1716) moved to New Haven and later changed its name in honor of its benefactor, Elihu Yale. A member of the Ivy League, it has some 10,000 students and about 4,000 faculty members. America's first Ph.D degrees were awarded by Yale in 1861. Although the campus is predominantly Gothic, there are also significant Georgian buildings, and quite a few outstanding modern structures by today's leading architects.

Enter the campus and pass **Connecticut Hall** on your left. Built in 1752, this is the university's oldest building. Nathan Hale lived here as a student, as did many other famous (and infamous) personages. Straight ahead is the **Harkness Tower** (2), a 220-foot-tall, highly ornamented bell tower in the Gothic Revival style. Built in 1920, it bears the famous inscription: "For God, for Country, and for Yale." Turn left on High Street to the:

*YALE CENTER FOR BRITISH ART (3), 1080 Chapel St., New Haven, CT 06520, ☎ (203) 432-2800. *Open Tues.–Sat. 10–5, Sunday noon–5. Closed Mon. and major holidays. Free. Gift shop.* ♿.

The largest collection of British art outside Great Britain resides right here in New Haven, housed in a stunning 1977 skylit building that was the last major work by architect Louis Kahn. Amassed over a period of forty years by art patron Paul Mellon, given to Yale in 1966 and later expanded, the paintings, sculptures, prints, and rare books comprise an exciting visual history of life in Britain from the reign of Henry VIII right down to the present. Among the artists represented are Hogarth, Gainsborough, Reynolds, Stubbs, Constable, and Turner.

Right across the street is the:

*YALE UNIVERSITY ART GALLERY (4), 1111 Chapel St., New Haven, CT 06520, ☎ (203) 432-0600. *Open Tues.–Sat. 10–5, Sun. 2–5. Closed Mon., major holidays, and Aug. Free.* ♿.

North America's oldest college art museum features some 75,000 works ranging from ancient times to the present. It was founded in 1832 and today occupies two handsome buildings: a 1928 structure in the Italian Romanesque style, and a modern 1953 addition by Louis Kahn. Whatever your tastes in art, you'll surely find something of interest here. On the ground floor, a collection of ancient art features a Mithraic temple from Roman Syria; Egyptian, Greek, Etruscan, and Roman sculptures; and a large selection of pre-Columbian artifacts. The first floor is mostly devoted to contemporary works and special exhibits, while Impressionists occupy much of the second floor. Pride of place among these goes to van Gogh's renowned **Night Café*, and there are works by Manet, Courbet, Millet, Corot, Degas, Renoir, and Matisse as well. Modern art is represented by such luminaries as Duchamp, Magritte, Stella, Dali, Tanguy, Ernst, Klee, Picasso, Kadinsky, Rothko, and de Kooning.

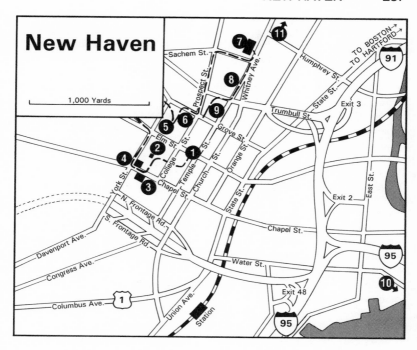

The third floor has a marvelous selection of medieval, Italian Renaissance, and Flemish Masters paintings. Perhaps the museum's greatest treasure is its ***Garven Collection** of early American furniture and decorative arts. There are also notable American paintings of the 19th and 20th centuries. Upstairs, the fourth floor is devoted to Asian art from ancient times to the present.

Turn right on York Street, first passing the boldly aggressive **School of Art and Architecture**, a 1964 work by Paul Rudolph noted for its spatial ingenuity, if not its interior comfort. Farther down the street, on the right, stands the **Wrexham Tower**, a duplicate of the historic 16th-century church tower in Wales near which Elihu Yale is buried. Bear left onto the recently revitalized Broadway, home to a thriving retail district that features the famous **Yale Co-op** store. To the right is **Ezra Stiles College**, designed by Yale graduate Eero Saarinen. The nearby **Payne Whitney Gymnasium** is one of the largest buildings in the world devoted to physical fitness.

Follow the map down Tower Parkway and around to the cathedral-like **Sterling Memorial Library** (5). With over four million volumes, manuscripts, archives, and even Babylonian tablets, Yale's main library offers plenty to look at. ☎ *(203) 432-2798. Open Mon.–Thurs. 8:30–midnight, Fri. 8:30–5, Sat. 10–5, Sun. 1 p.m.–midnight; shorter hours in summer. Free.* Even rarer volumes are displayed at the nearby **Beinecke Rare Book and Manuscript Library** (6). Translucent marble panels create an unusual lighting effect in this marvelous 1963 structure by Gordon Bunshaft. Inside, visitors can examine an original ***Gutenberg Bible**, Audubon prints, and changing exhibits. ☎ *(203) 432-2977. Open Mon.–Fri. 8:30–5, Sat. 10–5. Free.* &.

The **Grove Street Cemetery** has such illustrious permanent residents as Noah Webster, Eli Whitney, and Charles Goodyear, as well as a fine entrance gate. Head north on Prospect Street, turning right on Sachem Street to the:

*PEABODY MUSEUM OF NATURAL HISTORY (7), 170 Whitney Ave., New Haven, CT 06511, ☎ (203) 432-5050. *Open Mon.–Sat. 10–5, Sun. noon–5. Closed some major holidays. Adults $5, seniors and children (3–15) $3. Museum shop.* &.

Dinosaurs are the Peabody's specialty, and they've got plenty of them. Among the "terrible lizards" of yore on display are a 67-foot-long brontosaurus, a stegosaurus, and a horned beastie. A wonderful 110-foot-long mural by Rudolph Zallinger depicts the *Age of Reptiles* as it looked some 350 million years ago. Of course there's much more, including all manner of mammals and primates, artifacts of native cultures from the Americas and the Pacific, meteorites, minerals, and various flora and fauna.

Head south on Whitney Avenue to the **New Haven Colony Historical Society** (8), a good local history museum featuring exhibits of New Haven's cultural and commercial growth from 1638 to the present. ☎ *(203) 562-4183. Open Tues.–Fri. 10–5, weekends 2–5. Adults $2, seniors and students $1.50, children (6–16) $1. Gift shop.* &.

Heading back towards The Green on Hillhouse Avenue takes you past the intriguing **Yale Collection of Musical Instruments** (9). Ever see a Stradivarius? A real one? Or an oud, a koto, a moon guitar, or a stockflote? They're all here, along with harpsichords, virginals, fortepianos, and anything else that makes sweet music. With over 800 instruments from the 16th to the 20th centuries, the collection is rotated so that about a quarter of it is on display at any time. ☎ *(203) 432-0822. Open Sept. through June, Tues.–Thurs., 1–4. Closed during university recesses. Donation $1.*

ADDITIONAL SIGHTS:

The New Haven area boasts several other attractions, of which the following are especially recommended:

SHORE LINE TROLLEY MUSEUM (10), 17 River St., East Haven, CT 06512, ☎ (203) 467-6927. *Open Apr. & Nov., Sun. 11–5; May & Sept.–Oct., weekends 11–5; Memorial Day to Labor Day, daily 11–5; late Nov. to*

Christmas, weekends 11–5 with Santa on board. Adults $5, seniors $4, children (2–11) $2. Admission includes unlimited rides. Gift shop. Picnic area. From New Haven, take I-95 east to Exit 51, turn right onto Hemingway Avenue, then left onto River Street.

Nearly a hundred old trolley cars, interurbans, and rapid transit cars either clang their way along three miles of track or reside in the museum area, much to the delight of everyone. Not only can visitors ride them, they can also watch them being restored. Could anything be more fun?

ELI WHITNEY MUSEUM (11), 915 Whitney Ave. at Armory St., Hamden, CT 06517, ☎ (203) 777-1833. *Open Wed.–Fri. & Sun., noon–5; Sat. 10–3; closed Thanksgiving, Christmas, New Years. Adults $2.50, seniors & children $1.50. ♿. From New Haven, continue north on Whitney Avenue past the Peabody Museum and into Hamden.*

Besides inventing the cotton gin, Yale graduate Eli Whitney (1765–1825) pioneered the concept of mass production by being the first to use inter-changeable parts in the production of firearms. An amazingly inventive man, he altered the course of American history in more ways than one. This museum, complete with hands-on interactive exhibits, working models, and memorabilia, is devoted to the creative genius of a local lad who certainly made good.

Yale's Harkness Tower

Trip 37

Tobacco Valley

Here's an enjoyable scenic drive that neatly ties together several intriguing but often-overlooked sights in Connecticut's Tobacco Valley. Named for the "filthy weed" that long sustained its economy, the north central part of the state offers an unusually broad variety of attractions and lovely scenery within a compact area. Besides the historic homes there are also these highlights: The largest aviation museum in the Northeast, a chilling underground prison from Colonial days, and a marvelous collection of old-time trolleys that visitors can ride.

For a longer stay, why not combine this excursion with the ones to nearby Hartford, the Litchfield Hills, or Springfield in Massachusetts?

GETTING THERE:

By car, the Tobacco Valley lies nearly a hundred miles southwest of Boston. Take Route **I-90** (Massachusetts Turnpike) to Exit 9 at Sturbridge, then **I-84** south to Exit 73. From here head west on scenic route **CT-190** through Stafford Springs to Suffield, the beginning of the tour.

PRACTICALITIES:

Most of the attractions along the route are open from sometime in spring through the middle of fall; the minor ones only on specific days of the week. The New England Air Museum is, however, open daily all year round, except on Thanksgiving and Christmas. Your best bet is to make the tour toward the end of a week between Memorial Day and Labor Day. Be sure to check the opening times of any attractions that particularly interest you.

Attractions aside, this is a wonderful drive to make during the fall foliage season.

Visitors to the Old New-Gate site are advised to wear rubber-soled shoes, and to bring a sweater or light jacket for the damp underground section.

For further information contact **Connecticut's North Central Tourism Bureau**, 111 Hazard Ave., Enfield, CT 06082, ☎ (860) 763-2578 or (800) 248-8283, Fax (860) 749-1822. The Simsbury area is represented by the **Greater Hartford Tourism District**, 1 Civic Center Plaza, Hartford, CT 06103, ☎ (860) 520-4480 or (800) 793-4480, Fax (860) 520-4495.

FOOD AND DRINK:

Some choice places for lunch:

Simsbury 1820 House (731 Hopmeadow St., US-202, just south of Massacoh Plantation in Simsbury) This comfortable old country inn serves wonderful traditional American and Continental specialties. Reserve, ☎ (860) 658-7658. $$ and $$$

Albert's (159 Ella Grasso Tpk., CT-75, near the New England Air Museum) An excellent place for steak and seafood. ☎ (860) 292-6801. X: Sat. lunch. $$

Metro bis (928 Hopmeadow St., US-202, north from Massacoh Plantation in Simsbury) A French bistro decorated with artifacts of the Paris Metro. ☎ (860) 651-1908. X: Mon. $$

One-Way Fare (4 Railroad St. in Simsbury) Burgers, soups, chili and the like in a 19th-century railroad station. ☎ (860) 658-4477. $

LOCAL ATTRACTIONS:

Numbers in parentheses correspond to numbers on the map.

Begin your tour in **Suffield** (1), a small town established in 1670 on land purchased from the Indians. The main attraction here is the **Hatheway House** at 55 South Main Street (CT-75), the oldest section of which dates from 1761. A north wing in the new Federal style, added in 1794, reflects the growing prosperity of the region. Fancy French wallpaper, Hepplewhite, Sheraton, and Chippendale furniture, and a formal garden make this one of the most elegant mansions in Connecticut. ☎ *(860) 668-0055 or 247-8996. Open mid-May–June and Sept.–mid-Oct., Wed. and Sat.–Sun. 1–4; July & Aug., Wed.–Sun. 1–4. Adults $4, children under 18 $1.*

Another attraction in Suffield is the **King House Museum** at 232 South Main Street, a short stroll from the Hatheway House. Built in 1764, the house has original fireplaces, period furnishings, and a collection of tobacco artifacts to celebrate the local Colonial economy. ☎ *(860) 668-5286 or 668-2533. Open May through Sept., Wed. and Sat., 11–4. Nominal admission.*

Continue south on CT-75 to the area's most famous attraction, the:

*NEW ENGLAND AIR MUSEUM (2), Bradley International Airport, Windsor Locks, CT 06096, ☎ (860) 623-3305. *Open daily all year round, 10–5. Closed Thanksgiving and Christmas. Adults $6.50, children (6–11) $3. Gift shop.* ♿.

Over 70 magnificent flying machines, dating from 1909 to the near-present, are gathered together in two hangars and an outdoor area to form an exciting hands-on history of manned flight. World War II planes are especially well represented, with such proud examples as the B-25 Mitchell, the B-29 Superfortress, the P-47 Thunderbolt, the Corsair, the Wildcat, and the Hellcat. There are also warplanes from the Soviet Bloc, seaplanes, helicopters (a local specialty), a cockpit simulator, and videos to watch. Visitors coming on Open Cockpit Days can climb aboard some craft and live out their fantasies.

Turn west on CT-20 past East Granby, then north to the:

*OLD NEW-GATE PRISON and COPPER MINE (3), Newgate Rd., East Granby, CT 06026, ☎ (860) 653-3563 or 566-3005. *Open mid-May through Oct., Wed.–Sun. and holidays, 10–4:30. Adults $3, seniors and children (6–17) $1.50. Visitors are advised to wear rubber-soled shoes and a sweater or jacket; it's damp and chilly inside.*

What began in 1707 as America's earliest chartered copper mine became Connecticut's first state prison in 1773. The idea of housing convicts in these dark, damp subterranean dungeons might seem just a wee bit draconian today, but in Revolutionary War times it was a convenient (and probably cheap) place to dump them. During the conflict it held Tory sympathizers, and until 1827 was used for convicted criminals. Often considered the worst hell-hole in North America, the facility was named after London's notorious Newgate Prison—only here the inmates were confined some 50 feet underground, where they often succumbed to disease, insanity, or suicide. Today's visitors can probe the eerie passageways, and then make their escape!

Continue west on CT-20 to Granby, then turn south on US-202/CT-10 to **Simsbury** (4). Technically just outside Tobacco Valley and actually in the Farmington Valley, the small town still fits nicely into this trip. Settled in 1648 and totally destroyed during King Philip's War in 1676, Simsbury recovered quickly enough and prospered with the booming copper industry. Its main thoroughfare, Hopmeadow Street (US-202/CT-10), is named after the hops once grown in the area. Go down it to the town center, where you'll find the **Massacoh Plantation**, a complex of restored buildings representing three centuries of local history. Among them is a one-room schoolhouse of 1740; the 1771 **Phelps House**, once a tavern and now filled with period furnishings and costumes; a cottage and herb garden of 1795; and a Victorian carriage house of 1880. The only replica structure is the First Meeting House, originally built in 1683. There are many artifacts on display, perhaps the most interesting of which are the first copper coins struck in America, made locally in 1737. ☎ *(860) 658-2500. Open May–Oct., Sun.–Fri. 1–4, last tour at 3:30. Adults $5, seniors (60+) $4, children (5–18) $2.50.*

Continue south, then turn east on CT-185 for a few miles. A left turn on CT-178 leads to **Bloomfield**. By heading north on CT-189 for about four miles to just beyond the intersection with CT-187, you can visit the **Farm Implement Museum** (5) in North Bloomfield. Agricultural implements and hand tools dating as far back as 1790 are featured in this former tobacco barn, along with a working blacksmith shop and a petting zoo. ☎ *(860) 242-1130. Open Apr.–Oct., daily 9–5. Adults $2, seniors $1, under 12 free.* &.

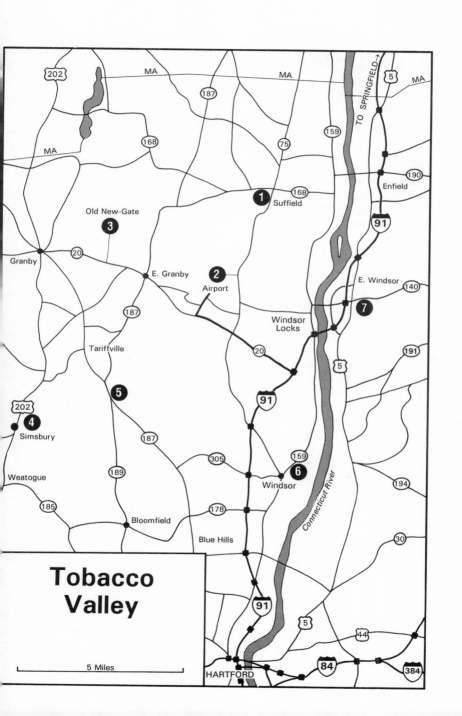

Tobacco Valley

5 Miles

Follow the map east to **Windsor**, home of the **Windsor Historical Society** (6) at 96 Palisado Avenue (CT-159, northeast of the intersection with CT-75). Windsor considers itself to be the oldest town in Connecticut, having been settled in 1633, but this claim is contested by Wethersfield. In any case, there's a lot of history on display in the two adjoining houses that make up this museum. The **Lieutenant Walter Fyler House** of 1640 is among the oldest surviving frame structures in the state, while the **Dr. Hezekiah Chaffee House** of 1765 is a lovely 3-story brick Colonial. Both are nicely restored and filled with period furniture and artifacts. Changing exhibits are featured, and there's a genealogical and historical library on the premises. ☎ *(860) 688-3813. Open Apr.–Nov., Tues.–Sat. 10–4; Dec.–March, Mon.–Fri. 10– 4. Closed major holidays. Adults $3, seniors $2, students and children under 12 free. Partially* &.

Head north on CT-159 and cross the Connecticut River on I-91. Get off at Exit 45 and go east on CT-140 a short distance to the:

*CONNECTICUT TROLLEY MUSEUM (7), 58 North Rd. (CT-140), East Windsor, CT 06088, ☎ *(860) 627-6540 or 627-6597. Open March– Memorial Day and Labor Day–Thanksgiving, weekends 11–5; Memorial Day to Labor Day, daily 11–5; special events in late Oct., late Nov., and Dec. Closed Easter, Thanksgiving Day, Dec. 24 & 25. Available for charters all year round. Unlimited rides: Adults $6, seniors (62+) $5, children (5–12) $3. Refreshments. Picnic area. Gift shop.*

Just about everyone loves to ride old trolley cars, especially these antiques. Some 50 trolleys and rail cars dating from around 1894 to 1949 are on display, with several carrying passengers on a three-mile round trip through the New England countryside. Don't miss this treat!

Just behind the Trolley Museum is the **Connecticut Fire Museum**, where the history of fire-fighting unfolds with a collection of vintage equipment dating from the 19th century to the mid-20th. There are also models and memorabilia on display. ☎ *(860) 623-4732. Open May–June and Sept.– Oct., weekends noon–5; and July–Aug., Mon.–Fri. 10–4, and weekends noon–5. Adults $2, seniors (65+) and children (5–12) $1.*

Hartford

Hartford may not be at the top of your destination list; America's Insurance City is hardly that exciting. On the plus side, however, it *is* blessed with several first-class attractions—and enough minor ones to make this a highly worthwhile excursion. Art lovers will surely enjoy the renowned Wadsworth Atheneum, while literary fans and history enthusiasts will revel in the colorful Mark Twain and Harriet Beecher Stowe houses. Along with its commercial prosperity, Hartford is also the capital of Connecticut, with all the attractions that entails. Having a history that stretches back over 350 years, it offers its share of well-preserved sites.

Yet another refuge from then-oppressive Massachusetts, Hartford—originally a Dutch trading post of 1633—was settled in 1635 by dissident followers of the Reverend Thomas Hooker, and named after Hertford in England. In 1639 it drew up a constitution, the first ever in the New World, which is why Connecticut calls itself the "Constitution State." Granted a good deal of independence by Charles II in 1662, the colony refused to surrender its charter to an English governor during the notorious Charter Oak incident of 1687.

Hartford's insurance business began in 1794 and has flourished ever since. By the late 19th century the city boasted the highest per capita income in the nation, attracting a talented population and resulting in a rich architectural and cultural heritage that serves it well today.

For those able to stay over a few days, this trip combines well with the ones to Tobacco Valley, the Connecticut River Valley, New Haven, or with Springfield in Massachusetts.

GETTING THERE:

By car, Hartford is about 102 miles southwest of Boston. Take **I-90** (Massachusetts Turnpike) to Exit 9 at Sturbridge, then **I-84** into Hartford. Get off at Exit 52 and park in a lot as close to Main Street or the Civic Center as possible.

After exploring downtown, you might want to use the car to reach the other attractions, instead of a longish walk or bus ride.

Trains operated by Amtrak provide service to Hartford from various points in New England, ☎ (800) USA-RAIL for details.

Buses connect Hartford's downtown Union Station Transportation Center with Boston and places all over New England. Check **Peter Pan Bus Lines**,

☎ (860) 724-5400 or (800) 237-8747; **Bonanza Bus Lines**, ☎ (860) 677-5466 or (800) 556-3815; or **Greyhound**, ☎ (860) 522-9267 or (800) 231-2222 for details.

PRACTICALITIES:

Avoid making this trip on a Monday or major holiday, when several of the best sights are closed. The State Capitol and the Museum of Connecticut History are closed on weekends and holidays, except that the capitol has tours on Saturdays from April through October. The fabulous Mark Twain House is closed on Tuesdays during the off-season. Hartford throbs with commercial vitality in weekdays; on weekends it is less crowded.

For further information contact the **Greater Hartford Tourism District**, 1 Civic Center Plaza, Hartford, CT 06103, ☎ (860) 520-4480 or (800) 793-4480, Fax (860) 520-4495, Web Site: http://www.travelfile.com/get?ghtd. Alternatively, contact the **Greater Hartford Convention & Visitors Bureau**, 1 Civic Center Plaza, Hartford, CT 06103, ☎ (860) 728-6789 or (800) 446-7811.

FOOD AND DRINK:

You'll find plenty of places for lunch all along the downtown walking tour, including food courts at State House Square, Civic Center, and The Richardson. Some choice restaurants are:

Gaetano's Ristorante (Civic Center, 2nd level) A casually elegant spot for Northern Italian cuisine. Reservations accepted, ☎ (860) 249-1629. X: Sat. lunch, Sun., holidays. $$ and $$$

Max on Main (205 Main St., south of the Butler-McCook House) Contemporary American/Italian dishes with a creative touch. Reservations suggested, ☎ (860) 522-2530. X: Sat. eve., Sun., holidays. $$ and $$$

Brown, Thompson & Company (942 Main St., in The Richardson) Housed in a historic building, this turn-of-the-century restaurant features a vast selection of American dishes. ☎ (860) 525-1600. X: Sat. lunch, Sun. lunch. $$

Museum Café (in the Wadsworth Atheneum) An unusually good museum restaurant. ☎ (860) 728-5989. X: Mon. $

SUGGESTED TOUR:

Numbers in parentheses correspond to numbers on the map. Begin your walk at the:

OLD STATE HOUSE (1), 800 Main St., Hartford, CT, ☎ (860) 522-6766. *Open Mon.–Sat. 10–5, Sun. noon–5; closed some major holidays. Free. Visitor information center, museums, gift shop, seasonal events.* ♿.

This elegant Federal structure was the first public commission of Charles

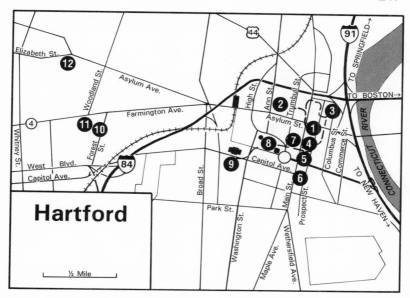

Bulfinch (1763–1844), one of America's best early architects. Bulfinch went on to design many other buildings, including the statehouse in Boston and the Massachusetts General Hospital, but is perhaps best remembered for bringing the Capitol building in Washington, D.C., to completion in 1830. The Old State House served as Connecticut's state capitol from 1796 to 1878, and as Hartford's city hall from 1879 to 1915. Today it is a National Historic Landmark, museum, and cultural center. A rare Gilbert Stuart full-length *portrait of George Washington hangs in the restored Senate Chamber. **Mr. Steward's Museum** of 1796 is still there, featuring such natural curiosities as a two-headed cow; and there's a fine **Museum of Connecticut History** in the new underground wing.

Stroll north along Main Street, possibly making a little side trip on lively old Pratt Street to the **Hartford Civic Center** (2). Whether you're here for a convention, entertainment, shopping, or dining, this vast modern complex has it all. An elevated skywalk leads to **CityPlace**, Connecticut's tallest building, a 1984 structure noted for its richly-landscaped atrium. Back on Main Street, **The Richardson** is a marvelous brownstone commercial building of 1877 that was salvaged and recycled as a shopping mall.

Follow the map around to **Constitution Plaza** (3). These dozen acres of elegant high-rises and landscaped promenades show the effects of urban renewal at its best. Completed in 1964, the plaza combines office space, shopping centers, and parking facilities. Among its features are the boat-shaped elliptical headquarters of the Phoenix Mutual Life, one of the few two-sided buildings on Earth, and the splashless fountain, designed to resists the fiercest provocations from the plaza winds.

Continue around to the **Travelers Tower** (4) of 1919, once the tallest structure in New England. The 527-foot tower was built by the Travelers Insurance Company, a venerable Hartford institution that got its start in 1863 by insuring a Captain James Bolter for $5,000 for a trip from his home to the post office at a premium of two cents. Plenty of other travelers put in their two cents' worth over the years, and the company grew to become one of the giants of the insurance field.

The Travelers Tower stands on a site once occupied by Sanford's Tavern, where in 1687 Sir Edmund Andros, James II's royal governor of New England, demanded the surrender of the original charter granted to the Connecticut colonists by Charles II in 1662. While Andros was engaged in heated debate with the colonists at Sanford's, Captain Joseph Wadsworth took the charter and squirreled it away in the hollow of an ancient white oak, where it remained safely hidden until the colonists succeeded in ridding themselves of the autocratic Andros. The Charter Oak, thought to have been more than 1,000 years old, succumbed to a storm in 1856, but the 1662 charter is on display in the Museum of Connecticut History, and the family tree lives on in the white oak on the grounds of the Center Church, just across Main Street.

Immediately south of the tower is the:

***WADSWORTH ATHENEUM** (5), 600 Main St., Hartford, CT 06103, ☎ (860) 278-2670. *Open Tues.–Sun. 11–5, closed Mon. and major holidays. Adults $5, seniors & students $4, children under 13 free. Free all day Thurs. and Sat. 11–noon. Gift shop.* ✕. ♿.

One of the nation's oldest and best public art museums, the Wadsworth Atheneum has a well-deserved reputation for the excellence and breadth of its collections. More than 45,000 art objects, from ancient Egyptian artifacts to contemporary sculptures, are on display here in spacious galleries occupying five interconnected buildings. There's an extensive selection of paintings representing every major period and style since the 15th century, with some particularly fine works by Monet, Renoir, and other 19th-century french artists. Also noteworthy are the collections of American and English silver, Meissen porcelain, furniture, and period costumes.

Directly south of the Atheneum is **Burr Mall**, a small park dominated by Alexander Calder's massive steel *Stegosaurus.* A little side trip can be made here by continuing south on Main Street to the:

BUTLER-McCOOK HOMESTEAD (6), 396 Main St., Hartford, CT 06103, ☎ (860) 247-8996. *Open mid-May to mid-Oct., Tues., Thurs., Sun. noon–4; closed holidays. Adults $4, children under 18 $1.*

This survivor of urban renewal stands in quaint contrast to the glittering office buildings of downtown Hartford. The oldest private home in the city (1782), it has been preserved as a museum of 18th- and 19th-century tastes in furnishings and decorative arts. On display are fine collections of silver, 19th-century American paintings, Chinese bronzes, Egyptian artifacts, toys, and dolls. The annual Victorian Christmas exhibit is a nice way to get into the spirit of the season.

Go back up Main Street. On the left, opposite Travelers Tower, is the **Ancient Burying Ground** (7), final resting place of some of Hartford's early settlers, with headstones dating back to 1640; look for the epitaph of Dr. Thomas Langrell, who "drowned in the glory of his years, and left his mate to drown herself in tears." Right by the cemetery stands the **Center Church** of 1807, patterned after London's St. Martin's-in-the-Fields, with stained-glass windows by Louis Tiffany. The church occupies the site where the U.S. Constitution was ratified by Connecticut in 1788.

Amble down Gold Street and into **Bushnell Park** (8). This was the first land in the United States to be claimed for park purposes under eminent domain, and was laid out according to a natural landscape design influenced by the ideas of Hartford native Frederick Law Olmsted. The **Pump House Gallery** in its southeast corner features exhibits by area artists. ☎ *(860) 722-6495. Open Tues.–Fri. 11–2. Free. H.* A popular spot for outdoor concerts and special events, the park is also the home of a restored **1914 Carousel**, a real beauty transported here from Canton, Ohio. For fifty cents you can ride one of the 48 brightly-painted hand-carved horses and try for the brass ring.

Dominating Bushnell Park is the:

STATE CAPITOL (9), 210 Capitol Ave., Hartford, CT 06106, ☎ (860) 240-0222. *One-hour tours begin at neighboring Legislative Office Building: Sept.–June, Mon.–Fri. 9:15 first tour, 1:15 last tour; July–Aug. Mon.–Fri. 9:15 first tour, 2:15 last tour. Open Sat. from Apr.–Oct., 10:15 first tour, 2:15 last tour. Closed state holidays. Free. ₺.*

Here is Hartford's most impressive building, seat of Connecticut government since 1879, housing the state executive offices and legislative chambers. A great gold-leaf dome presides over this eclectic architectural concoction by Richard Mitchell Upjohn. On the tour you'll see statues, murals, and historic displays featuring bullet-riddled flags, Lafayette's camp bed, and other reminders of Connecticut's past, as well as a plaster model of the Genius of Connecticut, which adorned the capitol spire until it was melted down during World War II.

From here you can either drive, take a bus, or hike to the:

HARRIET BEECHER STOWE HOUSE (10), Nook Farm, 77 Forest St.,

Hartford, CT 06105, ☎ (860) 522-9258. *Open Tues.–Sat. 9:30–4, Sun. noon–4; also on Mon. from June–Columbus Day and Dec. Closed major holidays. Adults $6.50, seniors (60+) $6, children (6–16) $2.75.*

Nook Farm is an old Hartford neighborhood that attracted a remarkable group of 19th-century writers and intellectuals connected by family ties and bonds of friendship. Among the distinguished company that settled here were women's-rights activist Isabella Beecher Hooker, playwright and thespian William Gillette (see Gillette Castle), Senator Joseph Hawley, and Charles Dudley Warner, editor of the *Hartford Courant* and coauthor with Mark Twain of *The Gilded Age.* Today most of Nook Farm has been torn down, but several of the original buildings remain, including the homes of its most famous residents: Harriet Beecher Stowe and Mark Twain.

Author Harriet Beecher Stowe settled into this Victorian "cottage" in 1873, and remained here until her death in 1896. The house certainly reflects the tastes of its owner: the design of the kitchen follows the specifications set forth in the book Stowe wrote with her sister, *The American Woman's Home;* some of her paintings hang on the walls; there are mementos of her career as a writer and reformer, and many original items of furniture, including the tiny desk at which she penned her most important work, *Uncle Tom's Cabin* (1852), a book that aroused popular sentiment against slavery and sold 300,000 copies within a year—a staggering figure in those days.

Whatever you do, don't miss seeing the nearby:

*MARK TWAIN HOUSE (11), Nook Farm, 351 Farmington Ave., Hartford, CT 06105, ☎ (860) 493-6411. *Open Mon. and Wed.–Sat. 9:30–5; also open Tues. from June–Columbus Day and in Dec. Closed New Year's, Easter, Thanksgiving, Dec. 24–25. Tours last 1 hour, last tour at 4. Adults $7.50, seniors (60+) $7, children (6–12) $3.50. Museum shop. Partially* ♿.

Mark Twain's house, designed by Edward Tuckerman Potter, is a colorful and idiosyncratic reflection of the author's personality, perhaps best appreciated by those who have read his works and know his humor. The south façade is modeled after a Mississippi River steamboat, the dressing room recreates a riverboat pilothouse, and the etched windows in the upstairs study, where Twain wrote *The Adventures of Tom Sawyer, The Adventures of Huckleberry Finn,* and five other books memorialize his great passions in life—smoking, drinking, and billiards. Twain lived at Nook Farm with his wife and three daughters from 1874 to 1891, when financial difficulties forced him to sell the house and take to the lecture circuit.

Game for more before calling it a day? It's only a hop to the:

CONNECTICUT HISTORICAL SOCIETY (12), 1 Elizabeth St., Hartford, CT 06105 ☎ (860) 236-5621. *Museum open all year Tues.–Sun. noon–5; library open all year Tues.–Sat. 9–5; both closed Mon. and holidays, also*

Mark Twain House

Sat. from Memorial Day to Labor Day. Combined admission: adults $3, children under 18 free. Partially &.

The leading repository of museum materials on state history, the Connecticut Historical Society has eight galleries of changing exhibits and permanent displays, including two particularly fine furniture collections: the Barbour Collection of Connecticut pieces from the Colonial and Federal periods, and the George Dudley Seymour Collection of 17th- and 18th-century pieces. You can also see Connecticut-made silver, pewter, toys, glassware, pottery, and stoneware. The art of the tavern sign is well represented by more than 70 specimens, suggesting that a fair number of past Connecticut residents were not customers of the Phoenix Mutual Life Insurance Company, which accepted only teetotalers when it was established in Hartford in 1851. The society also maintains a vast library of almost two million historical manuscripts, 100,000 books, 3,500 bound volumes of newspapers and periodicals, extensive genealogical holdings, and assorted maps, prints, and photographs.

Trip 39

The Litchfield Hills

As the Berkshires of western Massachusetts tumble south into Connecticut they change their name and, subtly, their character. This region, known as the Litchfield Hills, is the quintessential New England, perhaps more consistently pretty than any other spot in all six states.

Can you really get to know its special charms on a daytrip? Hardly, but the scenic drive outlined here will let you sample some of the best the region has to offer, and perhaps lure you into returning for a longer stay. Happily, the Litchfield Hills abound in quaint old inns, B & Bs, and other desirable lodgings.

There's no denying that this is a lengthy excursion from Boston; the total round trip is a bit over 300 miles, of which somewhat over 200 miles is via turnpike. Having a car that's fun to drive helps. Those starting from elsewhere in New England will most likely have a shorter way to go.

For longer stays, this trip combines well with either (or both) of the Berkshire trips in Massachusetts beginning on page 165.

GETTING THERE:

By car, the Litchfield Hills begin about a hundred miles southwest of Boston. Take **I-90** (Massachusetts Turnpike) west to Exit 3, then **US-202** south to Granby in Connecticut. **CT-20** takes you west around the Barkhamsted Reservoir to the first stop, Riverton. From there follow the tour description.

There are numerous options for the return journey. Routes US-44 and CT-8 in northwest Connecticut; and US-7, MA-8, and MA-23 in Massachusetts are particularly attractive roads leading back to the Massachusetts Turnpike.

PRACTICALITIES:

Good weather is a prerequisite for this scenic excursion. Glorious weather would be even better, especially during the fall foliage season. While there are no great cultural sights, the region is rich in low-key historic sites and charming, off-the-beaten-path-type attractions. Some are open year-round, but most close for the winter season. Check individual listings before making your plans as their schedules vary widely, and sometimes change. You will encounter more than a few antique shops, boutiques, country stores, and some unusually good restaurants along the way.

For further information, contact the **Litchfield Hills Travel Council**, P.O. Box 968, Litchfield, CT 06759, ☎ (860) 567-4506, FAX (860) 567-5214. They'll be happy to send you a variety of thorough, informative, lively brochures and a calendar of events for this very eventful region.

FOOD AND DRINK:

Some good places for lunch are:

Tollgate Hill Inn (US-202, Litchfield, 2½ miles north of The Green, at CT-118) An historic Colonial inn serving sophisticated cuisine in a romantic setting. Reservations, ☎ (860) 567-4545. X: Tues. & Wed. off-season. $$$

West Side Grill (43 West St., US-202, Litchfield) *The* place in town for creative cuisine. Reservations advised, ☎ (860) 567-3885. $$ and $$$

Hopkins Inn (22 Hopkins Rd., near New Preston) Austrian and American specialties overlooking a lake, with outdoor tables in season. Reservations suggested, ☎ (860) 868-7295. X: Mon., Jan.–Mar. $$ and $$$

Old Riverton Inn (CT-20 in Riverton) This old stagecoach stop has been offering hospitality and American cuisine since 1796. ☎ (860) 379-8678. X: Mon. off-season, Tues., early Jan. $$

Fife 'n Drum Inn (53 N. Main St., US-7, in Kent) Continental cuisine, Sunday brunches. ☎ (860) 927-3509. X: Tues. $$

Riverton General Store (CT-20 in Riverton) This is a great area for picnicking, and you can get all the makings—sandwiches to drinks—right here. ☎ (860) 379-0811. $

Skee's Diner (Main at N. Elm, Torrington) A really old, *old* diner of the type you hardly see anymore. ☎ (860) 496-0166. X: Mon., evenings. $

Litchfield Food Company (39 West St., US-202, Litchfield) Great sandwiches and deli specialties. ☎ (860) 567-3113. $

Villager Restaurant (Main St., US-7, Kent) A cozy place for simple, home-style lunches. ☎ (860) 927-3945. X: evenings. $

SUGGESTED DRIVE:

Numbers in parentheses correspond to numbers on the map.

Begin your tour at **Riverton** (1), once known as Hitchcocksville after its famous, early-19th-century product, the Hitchcock Chair. The concept of mass production, developed around New Haven by Eli Whitney, was here adapted to rugged, inexpensive pieces of household furniture that have since become collectors' items. Alas, founder Lambert Hitchcock went broke by mid-century, so the village changed its name. Then, nearly a century later, the factory reopened and resumed production of its unique offerings. A superb collection of the antique painted and stenciled pieces can be seen at the **Hitchcock Museum** in the former Old Union Church of 1829, along with a short film on their history. ☎ *(860) 738-4950. Open Apr.–Dec., Thurs.–Sun., noon–4. Donation.* You can also visit the **Hitchcock Chair Company Factory Store** in Lambert Hitchcock's original factory to see the modern reproductions, and perhaps purchase some. ☎ *(860) 379-4826. Open daily. Free.*

Head south on CT-20 and CT-8 to **Winsted** (2), hub of laurel season festivities. For a short side excursion, take US-44 west briefly to CT-263, following that west to the corner of Prospect Street. Here you can visit the **Solomon Rockwell House**, built in 1813 by a well-to-do iron manufacturer. Sometimes called "Solomon's Temple," the house is of interest today for its Greek Revival architecture and its collection of rare portraits, clocks, Hitchcock chairs, glass-plate negatives, and memorabilia from the Revolutionary and Civil wars. ☎ *(860) 379-8433. Open mid-June to mid-Oct., Tues. and Wed. 10–12, Thurs.–Sun. 2–4. Adults $2.*

Another little side trip leads west on CT-263 to **Winchester Center** (3), home of the truly unusual **Kerosene Lamp Museum**. Operated more as a hobby than a serious collection, the museum is filled to overflowing with some 500 lamps used in homes, schools, factories, and railroad cars from 1856 to 1880—that fateful year when the first light bulb appeared. ☎ *(860) 379-2612. Open weekends 9:30–4. Free.*

Torrington (4), a bit farther south on CT-8, was the birthplace of the abolitionist John Brown and a center of brass manufacturing. Before getting down to brass tacks, Torrington was known as "Mast Swamp" because the local pines supplied so many masts for sailing vessels. A local attraction here is the **Hotchkiss-Fyler House** on Main Street. A grand Victorian mansion built in 1900, the house features parquet floors, mahogany paneling, hand stenciling, and fine furnishings; local history exhibits are on view in the adjacent museum. ☎ *(860) 482-8260. Open Mon.–Fri., 9–4, Sat. 10–3. Closed Jan.–Mar. Adults $2.* Also on Main Street is the **Warner Theater**, a former art deco movie palace, now a National Historic Landmark offering a year-round schedule of concerts, as well as performances by the Nutmeg Ballet.

Turn left on US-202, following it to the lovely little town of ***Litchfield** (5). This is New England at its best, and in some ways most typical. Quite a prosperous place in the 18th century, Litchfield went to sleep in the 19th when it was bypassed by the railroad and missed out on the Industrial Revolution. Today it is a beautifully preserved vision of Colonial days, with just enough low-key attractions to keep you busy for a while. At its center, by the junction of US-202 and CT-118, is the picturebook village green and its pristine ***Congregational Church** of 1829—surely one of the most photographed sights in New England. Park as close to here as possible.

Stroll to the south side of the green, where you'll find the **Litchfield Historical Society Museum**. Unlike many local museums whose rooms are crammed full of Americana, this one has four spacious galleries where every

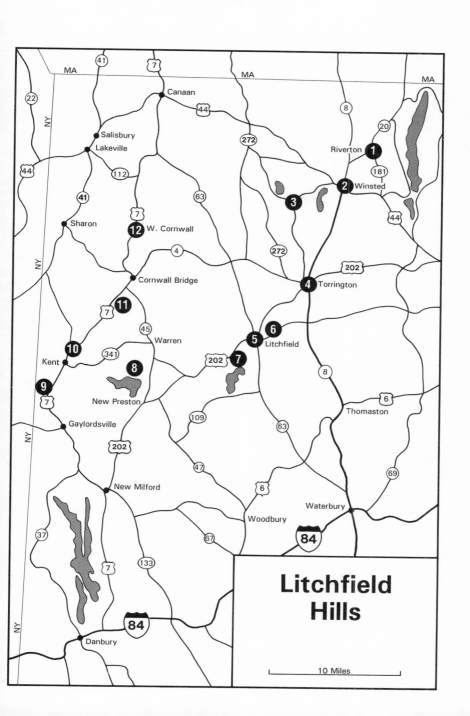

Litchfield Hills

10 Miles

article on display stands out. The exhibits include furniture, decorative arts, textiles, photographs, and paintings that together tell the story of Litchfield's history. Among the fine collection of paintings by Ralph Earl is a portrait of Mariann Wolcott, daughter of one of Litchfield's most prominent citizens, Oliver Wolcott Sr., who signed the Declaration of Independence, served in the Continental Congress, and was governor of Connecticut in 1796–97. You'll want time to browse here. ☎ *(860) 567-4501. Open mid–Apr. to mid–Nov., Tues.–Sat. 11–5, Sun. 1–5. Closed major holidays. Adults $3, includes Tapping Reeve House & School, below; children 16 and under free. Gift shop. ♿.*

Go down South Street to the **Tapping Reeve House and Law School**. America's first law school was established here in 1774 by Tapping Reeve, lawyer and jurist. He began by holding classes in the parlor, later moving to the school building next door. Reeve was married to Aaron Burr's sister, and Burr was one of his earliest pupils, the first in a long line of distinguished graduates that included Vice President John C. Calhoun, Horace Mann, three Supreme Court justices, six cabinet secretaries, and 130 members of Congress. The Tapping Reeve House is furnished to the late 18th and early 19th century period, while the Litchfield Law School building houses an exhibit on the school and its graduates. ☎ *(860) 567-4501. Open mid-May to mid-Oct., Tues.–Sat. 11–5, Sun. 1–5. Closed major holidays. Adults $3, includes Historical Museum, above, Children 16 and under free.*

Across the street is the Oliver Wolcott Sr. House, to which, during the Revolutionary War, came Washington, Lafayette, Alexander Hamilton, and the equestrian statue of George III, the latter toppled from its pedestal in Bowling Green, New York City, by the Sons of Liberty, dragged all the way to Litchfield, and melted down into bullets by the women of the town. Farther down South Street is Old South Road, a righthand fork that takes you to the Ethan Allen House, where the famed Revolutionary War hero and leader of the Green Mountain Boys once lived.

Go back to the green. Here look for a narrow road leading behind the shops on West Street to Cobble Court, a 19th-century cobblestone courtyard ringed by quaint shops. Continue up North Street to a number of other historic spots: the home of Benjamin Tallmadge, a Revolutionary War officer, confidential agent, and aide to George Washington; Sheldon's Tavern, another of Washington's many resting places; the site of the birthplace of Henry Ward Beecher and Harriet Beecher Stowe, whose father, the influential clergyman Lyman Beecher, preached at the earlier Congregational Church; and the site of Miss Pierce's Academy, the first girls' school in the United States, founded by Sarah Pierce in 1792.

Just east of Litchfield, to the left off Route CT-118, is the **Lourdes in Litchfield Shrine** (6) of the Montfort Missionaries. An outdoor chapel here faces a replica of the grotto at Lourdes, France, where the Virgin Mary is said to have appeared to Saint Bernadette in 1858. To one side, the Way of the

Cross starts up a wooded trail that winds to the top of the hill, ending with a flight of steps up to Calvary. ☎ *(860) 567-1041. Grounds open daily all year, Pilgrimage season May to mid-Oct.; call for schedule of services. Donation.* ♿. By continuing east on CT-118 a little bit and turning right on Chestnut Hill Road, you can visit the **Haight Vineyard and Winery** for free tours and tastings. ☎ *(860) 567-4045. Open Mon.–Sat. 10:30–5; Sun. noon–5.*

Head west from Litchfield on US-202. In about two miles you'll come to the **White Memorial Foundation** (7). Connecticut's largest nature sanctuary, on the shores of Connecticut's largest natural lake, offers 4,000 acres of forest, marshlands, ponds, and streams sheltering a diversity of trees, flowers, ferns, mosses, birds, fish, and wildlife. Some 35 miles of trails provide ample opportunity for hiking, horseback riding, birdwatching, nature study, or relaxed contemplation. Beautiful Bantam Lake offers its shore for picnicking and its waters for fishing. The **Conservation Center** is an excellent natural history museum with an extensive library, a children's room, and displays explaining the varied habitats and ecological systems within the sanctuary. ☎ *(860) 567-0857. Grounds open daily all year; free. Conservation Center open all year, Mon.–Sat. 9–5, Sun. noon–4, adults $2, children (6–12) $1.* ♿.

*At this point you might choose to take a **shortcut** directly to Kent (10) by soon turning right on CT-341 through Warren.*

If not, continuing west on US-202 quickly brings you to **New Preston**, noted for its unusual antique shops, and **Lake Waramaug State Park** (8), an area of great scenic beauty. Located along the north shore of the lake, on Hopkins Road, the **Hopkins Vineyard** offers free tours and tastings. ☎ *(860) 868-7954.* Head south on US-202 to **New Milford**, where you turn north on US-7, following the beautiful Housatonic River.

A few miles north of Gaylordsville, on a country road to the left, you can take in a truly lovely sight. ***Bull's Bridge** (9), one of the two covered bridges in Connecticut still open to automobile traffic, is well over 200 years old. Legend has it that George Washington lost his horse while passing over this span. Beneath it, the Housatonic tumbles over rocks; on its far side is a scenic overlook and parking area. What a fine place for a picnic!

For a village of its size, **Kent** (10) has an extraordinary number of craft shops, galleries, bookstores, and restaurants. It is also home to the ***Sloane-Stanley Museum** of early American farm implements and tools, brought together by famed author and artist Eric Sloane (1905–85) on land donated by the Stanley tool manufacturing company of New Britain. Captions accompany the tools, which are displayed in a way that demonstrates how they were used. In the early 18th century, Kent was a center of the iron ore industry, and ruins of the old Kent blast furnace are here on the museum grounds, along with a replica of Eric Sloane's studio. ☎ *(860) 927-3849 or 566-3005. Open mid–May through Oct., Wed.–Sun. 10–4. Adults $3, seniors and children (6–17) $1.50. Partially* ♿.

Bull's Bridge

Kent Falls State Park (11) is just a few miles north along US-7. Here Connecticut's loveliest waterfall cascades down several levels to a brook. A wide, winding path leads to the head of the falls, which are particularly beautiful in spring when the water is high, and in fall when the leaves turn. All around are pine forests with inviting trails for hiking. ☎ *(860) 927-3238. Open Apr.–Nov., daily 8–sunset. Parking fee on weekends and holidays, free other times. Partially ♿.*

Head north past Cornwall Bridge to the postcard-pretty village of **West Cornwall** (12), where you'll find the second covered bridge over the Housatonic, on Route CT-128. This one, designed by covered-bridge maven Ithiel Town, has been in continuous use since 1837. West Cornwall is a fine place to stop before heading back home, as there are several interesting crafts shops and eateries near the bridge.

Section VI

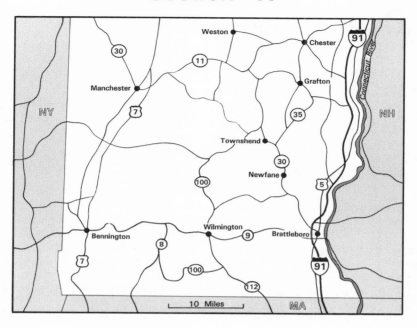

DAYTRIPS TO
VERMONT

Les Verts Monts, the Green Mountains of Vermont, were discovered in 1609 by the French explorer Samuel de Champlain, but remained almost uninhabited by Europeans until the British defeated the French at Québec in 1759. Border disputes plagued Vermont for decades; its land was claimed by both New Hampshire and New York, giving rise to militia actions by Ethan Allen's Green Mountain Boys. After playing an heroic role in the Revolution, the ever-rebellious, independently-minded (and some would say cantankerous) Vermonters decided to go it alone, forming the Republic of Vermont in 1777. Fourteen years later it finally joined the Union as the 14th state.

Vermont is a fascinating and extraordinarily beautiful place. Unfortunately, most of it is beyond reasonable daytrip range, but the two excursions described here will give you an enjoyable sampling of what lies farther to the north, an area you might want to explore at leisure.

Trip 40

Bennington

The Battle of Bennington, a major turning point of the American Revolution, was actually fought in nearby New York State, but it was this historic Vermont town and its military supplies that the British were after. They didn't succeed. On August 16, 1777, Patriots led by General John Stark, supplemented by Ethan Allen's Green Mountain Boys, soundly defeated the Redcoats in a victory that led to the British surrender at Saratoga a few weeks later. Artifacts of the battle, including the famous '76 flag, are proudly displayed in the Bennington Museum, while at the nearby Battle Monument visitors can get a bird's-eye view of the scene.

Bennington has other attractions, as well. Colonial and Victorian houses grace its older sections, and there are no fewer than three covered bridges near the lovely campus of Bennington College. Besides its historic exhibits, the Bennington Museum has a large section devoted to the life and works of Grandma Moses, one of America's all-time favorite artists. There's a wonderful Victorian mansion to explore, and a state park at which to relax. If your time and budget permit, why not stay over and combine this trip with the next one, a drive through Southern Vermont? This excursion also fits in well with the one to the Northern Berkshires (page 171) and Historic Deerfield (page 160).

GETTING THERE:

By car, Bennington is about 150 miles northwest of Boston. Take Route **MA-2** west to Williamstown, then **US-7** north into Bennington. Going by way of Brattleboro is a bit longer but may be slightly faster. Both routes are scenic most of the way.

PRACTICALITIES:

The Bennington Museum, a major attraction, is open every day except Thanksgiving and late December through New Year's Day. The Battle Monument can be ascended on any day from mid-April through October, and the Park-McCullough House visited on any day from late May through October.

Expect heavy traffic during the fall foliage season. Late spring would probably be an ideal time to visit.

For further information, contact the **Bennington Area Chamber of Commerce**, Veterans Memorial Drive, Route US-7, Bennington, VT 05201, ☎ (802) 447-3311. Free walking tour maps are available at their information booth.

FOOD AND DRINK:

Four Chimneys (21 West Rd., VT-9, a mile west of town) Elegant Continental cuisine in an old mansion, now an inn. Reservations suggested. ☎ (802) 447-3500. $$ and $$$

Bennington Station (150 Depot St., corner of River St., half-mile east of Bennington Museum) Bennington's former train station is now a popular restaurant specializing in regional American cuisine. ☎ (802) 447-1080. $$

Brasserie (324 County St., just east of North St., US-7, near tourist office) Creative cuisine in a contemporary setting, with indoor/outdoor dining. ☎ (802) 447-7922. $$

Alldays & Onions (519 Main St., east of US-7) This combination deli and restaurant features healthy salads, sandwiches, light lunches, and even full dinners. ☎ (802) 447-0043. $ and $$

Blue Benn Diner (US-7, a mile north of VT-9) A real 1940s diner with all kinds of food, from burgers to tofu. ☎ (802) 442-5140. $

LOCAL ATTRACTIONS:

Numbers in parentheses correspond to numbers on the map.

*THE BENNINGTON MUSEUM (1), West Main St. (Route VT-9), Bennington, VT 05201, ☎ (802) 447-1571. *Open daily 9–5. Closed Thanksgiving and from late Dec. to Jan 1. Adults $5, seniors $4.50, under 12 free. Gift shop. Partially &.*

What could be more American than the original ***'76 Flag** and the largest public collection of ***Grandma Moses paintings** anywhere? You'll find both at this marvelous museum, along with items of military history, period artifacts and costumes, rare pottery, 19th-century Vermont glass, New England furniture and clocks, early American paintings and sculptures, and even a locally-built automobile from the 1920s.

Anna Mary Robertson (1860–1961), a.k.a. **Grandma Moses**, was one of the most beloved artists that America ever produced. Completely self-taught, her work was quite primitive, but always captivating in its charmingly awkward way. That's what so endears her with art lovers everywhere, from layman to connoisseur. Visitors can enjoy a large selection of her works, then tour the adjacent ***Schoolhouse** that she attended as a child.

Just steps away stands the:

OLD FIRST CHURCH (2), West Main St. and Monument Ave., ☎ (802) 447-1223. *Open July–Columbus Day, Mon.–Sat. 10–noon and 1–4, Sun. 1–4; Memorial Day–June, Sat. 10–noon and 1–4, Sun. 1–4. Donations.*

This white clapboard Congregational church of 1805 is considered to be one of the most beautiful in all New England, and has been fully restored to its original appearance. Inside, there are box pews and a vaulted ceiling of plaster and wood supported by six wooden columns. Don't miss the adjacent **Old Burying Ground**, where you'll find the graves of Vermont's founders, Revolutionary soldiers, five governors, and the renowned poet Robert Frost (1874–1963). The latter left his own epitaph: "I had a lover's quarrel with the world."

You can't miss seeing the next attraction, the:

BENNINGTON BATTLE MONUMENT (3), 15 Monument Circle, ☎ (802) 447-0550. *Open mid-April through Oct., daily 9–5. Adults $1, children (6–11) 50¢. Gift shop.* ♿.

Completed in 1891 to commemorate the Battle of Bennington, this stark obelisk of blue dolomite marks the site of the Continental arsenal that the British failed to capture. It's 306 feet high but, for once, there's an elevator to the observation platform so you won't have to huff and puff your way up for a ***panoramic view** that covers parts of three states. On a clear day, a *really clear* day, you can see the actual site of the battle in New York State. In bad, or even windy, weather you won't see much of anything. Downstairs, at the base, there's a diorama of the battle, and a massive cooking kettle that the Brits left behind.

About two miles to the north you'll find three 19th-century **covered bridges** (4) spanning the mighty Walloomsac River. The Silk Road Bridge of 1840 and the Paper Mill Village Bridge of 1889 are just south of Route MA-67A, while the Bert Henry Bridge of 1840 is on nearby Murphy Road. All are supported by Town lattice trusses, perfected in 1820 by the Connecticut bridge master Ithiel Town (see page 258). Just north of these is the gorgeous 550-acre campus of **Bennington College** (5), a private four-year liberal-arts college founded in the 1930s. This was once a farm, and some of the current buildings were originally barns and stables. One of the most expensive schools in the nation, co-ed Bennington has about 520 students and stresses creativity in the arts. Tours may be arranged in advance, or you can just stroll around. ☎ *(802) 445-5401.*

About a mile northwest of the campus, at the intersection of West and Park streets, is the:

PARK-McCULLOUGH HOUSE (6), West St. off 67A, North Bennington, VT 05257, ☎ (802) 442-5441. *Open late May–Oct., daily 10–4; Dec. weekends 10–4. Guided tours on the hour, 10–3. Adults $5, seniors (60+) $4, youths (12–17) $3.*

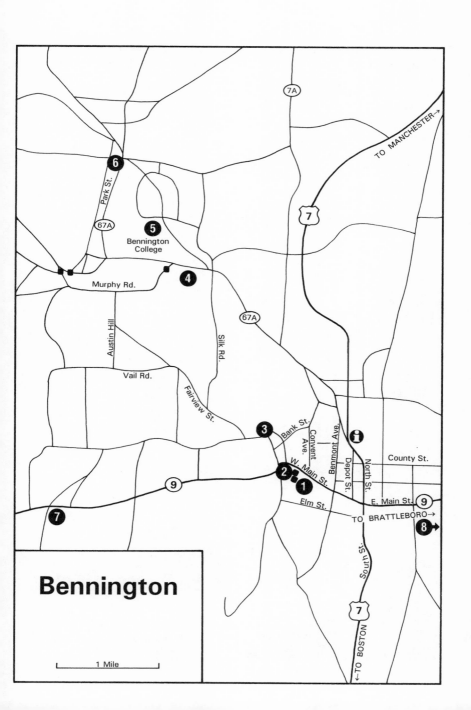

Bennington

1 Mile

Two Vermont governors lived in this magnificent Victorian mansion, completed in 1865 in the Second Empire style. At various times, it was also home to the founders of Bennington College, and to several business leaders. Set on a wooded six-acre site, the house has 35 rooms filled with period furniture, paintings, decorative arts, clothing, and family heirlooms. The estate includes a carriage house with sleighs and carriages, formal gardens, and a children's playhouse.

Before leaving Bennington, antique-car enthusiasts (and some normal folk, too) might want to stop at the offices of *Hemmings Motor News* (7) on VT-9, just west of town. Hemmings is the bible of the old car hobby, an essential publication for anyone who's trying to restore their old jalopy. There's a display of vintage vehicles at their nearby service station, and you can watch the magazine being put together. *Route VT-9, Bennington, VT 05201,* ☎ *(802) 442-3101. Open Mon.–Fri. 9–5. Free.*

Those returning via Route VT-9 might want to make a rest stop at **Woodford State Park** (8), about 10 miles east of Bennington. Picnicking, nature trails, swimming, boating, fishing, and even camping and hunting are offered on this 400-acre site on the edge of a reservoir. ☎ *(802) 447-7169. Open Memorial Day to Columbus Day, 10–dusk. Nominal fee.* ♿.

The Grandma Moses Schoolhouse and the Bennington Museum

A Drive Through Southern Vermont

Here's a rewarding day-long drive that leads you down the most scenic roads of Southern Vermont, halting at a variety of low-key attractions along the way. You'll have to choose your stops carefully as there are far more than you could possibly see in just one day, but of course it's nice to save some for a return visit or a longer stay.

Vermont is a particularly attractive state to drive in as its roads are largely rural and unencumbered by ugly billboards and other commercial signs. Instead, you'll see mountains, streams, covered bridges, forests, farms, and some of the most picturesque villages in all of New England. Not a bad way to spend a day.

If this trip seems a bit too long, you might want to stay overnight, possibly combining it with the previous excursion to Bennington. For longer stays, it also works well with the trips to Historic Deerfield (page 160) or the Northern Berkshires (page 171).

GETTING THERE:

By car, Brattleboro is about 117 miles northwest of Boston via routes **MA-2** and **I-91**. Taking the full circuit described here will add about 140 miles to that, although you can substantially reduce the distance by not going to Manchester, or by taking a shortcut from West Townshend to East Jamaica. Add to that your return trip.

PRACTICALITIES:

This is a long drive, best made in the late spring or summer when the hours of daylight are at their maximum. An early start is essential. Having another driver is a big help, too, as is having a car that's fun to drive.

The route is at its absolute prettiest during the fall foliage season, but that's also when you can expect the most traffic. For the current foliage report in Vermont, ☎ (802) 828-3239 from September to late October.

Further information is available from the **Vermont Department of Travel & Tourism**, 134 State St., Montpelier, VT 05602, ☎ (802) 828-3236 or (800) 837-6668. Web Site: www.genghis.com/tourism.vermont.htm. There's a handy **Vermont Welcome Center** on Route **I-91** at the Massachusetts border, ☎ (802) 254-4593.

FOOD AND DRINK:

Restaurants in this area tend to be open for dinner only; among those that do serve a good lunch are:

The Old Tavern at Grafton (in Grafton at VT-121) Regional cuisine in a landmark 1801 inn. Reservations suggested. ☎ (802) 843-2231. $$

Quality Restaurant (Main St. in Manchester) A traditional Vermont eatery, gussied up a bit for the tourists but still popular with the locals. ☎ (802) 362-9839. $ and $$

Garden Café and Gallery (Route VT-11 in Londonderry) Healthy lunches and fancier dinners in a rustic, plant-filled setting. ☎ (802) 824-6021. $ and $$

Mole's Eye Café (High St. at Main St., Brattleboro) A local favorite with an eclectic menu. ☎ (802) 257-0771. $

The Common Ground (25 Eliot St. in Brattleboro) Natural and vegetarian dishes from all over the world, served amid art with a social message. ((802) 257-0855. X: Tues. $

SUGGESTED DRIVE:

Numbers in parentheses correspond to numbers on the map.

The first town you'll come to in Vermont will probably be **Brattleboro** (1), the state's earliest Colonial settlement. Since the route brings you back this way, why not save it for the end and head directly for the boonies?

Take Route VT-30 north to the pretty little village of **Newfane** (2), founded in 1774 and noted for its traditional green, church, inns, and county courthouse of 1825. Continue north to **Townshend State Park** (3), where you can park your car and peacefully stroll across the historic **Scott Covered Bridge** of 1870. At 276 feet, this is the longest of Vermont's 114 wooden covered bridges, and uses three different truss systems: the Town Lattice Truss, the laminated Bow Truss, and the King Post Truss. It spans the West River below the Townshend Lake Dam, built in 1961 for flood control. Drive through the park and across the dam, which puts you back on VT-30. Turn right and return to the village of Townshend, where you turn left onto VT-35.

Continue north, bearing left in a few miles on the direct road to the beautifully restored village of ***Grafton** (4). Once a prosperous mill town whose industries thrived on water power, Grafton declined as steam took over in the mid-19th century. Its wool industry, based on some 10,000 grazing sheep, was no longer able to compete, and new transportation routes bypassed the area. Grafton's population plummeted dramatically,

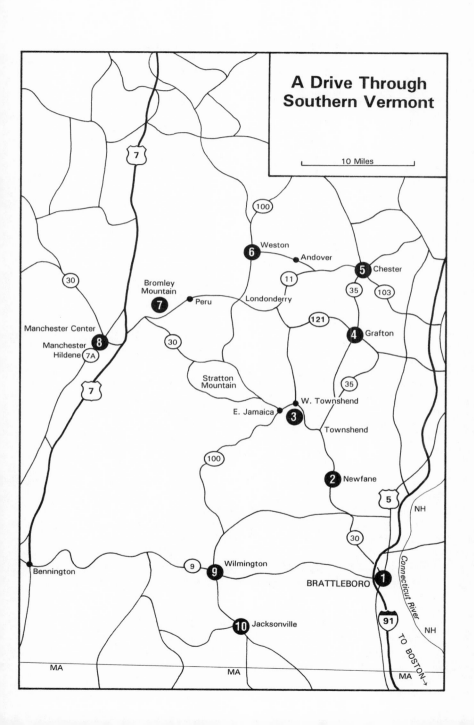

A Drive Through Southern Vermont

10 Miles

nearly turning it into a ghost town. Then, in 1963, salvation came in the form of the Windham Foundation, formed to revitalize the town and preserve its charm. Today a mecca for discriminating visitors, Grafton's story is documented at the **Historical Society Museum**, ☎ *(802) 843-2255. Open Memorial Day to Columbus Day, Sat. afternoons, also Sun. afternoons in July & Aug.* More history can be seen at **The Old Tavern**, still functioning as an inn after more than 180 years. Several presidents and authors have stayed here; memories of them are displayed near the entrance. If time permits, why not take a horse-drawn carriage ride through the village, or visit the local cheese works?

Keep heading north on VT-35 to **Chester** (5), a bit off the beaten path but a good discovery for those looking for New England charm without the tourist hordes. Chester has been home to the **National Survey**, a noted map publisher, since 1912, and you're welcome to visit their Victorian-style Charthouse, a delightful map store filled with all sorts of cartographic treasures. *Main St.,* ☎ *(802) 875-2121. Open Mon.–Sat. until 4.*

Turn west on VT-11, then right on a local road through Andover to **Weston** (6). Another small village that nearly disappeared from the map, Weston preserves its 19th-century quaintness for the delight of today's visitors. The famous **Vermont Country Store** is here, offering the kind of merchandise that your great-grandparents once purchased, but not at the same prices. There's penny candy, arcane bits of hardware, practical underwear, and much more. ☎ *(802) 824-3184. Open Mon.–Sat., 9–5.* The restored **Farrar-Mansur House** of 1797 was once a tavern but is now the local history museum, featuring period furnishings, paintings, and the like. *Route 100, north side of the village green,* ☎ *(802) 824-8190. Open daily afternoons, July–Aug.; weekend afternoons Memorial Day–June and Sept.–Columbus Day. Modest admission.* Another attraction here is the **Weston Mill Museum**, where old-time skills are still practiced for the enlightenment of visitors. *Open daily, Memorial Day–Columbus Day. Donation.*

Drive south on VT-100 to Londonderry, then west on VT-11 past Peru to **Bromley Mountain** (7). One of New England's oldest ski resorts, Bromley has been popular since the 1930s and still attracts a friendly crowd. During summer and fall it offers its famous ***Alpine Slide** rides down the same scenic slopes, starting from a height reached by chairlift. You can also cruise down a mountain trail on a wheeled Alpine cart. ☎ *(802) 824-5522. Snow skiing mid-Nov. to mid-April; Alpine Slide late May to mid-Oct., all daily.* ✗.

Manchester (8) is next, reached by heading west on VT-11 and VT-30 to VT-7A. There are actually two towns; Manchester Center comes first. Busy all year round, the Center abounds in upscale shops, restaurants, and even factory outlets. Continue south on VT-7A into ***Manchester Village**, a stately old resort town whose shady sidewalks are paved with marble from a local quarry. Just south of the village, along VT-7A, is ***Hildene**, the 412-acre summer estate of Abraham Lincoln's son, Robert Todd Lincoln (1843-1926),

The Scott Covered Bridge

who made his fortune as a lawyer and businessman. His descendants continued to live in this 24-room Georgian Revival mansion until 1975. The original furnishings are still there, along with family memorabilia, the massive Aeolian pipe organ, and the formal gardens with their mountain views. ☎ *(802) 362-1788. Open mid-May through Oct., daily tours on the half-hour from 9:30–4. Adults $7, children (6–15) $4. Partially ♿. Cross-country skiing in winter.*

Anglers will be hooked by the **American Museum of Fly Fishing** on VT-7A at Seminary Avenue. Tackle owned by famous Americans is featured, along with sporting prints, paintings, hundreds of rods, reels, and countless flies. ☎ *(802) 362-3300. Open May–Nov., daily 10–4; rest of year, Mon.–Fri. 10–4. Closed major holidays. Admission $3.* ♿. Manchester is also home to the Orvis Company, the oldest manufacturer of fishing tackle in America. Their retail shop and factory outlet store carry upscale outdoor clothing and home furnishings as well.

From Manchester's village green you can take West Road north for about a mile to the **Southern Vermont Art Center**, located on a 375-acre mountainside estate. The grounds are filled with unusual outdoor sculptures, and there's a wonderful botany trail for you to explore. Inside the mansion are changing exhibitions of paintings, prints, sculptures, photography, and the like. The Art Center also presents concerts, films, dances, and a variety of cultural events. ☎ *(802) 362-1405. Open late May to late Oct., Tues.–Sat. 10–5, Sun. noon–5; Dec. to March, Mon.–Sat. 10–5. Admission $3, $4 for special exhibits, reduced for students, under 13 free.* ☎. ♿.

Return north to Route VT-30 and follow it east, then southeast, past the Stratton Mountain ski area to East Jamaica. Turn right on VT-100 and continue south past the Mount Snow ski area to **Wilmington** (9), whose Main Street features an interesting group of 18th- and 19th-century buildings. A delicious side trip can be made from here by following VT-100 south to Jacksonville, then VT-112 to the **North River Winery** (10). Housed in an 1850 farmhouse, the winery offers tours and tastings of its unusual fruit wines made from apples and pears. ☎ *(802) 368-7557. Open Memorial Day through Dec., daily 10–5; rest of year Fri.–Sun. 11–5. Closed Easter, Thanksgiving, Christmas, New Year's. Free.*

The **Molly Stark Trail**, Route VT-9, winds its way east over mountains, passing the famed **Hundred Mile View**. You might want to stop here for a look before continuing on past Marlboro, West Brattleboro, and the Creamery Covered Bridge of 1879, just off the main road.

You are now back in **Brattleboro** (1), where this tour began. Vermont's oldest town was founded as Fort Dummer in 1724 by the folks from Massachusetts, who claimed the territory. Soon after that, New Hampshire grabbed the land, but this was contested by New York and given to it in 1764 by King George III. Vermont did not gain its own identity until 1777, first as an independent republic and 14 years later as a state.

During the 19th century, Brattleboro developed as a small industrial city with little of its Colonial past surviving. Since the 1960s it has become somewhat of a center for alternative lifestyles, and a home for aging (and mellowing) hippies. Stroll around, soaking up the slightly radical atmosphere, and then visit the **Brattleboro Museum and Art Center**. Housed in an old railroad station at Main and Vernon streets near the center of town, the museum celebrates the work of Vermont artists with permanent and changing exhibits. There are also many historical items including a collection of locally-produced Estey organs. ☎ *(802) 257-0124. Open May–Oct., Tues.– Sun., noon–6. Closed major holidays. Adults $2, seniors and students $1.* ♿.

Section VII

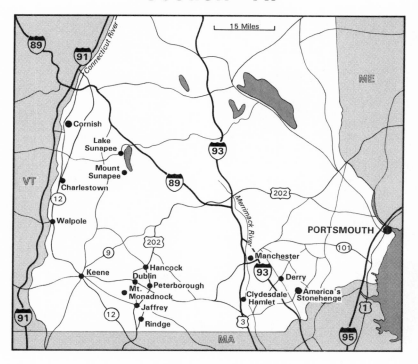

DAYTRIPS TO
NEW HAMPSHIRE

Their license plates shout "Live Free or Die," and they mean it. New Hampshire folk are different—fiercely independent, distrustful of Big Brother institutions, and proudly self-sufficient. This is a state that has no income tax, and no sales tax either; relying instead on "sin" taxes, the lottery, property and business levies, and taxes on tourist services such as restaurants and inns to fund their modest government. For such a small state, New Hampshire exerts an amazingly large influence on national politics every four years with its first-in-the-nation presidential primary, reported in excruciating detail by the media.

As is the case with Vermont, most of New Hampshire lies sadly beyond any reasonable daytrip range. Luckily, there are a few exceptions to this, and they'll be thoroughly explored in this section.

Trip 42

Portsmouth

New Hampshire actually has a seacoast, and you'll pass all 15 miles of it on the way to Portsmouth. This old maritime center, named after the Portsmouth in Hampshire, England, was first settled in 1630. At that time the land was covered with wild strawberries, accounting for the town's original name of Strawbery Banke—a moniker resurrected for its marvelous downtown restoration. Besides the historic structures here, Portsmouth also has several elegant mansions that may be visited, a colorful Old Harbor district complete with craft shops, restaurants, and several boat ride opportunities, a children's museum, and a maritime museum where you can climb aboard an experimental US Navy submarine from the 1950s. If that's not enough, visitors can take a cruise to the Isles of Shoals, or a drive to New Castle to see one of the earliest fortifications along the New England coast.

GETTING THERE:

By car, Portsmouth is about 65 miles northeast of downtown Boston via routes **US-1** and **I-95** (toll in NH) to Exit 7.

PRACTICALITIES:

Portsmouth's major attraction, Strawbery Banke, is open daily from May through October only. The other historic houses vary, but in general are open on Tuesdays through Sundays, from mid-June through mid-October. Check the individual listings. Cruises to the Isles of Shoals operate from June through Labor Day. The Children's Museum is open on Tuesdays through Sundays during the school year, daily in summer, while the Maritime Museum is open daily all year round.

For further information, contact the **Greater Portsmouth Chamber of Commerce**, 500 Market St., Portsmouth, NH 03802, ☎ (603) 436-1118. Another source is the **Seacoast Council on Tourism**, 235 West Rd., Portsmouth, NH, 03801, ☎ (603) 436-7678 or (800) 221-5623.

FOOD AND DRINK:

Portsmouth is noted for its fine restaurants, including:

> **Oar House** (55 Ceres St., east of Moffatt-Ladd House) Excellent cuisine, with an emphasis on seafood, is offered in this restored 1803 warehouse on the waterfront. Reservations suggested. ☎ (603) 436-4025. $$ and $$$

Metro (20 High St., west of Moffatt-Ladd House) American cuisine in a smart, old-time setting. ☎ (603) 436-0521. X: Sun. $$

Pier II (10 State St., just north of Strawbery Banke) A good value for seafood and steak, with outdoor dining and a harbor view. ☎ (603) 436-0669. $ and $$

Portsmouth Brewery (56 Market St.) This micro-brewery offers a variety of ales along with tasty pub food. ☎ (603) 431-1115. $ and $$

Stockpot (53 Bow St., near St. John's Church) Homemade soups, sandwiches, and full meals; overlooking the river. ☎ (603) 431-1851. $

Yoken's Thar She Blows (Lafayette Rd., US-1, 2 miles southwest of downtown) A family restaurant with seafood, steak, and the like. ☎ (603) 436-8224. $

LOCAL ATTRACTIONS:
Numbers in parentheses correspond to numbers on the map.

*STRAWBERY BANKE MUSEUM (1), Marcy St. on the waterfront, Portsmouth, NH 03802, ☎ (603) 433-1100. *Open May through Oct., daily 10–5. Adults $10, seniors $9, ages 7–17 $7, 6 and under free, families $25. Tickets valid two consecutive days. Gift shop.* X. *Partially* ♿.

Puddle Dock, site of the original Strawbery Banke settlement that later grew into Portsmouth, became derelict after World War II and was slated for demolition as part of an urban renewal program. Rather than forever lose such a rich heritage, public-spirited citizens got together during the 1950s to save the entire neighborhood as a living museum. Today, some 42 buildings dating from the 1690s to the 20th century have been preserved. Reflecting four centuries of architectural and social change, many of these are now furnished as they would have been in their prime, while others house exhibits and crafts demonstrations. Costumed role players reenact life in the various time frames, bringing to whole place to life for visitors—who can also enjoy the gardens, shops, and eatery.

Just east of the restored neighborhood, and bordering the broad Piscataqua River, is **Prescott Park** (2). Stroll over past the Liberty Pole to the **Sheafe Warehouse** of 1705, where naval hero John Paul Jones outfitted his ship, the *Ranger*, in 1777. His sailing out of Portsmouth Harbor later that year marked the first time that an American flag was flown at sea. The warehouse now houses the local Folk Art Museum. ☎ *(603) 431-8748. Museum open June–Labor Day, Wed.–Sun. 10–7. Free.*

Three blocks north of Strawbery Banke stands the magnificent ***Warner House** (3) of 1716, one of the finest mansions of its time in New England. According to legend, the lightning rod on its west wall was put there in 1762 by none other than that great electrical genius himself, Benjamin Franklin.

The house was built by Archibald Macpheadris, a Scottish sea captain, fur trader, and wealthy merchant, who settled in Portsmouth. It was later the home of one Jonathan Warner, who married the captain's daughter in 1760. ☎ *(603) 436-5909. Open June–Oct., Tues.–Sat. 10–4 and Sun. 1–4. Adults $4, children (7–12) $2.* Just a few steps up Chapel Street is **St. John's Church** (4), erected in 1807 to replace the original 1732 church destroyed in a fire. Before the Revolution, the earlier structure was called Queen's Chapel after the many gifts given it by Queen Caroline, consort of King George II. Her communion silver is still in use. Like so many churches in New England, its bell was cast by Paul Revere. Be sure to see the rare "Vinegar" Bible, so-called because of a misspelling of the word vineyard. ☎ *(603) 436-8283. Open daily 8–5, except during services.*

The **Moffatt-Ladd House** (5), near the harbor, was built in 1763 by a rich English sea captain named John Moffatt. His daughter married General William Whipple, a signer of the Declaration of Independence, and they lived here until his death in 1785. Besides the elegantly restored interior, there are also beautiful gardens and out buildings.

While in the neighborhood, you might be interested in taking an:

*ISLES OF SHOALS CRUISE (6), 315 Market St., Portsmouth, NH 03802-0311, ☎ (603) 431-5500 or (800) 441-4620. *Operates mid-June–Labor Day, limited service from May and until Oct., varying schedule and fares. Call ahead for information and reservations.*

The Isles of Shoals, four in New Hampshire and five in neighboring Maine, were discovered by Captain John Smith in 1614. Some believe, however, that European fishermen came here centuries before that! Strange tales of pirate treasure and ghostly goings-on abound on these tiny, remote islands, and add to the pleasure of a visit.

A similar service on a smaller vessel is offered by **Portsmouth Harbor Cruises**, Ceres Street Dock, ☎ (603) 436-8084 or (800) 776-0915. Again, call ahead for current information and reservations.

Continuing north on Market Street soon brings you to the **Port of Portsmouth Maritime Museum & Albacore Park** (7), where you can explore the innards of an experimental submarine. Launched in 1953 at the nearby Portsmouth Naval Shipyard, the **USS *Albacore*** was used until 1972 to test innovative designs in submarine technology. Significantly, it marked the end of the submarine as a surface ship that can dive briefly and maneuver underwater slowly, and the beginning of a new era of high-speed subs that remain submerged for long periods over great distances. Visits include an orientation film and tour. ☎ *(603) 436-3680. Open daily 9:30–5:30. Closed Thanksgiving, Christmas, New Year's. Adults $4, seniors $3, children (7–17) $2, families $10. Gift shop. Picnic facilities.*

Back in town, there are several other attractions that might interest you. The **John Paul Jones House** (8) of 1758 was twice the temporary residence of

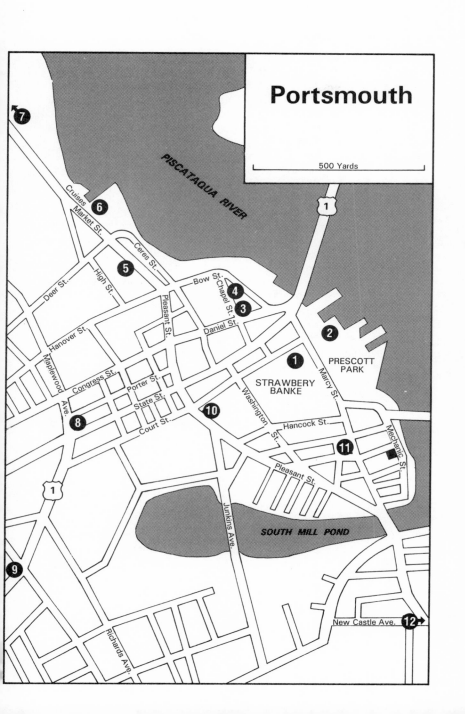

Portsmouth

500 Yards

PISCATAQUA RIVER

Cruises

Market St.

Ceres St.

Deer St.

High St.

Bow St.

Chapel St.

Daniel St.

Pleasant St.

Hanover St.

Maplewood Ave.

Congress St.

Porter St.

State St.

Court St.

STRAWBERY BANKE

PRESCOTT PARK

Marcy St.

Washington St.

Hancock St.

Mechanic St.

Pleasant St.

Junkins Ave.

SOUTH MILL POND

Richards Ave.

New Castle Ave.

the great naval hero; in 1777 as he oversaw completion of the sloop *Ranger* and again in 1781 to complete the *America*. Today this former boarding-house is the headquarters of the **Portsmouth Historical Society**, and serves as their museum. ☎ *(603) 436-8420. Open June to mid-Oct., Mon.–Sat. 10–4, Sun. noon–4. Adults $4, seniors $3.50, children (6–14) $2.*

The **Rundlet-May House** (9), a few blocks to the south, was built by a wealthy merchant in 1807 and occupied by his descendants until the 1970s. Maintaining much of its original character, the Federal-style mansion also reflects the changing lifestyles of successive family generations. It is espe-cially noted for its fine outbuildings, gardens, and setting. ☎ *(603) 436-3205. Open June through mid-Oct., Wed.–Sun. noon–5. Last tour at 4. Adults $4, seniors $3.50, children $2.*

Heading back towards Strawbery Banke, you'll come to the **Governor John Langdon House** (10) of 1784. George Washington once called this the finest home in Portsmouth, and it certainly is a handsome sight. Besides being a three-time governor of New Hampshire, John Langdon (1741–1819) was a Revolutionary leader, a signer of the U.S. Constitution, and the first president of the U.S. Senate. ☎ *(603) 436-3205. Open June to mid-Oct., Wed.–Sun. noon–5. Last tour at 4. Adults $4, seniors $3.50, children $2.*

If you happen to have any kids in tow, and they're getting a bit fidgety by now, why not stop at the nearby **Children's Museum of Portsmouth** (11)? Once a meetinghouse, this old building has also been a church, a school, and is now a museum filled with hands-on exhibits for learning and fun. Among the attractions is a space shuttle cockpit, a play submarine and a lobster boat, and of course the inevitable interactive science projects. *280 Marcy St.,* ☎ *(603) 436-3853. Open Tues.–Sat. 10–5, Sun. 1–5; also on Mon. during summer and school vacations. Admission $3.50, seniors $3, under 1 free.* ♿.

Before heading home, you could top off the day by taking a short drive out to **New Castle** (12), the first capital of Colonial New Hampshire. Now a quiet little village, the places fairly reeks of history. At its eastern tip is **Fort Constitution**, first built in the 1630s and called Fort William and Mary after England's joint sovereigns. In 1774 it saw the first openly hostile action of the Revolutionary War, set off by a little-known ride by Paul Revere who brought news of the British intent to fortify the fort. Rebuilt many times, this is most likely the only fortification in the United States to have garrisoned troops during every national conflict from the Revolutionary War through World War II. Much of it is open for exploration. ☎ *(603) 436-6607. Open mid-June to Labor Day, daily 9–5; rest of year weekends only. Free.*

America's Stonehenge, the Robert Frost Farm, and Manchester

From prehistoric mysteries to a resurrected city, from inspirational poetry to the brewing of glorious beer, this easy daytrip offers something wonderful for nearly everyone.

America's Stonehenge doesn't look much like England's, but it's just as enigmatic and probably just as ancient. You can ponder its riddle as you continue north to a thoroughly American landmark, the home of poet Robert Frost. Manchester, an old industrial city that almost died economically, is back on its feet and offers an excellent art museum along with unusual historic sites. The art of brewing combines with equestrian pleasures at the Anheuser-Busch Brewery and Clydesdale Hamlet, a tasty end to a delightful day's drive.

For those who can stay overnight, this trip combines well with the one to the Monadnock Mountain Area, or with Lowell and Andover in Massachusetts (see page 88).

GETTING THERE:

By car, the farthest point of the trip, Manchester, is about 58 miles northwest of Boston. Take Route **I-93** north to Exit 3, then **NH-111** east about 5 miles to Island Pond and Haverhill roads. Follow Haverhill Road south to America's Stonehenge.

Return to NH-111 and go west to **NH-28**, taking that north to the Robert Frost Farm, about 1½ miles south of the intersection with NH-102.

Head west to the town of Derry and get back on I-93 at Exit 4. Go north to Exit 7 and follow Bridge Street west into Manchester and its downtown attractions.

Cross the Merrimack River and head south on **I-293** (Everett Tpk., toll) to Exit 10, then **US-3** south to the Anheuser-Busch Brewery.

US-3 takes you back towards Boston.

PRACTICALITIES:

America's Stonehenge is open daily from April through November, and on some weekends in March and December. The Robert Frost Farm may be visited on Wednesdays through Sundays from mid-June until early September, and on weekends from mid-May to mid-June and Labor Day to Columbus Day. Manchester's major attraction, the Currier Gallery, is open from Wednesdays through Mondays, but not on holidays. Lastly, the Anheuser-Busch tours are held daily from May through October, and on Wednesdays through Sundays the rest of the year, except on major holidays.

For further information contact the **Southern New Hampshire Convention and Visitors Bureau**, Box 115, Windham, NH 03087, ☎ (603) 635-9000 or (800) 932-4282. You might also try the **Manchester Chamber of Commerce**, 889 Elm St., Manchester, NH 03101, ☎ (603) 666-6600.

FOOD AND DRINK:

Renaissance (1087 Elm St., US-3, downtown Manchester) American, Greek, and Italian specialties. ☎ (603) 669-7000. $$

Café Pavone (75 Arms Park, downtown Manchester, on the river just off Commercial St.) Good Italian food near the old mills overlooking the Merrimack. ☎ (603) 622-5488. X: Sat. lunch, Sun. lunch. $$

Newick's Seafood (696 Daniel Webster Hwy., US-3, between Manchester and Merrimack) Fresh seafood in a very casual setting. ☎ (603) 429-0262. $$

Shorty's Mexican Roadhouse (1050 Bicentennial Dr., in Northside Shopping Center near Exit 9S of I-93) Features a wide variety of Mexican dishes. ☎ (603) 625-1730. $

LOCAL ATTRACTIONS:

Numbers in parentheses correspond to numbers on the map.

*AMERICA'S STONEHENGE (1), Mystery Hill, Haverhill Rd., North Salem, NH 03079, ☎ (603) 893-8300. *Open late June to Labor Day, daily 9–7; April to late June and day after Labor Day through Nov., daily 10–5; variable times and dates in March and Dec. Last admission one hour before closing. Adults $7, seniors $6, youths (13–18) $5, children (6–12) $3.50. Gift shop. Picnic facilities.* ☎.

No one knows who built this giant megalithic astronomical complex some 4,000 years ago. Or why. Radiocarbon dating establishes the age, but its purpose remains pure speculation. The layout suggests a calendar that can determine specific solar and lunar events throughout the year, raising all sorts of questions regarding so-called primitive people. Whatever else, this is almost certainly the oldest man-made construction in the United States, and a must-see for anyone with an open mind.

A visit to America's Stonehenge requires that you pay close attention to the theories given on the orientation video and the printed guide; otherwise you won't see much more than stone ruins. But exciting possibilities can fire the imagination as the significance of the layout becomes apparent. Was there a Native American culture with advanced science? Was this the work of prehistoric wandering Celts from Europe? Did aliens from outer space

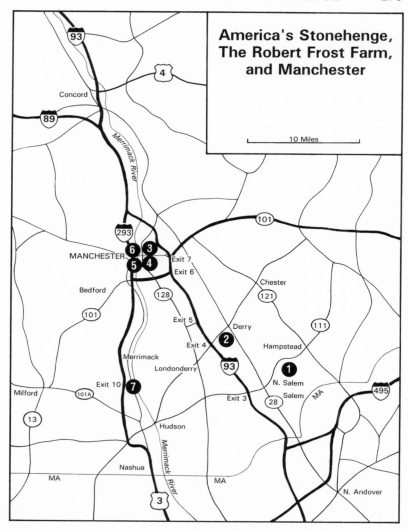

colonize here? Why have you never heard of the place before? The latter, at least, can be answered. Research on the site is relatively recent, the setting is not nearly as spectacular as England's Stonehenge, and—of course—there are no Druids to add to the drama. But it's still a memorable place to visit.

A rewarding stop on the way north to Manchester is at the **Robert Frost Farm** (2) on NH-28 in Derry. The beloved poet Robert Frost (1874–1963) lived here from 1900 to 1909, drawing inspiration from the setting that later formed the core of his writing. Now restored to that time frame, the simple two-story white clapboard house has original family possessions and period furnishings. Out in the barn, there are displays on the poet's life and video-taped readings of his works. A nature-poetry trail leads through fields and woodlands, offering a quiet place for contemplation. ☎ *(603) 432-3091. Open mid-June to the day before Labor Day, Wed.–Sun. 10–5; mid-May to mid-June and Labor Day to Columbus Day, weekends 10–5. Adults $2.50, under 18 free.*

Up ahead lies the industrial city of **Manchester** (3–6), whose 19th-century textile mills thrived on the abundant waterpower of the Merrimack River. The brick façades of the old **Amoskeag Mills**, once the largest in the world, still stretch a mile along the waterway. The company, employing some 17,000 workers, went bankrupt in 1935. Manchester was plunged into destitution at the very peak of the Great Depression. Out of this misery came a glimmer of hope when a group of businessmen purchased the mills and brought new activities, most notably financial services, to town.

Once again fairly prosperous, Manchester has several attractions to tempt visitors. Head straight for the newly-renovated ***Currier Gallery of Art** (3), a museum whose fine collections might surprise you. The European section spans the 13th through the 20th centuries, with notable works by Tiepolo, Gossaert, Degas, Monet, and others. Modern American art is repre-sented by Edward Hopper, Andrew Wyeth, Georgia O'Keeffe, Louise Nev-elson, Alexander Calder, and the like. An American decorative art section features furniture and furnishings from the 18th and 19th centuries, along with paintings by Copley, Bierstadt, and Church—to name a few. A wonder-ful little excursion can be made by van to the **Zimmerman House**, one of Frank Lloyd Wright's idealistic "Usonian" houses of the 1940s and '50s. This is shown by tour only, with an extra charge, and reservations must be made at the museum admission desk. *201 Myrtle Way, 3 blocks north of Bridge St. at Walnut St.* ☎ *(603) 669-6144. Open Wed.–Mon. 11–5 (9 p.m. on Fri.), closed some holidays. Adults $5, seniors and students $4, under 18 free. Gift shop.* &.

Nearby, the **Manchester Historic Association** (4) maintains a library and museum devoted to the city's proud past. Here you'll find Native American artifacts, firefighting equipment, costumes, furnishings, and—most important—material relating to the world-famous Amoskeag Mills that first brought prosperity and then devastation to Manchester. This is a vital source of information if you plan to explore around the handsome old mills and waterways. *129 Amherst St.,* ☎ *(603) 622-7531. Open Tues.–Fri. 9–4, Sat. 10–4. Free.*

Science comes alive, especially for young people, at the **See Science Center** (5), an interactive, hands-on facility designed to promote the under-standing and enjoyment of scientific principles. *324 Commercial St.,*

The sacrificial table at America's Stonehenge

☎ *(603) 669-0400. Open weekends year round, noon–5, plus Mon.–Fri. in summer, 10–3. Admission $3.*

Having gotten information at the Historic Association (above), you might want to poke around the resurrected, mile-long, 19th-century **Amoskeag Mills** (6). Once the largest textile factory in the world, Amoskeag totally dominated the city's economy until falling on hard times in the late 1920s, and going bankrupt in 1935. Today, happily, they have been put to contemporary use and Manchester thrives once again.

If you love beer or horses, or both, head straight south to Merrimack and the:

ANHEUSER-BUSCH BREWERY TOURS (7), 221 Daniel Webster Highway (US-3), Merrimack, NH 03054, ☎ (603) 595-1202. *Open May–Oct., daily 9:30–5; rest of year Wed.–Sun. 10–4. Closed Easter, Thanksgiving (Wed. & Thurs.), Dec. 24–25 & 31, New Year's. Free. Children must be accompanied by an adult. Tours, samples. Gift shop.*

Visitors can watch beer being brewed and bottled, get an understanding of the process, and then settle down in the Hospitality Room to enjoy the results (or a soft drink). From there, they can amble over to the **Clydesdale Hamlet**, a re-created 19th-century European-style farm, for a good look at those big, sturdy horses and their wagons.

Trip 44

Monadnock Mountain Area

Neither too high nor too low, neither too difficult nor too easy, Mount Monadnock is the perfect peak for ordinary mortals to climb. Its surroundings are perfect, too, for a delightful excursion into rural New Hampshire at its best. Charming New England villages, white-steepled churches, antique and craft shops, old mills, narrow country roads, stone fences, and covered bridges help explain why this region is often called the "Currier & Ives Corner." This is, in fact, the land that inspired Thornton Wilder's play *Our Town*, and that is celebrated by its local *Yankee* Magazine.

The best time to take this trip is during the fall foliage season, probably in early October. You won't be alone then, but the splendor of it all is well worth a bit of traffic. Other seasons have their charms; the view from the peak is always glorious. And even if you don't plan to climb the mountain, the drive itself is rewarding enough.

By staying overnight, preferably at a country inn, you could easily combine this trip with the ones to the Manchester area and the Saint-Gaudens National Historic Site.

GETTING THERE:

By car, Monadnock is about 70 miles northwest of Boston; the total round-trip will be a bit more than double that. Take routes **MA-2**, **MA-2A**, **MA-225**, **MA-119**, and **NH-119** to Rindge, then follow directions in the text and on the map.

PRACTICALITIES:

Those climbing the mountain should be equipped with adequate hiking boots offering good ankle support. Bring a light jacket or sweater as it can get chilly at the top. You should also carry along a water bottle and trail snacks, plus of course your camera and binoculars. Only people in good physical condition should make the climb, and they should allow a total of three to four hours for the round-trip.

For current foliage conditions during September and October, ☎ (800) 258-3608 or (800) 262-6660, or visit the Web Site: www.visitnh.gov.

For further information contact the **Monadnock Travel Council**, 48 Central Square, Keene, NH 03431, ☎ (603) 352-1308 or (800) 432-7864. You might also try the **Jaffrey Chamber of Commerce**, Jaffrey, NH 03452,

☎ (603) 532-4549, and/or the **Peterborough Chamber of Commerce**, Box 401, Peterborough, NH 03458, ☎ (603) 924-7234.

FOOD AND DRINK:

There are good picnic facilities at Mount Monadnock. As for restaurants, here are a few choices:

Monadnock Inn (NH-124, 2 miles west of Jaffrey) Continental cuisine at a country inn. Reservations essential, ☎ (603) 532-7001. X: Sat. lunch. $$

Latacarta (6 School St. in Peterborough) Creative and healthy cuisines, with touches from around the world, all served in a fashionable setting. Reservations suggested, ☎ (603) 924-6878. $$

Boilerhouse (on US-202, 2 miles south of Peterborough, at Noone Falls) It's open for dinner only (except Sunday brunch), but it's a great place to end the day. Gourmet dining in a converted 19th-century factory overlooking a waterfall. Reservations suggested, ☎ (603) 924-9486. X: Mon. $$

SUGGESTED DRIVE:

Numbers in parentheses correspond to numbers on the map.

Starting at the village of **Rindge** (1), home of Franklin Pierce College, turn north on Cathedral of the Pines Road to the inspiring **Cathedral of the Pines** (2). This non-denominational outdoor church honors all Americans killed in war from 1775 to the present. Its **Altar of the Nation**, facing Mount Monadnock, is made of stones donated by American presidents, military leaders, and all 50 states plus the territories. The **Memorial Bell Tower**, with plaques by Norman Rockwell, commemorates American women who served in wartime. Gardens, chapels, and a **museum** of military memorabilia further enhance the lovely hilltop site. *☎ (603) 899-3300. Open May–Oct., daily 9–dusk. Donation.* ♿.

Continue north on Prescott Road past Squantim and turn left on NH-124. Just before Jaffrey is the **Silver Ranch Airpark**, offering scenic airplane rides over the Monadnock region. If you're not up to climbing the mountain, you can still get a great view this way! *☎ (603) 532-8870 for rates and reservations.* Beyond Jaffrey is **Jaffrey Center** (3) with its old meetinghouse from Revolutionary times. Lectures held here every July and August honor one Amos Fortune, a former slave who purchased his freedom, prospered, and left his fortune to the Jaffrey School in 1801. He is buried in the cemetery here, as is the author Willa Cather.

Turn right on Dublin Road to:

*MONADNOCK STATE PARK (4), Jaffrey, NH 03452, ☎ (603) 532-8862. *Open year round, daily 8–dusk. Fee $2.50. Visitor Center, picnicking, camping, hiking trails, cross-country skiing, park store. No pets. ☎. Partially* ♿.

This is where your trek to the summit of glorious ***Mount Monadnock** begins. One of the most climbed mountains in the world, Monadnock may be second in popularity only to Japan's Mount Fuji. At 3,165 feet, it is considerably lower but offers the only ***view** anywhere that takes in parts of each of the six New England states. Yes, you can allegedly see Connecticut from here on a clear day. A very clear day.

Several trails lead to the summit. The quickest way up is via the **White Dot Trail**, which has a few fairly steep sections and takes at least three hours round-trip. The **White Cross Trail** is about the same length but slightly more difficult. Ask at the Visitor Center for advise, current trail conditions, and a map. With luck, at the top you'll be able to enjoy a panorama that includes Mount Washington in the north and Boston to the southeast.

Continue north on what is now called Upper Jaffrey Road to the village of **Dublin** (5), the home of *Yankee* Magazine and the *Old Farmer's Almanac*. At an elevation of 1,493 feet, this is supposed to be the highest town in New England. **Harrisville** (6), a few miles farther north, is a tiny old mill town with handsome 19th-century red-brick industrial buildings reflected in its village pond. Hand-spun yarns made from local sheep, along with looms and finished fabrics, are displayed and sold at **Harrisville Designs**, an interesting stop for the serious weaver. ☎ *(603) 827-3996. Open Tues.–Sat., 10–5.*

Take Hancock Road east past Eastview, turning north on NH-137 to **Hancock** (7). Park your car and stroll around its archetypal New England village center, graced with a picturesque green, a meeting house, a bandstand, a general store, and the John Hancock Inn of 1789—New Hampshire's oldest operating inn.

Head south on NH-123. In a few miles, after the road joins US-202, a country lane to the left leads to a covered bridge. Continue south to **Peterborough** (8), the cultural center of the region. The composer Edward MacDowell (1860–1908) lived nearby and founded an arts colony here that is still going strong, attracting leading painters, sculptors, filmmakers, writers, and composers to its quiet retreat. Very little of this is open to the public, but you can visit the library and MacDowell's grave by checking at Colony Hall. *100 High St.,* ☎ *(603) 924-3886. Open Mon.–Fri. 1–4.* Other cultural pursuits in Peterborough include a lively summer theater scene, and the highly unusual **New England Marionette Opera** with performances on weekends in season. ☎ *(603) 924-4333.* The town is also noted for its shops, galleries, and fine restaurants.

Take NH-101, and then NH-123 south into **New Ipswich** (9), a local trading center with several Colonial buildings. Here you can visit the **Barrett House**, otherwise known as Forest Hall. This Federal-style mansion from around 1800 features a grand ballroom, period furnishings, a Gothic Revival summer house, and extensive grounds. *Main St.,* ☎ *(603) 878-2517. Open June to mid-Oct., Thurs.–Sun., noon–4. Adults $4, seniors $3.50, ages 6–12 $2.* Continuing south on NH-124 will head you in the direction of Boston.

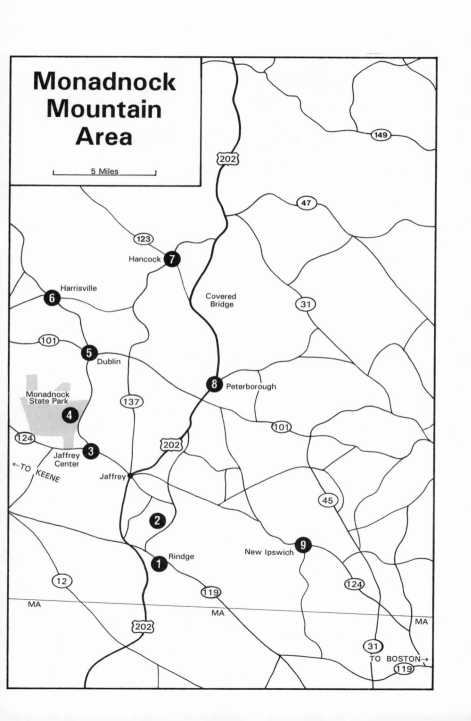

Monadnock
Mountain
Area

5 Miles

Trip 45

Keene, the Saint-Gaudens National Historic Site, and Lake Sunapee

Although it's a bit of a drive from Boston, this day's outing takes you to some of the prettiest scenery in New Hampshire, and to several intriguing historic sites as well. The focus is on the marvelous Saint-Gaudens National Historic Site, but along the way you'll be treated to the bustling center of Keene, and to the small historic towns of Walpole, Charlestown, and Claremont. The Fort at Number 4 is a living history museum that brings the French and Indian War of the early 18th century to life. One of the longest covered bridges in the world spans the Connecticut River at Cornish, linking New Hampshire to Vermont. After enjoying the Saint-Gaudens site, you can end the day at Lake Sunapee—perhaps on a sunset dinner cruise—before returning home via the Interstate.

This daytrip could be converted into a mini-vacation by staying overnight and combining it with the previous one to the Monadnock Mountain Area, or with the Drive Through Southern Vermont (page 265).

GETTING THERE:

By car, the Saint-Gaudens site is roughly 150 miles northwest of Boston via the route described in the text. The shorter (and much faster) return route is about 133 miles, making a total of 288 miles for the day.

PRACTICALITIES:

The Saint-Gaudens site is open daily from Memorial Day through October, while the Fort at Number 4 operates from May through October, daily except on Tuesdays. Other sites have varying times; check the individual listings if you plan to stop at them.

For additional information contact the **Keene Chamber of Commerce**, 8 Central Square, Keene, NH 03431, ☎ (603) 352-1303; or the **Claremont**

A sculpture at the Saint-Gaudens Site

Chamber of Commerce, Claremont, NH 03743, ☎ (603) 543-1296; or the **Sunapee Business Association**, Box 400, Sunapee, NH 03782, ☎ (603) 763-2495 or (800) 258-3530.

FOOD AND DRINK:

Bryanna's (NH-103, 2 miles south of NH-11, west of Sunapee) A great place for dinner near the lake. Italian and American cuisine, outdoor dining in season. Reservations suggested, ☎ (603) 863-1820. X: Mon. $$

Henry David's (81 Main St. in Keene) Henry David Thoreau's grand-mother operated this 1785 tavern for many years, and his mother lived here. There's a pleasant atrium and contemporary food. ☎ (603) 352-0608. $ and $$

One-Seventy-Six Main (176 Main St. in Keene) An old tavern with American, Italian, and Mexican dishes, plus a great selection of quality beers. ☎ (603) 357-3100. $ and $$

The Pub (Winchester & Ralston sts., Keene, ½ mile north of intersec-tion of NH 9/10/101) Greek, Italian, and American dishes. ☎ (603) 352-3135. $ and $$

Timoleans (27 Main St. in Keene) A classic diner, very popular. $

SUGGESTED DRIVE:

Numbers in parentheses correspond to numbers on the map.

Begin your day at **Keene** (1), easily reached from Boston via routes MA-2 to Fitchburg, then MA-12 and NH-12. Most of the attractions in this old manufacturing town are on Main Street, including the **Wyman Tavern Museum** of 1762. In 1770 it was the venue for the initial meeting of the trustees of Dartmouth College, and five years later the departure point for the local Minute Men as they marched off to Lexington to fight the first battle of the Revolution. *339 Main St.,* ☎ *(603) 352-1895. Open June–Labor Day, Thurs.–Sat. 11–4. Admission $2.* Nearby, the **Historical Society of Cheshire County** maintains a museum that specializes in locally-produced glass and pottery, some of which is of extraordinary quality. There are also rotating exhibits of local history. *246 Main St.,* ☎ *(603) 352-1895. Open all year, Mon.–Fri. 9–4. Donation.* Also on Main Street, the **Horatio Colony House Museum** displays the vast collection of minor cultural treasures, world travel souvenirs, and just plain things accumulated over a lifetime by an early 19th-century collector named Horatio Colony. *199 Main St.,* ☎ *(603) 352-0460. Open June to mid-Oct., Tues.–Sat. 11–3; rest of year Sat. 11–3. Free.*

Covered Bridge mavens will want to take a short detour south on NH-10 past West Swanzey, an area rich in these picturesque wooden spans. Local signs point the way.

Continue north on NH-12 to **Walpole** (2), a prosperous little village with a delightful town green. The route now follows the Connecticut River to **Charlestown** (3). Founded in 1744 and abandoned during the French and Indian War, the town prospered after the Revolution and is today blessed with one of the best collections of Federal, Greek Revival, and Gothic Revival houses in New England. A mile or so to the north is the reconstructed **Fort at Number 4** (4), the only living history museum devoted to the French and Indian War. Interpreters' in period costumes act out the day-to-day adventures of 18th-century frontier life amid more than a dozen re-created structures within the fort's walls. Those coming at the right time can experience battle reenactments, militia musters, festivals, and the like; call in advance for times. ☎ *(603) 826-5700. Open Memorial Day weekend to Labor Day and late Sept. to mid-Oct., Wed.–Mon. 10–4; also early-to-mid-Sept., weekends 10–4. Adults $6, children (6–11) $4, families $20.*

Continue north along the river, bearing left on NH-12A towards Cornish. The **Cornish-Windsor Bridge** (5) of 1866 spans the Connecticut River here, joining New Hampshire and Vermont with one of the longest covered bridges in the world. During the first decade of the 20th century, Cornish was home to a leading art colony that centered around the talents of sculptor Augustus Saint-Gaudens, painter Maxfield Parrish, and many others. Reminders of this illustrious past can be seen at the marvelous:

*SAINT-GAUDENS NATIONAL HISTORIC SITE (6), off NH-12A, Cornish, NH 03745, ☎ (603) 675-2175. *Grounds open daily. Buildings open Memo-*

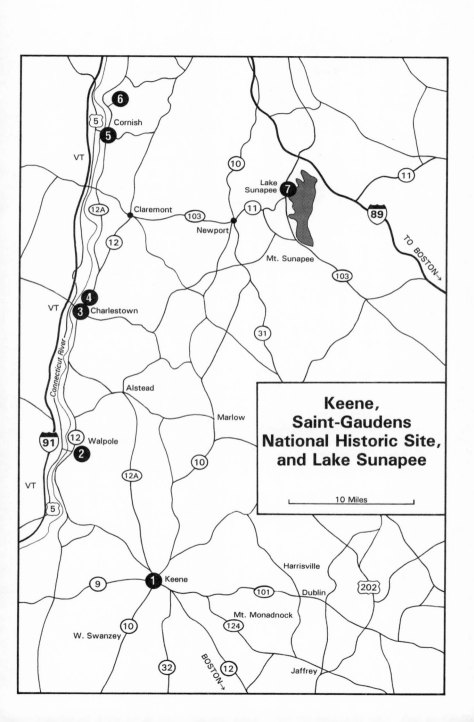

**Keene,
Saint-Gaudens
National Historic Site,
and Lake Sunapee**

10 Miles

rial Day–Oct., daily 9–4:30. Adults $2, seniors and children under 17 free. Picnic facilities. Nature trails. &.

Augustus Saint-Gaudens (1848–1907) was considered to be the greatest American sculptor of his era, with many public works enhancing cities from Chicago to Edinburgh. Born in Ireland, he came to the United States as an infant, studied at the Ecole des Beaux-Arts in Paris, returned to America in 1875, and summered here in Cornish from 1885 until 1900, after which this became his permanent residence. Originally an old inn that had fallen on hard times, the property—renamed "Aspet" after his father's birthplace in France—was transformed by Saint-Gaudens into a magnificent country estate complete with studios, gardens, pools, fountains, a grand ***view** of Vermont's Mount Ascutney, and even a golf course. The golf is long gone, as is the toboggan run, but there's plenty to see here, especially in the studios and galleries. Exact copies of his works reveal a talent that has hardly ever been matched; don't miss the exhibit of 1907 U.S. gold coinage designed by Saint-Gaudens at President Theodore Roosevelt's request.

Return south on NH-12A, turning left (east) on NH-103 through lovely Claremont. This heads you directly towards speedy Route I-89, the quick way back to Boston. Before getting on the Interstate, however, you might want to finish off the day at **Lake Sunapee** (7). Mount Sunapee State Park, at the southern end of the lake, features a multitude of visitor facilities, including a chairlift to the 2,743-foot summit of **Mount Sunapee** for a breathtaking panoramic ***view**. ☎ *(603) 763-2356. Summer lift service operates mid-June to Labor Day, Wed.–Sun. noon–7; Memorial Day to mid-June and mid-Sept. to Columbus Day, weekends 9–5. Fares: Adults $5.50, children (6–12) $2.50. Park open daily, free. Beach $2.50. Ski service in winter. Hiking, swimming, picnicking.* If that doesn't tempt you, how about a **dinner cruise** on the lake? The MV *Kearsarge* departs Steamboat Landing, at Sunapee Harbor near the junction of NH-103B and NH-11, once or twice each evening from mid-June through Labor Day. *Reservations suggested,* ☎ *(603) 763-5477. Fare with dinner: Adults $17.50, children (3–11) $8.50.*

Section VIII

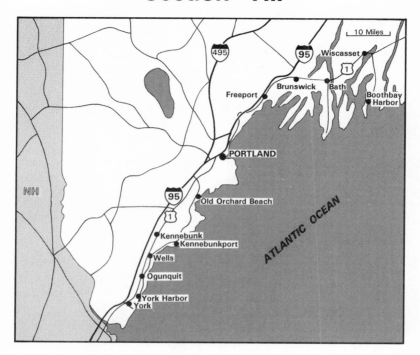

DAYTRIPS TO
MAINE

Only a small part of Maine lends itself to convenient daytrips from the rest of New England; fortunately the areas that do lie within easy reach are well worth exploring. This, of course, is not the backwoods Maine of an L.L. Bean catalog, nor the lonely coastal reaches of maritime novels—although you will find traces of the latter on the last trip of this section. Rather, this is historic Maine, with Colonial towns, restored urban areas, lighthouses, beaches, nature preserves, and a multitude of enjoyable tourist attractions including numerous boat cruises. Hopefully, these will whet you appetite for the treats that lie farther north, which require at least a few days to enjoy.

Many people travel to southern Maine for the shopping alone. Freeport is especially renowned in this regard, and Route US-1 from the New Hampshire border to The Yorks is positively infested with factory outlets, some of which can be real bargains.

Trip 46

The Yorks
and Ogunquit

Amid the commercialization of Maine's southern coast lurk two gems; both largely unspoiled and well worth seeking out. The Yorks, actually three towns with different personalities, were first settled by Europeans in 1624 as Agamenticus, and in 1642 became the first chartered English "city" in America. Then known as Gorgeana, the town was unable to govern itself effectively, so in 1652 it joined Massachusetts and changed its name to York. There's a lot of history here, with several wonderfully-restored 18th- and 19th-century buildings to explore in the heart of York Village. Nearby York Harbor has its own charms, and hums with maritime activity. One of the most photographed sights in Maine is the Cape Neddick Lighthouse on a tiny island off Nubble Point.

Ogunquit, whose name means "beautiful place by the sea" in the Algonquin language, is both a quality summer resort and a thriving art colony, with an excellent Museum of American Art and several galleries. It also offers a scenic coastal footpath along a cliff, and a picturesque harbor from which short cruises are available. The public beach is among the finest on the Atlantic coast; a delightful way to end the day.

You could, of course, make a real vacation out of this by staying over a few nights (reserve!) and combining it with any or all of the following four trips along the Maine coast, or with Portsmouth in New Hampshire (page 272).

GETTING THERE:

By car, The Yorks are about 75 miles northeast of downtown Boston via routes **US-1** and **I-95** (toll in NH) to Exit 4 in Maine. Follow **US-1A** east into York Village for the first attractions, then follow the map and the directions in the text.

PRACTICALITIES:

This is really a summer place, where most of the attractions are closed during the long off-season. The best time to come is from mid-June through September, although this can be extended a few weeks at either end without missing too much. Avoid coming on a Monday if the historic sites are important to you; at least one of these is also closed on Tuesdays. Be sure to bring sun-block lotion, and maybe your bathing togs.

For more information contact the **Southern Maine Coast Information Center**, ☎ (800) 639-2442; the **York Chamber of Commerce**, ☎ (207)

363-4422, or the **Ogunquit Chamber of Commerce,** ☎ (207) 646-2939. The statewide **Maine Publicity Bureau** has an information center along routes I-95 and US-1 just above the New Hampshire border, ☎ (207) 439-1319.

FOOD AND DRINK:

Among the places open for lunch are:

York Harbor Inn (US-1A, York St., in York Harbor) Continental cuisine overlooking the harbor. ☎ (207) 363-5119. X: Sat. lunch, also Mon.–Thurs. from Jan.Apr. $$

Barnacle Billy's (Shore Rd. in Perkins Cove) Seafood and a few other dishes, self-serve, indoor/outdoor dining overlooking a working harbor. There is also a Barnacle Billy's Etc. restaurant next door. ☎ (207) 646-5575. $$

Ogunquit Lobster Pound (US-1, ½ mile north of Ogunquit) Pick your own lobster and eat it in rustic surroundings, indoors or out. ☎ (207) 646-2516. X: Lunch in May & June, and Labor Day to Columbus Day. Closed late Oct. to Apr. $$

Jama's Café (433 US-1, a mile south of turnpike exit) A casual, friendly place for well-prepared American dishes. ☎ (207) 363-7980. $

Hayloft (US-1, 2½ miles north of Ogunquit) Good-value seafood, chicken, or beef in a country setting. ☎ (207) 646-4400. X: Dec.–Jan. $

LOCAL ATTRACTIONS:

Numbers in parentheses correspond to numbers on the map.

Begin in **York Village**, whose treasured past is maintained by the:

*OLD YORK HISTORICAL SOCIETY (1), P.O. Box 312, York, ME 03909, ☎ (207) 363-4974. *Sites open mid-June through Sept., Tues.–Sat. 10–5, Sun. 1–5. Individual sites: Adults $2, ages 6–16 $1. Combination ticket for all six sites: Adults $6.50, ages 6–16 $2.50, families $16. Purchase tickets and begin tours at Jefferds Tavern, Lindsay Rd. at US-1A (York St.). Partially* &.

Jefferds Tavern was originally built in 1750 on the King's Highway in Wells as a "Publick House," and was moved here in the early 1940s. Its restored taproom no longer quenches the thirst of travelers, at least not for rum. The venerable building now serves as an orientation and educational center, with exhibits on early York life, and a gift shop.

Practically adjacent to the tavern is the **Old Schoolhouse** of 1745, thought to be the state's oldest surviving one-room school. It's furnished as it would have been in the past, only today's visitors learn about the history of education in Colonial York.

The **Emerson-Wilcox House** of 1742, just across the street, has seen a variety of uses down through the years. It's been a tavern, a post office, a general store, a tailor shop, and a private dwelling. Today, the house is furnished with period antiques, and is especially noted for its crewelwork bed hangings created well over two centuries ago. Built on land leased for 999 years, the house still pays rent to the **First Parish Church** of 1747, across the street.

In the same immediate neighborhood is the ***Old Gaol**, built in 1719 and used as a prison until 1860. Its two-foot-thick walls housed both debtors and hardened criminals, the latter in the cavelike dungeon. Since 1900 it's been a museum devoted to local historical artifacts, with cells and jailer's quarters furnished as they would have been around 1790.

Stroll down Lindsay Road and cross **Sewall's Bridge**, built in 1761 as New England's first pile drawbridge. In 1775, Maine's Minutemen crossed this span as they marched off to Lexington. You should cross it too, and visit the **Elizabeth Perkins House** of 1732, the Colonial Revival summer house of the prominent preservationist who died in 1952.

Recross the bridge and bear right to the **John Hancock Warehouse**, owned in part by the famous patriot until 1794. Once used as a customs house, it now contains exhibits on local maritime and agricultural history. From here you can take a short walk along a river path, passing through a nature preserve to **Wiggley Bridge**. This is one of the smallest suspension bridges in the world, and if you cross it you'll discover how it got its name. Return to Lindsay Road and your car.

Head south along US-1A (York St.) towards **York Harbor**. Along the way, a turn to the right onto Barrell Lane leads to the **Sayward-Wheeler House** (2) of 1718. Owned by a prosperous 18th-century trader, it remained in the family for generations and is filled with heirlooms and original furniture. ☎ *(207) 363-5204. Open June to mid-Oct., Wed.–Sun. noon–4. Adults $4, seniors $3.50, children (6–12) $2.*

The **Town Wharf** (3) of **York Harbor** lies across the river; cross the bridge on ME-103, then turn left onto Harris Island Road. There are all sorts of maritime activities here, including boat rides.

Back on the north side of the York River, continue south on US-1A and turn right on Harbor Beach Road to reach the beautiful **Cliff Walk** (4). This winding trail, crossing private land but open to the public, offers spectacular ***views** of the ocean.

Continue along US-1A past Long Sands Beach, then turn right on Nubble Road to Nubble Point and the delightful ***Cape Neddick Lighthouse** (5). Built in 1879 after a terrible shipwreck, the light is on a tiny island just off shore, so you can't quite reach it. Still, it's a great sight; one of the most photographed along the Maine coast.

Continuing around on Nubble Road and Broadway eventually gets you back on US-1A. Heading north past **York Beach**, bear right on Shore Road and follow it into the town of **Ogunquit**. This "beautiful place by the sea," as

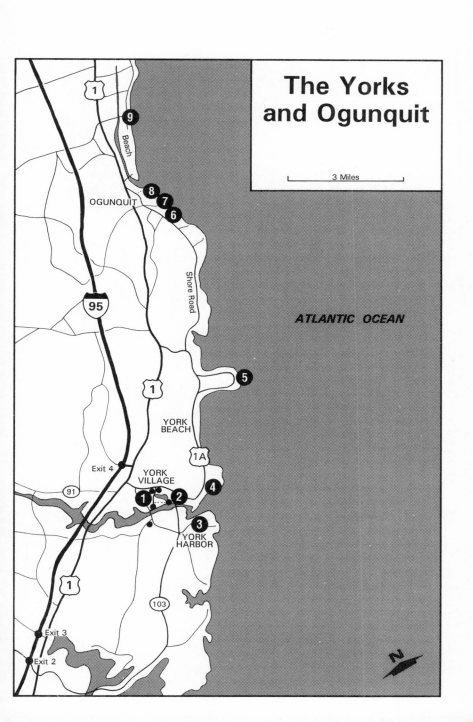

The Yorks
and Ogunquit

3 Miles

ATLANTIC OCEAN

OGUNQUIT

Beach

Shore Road

95

YORK
BEACH

1A

Exit 4

YORK
VILLAGE

91

YORK
HARBOR

103

Exit 3

Exit 2

N

On the Wiggley Bridge

the Abenaki Indians so aptly called it, is today both a fine resort and a thriving art colony. The first attraction you'll come to is the ***Ogunquit Museum of American Art** (6) on Shore Road. Among the 20th-century American artists represented here are Rockwell Kent, Reginald Marsh, Walt Kuhn, Marsden Hartley, and many others. The museum is set in a three-acre sculpture garden, with rugged views of the ocean and cliffs. ☎ *(207) 646-4909. Open July–Sept., Mon.–Sat. 10:30–5, Sun. 2–5. Closed Labor Day. Adults $3, seniors and students $2, under 12 free.*

Turn right on Oarweed Road to visit ***Perkins Cove** (7), a tiny harbor with immense charm that offers a good variety of craft shops, boutiques, galleries, and restaurants. You may have to park a short distance away and take the town's "trolley" as space near the cove is limited. Be sure to stroll across Maine's only pedestrian drawbridge, which rises for nearly every passing boat. Sightseeing **cruises** are offered on a number of vessels, including lobster boats, sailboats, and yachts. These can be as short as one hour, and include such delights as evening cocktail cruises. *Finestkind Scenic Cruises,* ☎ *(207) 646-5227.*

Marginal Way (8) is a mile-long footpath leading north from Perkins Cove, with stunning ***views** of the rocky shore, passing boats, lobster traps, and the like. To visit **Ogunquit Beach** (9), continue north on Shore Road through the town, then turn right on Beach Street.

Wells and the Kennebunks

Just a bit farther up the shore, the resort town of Wells offers three unusual attractions that might compel a stop. Car enthusiasts are as drawn to the Wells Auto Museum as nature lovers are to the National Estuarine Research Reserve and the Rachel Carson National Wildlife Refuge. The nearby Kennebunks became famous a few years back when then-President Bush established his summer White House there. Today they offer a variety of treats, ranging from historic houses to the Seashore Trolley Museum, where you can ride antique streetcars along an old right-of-way. To finish off the day, you might head north to Old Orchard Beach, one of the finest and oldest on the Maine coast, to have fun at the old-fashioned amusement area.

If time permits, why not stay overnight and combine this trip with the previous one, or the three that follow?

GETTING THERE:

By car, Wells is about 90 miles northeast of downtown Boston via routes **US-1** and **I-95** (toll in NH and ME) to Exit 2 of the **Maine Turnpike**, which is what I-95 is called north of the toll booth near York.

From there, it's 8 miles north to Kennebunk, then 6 miles east to Kennebunkport. Those going to Old Orchard Beach will add another 20 miles.

PRACTICALITIES:

Most of the attractions are open from about Memorial Day through September, although you should check the individual listings to be sure. Those making the trip in the late spring or early fall would do well to make a few phone calls first, as even the published schedules vary a bit from year to year. Don't forget the sun-block lotion, and perhaps an insect repellant if you're going into either of the nature preserves.

For further information contact the **Southern Maine Coast Information Center**, ☎ (800) 639-2442; the **Wells Chamber of Commerce**, ☎ (207) 646-2451; or the **Kennebunk and Kennebunkport Chamber of Commerce**, 173 Port Road (ME-35) in Lower Village, ☎ (207) 967-0857. The statewide **Maine Publicity Bureau** has an information center along routes I-95 and US-1 just above the New Hampshire border, ☎ (207) 439-1319.

FOOD AND DRINK:

Billy's Chowder House (216 Mile Rd., between the Auto Museum and Wells Beach) A rustic seafood place with a great view of the tidal marshes. ☎ (207) 646-7558. $$

Litchfield's Seafood Restaurant (US-1, 1½ miles north of Wells) Seafood, steak, and pasta in a casual setting. ☎ (207) 646-5711. $$

Bartley's Dockside (ME-9, by the bridge in Kennebunkport) Seafood and other dishes, indoor/outdoor dining, with a view of the harbor. ☎ (207) 967-5050. $ and $$

Arundel Wharf (43 Ocean Ave., by the marina in Kennebunkport) Sandwiches, seafood, and meat dishes on a wharf overlooking the water; indoor/outdoor seating. ☎ (207) 967-3444. $ and $$

LOCAL ATTRACTIONS:

Numbers in parentheses correspond to numbers on the map.

From the Turnpike exit take ME-109 east into Wells, then turn right on US-1 and follow it south about a mile to the:

WELLS AUTO MUSEUM (1), US-1 at Bay View Terrace, Wells, ME 04090, ☎ (207) 646-9064. *Open mid-June through Sept., daily 10–5; late May to mid-June and early Oct., weekends 10–5. Adults $3.50, children (6–12) $2. Model T rides $1 extra.* ♿.

A fabulous collection of antique and classic cars dating from around 1900 to the 1960s celebrates the glorious history of motoring, along with other bits of period Americana such as nickelodeons, arcade games, and the like. Visitors can even go for a short ride in a Model T Ford of 1911, and watch exciting flicks on the coin-operated picture machines. Among the automotive treasures are examples by such once-famous manufacturers as Pierce-Arrow, Stanley Steamer, Maxwell, and Packard—as well as strange vehicles such as the long-forgotten Grout Steamer, the Orient Buckboard, and the original Snowmobile of 1923, the latter an ingenious answer to New Hampshire's winters.

Return north along US-1, passing the intersection with ME-109. After almost two miles, a right turn on Laudholm Farm Road leads to the:

WELLS NATIONAL ESTUARINE RESEARCH RESERVE (2), Laudholm Trust, P.O. Box 1007, Wells, ME 04090, ☎ (207) 646-1555, Internet: http://inlet.geol.edu/WEL. *Reserve open all year, daily 8–5. Visitor Center open May–Oct., Mon.–Sat. 10–4 and Sun. noon–4; rest of year Mon.–Fri. 10–4. Reserve free, tours $2.50. Parking fee $5 in July–Aug., free other times. Exhibits. Gift shop.*

Laudholm Farm, a 1,600-acre spread of saltwater marshes and scenic upland, was started in 1643. Its splendid Greek Revival farmhouse dates

In the Wells Auto Museum

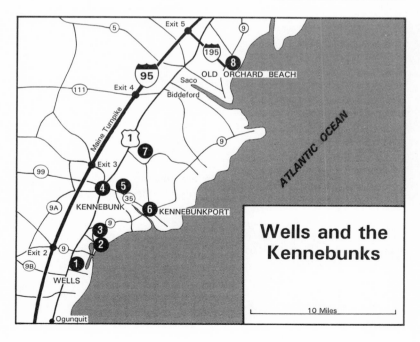

from the 19th century, and today houses educational, environmental, and research facilities. Seven miles of trails and boardwalks meander through marshes, fields, coast, and forest, offering magnificent *views and bird-watching opportunities. Pick up a trail map and brochure guide at the visitor center, watch the slide show, see the exhibits, and then go off exploring either on your own or on a tour.

Nearby is the associated:

*RACHEL CARSON NATIONAL WILDLIFE REFUGE (3), Route ME-9 a mile east of US-1, Wells, ME 04090, ☎ (207) 646-9226. *Open daily, dawn to dusk. Free, donations appreciated.*

Rachel Carson (1907–64) was an American biologist whose famous book *Silent Spring* helped trigger the modern environmental movement in the 1960s. She is honored with this 4,500-acre refuge of salt marshes, upland, and coastal habitats—quite a world apart from the surrounding resort areas. Visitors can hike the mile-long interpretive nature trail with its delightful views, stopping first at the office near the parking area for a free trail map and brochure.

Return to Route US-1 and continue north into **Kennebunk**, an old ship-building community first settled around 1650. Its economy peaked in the early 19th century, leaving behind a rich heritage of architectural gems that make for an interesting little walking tour. Start your exploration at the **Brick Store Museum** (4) at 117 Main Street (US-1), opposite the library. Spread through an entire block of restored 19th-century buildings, the museum is devoted to local history, maritime exhibits, and the decorative arts. The nearby **Taylor-Barry House** of 1803 is also a part of the museum. Guided tours of the historic district are offered, as are self-guided tour booklets. ☎ *(207) 985-4802. Museum open Tues.–Sat. 10–4:40, closed holidays. House open July–Sept., Tues.–Fri. 1–4. Museum: adults $3, children (6–16) $1. House: adults $2, children $1. Combination ticket available. Partially &.*

Head down Landing Road (ME-9A), passing the incredible **Wedding Cake House** (5) in about a mile on the left. Built in 1826, this otherwise undistinguished house is completely festooned in fancy fretwork, sup-posedly as compensation by a sea captain to his bride for the wedding cake she never had.

Continue down ME-9A and turn left on ME-9, crossing the bridge into **Kennebunkport**. Popular as a resort, the old town is also noted as an art and literary colony. During the Bush administration (1989–93), it was the sum-mer home of the 41st President of the United States. Much of its past can be appreciated at the gloriously Victorian **Nott House** (6) of 1853, a.k.a. **White Columns**. Nothing, but nothing, has been changed here for generations; in fact it still contains the original wallpaper, carpeting, and furnishings. Guided tours of the town's historic district are offered on Wednesdays and

Fridays in July and August. *Maine St.,* ☎ *(207) 967-2751. Open mid-June to mid-Oct., Wed.–Sat. 1–4. Adults $3, children $1.*

If you enjoyed the Auto Museum in Wells, you'll probably love the nearby:

SEASHORE TROLLEY MUSEUM (7), Log Cabin Rd., about 3 miles north via North St., Kennebunkport, ME 04046, ☎ (207) 967-2800. *Open May to mid-Oct., daily 10 or 11 to 3:30 or 4:30; schedule varies, check first. Adults $6, seniors $5, children $4, families $20.*

One of the world's largest collections of street cars is right here in Maine, and features some 50 restored trolley cars that originally served in such exotic places as Sydney, Nagasaki, Budapest, Rome, Glasgow, New York, and New Orleans. There are also unusual cars from Manchester, NH, New Bedford, MA, and even nearby Boston. Best of all, you can ride whichever ones are running that day, for several miles over a restored right-of-way. Besides those that run, there are many others in various states of repair, and visitors can watch them being restored. Lots of fun, laced with more than a little bit of nostalgia!

While in a nostalgic mood, why not finish the day at a real, old-fashioned oceanside amusement area? **Old Orchard Beach** (8) is some 20 miles farther up the coast, and well worth the drive. Take Route ME-9 all the way, then step back in time to an earlier era reminiscent of what Coney Island once was like. There's an old carousel, a Ferris wheel, arcade games, all sorts of amusement rides, and enough greasy food to keep the child in you happy.

At the Seashore Trolley Museum

Trip 48

Portland

Maine's largest city is hardly a metropolis, but it's still a very urbane, civilized place. Surprisingly, this town of some 65,000 souls boasts attractions that many a big city would envy. First and foremost, its Old Port Exchange area is a revitalized waterfront neighborhood that had long ago gone to seed. Today, it's a fashionable place whose 19th-century Victorian commercial buildings overflow with fine shops and eateries as well as offices. Cruises are offered to nearby Casco Bay and the Calendar Islands; some of these are short enough to fit into your daytrip. As the cultural center of the state, Portland has a superb art museum along with a number of restored historic houses and impressive mansions. There's also a children's museum, an observatory, and several nearby lighthouses with scenic views.

GETTING THERE:

By car, Portland is about 115 miles northeast of downtown Boston via routes **US-1** and **I-95** (toll in NH and ME), which becomes the Maine Turnpike. Take the latter to Exit 6A, then **I-295** to Exit 5 and Congress Street east into the Old Port area. Most of the attractions are within walking distance of here.

Buses operated by Concord Trailways provide daily express service between Boston and Portland. For information, ☎ (800) 639-3317.

PRACTICALITIES:

Portland is best visited between mid-June and Labor Day, when things are in full swing. Several places open a few weeks earlier and remain open into October; a few operate all year round. Check the individual listings. The renowned Portland Museum of Art and most of the historic houses are closed on Mondays and some holidays.

For further information, contact the **Convention & Visitors Bureau of Greater Portland**, 305 Commercial St., Portland, ME 04101, ☎ (207) 772-5800. The statewide **Maine Publicity Bureau** has an information center along routes I-95 and US-1 just above the New Hampshire border, ☎ (207) 439-1319.

Along Portland's waterfront

FOOD AND DRINK:

DiMillo's Floating Restaurant (25 Long Wharf at Commercial St.) This former ferryboat now serves seafood, steak, and the like—indoors or out. ☎ (207) 772-2216. $$

Sapporo (230 Commercial St. at Union Wharf, on the waterfront) Japanese cuisine in the Old Port Exchange area. ☎ (207) 772-1233. $$

F. Parker Reidy's (83 Exchange St., near the north end of the Old Port Exchange) Friendly, casual dining in an 1866 Victorian bank, with both seafood and meat dishes. ☎ (207) 773-4731. X: Sun. lunch, major holidays. $$

Seamen's Club (375 Fore St. at Exchange St., in the Old Port Exchange area) This landmark establishment is tremendously popular for its seafood, and there are meat dishes too. Harbor view. Reservations accepted, ☎ (207) 772-7311. $ and $$

Valle's Steak House (1140 Brighton Ave. at I-95 Exit 8, junction of ME-25) Seafood, steak, and the like. ☎ (207) 774-4551. $ and $$

LOCAL ATTRACTIONS:

Numbers in parentheses correspond to numbers on the map.

Begin your tour at the **Visitor Information Center**, 305 Commercial Street (US-1A), on the waterfront just west of the Old Port Exchange. Here you can pick up a walking tour map for exploring the historic ***Old Port Exchange** (1), a colorful neighborhood that has once again come back to life. Destroyed by Indian raids in the 1670s, reduced to rubble by the British in 1775, and burned to the ground in 1866, the Old Port was economically devastated as 20th-century business moved elsewhere. But those sturdy Victorian buildings, cobblestoned streets, and old gas lamps had their attractions, and by the 1970s once again became fashionable. No wonder that the town's motto is *Resurgam*—I Shall Rise Again!

One of the most interesting sights in the Old Port Exchange is the *trompe l'oeil* **mural** at the corner of Middle and Exchange streets; you'll have to look twice to determine what parts of it are real. Just north on Exchange Street is a wonderful block of Italianate buildings. The French style with its Mansard roofs dominates around the corner at Middle and Pearl streets, while to the south at 312 Fore Street the **United States Custom House** of 1868 reveals the optimism of the Victorian era. Heading west on Fore Street, the **Mariner's Church** at number 368 was built in 1828 and luckily survived the great conflagration of 1866. Even from the beginning, first-floor space in this Greek Revival structure was rented out to businesses to support the holy goings-on upstairs. The shops are still there, but the church is no more. Just across the street, the Gothic Revival **Seamen's Club**—built shortly after the fire—is now a popular restaurant.

This is just a sampling of the area's treasures; there are many more to discover before heading down to the **Waterfront** (2). Several firms along here offer enjoyable **cruises** around Casco Bay and to the nearby **Calendar Islands**, which allegedly number 365. At low tide, perhaps. A very low tide. But even if the count falls short, these are still interesting sights and the ride to them a lot of fun. Among the cruise operators are: **Casco Bay Lines**, on Commercial Street just east of the Custom House, ☎ (207) 774-7871; **Eagle Tours**, Long Wharf near Exchange Street, ☎ (207) 774-6498; and **Bay View Cruises**, Fisherman's Wharf at 184 Commercial Street, ☎ (207) 761-0496. A really long cruise is offered aboard the MS *Scotia Prince*, a huge car ferry that goes to Yarmouth, Nova Scotia, in about 11 hours with all the comforts of an ocean liner—casino, shops, entertainment, restaurant, the works. ☎ (207) 775-5616, (800) 341-7540 nationwide, or (800) 482-0955 (in Maine).

Back on the mainland, near the northwest corner of the Old Port Exchange, is the **Wadsworth-Longfellow House** (3). The great poet, Henry Wadsworth Longfellow (1807–82), spent much of his childhood in this simple brick dwelling built by his maternal grandfather in 1785. Furniture, possessions, and records of both the Wadsworth and Longfellow families can be seen, and there's a garden. To the rear is the **Maine Historical Society**

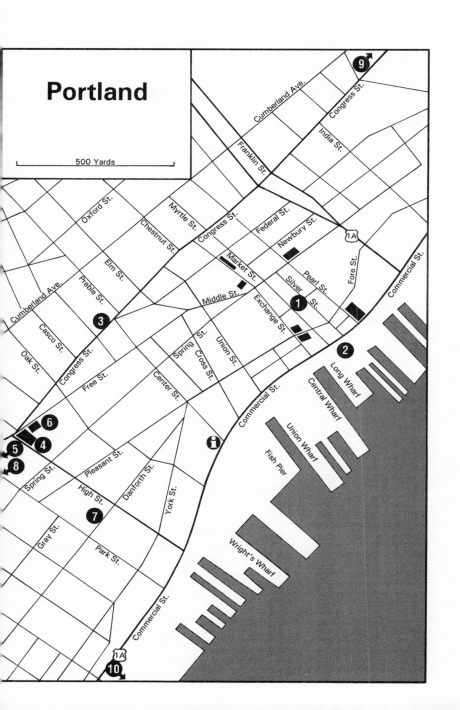

Portland

500 Yards

Library, featuring all sorts of material on Maine's history. *487 Congress St.,* ☎ *(207) 879-0427. Open June–Oct., Tues.–Sun. 10–4. Closed July 4 and Labor Day. Adults $4, under 12 $2.*

From here, it's about five blocks down Congress Street to the:

*PORTLAND MUSEUM OF ART (4), 7 Congress Sq., Portland, ME, ☎ (207) 775-6148 or 773-ARTS (recording). *Open Tues.–Sat. 10–5, Sun. noon–5, remaining open on Thurs. until 9. Closed holidays. Tours daily at 2, also at 5:30 on Thurs. Adults $6, seniors and students $5, children (6–12) $1. Museum shop.* ♿.

American artists associated with Maine are featured in this thoroughly modern museum, designed by Henry N. Cobb of I.M. Pei & Partners in 1983. Among the most notable paintings are those by Andrew Wyeth, Winslow Homer, Edward Hopper, and John Marin. There are also European works by Renoir, Monet, Picasso, and others. American and English ceramics, Portland glass, Federal furniture and decorative arts, silver and the like round out the collections.

A few blocks farther west on Congress Street is an 1829 house that recalls a strange chapter in Maine's history. The **Neal Dow Memorial** (5), a Federal-style mansion of 1829, was the residence of one Neal Dow (1804–97), Mayor of Portland, outspoken foe of "Demon Rum," leader of the temperance movement, and candidate of the Prohibition Party for President of the United States in 1880. In 1851 he succeeded, almost single-handedly, in prohibiting the sale of spirits throughout Maine. Some people were understandably opposed to this, and tried to smash their way into the house to have a little discussion with him. Despite enemies, he lived a long life and in the end bequeathed his mansion to the Maine Women's Christian Temperance Union, which occupies it today. The first floor is maintained as it was in his time, complete with his furniture, mementos, and priceless antiques. On request, visitors are shown Mr. Dow's death mask, made immediately after his demise. *714 Congress St.,* ☎ *(207) 773-7773. Open Mon.– Fri. 10–4. Closed major holidays. Donations accepted.*

Those with kids to tow might want to head straight to the **Children's Museum of Maine** (6), close to the Museum of Art (above). Highlights include the inevitable interactive science exhibits, a lobster boat, a farming display, a grocery store, a huge globe, a model space shuttle, and more goodies including the fascinating Camera Obscura. *142 Free St.,* ☎ *(207) 828-1234. Open Mon. and Wed.–Sat. 10–5, remaining open on Fri. until 8, Tues. and Sun. noon–5. Admission $4, under 1 free. Free to all on Fri. evening.*

Lovers of Victoriana should head south a few blocks to the **Victoria Mansion** (7), a.k.a. the **Morse-Libby House**. Built between 1859 and 1863 in the exuberant Italianate Villa style, the house is literally covered with layer upon layer of decoration. Inside, there are *trompe l'oeil* walls and ceilings, stained-glass windows, hand-carved staircases, ornate chandeliers, marble fireplaces, original carpets and furnishings, rare porcelains, and much more. *104 Danforth St., between High and Park streets,* ☎ *(207) 772-4841. Open late May to day before Labor Day, Tues.–Sat. 10–4, Sun. 1–5; day after Labor Day through Oct., Fri.–Sat. 10–4, Sun. 1–5. Closed July 4 and Labor Day. Adults $4, seniors $3.50, ages 6–17 $1.50.*

The **Tate House** (8) is out near the airport, but worth the journey for aficionados of elegant 18th-century interiors in the English manner. If that's you, get in the car and drive west on Congress Street for about three miles, passing Route I-295 along the way, then turn left on Westbrook Street to number 1270, just south of Congress. George Tate, Mast Agent for the King of England, built this impressive dwelling in 1755. A mast agent supplied tall trees to be used as masts for Royal Navy ships; any suitable tree was automatically crown property, not to be felled by colonists for their own use on pain of the king's displeasure. The Georgian-style house is quite elegant, preserving much of the atmosphere of a London townhouse. ☎ *(207) 774-9781. Open July to the day before Labor Day, Tues.–Sat. 10–4 and Sun. 1–4; day after Labor Day through Oct., Fri.–Sun. 10–4. Closed July 4. Adults $4, under 12 $1.*

At the opposite end of town, a mile or so northeast of the Museum of Art, is the **Portland Observatory** (9). Set atop Munjoy Hill, this strange building was erected in 1807 as a signal tower to announce with flags the arrival of ships in the harbor. It's 86 feet tall, and visitors can climb it whenever the flags are flying for a glorious ***view**. *138 Congress St.,* ☎ *(207) 774-5561. Open July–Labor Day, Wed.–Sun. afternoons; June and early Sept.–Oct., Fri.–Sun. afternoons. Adults $1.50, under 12 50¢.*

Cape Elizabeth (10) lies about 10 miles south of Portland. Take Route ME-77 to South Portland, then turn left on Cottage Road, which becomes Shore Road. This soon brings you to Fort Williams Park and the **Portland Head Lighthouse** of 1791, the first to be built in the newly-independent United States. There's a great ***view** from here, hiking paths, picnic facilities, and even a little museum. ☎ *(207) 799-2661. Park open daily, dawn to dusk, free. Museum open June–Oct., daily 10–4; Apr.–May and Nov.–Dec., weekends 10–4. Museum: adults $2, ages 6–18 $1.* Two more lighthouses can be found a bit to the south at Two Lights, by the **Two Lights State Park**.

Trip 49

Freeport, Brunswick, and Bath

There's not much that's free in Freeport, and it isn't all that much of a port either, but the "Birthplace of Maine" is renowned throughout the world as the source of those homely-but-eminently-practical boots developed in 1912 by one Leon Leonwood Bean. The success of the L.L. Bean firm has been so astounding that today countless visitors descend on this small town, and millions of others shop there by mail, phone, or fax every day of the year. In their wake, aspiring to similar sales figures, are over 100 factory outlet stores mostly lined up along Main Street. When you grow weary of shopping, why not explore the nearby Desert of Maine, or take a short cruise along the coast?

Brunswick, home of Bowdoin College, offers excellent museums devoted to art, Arctic exploration, and local history. Bath, still a major shipbuilding center, celebrates its seagoing past at the wonderful Maine Maritime Museum, a ten-acre shipyard where visitors can witness traditional boat construction while learning about life at sea. You can finish off your day at Popham Beach, either frolicking on the sand or visiting the intriguing Fort Popham State Historic Site.

For those staying overnight, this trip combines well with the previous one to Portland, or with the following one to Wiscasset and Boothbay Harbor.

GETTING THERE:

By car, Freeport is about 135 miles northeast of downtown Boston via routes **US-1** and **I-95** (toll in NH and ME), which becomes the Maine Turnpike. At Exit 9 (Portland), I-95 leaves the turnpike and continues northeast toward Freeport and Brunswick. Follow this and get off at Exit 19, Freeport.

From there follow the route in the text and on the map. From Freeport to Brunswick is about 10 miles, and another 10 to Bath. Popham Beach lies 16 miles south of Bath.

PRACTICALITIES

Shopping in Freeport is a year-round activity, but some other attractions are seasonal. The Desert of Maine operates from early May until mid-October, as do the cruises. The college museums of Brunswick are closed on Mondays and holidays. Bath's Maine Maritime Museum is open every day except Thanksgiving, Christmas, and New Year's.

For further information contact the **Freeport Merchants Association**, 10 Morse St., Freeport, ME 04032, ☎ (207) 865-1212 or (800) 865-1994, online freeportcc@Maine.com; the **Chamber of Commerce for Brunswick/Bath Region**, 59 Pleasant St., Brunswick, ME 04011, ☎ (207) 725-8797; or the **Bath Region Chamber of Commerce**, 45 Front St., Bath, ME 04530, ☎ (207) 443-9751. The statewide **Maine Publicity Bureau** has an information center along routes I-95 and US-1 just above the New Hampshire border, ☎ (207) 439-1319.

FOOD AND DRINK:

Jameson Tavern (121 Main St. in Freeport, near L.L. Bean) The documents separating Maine from Massachusetts were signed in this historic 1779 tavern. Seafood, steak, and chicken with lots of atmosphere. Reservations suggested, ☎ (207) 865-4196. $$

Ocean Farms (23 Main St., US-1, in Freeport) Seafood and steak, indoors or out. ☎ (207) 865-3101. $$

Kristina's (160 Centre St. in Bath) Creative American cuisine and great pastries, with outdoor dining in season. ☎ (207) 442-8577. $$

Lobster Cooker (39 Main St., US-1, in Freeport) Seafood in an early-19th-century building, or outdoors. ☎ (207) 865-4349. $ and $$

Great Impasta (42 Maine St. in Brunswick) A good value in pasta dishes. ☎ (207) 729-5858. X: Sun. lunch. $ and $$

Taste of Maine (US-1 in Woolwich, a mile north of Bath) Seafood, lobster, and steak overlooking the Kennebec River. ☎ (207) 443-4554. $ and $$

LOCAL ATTRACTIONS:

Numbers in parentheses correspond to numbers on the map.

Freeport (1) is known as the "Birthplace of Maine" because it was here that Maine gained its independence from Massachusetts, becoming the 23rd state in 1820. History aside, the small town is famous around the world for its fantastic shopping opportunities. Blame it all on Leon Leonwood Bean, who in 1912 developed a highly practical, if somewhat ugly, hunting boot and opened shop here in Freeport to manufacture and sell it. Today, **L.L. Bean** dominates the town, attracting a vast number of customers to its store, which is open 24 hours a day, every day of the year. Legend has it that its doors were only ever closed once. Bean's clothing, sporting goods, and housewares have their own distinctive style, are the height of fashion in certain circles, are very well made, represent good value, and are marketed with a degree of integrity that is all too rare today. The retail store has numerous items that are not in the catalog, while Bean's outlet store (across the street) sells seconds and end-of-season merchandise at bargain prices.

Drawn by Bean's success, well over a hundred other factory outlets, discounters, and specialty stores have set up shop in and around Freeport in recent years. If shopping is your thing, this is Heaven. If not, you might want to head out to the strange **Desert of Maine** (2), an ecological phenomenon in which once-fertile farmland is gradually becoming a barren desert of wind-swept sand. From the center of town, head south on Main Street (US-1) and turn right on Desert Road. Pass Exit 19 of I-95 and continue for about two miles, following signs. With dunes as high as 70 feet, the desert continues to grow, swallowing up forests and buildings in its wake. Guided tours are offered, on which the natural forces at work here are explained. ☎ *(207) 865-6962. Open early May to mid-Oct., daily 9–dusk. Adults $6, youths (13–16) $4, children (6–12) $3. Gift shop. Camping facilities.* ♿.

Going from desert dry to ocean wet, you might like to try an interesting **cruise** from the harbor in **South Freeport** (3). Tours vary in length, but the most adventurous is the three-hour excursion to **Eagle Island**, where you can visit the unusual summer home of Admiral Robert E. Peary (1856–1920). The great Arctic explorer is considered to be the first man to ever set foot on the North Pole, an achievement reached in 1909 after several previous failures. *Atlantic Seal Cruises, 25 Main St., South Freeport,* ☎ *(207) 865-6112. Eagle Island tour: adults $20, children (1–12) $15. Other tours vary. Reservations recommended.*

Head north on US-1 to **Brunswick** (4), first settled in the 1620s as Pejepscot and twice destroyed by Indian raids. Changing its name to the more easily pronounced Brunswick in the late 1700s, the town became home to Bowdoin College as early as 1794. This private liberal arts school is highly regarded and has a student enrollment of about 1,350. Among its alumni are Nathaniel Hawthorne, Henry Wadsworth Longfellow, Arctic explorers Robert Peary and Donald MacMillan, and President Franklin Pierce.

A stroll around the 110-acre campus brings you to the **Bowdoin College Museum of Art**, whose collections range all the way from Greek and Roman antiquities to contemporary 20th-century American paintings. There are pieces from Africa and Asia, Old Masters from Holland, France, and Italy, and American portraits from the Colonial and Federal periods. Every summer the Winslow Homer Gallery is opened, revealing paintings, graphics, and memorabilia of the great artist. ☎ *(207) 725-3275. Open Tues.–Sat. 10–5, Sun. 2–5. Closed major holidays. Free, donations accepted.* ♿.

Not only does this small college support an excellent art museum, it also boasts the intriguing **Peary-MacMillan Arctic Museum**. Both Admiral Robert E. Peary and his assistant, Donald B. MacMillan (1874–1970) studied at Bowdoin. If you took the Eagle Island tour, above, you already have some sense of Peary's life, but it is brought to life in a different way in these displays focusing on the first successful expedition to the North Pole. ☎ *(207) 725-3416. Open Tues.–Sat. 10–5, Sun. 2–5. Closed major holidays. Free, donations accepted.* ♿.

On the Desert of Maine

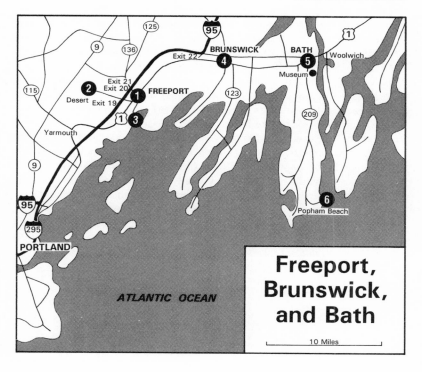

Freeport, Brunswick, and Bath

10 Miles

While in Brunswick, you can investigate the town's fascinating past at the nearby **Pejepscot Museum**, whose name reflects what the Native Americans originally called this area. Although it is hundreds of miles to the north, Brunswick has a double relationship with the Civil War. It seems that Harriet Beecher Stowe wrote *Uncle Tom's Cabin* here, which some consider a major cause of the conflict, and that Bowdoin College professor Joshua Lawrence Chamberlain was the man who accepted General Lee's surrender sword at Appomattox, ending the war. The latter's house may also be visited; ask at the museum. The other half of the museum's building, the **Skolfield-Whittier House**, is a Victorian capsule, frozen in time, that may be seen in summer. *159-161 Park Row,* ☎ *(207) 729-6606. Open Memorial Day to Labor Day, Mon.–Fri. 9–5, and Sat. 1–4; rest of year Mon.–Fri. 9–5. Donation. Skolfield-Whittier House open Memorial Day to Labor Day, Tues.–Fri. 10–3, and Sat. 1–4. Tour $3, appointment suggested.*

Continue east on US-1 to **Bath** (5), home of the marvelous ***Maine Maritime Museum and Shipyard**. Bath, of course, is still a major shipbuilding center, as it has been since the 17th century. Located on the waterfront, this 10-acre former shipyard is alive with activity as classic sailing ships are restored. Visitors can watch as boat construction and repair skills are taught to apprentices, and see exhibits tracing the history of shipbuilding. Short **cruises** are offered from June through October for an extra fee, and for the kids there's a children's playship. A museum building houses models, seafaring artifacts, and exhibits of life at sea. Visiting vessels may often be boarded. *243 Washington St.,* ☎ *(207) 443-1316. Open daily 9:30–5. Closed Thanksgiving, Christmas, and New Year's Day. Adults $7, seniors $6.50, ages 6–17 $4.50, families $20. Picnic facilities.* ☎. ♿.

If time permits, continue south on ME-209 to **Popham Beach** (6) at the tip of a 16-mile finger that pokes its way into the ocean. The first English colony in New England was started here in 1607, the same year as Jamestown in Virginia, but it only lasted long enough to construct the first English ship built in America. In the summer of 1608 the disenchanted settlers who survived went back to Britain. Today, there's virtually nothing to see of this historic footnote, but you can go swimming at **Popham Beach State Park**, or visit historic **Fort Popham**, built during the Civil War to defend Bath's shipyards against Confederate attack. *Beach open mid-Apr. to Oct., daily 9–dusk. Fee $2. Picnic facilities.* ♿. *Fort open Memorial Day through Sept., daily 9–dusk. Picnic facilities. Free.* ♿.

Wiscasset and Boothbay Harbor

It's about as far as you can go on a daytrip, but this longish excursion to Wiscasset and Boothbay Harbor finally gets you beyond the congested coastal areas of Maine and into the kind of landscape that the state is famous for. It also hints at the charms that lie beyond, perhaps inspiring thoughts of an extended vacation.

Exploring the region presents a bit of a challenge, as even a cursory glace at a road map will reveal. The coastline is deeply indented, with the most attractive spots at the end of long fingers of land extending south from the mainland. To get from one place to another usually requires retracing your miles back to US-1, or taking a boat, or swimming there. It's worth the small effort, however, to enjoy the magnificent, unspoiled, and uncrowded scenery, possibly ending with a boat trip to a nearby island before heading home.

This trip could, of course, be combined with any or all of the earlier Maine daytrips to form a real vacation by staying over for a few nights. Be sure to make reservations!

GETTING THERE:

By car, Wiscasset is about 160 miles northeast of downtown Boston via routes **US-1** and **I-95** (toll in NH and parts of ME), which becomes the Maine Turnpike for a stretch. At Exit 9 (Portland), I-95 leaves the turnpike and continues northeast. Follow this and get off at Exit 22, Brunswick. From there take US-1 through Bath to Wiscasset.

From Wiscasset it's another 12 miles south on **ME-27** to Boothbay Harbor.

PRACTICALITIES:

You'll need to make an early start to cover this much distance, even though it's fast highways nearly all the way. Any fine day from late May until mid-October will do, but try to avoid weekend traffic. A few of the minor sights are open in July and August only, and closed on Sundays and Mondays.

313

For further information contact the **Boothbay Harbor Region Chamber of Commerce**, Route ME-27, Boothbay Harbor, ME 04538, ☎ (207) 633-2353 or 633-4232. The statewide **Maine Publicity Bureau** has an information center along routes I-95 and US-1 just above the New Hampshire border, ☎ (207) 439-1319.

FOOD AND DRINK:

Le Garage (Water St., a block south of US-1, just before the bridge in Wiscasset) Meat, chicken, and seafood with a view of the ship-wrecked schooners, indoors or out. ☎ (207) 882-5409. X: Mon. off-season. $$

Andrew's Harborside (8 Bridge St., by the harbor in Boothbay Harbor) Seafood overlooking the water. ☎ (207) 633-4074. X: Late Oct.–Apr. $$

Bravo's Mexican (2 Boothbay House Hill, at the harbor in Boothbay Harbor) Mexican cuisine, steaks, and seafood in a rustic setting. ☎ (207) 633-7323. X: weekdays from mid-Oct. to late May. $$

Sarah's Café (Main St., US-1, in Wiscasset) Locally popular for its American, Mexican, and other dishes. ☎ (207) 882-7504. $

Ebb Tide (67 Commercial St. in Boothbay Harbor) A diner with all kinds of American favorites. ☎ (207) 633-5692. $

LOCAL ATTRACTIONS:

Numbers in parentheses correspond to numbers on the map.

*Wiscasset (1) calls itself "the prettiest village in Maine," an assertion that you might well agree with. Its picturesque harbor is visually enlivened by the decaying hulks of two four-masted schooners, the *Luther Little* and the *Hesper*, abandoned there in 1932. Once a prosperous international port and home to wealthy sea merchants, Wiscasset preserves its stately mansions and historic structures. Today, its broad, tree-lined streets shelter artists and writers, as well as antique shops and restaurants.

Perhaps the most unusual, and unexpected, attraction in Wiscasset is the utterly delightful ***Musical Wonder House**, occupying an 1852 Georgian dwelling at 18 High Street, just south of US-1. Some 500 player pianos, music boxes, gramophones, and other antique contraptions from Europe and America that make joyful, glorious music all by themselves are gathered together for visitors to enjoy. These are not just tinkly little music boxes, either. They range from tiny, delicate things mimicking bird songs to full orchestral devices complete with organ, drums, chimes, and bells. ☎ *(800) 339-7163 in Maine, (800) 336-3725 out-of-state. Open Memorial Day to mid-Oct., daily 10–5. Tours on the hour, minimum 2 people. Longer comprehensive tours by advance reservation. Standard tour: adults $12.50, seniors $10.50, under 12 $8.50. Gift shop.*

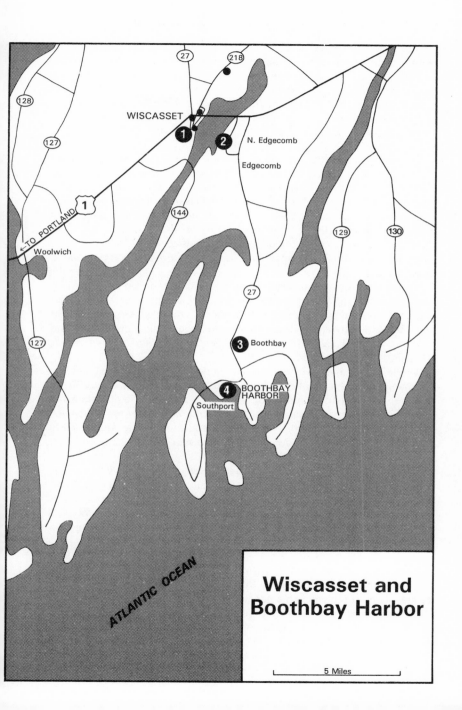

128

27 218

127

WISCASSET

1

2

N. Edgecomb

Edgecomb

1

TO PORTLAND

144

129 130

Woolwich

127

27

3 Boothbay

4 BOOTHBAY HARBOR

Southport

ATLANTIC OCEAN

Wiscasset and Boothbay Harbor

5 Miles

Just down the street, at the corner of Lee Street, is the **Castle Tucker House**, an architecturally unusual mansion of 1807 that was greatly modified in 1860 by one Richard Tucker, a wealthy sea captain. Some of his descendants still live here, and they invite visitors in for a good look at the life of a 19th-century sea captain. The furnishings are Federal and Victorian, and there's a marvelous free-standing elliptical staircase. ☎ *(207) 882-7364. Open July and Aug., Tues.–Sat. 11–4, and by appointment in Sept. Adults $3, children (6–12) 50¢.*

Across US-1, nearly a mile out on Federal Street, stands the **Old Lincoln County Jail**, now a local museum. Built in 1811 in response to growing criminality—and the misbehavior of sailors—it remained a place of grim incarceration until 1913. The three-story prison is built of granite slabs up to 40 inches thick, with tiny airless cells for real miscreants, and slightly more humane accommodations for debtors. Visitors are also shown the adjoining jailer's house, and a collection of appropriate artifacts. ☎ *(207) 882-6817. Open July and Aug., Tues.–Sun. 11–4:30; rest of year by appointment. Adults $2, under 14 $1.*

The nearby **Nickels-Sortwell House**, at the corner of Federal and Main streets, was built in 1807 by one William Nickels, a shipmaster in the lumber trade. Later owned by Alvin Sortwell, mayor of Cambridge, MA, the restored house features Sortwell family furnishings, an elegant elliptical staircase, and a garden. ☎ *(207) 882-6218. Open June–Sept., Wed.–Sun. noon–4. Adults $4, seniors $3.50, children (6–12) $2.*

While in Wiscasset, why not take a train ride? The **Maine Coast Railway** will haul you to Newcastle and back along the scenic Sheepscot River. Restored 1930s coaches are used, and there's a special combination rail and sail tour offered at peak times. *Waterfront Park, Water St., Wiscasset,* ☎ *(207) 882-8000 or (800) 795-5404. Operates daily, late June to early Sept.; weekends only, late May to late June and mid-Sept. to mid-Oct. Train fare $10, children (5–15) $5.*

Cross the river on US-1 and immediately turn right onto Eddy Road. This will take you south to **Fort Edgecomb** (2). Built during the War of 1812 to protect Wiscasset's vital shipyards, the wooden octagonal blockhouse offers magnificent ***views** along with historic remains and picnic facilities. ☎ *(207) 882-7777. Open Memorial Day to Labor Day, daily 9–5. Adults $1, ages 5– 12 50¢.*

Continue south, soon joining MA-27, to the hamlet of **Boothbay** (3). Here you'll find the **Boothbay Railway Village**, a re-created turn-of-the-century Maine village complete with a general store, little red schoolhouse, blacksmith shop, and many other old-time buildings. Rides are offered on a narrow-gauge steam train, and there's a wonderful display of antique automobiles and trucks. ☎ *(207) 633-4727. Open early June to mid-Oct., daily 9:30–5; late May to early June, weekends 9:30–5. Adults $6, under 12 $3.*

Boothbay Harbor

A few miles farther south, at the tip of the craggy, narrow peninsula, lies **Boothbay Harbor** (4). A real working seaport, Boothbay preserves a great deal of Maine's colorful past, and blends it with the emerging resort of today. This is a great place to just wander around on foot, aimlessly poking into whatever catches your interest. **Cruises**, some as short as an hour, are offered from the various piers.

If time permits, or you're staying overnight, you might consider the marvelous cruise to ***Monhegan Island**, a rugged, rocky place some 10 miles offshore. Artists have been flocking here for decades, followed in recent years by knowledgeable tourists. There are some 17 miles of hiking trails and, of course, a lighthouse overlooking the whole delicious ***panorama** of sea and rocks. *For boat information contact Balmy Day Cruises, Pier 8, Boothbay Harbor, ME 04538, ☎ (207) 633-2284.*

Section IX

Concord, April 19, 1775 . . . the Revolutionary War begins

HISTORICAL
PERSPECTIVES

This brief chronological outline of New England's history should help place events in context with each other.

PERIOD OF EXPLORATION:

c. 8000 B.C.	Wandering tribes arrive from Asia via a land bridge.
c. 2000 B.C.	Megalithic constructions begun at America's Stonehenge by unknown people.
c. A.D. 1000	New England coast partially explored by Norse sailors.
1492	New World "discovered" by Christopher Columbus.
1497	John Cabot (Giovanni Cabato) explores North American coast, claims land including New England for the King of England.
1509	Henry VIII accedes to the throne of England.
1524	North American coast explored for France by Giovanni da Verrazano.
1558	Queen Elizabeth I accedes to the throne of England.
1602	English explorer Bartholomew Gosnold discovers Cape Cod and Martha's Vineyard.
1604	French explorer Samuel de Champlain discovers Maine.
1605	Five American Indians brought from Maine to England.
1607	First successful English settlement in North America established at Jamestown, VA; another attempted in Maine fails.
1609	French explorer Samuel de Champlain discovers Vermont.
1614	Capt. John Smith return to England with fish and furs; makes first reference to "New England."

COLONIAL PERIOD:

1620	Pilgrims arrive at Plymouth aboard the *Mayflower*.
1625	Charles I becomes King of England.
1626	Puritan colony established at Salem, MA.
1630	Boston settled by Puritans.
1635	Hartford Colony established in Connecticut Valley.
1636	Harvard College founded; Providence, RI, established.
1638–39	Portsmouth, RI, founded; Connecticut Colony established.
1653–58	England ruled by Oliver Cromwell.
1660	Charles II becomes King of England.
1689	William III and Mary II become joint sovereigns of England.
1692	Salem witch trials.
1701	Yale University founded as the Collegiate School.
1702	Anne becomes Queen of England.

1714	George I accedes to the British throne.
1756–63	French & Indian War (Seven Years War) establishes British supremacy in North America.

INDEPENDENCE:

1765–67	The Stamp Act and Townshend Acts cause civil unrest in North America.
1770	Boston Massacre.
1773	Boston Tea Party.
1774	The Intolerable Acts passed by Parliament in retaliation.
1775	Battles of Lexington, Concord, and Bunker Hill; the Revolutionary War begins.
1776	Declaration of Independence.
1777	Battle of Bennington, Vermont declares itself a republic.
1781	Colonists defeat the British at Yorktown, VA; last battle of the war.
1783	Treaty of Versailles, Britain recognizes United States as an independent nation.
1788	Connecticut, Massachusetts, and New Hampshire join the Union.
1789	George Washington becomes first President of the United States.
1790	Rhode Island joins the Union.
1791	Vermont joins the Union.

19TH CENTURY:

1812	War of 1812.
1820	Maine joins the Union.
1845	Henry David Thoreau moves into his cabin at Walden Pond.
1851	Harriet Beecher Stowe writes *Uncle Tom's Cabin*.
1857	Discovery of oil in Pennsylvania puts an end to New England's rich whaling business.
1861–65	Civil War.

20TH CENTURY:

1917–18	U.S. participation in World War I.
1929	Stock market crash.
1941–45	World War II.
1944	World monetary conference at Bretton Woods, NH.
1954	First nuclear-powered submarine built at Groton, CT.
1961	John F. Kennedy of Massachusetts becomes President of the United States.

Index

Special interest attractions are also listed under their category headings.

322   INDEX

Daytrips

•OTHER TITLES NOW AVAILABLE•

DAYTRIPS LONDON
Explores the metropolis on 10 one-day walking tours, then describes 40 daytrips to destinations throughout southern England—all by either rail or car. 5th edition, 336 pages, 57 maps, 94 photos.

DAYTRIPS FRANCE
Describes 45 daytrips—including 5 walking tours of Paris, 23 excursions from the city, 5 in Provence, and 12 along the Riviera. 4th edition, 336 pages, 55 maps, 89 photos.

DAYTRIPS GERMANY
55 of Germany's most enticing destinations can be savored on daytrips from Munich, Frankfurt, Hamburg, and Berlin. Walking tours of the big cities are included. 4th edition, 336 pages, 62 maps, 94 photos.

DAYTRIPS HOLLAND, BELGIUM AND LUXEMBOURG
Many unusual places are covered on these 40 daytrips, along with all the favorites plus the 3 major cities. 2nd edition, 288 pages, 45 maps, 69 photos.

DAYTRIPS ITALY
Features 40 one-day adventures in and around Rome, Florence, Milan, Venice, and Naples. 3rd edition, 304 pages, 45 maps, 69 photos.

DAYTRIPS ISRAEL
25 one-day adventures by bus or car to the Holy Land's most interesting sites. Includes Jerusalem walking tours. 2nd edition, 206 pages, 40 maps, 40 photos.

DAYTRIPS WASHINGTON, DC
50 one-day adventures in the Nation's Capital, and to nearby Virginia, Maryland, Delaware, and Pennsylvania. Both walking and driving tours are featured. 352 pages, 60 maps, 48 photos.

DAYTRIPS NEW YORK
107 easy excursions by car throughout southern New York State, New Jersey, eastern Pennsylvania, Connecticut, and southern Massachusetts. 7th edition, 336 pages, 44 maps, 46 photos.

"Daytrips" travel guides, written or edited by Earl Steinbicker, describe the easiest and most natural way to travel on your own. Each volume in the growing series contains a balanced selection of enjoyable one-day adventures. Some of these are to famous attractions, while others feature little-known discoveries. For every destination there are historical facts, anecdotes, usually a suggested do-it-yourself walking tour, a local map, travel directions, time and weather considerations, and concise background material.

SOLD AT LEADING BOOKSTORES EVERYWHERE

Or, if you prefer, by mail direct from the publisher. Use the coupon below or just jot your choices on a separate piece of paper.

Hastings House
141 Halstead Avenue
Mamaroneck, NY 10543

Please send the following books:

_____copies   DAYTRIPS LONDON @ $14.95   _____
                    (0-8038-9367-1)

_____copies   DAYTRIPS FRANCE @ $14.95   _____
                    (0-8038-9366-3)

_____copies   DAYTRIPS GERMANY @ $14.95   _____
                    (0-8038-9369-8)

_____copies   DAYTRIPS HOLLAND, BELGIUM
                    AND LUXEMBOURG @ $14.95   _____
                    (0-8038-9368-X)

_____copies   DAYTRIPS ITALY @ $14.95   _____
                    (0-8038-9372-8)

_____copies   DAYTRIPS ISRAEL @ $14.95   _____
                    (0-8038-9374-4)

_____copies   DAYTRIPS WASHINGTON DC @ $14.95   _____
                    (0-8038-9373-6)

_____copies   DAYTRIPS NEW YORK @ $14.95   _____
                    (0-8038-9371-X)

_____copies   DAYTRIPS NEW ENGLAND @ $14.95   _____
                    (0-8038-9379-5)

New York residents add tax: _____
Shipping and handling @ $2.50 per book: _____
Total amount enclosed (check or money order)   _____
Please ship to: _____
_____
_____

ABOUT THE AUTHOR:

EARL STEINBICKER is a born tourist who believes that travel should be a joy, not an endurance test. For over 30 years he has been refining his carefree style of daytripping while working in New York, London, Paris, and other cities; first as head of a firm specializing in promotional photography and later as a professional writer. Whether by public transportation or private car, he has thoroughly probed the most delightful aspects of countries around the world— while always returning to the comforts of city life at night. A strong desire to share these experiences has led him to develop the "Daytrips" series of guides, which he continues to expand and revise. Besides this book, these now include London, France, Germany, Italy, Israel, Washington, DC, New York, and one volume combining Holland, Belgium and Luxembourg. Recently, he has been assisting other authors in developing additional "Daytrips" books, further expanding the series.